Animals in Ancient Greek Religion

This book provides the first systematic study of the role of animals in different areas of the ancient Greek religious experience, including in myth and ritual, the literary and the material evidence, the real and the imaginary.

An international team of renowned contributors shows that animals had a sustained presence not only in the traditionally well-researched cultural practice of blood sacrifice but across the full spectrum of ancient Greek religious beliefs and practices. Animals played a role in divination, epiphany, ritual healing, the setting up of dedications, the writing of binding spells, and the instigation of other 'magical' means. Taken together, the individual contributions to this book illustrate that ancient Greek religion constituted a triangular symbolic system encompassing not just gods and humans, but also animals as a third player and point of reference.

Animals in Ancient Greek Religion will be of interest to students and scholars of Greek religion, Greek myth, and ancient religion more broadly, as well as for anyone interested in human/animal relations in the ancient world.

Julia Kindt is Professor of Ancient Greek History in the Department of Classics and Ancient History at the University of Sydney, Australia, and a current Australian Research Council Future Fellow (2018–22). Her publications include *Rethinking Greek Religion* (2012) and *Re-visiting Delphi: Religion and Storytelling in Ancient Greece* (2016), as well as several co-edited volumes including *The Oxford Handbook of Ancient Greek Religion* (2015).

Routledge Monographs in Classical Studies

Titles include:

Robert E. Sherwood and the Classical Tradition
The Muses in America
Robert J. Rabel

Text and Intertext in Greek Epic and Drama
Essays in Honor of Margalit Finkelberg
Edited by Jonathan Price and Rachel Zelnick-Abramovitz

Animals in Ancient Greek Religion
Edited by Julia Kindt

Classicising Crisis
The Modern Age of Revolutions and the Greco-Roman Repertoire
Edited by Barbara Goff and Michael Simpson

Epigraphic Culture in the Eastern Mediterranean in Antiquity
Edited by Krzysztof Nawotka

Proclus and the Chaldean Oracles
A Study on Proclean Exegesis, with a Translation and Commentary of Proclus'
Treatise On Chaldean Philosophy
Nicola Spanu

Greek and Roman Military Manuals
Genre and History
Edited by James T. Chlup and Conor Whately

.For more information on this series, visit: https://www.routledge.com/classi-calstudies/series/RMCS

Animals in Ancient Greek Religion

Edited by
Julia Kindt

Routledge
Taylor & Francis Group

LONDON AND NEW YORK

First published 2021
by Routledge
2 Park Square, Milton Park, Abingdon, Oxon OX14 4RN

and by Routledge
52 Vanderbilt Avenue, New York, NY 10017

Routledge is an imprint of the Taylor & Francis Group, an informa business

British Library Cataloguing-in-Publication Data
A catalogue record for this book is available from the British Library

Library of Congress Cataloging-in-Publication Data
Names: Kindt, Julia, 1975- editor.
Title: Animals in ancient Greek religion / edited by Julia Kindt.
Description: Abingdon, Oxon ; New York, NY : Routledge, 2020. |
Includes bibliographical references and index. Identifiers: LCCN 2020010825
(print) | LCCN 2020010826 (ebook) | ISBN 9781138388888 (hardback) |
ISBN 9780429424304 (ebook)
Subjects: LCSH: Animals--Religious aspects. | Cults--Greece. | Mythology,
Greek. | Greece--Religion. | Greece--Religious life and customs.
Classification: LCC BL795.A54 A55 2020 (print) | LCC BL795.A54 (ebook)
| DDC 292.2/12--dc23
LC record available at https://lccn.loc.gov/2020010825
LC ebook record available at https://lccn.loc.gov/2020010826

ISBN: 978-1-138-38888-8 (hbk)
ISBN: 978-0-429-42430-4 (ebk)

Typeset in Bembo
by Taylor & Francis Books

Contents

Illustrations

Figures

Table

Contributors

Jan N. Bremmer is Professor Emeritus of Religious Studies at the University of Groningen, Netherlands. He has been a guest professor or fellow in, amongst others: the Centre for Hellenic Studies, the Getty Villa, the University of Edinburgh, Morphomata (Cologne), Ludwig Maximilian University (Munich), Max Weber College (Erfurt), Käte Hamburger College (Bochum), the Centre for Advanced Study (Oslo), and the Centre for Advanced Study 'Beyond Canon' (Regensburg). He has published widely on Greek, Roman, and early Christian religion as well as their historiography in modern times. His latest books are *Initiation into the Mysteries of the Ancient World* (de Gruyter, 2014) *Maidens, Magic and Martyrs in Early Christianity. Collected Essays I* (Mohr Siebeck, 2017), and *The World of Greek Religion and Mythology. Collected Essays II* (Mohr Siebeck 2019). He is also the co-editor (with M. Formisano) of *Perpetua's Passions* (Oxford University Press, 2012), (with D. Boschung) *The Materiality of Magic* (Brill, 2015), (with T. Karman and T. Nicklas) *The Ascension of Isaiah* (Peeters, 2016), *Thecla: Paul's Disciple and Saint in the East and West* (Oxford, 2016), (with V. Hirschberger and T. Nicklas) *Figures of Ezra* (Peeters, 2018), (with L. Feldt) *Marginality, Media, and Mutations of Religious Authority in the History of Christianity* (Peeters, 2019), and (with J. A. Doole *et al.*) *The Protevangelium of James* (Peeters, forthcoming).

James Henderson Collins II is Fellow in Ancient Greek Literature and Philosophy at the Center for Hellenic Studies at Harvard University and Interdisciplinary Senior Lecturer in the Department of Classics and Ancient History at the University of Sydney. He uses a variety of literary, philosophical, sociological, and neuroscientific approaches to study the pragmatics of intellectual life in antiquity, with a principal focus on philosophical recruitment and ancient education, including choral training and performance. He is Founder and Director of the interdisciplinary 'Performing Wisdom' programme, which develops strategies for introducing people of all backgrounds and ages to philosophy as an active – often public – discipline through dramatic and rhetorical training and performance. His publications include *Exhortations to Philosophy. The Protreptics of Plato, Isocrates, and Aristotle* (Oxford University Press, 2015) and 'Dancing the virtues, becoming virtuous: procedural memory and ethical presence', *Ramus* 42 (2013), 183–206. He does not remember being a bird or a bush in a past life.

Korshi Dosoo is currently junior team leader of the project 'The Coptic Magical Papyri: Vernacular Religion in Late Roman and Early Islamic Egypt' at the Julius Maximilian University of Würzburg. Previously, he worked as a postdoctoral researcher on the Paris-based Labex Laboratoire d'Excellence (RESMED) project 'Les Mots de la Paix' and lectured at the University of Strasbourg. He received his doctorate in ancient history from Macquarie University, Australia, in 2015 after completing his thesis on 'Rituals of Apparition in the Theban Magical Library', which examined the divination rituals found in the magical papyri of Roman Egypt.

Milette Gaifman is Professor of Greek Art and Archaeology, jointly appointed in the Departments of Classics and History of Art at Yale University. She is also the co-editor-in-chief of the *Art Bulletin*, the flagship journal of art history globally, for the years 2019–22. Her scholarship focuses primarily on Greek antiquity of the archaic and classical periods. Research interests include: the interaction between visual culture and religion, the variety of forms in the arts of antiquity (from the naturalistic to the non-figural), the interactive traits of various artistic media, and the reception of Greek art in later periods. She is the author of *Aniconism in Greek Antiquity* (Oxford University Press, 2012) and *The Art of Libation in Classical Athens* (Yale University Press, 2018). She is also co-editor (with M. Aktor) of *Exploring Aniconism*, a special issue of the journal *Religion* 47 (2017, reissued by Routledge in 2019), and (with M. Squire and V. Platt) of *The Embodied Object in Classical Antiquity*, a special issue of *Art History* (June 2018).

Ingvild Sælid Gilhus is Professor of the Study of Religion at the University of Bergen, Norway. She works in the areas of religion in late antiquity and new religious movements. Her publications include *Laughing Gods, Weeping Virgins* (Routledge, 1997) and *Animals, Gods and Humans. Changing Attitudes to Animals in Greek, Roman and Early Christian Ideas* (Routledge, 2006). She has co-edited several volumes, including (with S. J. Sutcliffe) *New Age Spirituality. Rethinking Religion* (Acumen 2013), (with S. E. Kraft and J. R. Lewis) *New Age in Norway* (Equinox 2017), (with A. K. Petersen *et al.*) *Evolution, Cognition, and the History of Religion. A New Synthesis* (Brill, 2019), and (with A. Taskos and M. C. Wright) *The Archangel Michael in Africa. History, Cult, and Persona* (Bloomsbury, 2019).

Fritz Graf is Distinguished University Professor of Classics and Director of Epigraphy at Ohio State University. He has published mainly on Greek and Roman religions, with a special interest in mystery cults, magic, and the epigraphical documentation of religion. His most recent book is *Roman Festivals in the Greek East* (Cambridge University Press, 2016). At present he is working on a history of Greek religion to be published by Yale University Press.

Emily Kearns is a lecturer and senior research fellow at St Hilda's College, Oxford. Her research interests lie mainly in the field of Greek religion, but she has also written on many aspects of Greek and Latin literature. She is the author of *The Heroes of Attica* (Institute for Classical Studies, 1989) and *Ancient Greek Religion: A Sourcebook* (Wiley Blackwell, 2010). She is currently working on a commentary on Euripides' *Iphigenia in Tauris*.

Julia Kindt is Professor of Ancient Greek History in the Department of Classics and Ancient History at the University of Sydney and a current ARC Future Fellow (2018–22). Her publications include *Rethinking Greek Religion* (Cambridge University Press, 2012) and *Re-visiting Delphi. Religion and Storytelling in Ancient Greece* (Cambridge University Press, 2016) as well as several co-edited volumes, including (with E. Eidinow) *The Oxford Handbook of Ancient Greek Religion* (Oxford University Press, 2015) and (with E. Eidinow and R. Osborne) *Theologies of Ancient Greek Religion* (Cambridge University Press, 2016). She is a member of the editorial board of the *Journal of Ancient History*, the editorial advisor board of Sydney University Press, and a senior editor of the *Oxford Research Encyclopaedia of Religion (ORE)*. She is currently completing a monograph entitled *Trojan Pigs and Other Stories: Ten Ancient Creatures that Make Us Human*, which investigates how conceptions of what it means to be human have emerged through our 'entanglements' with non-human creatures in antiquity and the present.

Jeremy McInerney is Professor of Classical Studies at the University of Pennsylvania. He has done research on ethnicity and landscape, and his current work is focused on the function of hybridity in Greek culture. He is also completing a study of Athenian relations with the island of Lemnos, as part of which he re-examines the temple of Hephaistos at Athens. His other recent research projects include studies of Greek gastronomical texts as well as work on the 'Pride of Halikarnassos' inscription. He is the author of a book on state formation in archaic Greece, *The Folds of Parnassos. Land and Ethnicity in Ancient Phokis* (University of Texas Press, 1999), and *The Cattle of the Sun* (Princeton University Press, 2010), a book dealing with the importance of cattle-raising, meat, and sacrifice in the culture of ancient Greece. He is editor of Blackwell's *Companion to Ethnicity in the Ancient Mediterranean* (Blackwell, 2014) and co-editor (with Ineke Sluiter) of *Valuing Landscape in Classical Antiquity. Natural Environment and Cultural Imagination* (Brill, 2016).

Florian Steger is Full Professor at and Director of the Institute of the History, Philosophy, and Ethics of Medicine at the University of Ulm, Germany, where he also chairs the Research Ethics Committee. From 2011 to 2016 he was Director of the Institute for History and Ethics of Medicine at Martin Luther University, Halle-Wittenberg. He is a member of the Saxon Academy of Sciences and Humanities and the Göttingen Academy of Sciences and Humanities. He studied medicine, classical philology, and history at the University of Würzburg and at Ludwig Maximilian University,

Munich. His main areas of expertise are ancient medicine and its reception, the intersection of medicine and the arts, problems of injustice in politicised medicine, and current ethical questions in medicine. His publications in the field of ancient medicine include *Asclepius. Medicine and Cult* (Steiner, 2018) and *Antike Medizin. Bibliothek der griechischen Literatur* (Hiersemann forthcoming), as well as numerous articles on ancient medicine.

Frank Ursin is a research associate ('Wissenschaftlicher Mitarbeiter') at the Institute of the History, Philosophy, and Ethics of Medicine at the University of Ulm, Germany. He studied ancient history, philosophy, and journalism at the University of Leipzig. He completed a Ph.D. in ancient history at Martin Luther University in Halle-Wittenberg in 2016 with a thesis on Greek memory culture at the time of the Second Sophistic, funded by the Gerda Henkel Foundation. Recent research interests include the pre-modern history of medicine and current ethical challenges of medicine. His publications include *Freiheit, Herrschaft, Widerstand. Griechische Erinnerungskultur in der Hohen Kaiserzeit* (Steiner, 2019).

Hannah Willey is Lecturer in Ancient History at the University of Cambridge and a fellow of Murray Edwards College, having previously held the W. H. D. Rouse Fellowship at Christ's College, Cambridge. Her research focuses on Greek cultural history and the interaction of different social groups within the polis, particularly in the religious sphere. She is currently working on a monograph on the interrelation of law and religion in the Greek city state. Other projects, published and in progress, include articles and chapters on religious pollution in Plato's *Euthyphro*, the lawgiver traditions, religion and theology in the speeches of Demosthenes, Thucydides' treatment of religion, cult communities during the Peloponnesian War, Xenophon's religious self-characterisation, and a large-scale study of cult foundation in the ancient world.

Acknowledgements

I thank the contributors to this volume for bringing their expertise to the project and for their patience and goodwill in responding to my editorial suggestions. At the same time, I would also like to thank the readers who have commented on drafts of individual chapters. I am very grateful to Amy Davis-Poynter and Ella Halstead from Routledge for their guidance and enthusiasm for this project, Philip Parr for his invaluable copy-editing, and my colleague James Collins II for his help in bringing the book into final shape. In addition, I would like to thank my wonderful team of research assistants, who helped me to get this book over the line in a relatively short period of time: Edward Armstrong, Alyce Cannon, Billy Kennedy, Brennan Nicholson, and Lucian Tan. Finally, I thank Maria Merkeling for help with English editing and Daniel Hanigan for translating a chapter from German into English. Work on this book has been funded by a Future Fellowship grant (2018–22), awarded by the Australian Research Council.

Abbreviations

General

ad loc.	*ad locum*
BP	before present
ca.	circa
cent.	century
cf.	confer/conferatur
ed./eds.	edited by/editor(s)
edn.	edition
e.g.	exempli gratia
et al.	*et alii*
esp.	especially
etc.	*et cetera*
Fig(s).	figure(s)
fr./frr.	fragment(s)
i.a.	*inter alia*
l./ll.	line/lines
Lin B.	Linear B
n./ns.	Note/Notes
no./nos.	number/numbers
orig.	original
p./pp.	page/pages
pl.	plate
repr.	reprint/reprinted
rev.	revised
sc.	scilicet
schol.	scholion
trans.	translated by

Secondary sources and reference works

ANRW	H. Temporini-Gräfin Vitzthum and W. Haase (eds.) (1972–) *Aufstieg und Niedergang der römischen Welt*

Arch. Deltion	*Archaiologikon Deltion*
BMC	
Peloponnesus	P. Gardner (1963) Catalogue of *Greek Coins in the British Museum. Peloponnesus (Excluding Corinth)*, ed. R. S. Poole. Bologna (repr. of the orig. 1887 edn.)
CGRN	*Corpus of Greek Ritual Norms*
CIL	*Corpus Inscriptionum Latinarum (1863–)*
CIRB	*Corpus Inscriptionum Regni Bosporani*
CRAI	*Comptes rendus de l'Académie des Inscriptions et Belles-Lettres*
DK	H. Diels and W. Kranz (1952) *Fragmente der Vorsokratiker*. 6th edn.
DNP	*Der neue Pauly*
DT	A. Auguste Audollent (1904) *Defixionum Tabellae*
FGrH	F. Jacoby (1923–) *Fragmente der griechischen Historiker*
IEph.	*Inscriptions from Ephesus*
IG	*Inscriptiones Graecae*
IOSPE	*Inscriptiones antiquae Orae Septentrionalis Ponti Euxini graecae et latinae*
LM	A. Laks and G. Most (2016) Early Greek Philosophy. 9 vols.
LIMC	J. C. Balty and J. Boardman (eds.) (1981–99) *Lexicon Iconographicum Mythologiae Classicae*. 8 vols., 2 indices, 1 supplement
LSJ	H. G. Liddell and R. Scott (1968) *Greek–English Lexicon*, 9th edn., rev. H. Stuart-Jones, suppl. E. A. Barber *et al.*
MEFRA	*Mélanges d'archéologie et d'historie de l'École Française de Rome*
PBad.	F. Bilabel and A. Grohmann (eds.) (1934) *Griechische, koptische und arabische Texte zur Religion und religiösen Literatur in Ägyptens Spätzeit*
PDM	*Papyri Demoticae Magicae* (for numbering and bibliography, see H. D. Betz (ed.) *The Greek Magical Papyri in Translation Including the Demotic Spells*, Chicago, 1986)
PG	J. P. Migne (1857–66) *Patrologiae Cursus, series Graeca*
PGM	K. Preisendanz and A. Henrichs (eds.) (1973–4) *Papyri Graecae Magicae. Die Griechischen Zauberpapyri*. 2 vols.
POxy	*Oxyrhynchus Papyri* (1898–)
RE	A. Pauly, G. Wissowa, and W. Kroll (eds.) (1893–) *Real-Encyclopädie der classischen Altertumswissenschaft*
RO	P. J. Rhodes and R. Osborne (eds.) (2003, rev. edn. 2007) *Greek Historical Inscriptions, 404–323 BC*
SEG	*Supplementum epigraphicum Graecum (1923–)*
SHA	Scriptores Historiae Augustae
SM	R. W. Daniel and F. Maltomini (1990–2) *Supplementum Magicum*. 2 vols.
Syll.3	W. Dittenberger (1915–24) *Sylloge Inscriptionum Graecarum*. 3rd edn.
ThesCRA	*Thesaurus Cultus et Rituum Antiquorum (2004–14)*. 9 vols.
TrGF	B. Snell, R. Kannicht, and D. Radt (eds.) (1971–2004) *Tragicorum Graecorum Fragmenta*. 6 vols.

On gods, humans, and animals

J. Kindt

In his influential essay 'Why Look at Animals?' the cultural critic John Berger described a deep rupture that emerged in the previously close relationship between humans and animals during the 19th and 20th centuries.[1] Most wild and domesticated animals, he argued, have now disappeared from our lives; others have been subsumed in unprecedented numbers into our households as pets. A third group encompassing exotic animals has been relegated to an institution dedicated to the public viewing of animals: the zoo.[2] All these observations led Berger to diagnose a fundamental shift in the way we humans relate to animals: with the exception of a chosen few, we no longer share our lives with most animals, yet animal images and animal representations are everywhere – in film, literature, in high and low culture, in advertising and art, and in numerous nature documentaries and investigative case studies. After Berger, it would seem that we compensate for the absence of real animals from our lives with an abundance of representations and appropriations.

The modern-day disconnect between humans and animals noted by Berger differs fundamentally from the situation of earlier periods – most notably, perhaps, from classical antiquity.[3] Domestic animals were an important part of everyday life in the ancient Greek city.[4] As companions, foodstuffs, and means of transportation, they lived in constant close proximity to humans.[5] They provided comfort and companionship, and they sustained human livelihoods in myriad different ways. They served as entertainment, in warfare, as luxury and prestige items. Wild animals, in turn, constituted an additional source of food, an opportunity to prove oneself in hunting rituals, and a potential threat to human life.[6]

In short, the lives and worlds of animals intersected variously with those of the ancient Greeks, providing numerous opportunities for first-hand experiences of – and encounters with – animals, both domestic and wild. As a result, the ancient Greeks developed a considerable interest in, and knowledge of, animal physiology, modes of life, and typical behaviours as evidenced in the naturalistic literature from the ancient world.[7] The knowledge of individual species compiled by this tradition provided the foundation for their many roles and functions in Greek thought and literature.[8]

Greek thought and literature is full of examples of how the ancient Greeks and Romans grappled with animals and animal nature in their own right and – more frequently – in relation to humans: from the argument that man stands out from all other creatures in classical philosophy (the so-called 'man-only *topos*') to endearing accounts of human/animal friendship explored in Greek storytelling;[9] from the Homeric animal similes to the animal imagery of Greco-Roman drama; from the genre of fable to the naturalistic and pseudo-naturalistic observations of Aristotle, Aelian, and Pausanias. In the ancient world animals provided a ubiquitous counterpart for humans to engage with questions of their humanity, and their own animality.

The prominent role of animals in Greek thought and literature indicates that the appropriation of animals for a variety of cultural and symbolic purposes is not predominantly a symptom of modernity. Rather, the greater proximity of humans and animals in the ancient world also nurtured a desire to engage with animals to explore their lives and their ways of being in the world. The resulting 'entanglements' are invariably productive stores of cultural meaning and go beyond the role of animals as the quintessential 'other':[10] they articulate themselves in multilayered relationships of likeness and difference which allow for the emergence of nuanced and diverging concepts of humanity in ways that we have only started to comprehend in all their complexity.[11] At the same time, these 'entanglements' affect interactions between Greeks and animals in a number of real-life contexts – from the husbandry of domestic animals to contact with those in the wild.

This book considers the role of animals in one particular area of ancient Greek culture and society that itself extends seamlessly from the real into the imaginary and symbolic: that of ancient Greek religion.[12] It offers the first systematic account of the way in which animals feature in different areas of the ancient Greek religious experience. To this end, it speaks to a number of questions that aim at capturing different facets of their role in ancient Greek religion. Which animals feature in ancient Greek religious beliefs and practices, why, and how? What role do they play in religion as a symbolic medium ('a language') that allowed the ancient Greeks to engage with each other in order to make complex statements about the world and the human place within it?[13] How is this symbolic role shaped by real human/animal interactions in ancient Greek culture and society? And, in turn, how does it affect such interactions?

The insight that animals are part of the fabric of ancient Greek religion is, of course, not new. From the beginning of academic interest in the religions of the ancient world in the 19th century, classical scholars discussed the role of animals in different areas of the ancient Greek religious experience. As Emily Kearns shows in her chapter on the representation of animals in scholarship on ancient Greek religion (this volume, Chapter 3), the ways in which non-human creatures feature in classical scholarship on ancient Greek religion underwent a number of changes in line with the larger research paradigms in the field. And yet, in most instances, and with the exception of a few pioneering works in this area, the interest of classical scholars in the real and symbolic roles of animals in Greek religion remained subordinate to other research questions and paradigms.[14]

As a result, the overall picture is uneven, at best. While the presence and significance of animals has been well researched in certain areas of the Greek religious experience – most notably in the context of blood sacrifice as the 'central' ritual of ancient Greek religion – there has been much less research, if anything, on the role of animals in other areas of religious beliefs and practices.[15] Even the influential work of the French structuralists did not fundamentally alter the picture. Of course, the famous 'culinary triangle' of Claude Lévi-Strauss did trigger some interest in the symbolism of meat, its ritual origins, and consumption in classical scholarship.[16] In particular the adherents of the so-called 'Paris School' around Jean-Pierre Vernant explored its symbolic implications and found them in the creation of group cohesion.[17] But their method was never applied to a systematic study of the symbolic value of other animals in contexts beyond animal sacrifice. Walter Burkert's competing explanation of Greek sacrificial practices did not change the larger picture either as it concerned the same area – sacrifice and, shared with the adherents of the 'Paris School', a specific focus on its function in human society.[18] Debates on ancient Greek blood sacrifice have now moved well beyond the impasse between the interpretations of Burkert and Vernant.[19] Yet, despite some promising early works exploring aspects of this relationship, there is no comprehensive study that takes up recent developments in this area of study and explores the place and significance of animals in different areas of the ancient Greek religious experience.

This book seeks to fill this gap by offering exemplary studies of the roles, functions, and meanings of animals in different areas of the ancient Greek religious experience. It investigates the presence and function of real and symbolic animals in the different ways the ancient Greeks interacted with the supernatural. To this end, it focuses on the way in which animals feature in such disparate religious (or religiously motivated) practices as divination, healing, and magical rituals. It traces the way in which animals make an appearance across different media, texts, and contexts with the ultimate aim of deriving a comparative picture of the kind of human/animal 'entanglements' at the core of the ancient Greek religious experience. As such, it extends the recent surge of interest in human/animal studies as an emerging interdisciplinary field of study into the realm of ancient Greek religion as a sphere that was 'embedded' in ancient society.[20]

Structure of the book

The chapters in this book are arranged into three parts. Part 1, 'Perspectives', brings together three chapters that look at the ways in which animals feature in ancient Greek religion from a larger, more global perspective than the chapters that follow. In Chapter 1 ('The 'Entanglement' of Gods, Humans, and Animals in Ancient Greek Religion'), Jeremy McInerney begins the investigation by developing the notion of 'entanglement' ('*Verschränkung*') at the core of this study. By running us through some examples of the different forms this 'entanglement' takes in the ancient Greek world, he shows what is at stake in expanding our notion of ancient Greek religion to include the animal as the third point of reference along with gods and humans. More specifically, he illustrates that the human category emerges in ever-new forms and definitions in relation to those of the divine and the animal. His contribution thus introduces this volume not only by laying out its methodological and conceptual focus; it also touches on a number of themes that feature in more detail in the subsequent chapters. These include the malleability of the different ontological categories of being as they emerge in different texts and contexts, the theological considerations included in notions of hybridisation and metamorphosis, and the question of how far their symbolic use relates to the lives of real animals in the ancient Greek world. In touching on these and other issues emerging from the 'entanglement' of gods, humans, and animals in Greek religious beliefs and practices, McInerney's contribution opens up the conversation to a wide range of new conceptual considerations that emerge as soon as we include the animal in the picture of human/divine relations.

Chapter 2 ('Sources for the Study of Animals in Ancient Greek Religion') by Ingvild Sælid Gilhus introduces us to the different kinds of evidence available for the study of animals in ancient Greek religion. She shows that these transcend the typical subdivisions of classical scholarship by including literary and historical sources, iconographic representations, archaeological remains, and zooarchaeological evidence (animal remains). Her chapter revolves around the notion of 'redirecting the gaze' – a call to consider the whole spectrum of relationships connecting gods, humans, and animals in ancient Greek religion. This call pertains to physical and material human/animal relationships as well as emotional ones. It includes the need to read between the lines and beyond the obvious meaning of images – both pictographic and literary – to advance to the deeper and possibly concealed layers of cultural significance (including those sympathetic to animals), and involves taking a fresh look at well-known sources as well as exploring new types of evidence (such as zooarchaeological remains and magical artefacts). At the same time, Gilhus points to the larger paradigms in classical scholarship as possible explanations for why certain types of sources and the divine/human/animal relationships represented therein have traditionally received more attention than others. This applies in particular to the ancient Greek cultural practice of blood sacrifice, which has traditionally been well researched. But here, too, 'redirecting the gaze' matters. As Gilhus shows, different kinds of evidence represent a different picture as to what kind of animals were sacrificed, thereby revealing different aspects of the triangular symbolic relationship between gods, humans, and animals as enacted in the ritual practice of blood sacrifice.

The paradigms under which classical scholarship has investigated the role of animals in ancient Greek religion already mentioned by Gilhus come fully to the fore in Chapter 3 ('Approaches: The Animal in the Study of Ancient Greek Religion') by Emily Kearns. Kearns explains why the great scholarly interest in animal sacrifice did not result in greater scrutiny of the role of animals in other areas of the ancient Greek religious experience by pointing

to a move away from the principles and practices of cult and towards its recipients (the gods) and what she calls 'human mentalities'. The main part of the
chapter then synthesises how animals come into focus in an array of scholarly
works and approaches that did not make them a main concern but nevertheless
touched on their various roles and functions. Overall, Kearns synthesises past
debates just as much as she identifies areas of further interest. These include
cognitive approaches to the study of animals and animal forms in ancient
Greek religion, and the need to differentiate between individual animal species
when it comes to thinking about their symbolic functions. In particular, she
draws our attention to the different ways in which the triangular relationship
between gods, humans, and animals has been conceived in the history of
scholarship.

Part 2, 'Representations', is concerned with the way in which animals or
animal parts feature in the realm of divine representation. In Chapter 4 ('Gods
and Heroes, Humans, and Animals in Ancient Greek Myth') Hannah Willey
explores how myth enacts multiple kinds of symbolic relationships between
gods, humans, and animals. A particular focus of her chapter is the role of
narrative in bringing these three players or points of reference in relation to
each other in new constellations. Two extended case studies illustrate how this
pans out in particular texts and contexts. First, Willey considers the scene in the
Iliad in which Achilles' horse Xanthus prophesises the hero's death to investigate how an animal helps complicate the boundary between gods and humans.
She argues that the transgression reflected by a speaking animal mirrors
Achilles' own special status, which transcends that of a normal human being.
Second, she explores foundation stories, in particular narratives that feature
oracles including animal signs as part of their imagery. She shows that animals
here serve in a variety of symbolic roles: for example, they can indicate a certain place of settlement as embraced by the gods, and they can also serve as
intermediaries between the colonists and the supernatural. In highlighting such
functions, Willey's contribution anticipates Chapter 9 (on oracles and divination), which considers the same topic from another perspective.

Chapter 5 ('The Theriomorphism of the Major Greek Gods') by Jan Bremmer
is at once broader and narrower than the previous two chapters. It is broader in
that Bremmer moves beyond the realm of myth and representation by including
the link to ritual practices; and it is narrower because he considers one particular
aspect of how gods and animals come together in ancient Greek religion –
through the full or partial divine zoomorphism of some of the major Olympian
deities. In doing so, Bremmer takes up strands of argument featured in earlier
chapters, most notably those relating to the possibility of divine metamorphosis.
The question of how theriomorphic and anthropomorphic forms of the major
Greek deities relate to each other – and, indeed, the otherworldly nature (or
'essence') of the gods – takes centre stage here. Bremmer takes the reader through
the way in which it has been answered by classical scholars past and present. He
concludes that full or partial divine theriomorphism brings out particular aspects of
the otherworldly nature of the gods and goddesses in question.

The possibility of divine representation in animal form also features in Chapter 6 ('Greek Anthropomorphism versus Egyptian Zoomorphism: Conceptual Considerations in Greek Thought and Literature'). The chapter considers how the zoomorphism of the Egyptian deities was conceived of and explained in the writings of several ancient Greek authors (Herodotus, Plutarch, and Philostratus). The chapter shows that, more often than not, the encounter with non-anthropomorphic deities in Egyptian religion raised fundamental questions about the principles and practices of divine representation in the human sphere. And these questions could be answered only with the help of broader conceptions about the universal nature of the gods and their representation among different peoples. Thus, a question already flagged by Bremmer – how divine anthropomorphism relates to divine theriomorphism – takes centre stage here, too, except that this time the focus is on how ancient Greek authors themselves answered it. All three case studies at the core of the chapter, in distinctive ways, distinguish those aspects of religion that are culturally specific (and thus diverse) from those that are universal. They differ in how they evaluate the suitability of anthropomorphism and theriomorphism to represent the true nature of the divine.

In Chapter 7 ('Philosophers on Animals in Ancient Greek Religion') James Collins spotlights conceptual and abstract considerations involving the role of animals in various Greek religious beliefs and practices. By investigating how ancient Greek philosophers discuss the place of animals in ancient Greek religion, Collins is able to show that the philosophical debate relates to their traditional roles and functions both within and outside of ancient Greek religion to develop alternative cosmologies and moral frameworks. The favoured vegetarianism of some philosophical schools (most notably the Pythagoreans) is merely the most obvious example here, as it openly dismisses the collective consumption of sacrificial meat. The vegetarian identity of the philosopher/thinker thus stands in sharp contrast to the civic ideology of the meat-eating and feasting citizens. Collins's chapter concludes this part of the book by exploring philosophy as an area of thought (about gods, humans, and animals as different categories of being) that relates to the principles and practices of ancient Greek religion without being identical to them. The philosophical perspectives on the roles and symbolic values of animals in certain areas of the ancient Greek religious experience can thus further illuminate mainstream religious practices. At the same time, they also provide an invaluable contemporary perspective in their own right.

Part 3, 'Beliefs and Practices', comprises six chapters that investigate the use and function of animals in the major forms of human/divine contact in the ancient Greek world. Chapter 8 ('Caloric Codes: Ancient Greek Animal Sacrifice') by Fritz Graf provides a central contribution to the book. Most of the other chapters point to it in one or the other way, thus confirming the centrality of blood sacrifice to the ancient Greek religious experience. The chapter begins with a succinct survey of how animal sacrifice has featured in classical scholarship to describe the *status quaestionis*. Graf then goes on to illustrate how our perception of blood sacrifice changes if it is considered in the larger context of Greek religious beliefs and practices concerning gods, humans, *and* animals. He shows, for example, that in most instances it is too simplistic to think of the role of the animal as such. A more nuanced picture distinguishes between the symbolic value of different animal species as sacrificial animals (such as the victim's age, gender, or colour of its fur). Further differentiation of the normative practice is derived by considering the evidence for the sacrificing of animals without the subsequent consumption of sacrificial meat, sacrifices to heroes rather than the major Greek deities, the principles and practices of Minoan and Mycenean animal sacrifice, as well as the myths associated with the origins of the practice. A section on philosophical attitudes towards animal sacrifice takes up some of the considerations raised in the previous chapter and presents them in the larger context of actual ritual practice. Most notably, this applies to the rejection of the idea that animals constitute a suitable gift to the gods – a thought that anticipates the outright rejection of animal sacrifice discussed in the final section of the chapter.

Chapter 9 ('Animals in Ancient Greek Divination: Oracles, Predictions, and Omens') moves on from animal sacrifice to divination as another set of beliefs and practices drawing on animals. It shows that animals do not feature merely in certain forms of technical divination – most notably in ornithomancy (the observation of birds) and extispicy (the reading of entrails) – but also in dreams, oracles, and omens of all kinds. The chapter begins with a general introduction to how ancient Greek cultural practices designed to anticipate future events draw on the natural environment in general, and animals in particular, to generate meaning. Some comments on how this pans out in ornithomancy and extispicy/hepatomancy are followed by a discussion of the roles of animals in dreams, oracles, and omens. Next, the chapter explores the complex roles animals play as intermediaries in ancient attempts to access the superior knowledge of the gods. Overall, it shows that oracles, predictions, and omens have more in common than we are sometimes prepared to acknowledge. It thus raises the question of whether it makes sense to think of oracular and 'technical' divination as separate strategies of invoking the gods in the intent to participate in the supernatural knowledge of the divine, as is frequently the case in classical scholarship.

The capacity of animals to mediate between the human and the divine realms also features prominently in Chapter 10 ('Animals in Ancient Greek Dedications'). Here, Milette Gaifman outlines the way the divine, human, and animal realms intersect in the material evidence attesting to the ancient Greek cultural practice of offering dedications to the gods. A particular focus is on some of the items depicting animals dedicated in the sanctuary of Zeus at Olympia between the eighth and fourth centuries BCE. These dedications illustrate various ways in which religion drew on the place of certain animals in Greek culture and society and rendered them into effective symbols in human interactions with the supernatural. Gaifman explores the scope and limits of what dedicatory objects can and cannot reveal about the intentions and motivations of those dedicating them, and variously emphasises the centrality of context in the reading of these objects. The consideration of place in both a literal and a more general *Platz im Leben* sense, together with comparisons with similar objects, allows us to understand some of the manifold ways in which dedications depicting animals, or humans and animals, facilitate real and symbolic transactions with the supernatural.

Chapter 11 ('Animals in Asclepian Medicine: Myth, Cult, and Miracle Healings') by Florian Steger and Frank Ursin investigates the way in which certain animals feature in the context of myths and ritual practices pertaining to Asclepian medicine. The authors illustrate that in the intersecting realms of healing and miracle work, animals variously help to describe the figure of the doctor/healer and the process of healing itself. The figure of the doctor/healer frequently combines human, animal, and divine aspects or powers. Asclepius, arguably the most prominent example of an ancient Greek doctor, whose persona came to represent the practice of medicine itself, serves as a case in point. The way in which the divine, human, and animal realms intersect in his case and the practices attributed to him offers insight into an often-neglected area of influence of the religious in the ancient world (medicine or temple healing) and reveals the origins of a tradition that continues to resonate in the present (in the form of the snake coiling around a staff and the so-called Hippocratic oath).

Questions of legitimacy that feature prominently in Chapter 11, such as ancient doctors' struggles to establish their authority amid rival explanations of disease, resurface in Chapter 12 ('Circe's Ram: Animals in Ancient Greek Magic'). Here, Korshi Dosoo explores the way in which magical practices and the beliefs sustaining them draw on the tripartite symbolic structure of ancient Greek religion featuring gods, humans, and animals and instrumentalise it for their own ends. Dosoo shows that (real and imagined) magical rituals conceptualise humans and animals in a variety of ways. At times (as in curse tablets), they stress the isomorphism between human and animal bodies; at other times, they foreground the ontological difference between humans and animals with the ultimate intention of animalising the human. A particular focus here is on the role and function of the transformation of humans into animals through magical means as part of the larger transgressions some magical practices promote. Transgression also features in the way certain representations of magical sacrifice collapse the distinction between human and animal bodies, again inverting the conventions and structures of official religion.

A short concluding chapter (Chapter 13: 'Gods, Humans, and Animals Revisited') pulls together some of the threads that run through the previous chapters. It addresses the question of change in the perception and use of animals in ancient Greek religious beliefs and practices over time and conclude with a few remarks on promising avenues of further enquiry.

This introductory chapter began with a discussion of John Berger's influential essay 'Why Look at Animals?' and his diagnosis of a growing dissociation between humans and animals in the modern world. I took issue with his implicit conclusion that it was, above all, this dissociation that opened up the possibility of the use of animals as representations and symbols. The human appropriation of non-human creatures is not primarily a symptom of modernity; it is as old as humanity itself. The individual contributions to this book show that the ancient Greeks, for example, regularly drew on animals and animal parts to make complex statements about the world. It is simply that in the modern world this appropriation can distance itself from the lives of real animals (due to the fact that most people now lack any authentic experience of them) while in the ancient it remained much more closely aligned with them.

Research into accounts of the relationships between humans and animals in ancient philosophical texts has shown that, despite the close proximity of humans and animals in the ancient Greek world, there was already a deep rupture between man and beast. This rift articulated itself above all in humans' attempts to distinguish their own humanity as much as possible from their animal natures.[21] As Richard Sorabji has argued, from the moment when the ancient Greek philosopher Aristotle denied animals *logos*, a fundamental ontological abyss opened up which allowed humans to think of and align ever more distinguishing criteria along the same fundamental divide.[22] In Greek and Roman thought and literature, animals were said to lack a long list of attributes, including speech, memory, and forethought.[23] And yet, in the background to this conversation, there was always the knowledge that what unites us with our furry, feathered, or scaly fellow creatures is greater than what separates us. In the ancient world, this knowledge articulated itself, for example, in the medium of storytelling, which explored the various ways our human and animal natures intersect.[24]

The beliefs and practices that constitute ancient Greek religion are no exception here. As we will see, relationships of both likeness *and* difference shape the way in which animals feature in different areas of the ancient Greek religious experience (including myth). Taken together, they point to the need for us to include animals as a third player and point of reference, alongside gods and humans. It is ultimately this tripartite 'entanglement' between gods, humans, *and* animals that makes ancient Greek religion such a powerful medium of sense making in the ancient world.

A note on conventions

We use British spelling throughout this book. Abbreviations of Greek and Roman authors' names and their works follow the conventions set out in the fourth edition of the *Oxford Classical Dictionary*.[25] A list of abbreviations used for secondary literature and scholarly reference works appears at the start of this book. We use the Latinised versions of all Greek and Roman authors' names (Herodotus, Dionysus, etc.), except when the Greek name is more common and established. We have tried to make the book accessible and interesting to both classical scholars with knowledge of the ancient languages and general readers with no such knowledge. For this reason, all quotes from the ancient literature in the main text are also offered in translation. Similarly, individual words or short phrases are transliterated from the ancient Greek for greater accessibility. We have rendered κ as k (not c), αι as ai (not ae), οι as oi (not oe), etc. We have transcribed η as ē and ω as ō but have not marked long α, ι, or υ unless the author has specifically marked the length of these vowels in the Greek. Cross-references ('this book, Chapter …') point to overlaps and themes that emerge between the individual chapters. Such themes are discussed in Chapter 13. The individual chapters' bibliographies include all items referenced in the notes as well as other relevant works on the topic in question that may be helpful. Names including a particle (e.g. 'van', 'von', 'de') are listed alphabetically according to the first letter of the surname (e.g. van Straten is listed under 'S', not 'V').

Notes

1 Berger 1980.
2 The relatively recent emergence of displays of domestic animals (pigs, goats, rabbits, cattle) in many Western zoos shows that these once-familiar animals have now also become exotic creatures.
3 Berger himself refers to the ancient world as a contrast to modernity: Berger 1980: 6–9.
4 Human/animal relations in antiquity: e.g. Dumont 2001: 11–43, 437–452. On domestic animals in the ancient world, see: Clutton-Brock 2007; Howe 2014; Kron 2014b.
5 Companions: MacKinnon 2014b. Foodstuffs: Kron 2014a; McInerney 2014.
6 Hunting in the ancient world: e.g. Hughes 2007; MacKinnon 2014a.
7 The ancient naturalistic tradition is discussed in Bodson 2014 (with further literature).
8 Some exemplary works on animals in ancient Greek thought and literature: Osborne 2007; Rothwell 2007; Payne 2010 (with a comparative ancient and modern edge); Lefkowitz 2014; Thumiger 2014.
9 See, e.g., Hom. *Od.* 17.290–315; Plut. *Them.* 10; Diod. Sic. 17.92 to illustrate this point with three ancient tales of outstanding canine loyalty to their human owners. On the 'man-only *topos*', see, in detail, Newmyer 2017.
10 By 'entanglements', I mean the manifold ways in which the lives, identities, and conceptions of humans and other animals are inextricably bound up with each other. On the notion of 'entanglement', see also this volume, Chapter 1.
11 On ancient attitudes towards animals: Lonsdale 1979.
12 By 'symbolic', I mean that religious beliefs and practices have the capacity to point to (or represent) realities and worlds that lie beyond themselves. Both the immanent (this-worldly) and the transcendent (otherworldly) dimensions of the religious rely on this capacity to signify.
13 On religion as a 'language': Geertz 1973: 87–125 ('religion as a cultural system'). On ancient Greek religion as a symbolic 'language': Gould 2001 with Kindt 2012: 70–82.
14 For an early, pioneering work on the role of animals in ancient Greek religion prior to the recent wave of interest, see Bodson 1975, who considered the use and function of animals according to their species. More recent foundational works on the role of animals in certain areas of the ancient Greek religious experience: e.g. Gilhus 2006; McInerney 2020, esp. 97–122, 123–145, 196–216; Aston 2011; Struck 2014; Ogden 2014; as well as the Greek essays collected by Johnston *et al.* 2013.
15 On animals in ancient Greek blood sacrifice see, e.g., Ekroth 2014, 2019 and Osborne 2016 (all with further literature). See also this volume, Chapter 8 (including an extensive bibliography on ancient Greek blood sacrifice).

16 On the 'culinary triangle': Lévi-Strauss 2008. The culinary triangle offers an anthropology based on the distinction of cooked, raw, and rotten foods.
17 Detienne and Vernant 1989.
18 Burkert 1986.
19 See, e.g., Faraone and Naiden 2012; Naiden 2013.
20 On Classics and human/animal studies: Kindt 2017. On the 'embeddedness' of ancient Greek religion: e.g. Bremmer 1994: 2–4; Kindt 2012: 16–19.
21 The philosophical literature of the ancient world engaged in an extended discussion of what is generally referred to as 'the question of the animal' (what separates animals from humans). On this question, see Wolfe 2003. On ways of answering it in ancient philosophy, see Sorabji 1993; Newmyer 2005, 2007, 2017; Osborne 2007.
22 Sorabji refers to various passages in Aristotle's writing, including *DA* 1.2 (404b4–6). See, in detail, Sorabji 1993: 12, n. 39 (with further references).
23 For an extensive account of such essentialist distinguishing features, see Sorabji 1993.
24 I am thinking here, for example, of the Homeric animal similes (see, e.g., Minchin 2001; Hawtree 2014), the genre of fable (see, e.g., Lefkowitz 2014), or, indeed, the animal choruses of Old Attic comedy (see, e.g., Rothwell 2007). On the representation of this conversation in Homer, Aeschylus, and Plato, see also Heath 2005. Ancient Greek religion as a religion of the story: Kindt 2016, esp. 153–155.
25 See https://oxfordre.com/classics/page/abbreviation-list/.

Bibliography

Aston, E. (2011) *Mixanthropoi. Animal–Human Hybrid Deities in Greek Religion.* Liège.

Berger, R. (1980) 'Why look at animals?', in J. Berger (ed.) *On Looking.* New York, N.Y., 1–26 (repr. as a short stand-alone monograph: Berger, J. (2009) *Why Look at Animals?* London).

Bodson, L. (1975) *Hiera zôia. Contribution à l'étude de la place de l'animal dans la religion grecque ancienne.* Brussels.

Bodson, L. (2014) 'Zoological knowledge in ancient Greece and Rome', in G. L. Campbell (ed.) *The Oxford Handbook of Animals in Classical Thought and Life.* Oxford, 556–578.

Bremmer, J. (1994) *Ancient Greek Religion.* Cambridge.

Burkert, W. (1983) *Homo Necans. The Anthropology of Ancient Greek Sacrificial Ritual and Myth*, trans. P. Bing. Berkeley, Calif. (German orig. 1972).

Clutton-Brock, J. (2007) 'How domestic animals have shaped the development of the human species', in L. Kalof (ed.) *A Cultural History of Animals in Antiquity.* London, 71–96.

Detienne, M. and J.-P. Vernant (eds.) (1989) *The Cuisine of Sacrifice among the Greeks*, trans. P. Wissing., Ill (French orig. 1979).

Dumont, J. (2001) *Les Animaux dans l'antiquité grecque.* Paris.

Ekroth, G. (2014) 'Animal sacrifice in antiquity', in G. L. Campbell (ed.) *The Oxford Handbook of Animals in Classical Thought and Life.* Oxford, 324–354.

Ekroth, G. (2019) 'Why does Zeus care about thighbones from sheep? Defining the divine and structuring the world through animal sacrifice in ancient Greece', *History of Religions* 58, 225–250.

Faraone, C. and F. Naiden (eds.) (2012) *Modern Perspectives on Ancient Animal Sacrifice.* Cambridge.

Geertz, C. (1973) *The Interpretation of Cultures. Selected Essays.* New York, N.Y. (orig. published 1966).

Gilhus, I. S. (2006) *Animals, Gods and Humans. Changing Attitudes to Animals in Greek, Roman and Early Christian Ideas*. London.

Gould, J. (2001) 'On making sense of Greek religion', in P. E. Easterling and J. Muir (eds.) *Greek Religion and Society*. Oxford, 1–33.

Hawtree, L. (2014) 'Animals in epic', in G. L. Campbell (ed.) *The Oxford Handbook of Animals in Classical Thought and Life*. Oxford, 73–83.

Heath, J. (2005) *The Talking Greeks. Speech, Animals, and the Other in Homer, Aeschylus, and Plato*. Cambridge.

Howe, T. (2014) 'Domestication and breeding of livestock: horses, mules, asses, cattle, sheep, goats, and swine', in G. L. Campbell (ed.) *The Oxford Handbook of Animals in Classical Thought and Life*. Oxford, 99–108.

Hughes, J. D. (2007) 'Hunting in the ancient Mediterranean world', in L. Kalof (ed.) *A Cultural History of Animals in Antiquity*. London, 47–70.

Johnston, P., A. Mastrocinque and S. Papaionannou (eds.) (2013) *Animals in Greek and Roman Religion and Myth. Proceedings of the Symposium Grumentinum Grumento Nova (Potenza) 5–7 June 2013*. Cambridge.

Kindt, J. (2012) *Rethinking Greek Religion*. Cambridge.

Kindt, J. (2016) *Revisiting Delphi. Religion and Storytelling in Ancient Greece*. Cambridge.

Kindt, J. (2017) 'Capturing the ancient animal: human/animal studies and the classics', *Journal of Hellenic Studies* 137, 213–225.

Kron, G. (2014a) 'Ancient fishing and fish farming', in G. L. Campbell (ed.) *The Oxford Handbook of Animals in Classical Thought and Life*. Oxford, 192–202.

Kron, G. (2014b) 'Animal husbandry', in G. L. Campbell (ed.) *The Oxford Handbook of Animals in Classical Thought and Life*. Oxford, 109–135.

Lefkowitz, J. B. (2014) 'Aesop and animal fable', in G. L. Campbell (ed.) *The Oxford Handbook of Animals in Classical Thought and Life*. Oxford, 1–23.

Levi-Strauss, C. (2008) 'The culinary triangle', in C. Counihan and P. van Esterik (eds.) *Food and Culture. A Reader*, trans. P. Brooks. London, 36–43 (orig. published in *Partisan Review* 33 (1966), 586–596).

Lonsdale, S. H. (1979) 'Attitudes towards animals in ancient Greece', *Greece and Rome* 26, 146–159.

MacKinnon, M. (2014a) 'Hunting', in G. L. Campbell (ed.) *The Oxford Handbook of Animals in Classical Thought and Life*. Oxford, 203–215.

MacKinnon, M. (2014b) 'Pets', in G. L. Campbell (ed.) *The Oxford Handbook of Animals in Classical Thought and Life*. Oxford, 269–281.

McInerney, J. J. (2014) 'Civilization, gastronomy, meat-eating', in G. L. Campbell (ed.) *The Oxford Handbook of Animals in Classical Thought and Life*. Oxford, 248–268.

McInerney, J. J. (2020) *The Cattle of the Sun. Cows and Culture in the World of the Ancient Greeks*. Princeton, N.J.

Minchin, E. (2001) 'Similes in Homer: image, mind's eye, and memory', in J. Watson (ed.) *Speaking Volumes. Orality and Literacy in the Greek and Roman World*. Leiden, 25–52.

Naiden, F. (2013) *Smoke Signals for the Gods. Ancient Greek Sacrifice from the Archaic through Roman Periods*. Oxford.

Newmyer, S. T. (2005) *Animals, Rights, and Reason in Plutarch and Modern Ethics*. London.

Newmyer, S. T. (2007) 'Animals in ancient philosophy: conceptions and misconceptions', in L. Kalof (ed.) *A Cultural History of Animals in Antiquity*. London, 151–174.

Newmyer, S. T. (2017) *The Animal and the Human in Ancient and Modern Thought. The 'Man Alone of Animals' Concept*. London.

Ogden, D. (2014) 'Animal magic', in G. L. Campbell (ed.) *The Oxford Handbook of Animals in Classical Thought and Life*. Oxford, 294–309.

Osborne, R. (2016) 'Sacrificial theologies', in E. Eidinow, J. Kindt and R. Osborne (eds.) *Theologies of Ancient Greek Religion*. Cambridge, 233–248.

Osborne, C. (2007) *Dumb Beasts and Dead Philosophers. Humanity and the Humane in Ancient Philosophy and Literature*. Oxford.

Payne, M. (2010) *The Animal Part. Human and Other Animals in the Poetic Imagination*. Chicago, Ill.

Rothwell, K. S. (2007) *Nature, Culture, and the Origins of Greek Comedy. A Study in Animal Choruses*. Cambridge.

Sorabji, R. (1993) *Animal Minds and Human Morals. The Origins of a Western Debate*. Ithaca, N.Y.

Struck, P. (2014) 'Animals and divination', in G. L. Campbell (ed.) *The Oxford Handbook of Animals in Classical Thought and Life*. Oxford, 310–323.

Thumiger, C. (2014) 'Animals in tragedy', in G. L. Campbell (ed.) *The Oxford Handbook of Animals in Classical Thought and Life*. Oxford, 384–440.

Wolfe, C. (ed.) (2003) *Zoontologies. The Question of the Animal*. Minneapolis, Minn.

Part 1
Perspectives

1 The 'entanglement' of gods, humans, and animals in ancient Greek religion

J. McInerney

In one of the most famous thought experiments of the 20th century, Erwin Schrödinger imagined the case of a cat in a box containing a small amount of radioactive matter which, upon breaking down, causes a hammer to shatter a flask of hydrocyanic acid, killing the cat. Schrödinger's elegantly conceived scenario was designed to expose flaws in the superposition principle of quantum mechanics by revealing the absurdity of imagining the cat to be both dead and alive at the same time.[1] The complexities of quantum mechanics might seem more appropriate to a paper on Plato than a chapter on the spheres of the human, animal, and divine but in the course of another paper written in the same year, Schrödinger employed the term *Verschränkung* ('entanglement') to describe what Einstein and others called a 'spooky' aspect of quantum theory: namely, the observation that the quantum state of some particles cannot be described without reference to the quantum state of certain other particles.[2]

Without wishing to press the analogy too far, and certainly without wishing to harm any cats, I propose that 'entanglement' is, in fact, a useful way of analysing the triad of human, animal, and divine in ancient Greek religion. Rather than postulating that animals are creatures lower down the food chain or the chain of consciousness, or that they are simply a medium for communicating with the divine through sacrifice, oracles, and omens, I suggest that all three are recursively linked, that the boundaries between them are permeable, and that Greek culture recognised that behind the seemingly obvious and firm distinctions between them, the three classes of living beings were actually in a constant state of flux.

In his description of Arcadia, the nearest to a primeval landscape available to a second-century CE Greek, Pausanias offers the following description of the statue of Black Demeter, located 30 stades from Phigaleia, in a cave sanctuary:[3]

> καθέζεσθαι μὲν ἐπὶ πέτρᾳ, γυναικὶ δὲ ἐοικέναι τἆλλα πλὴν κεφαλήν· κεφαλὴν δὲ καὶ κόμην εἶχεν ἵππου, καὶ δρακόντων τε καὶ ἄλλων θηρίων εἰκόνες προσεπεφύκεσαν τῇ κεφαλῇ...Μέλαιναν δὲ ἐπονομάσαι φασὶν αὐτήν, ὅτι καὶ ἡ θεὸς μέλαιναν τὴν ἐσθῆτα εἶχε.

> It was seated on a rock, like to a woman in all respects save the head. She had the head and hair of a horse, and there grew out of her head images of

serpents and other beasts...They say that they named her Black because the goddess had black apparel.[4]

Far from being unique, Black Demeter was part of a cluster of myths and cults that reflected a very fluid boundary between the animal and the divine in Arcadia. At Lykosoura, for example, the cult statue of Despoina was adorned with an elaborately carved veil that appears to show animals in human dress dancing in the goddess's honour.[5] Nearby Konstantinos Kourouniotis found a number of terracotta animal-headed figurines, presumably representations of the initiates to the Mysteries held at Lykosoura.[6] Nor was transformation confined to the human initiates. Pausanias tells the story of Demeter pursued by Poseidon.

πλανωμένη γὰρ τῇ Δήμητρι, ἡνίκα τὴν παῖδα ἐζήτει, λέγουσιν ἕπεσθαί οἱ τὸν Ποσειδῶνα ἐπιθυμοῦντα αὐτῇ μιχθῆναι, καὶ τὴν μὲν ἐς ἵππον μετα-βαλοῦσαν ὁμοῦ ταῖς ἵπποις νέμεσθαι ταῖς Ὀγκίου, Ποσειδῶν δὲ συνίησεν ἀπατώμενος καὶ συγγίνεται τῇ Δήμητρι ἄρσενι ἵππῳ καὶ αὐτὸς εἰκασθείς.

When Demeter was wandering in search of her daughter, she was followed, it is said, by Poseidon, who lusted after her. So she turned, the story runs, into a mare, and grazed with the mares of Oncius; realizing that he was outwitted, Poseidon too changed into a stallion and enjoyed Demeter.[7]

The cults of Arcadia may not have been typical (if such an adjective is in any way applicable to Greek religious practice), but they powerfully remind us that Greek religion was polymorphous and that the gods were, to use Marcel Detienne's useful term, polyhedrous.[8] If, as Xenophanes complained, the gods' behaviour was characterised by Homer and Hesiod as resembling the 'stealings and adulteries and deceivings of one another', the tain of the mirror revealed quite a different picture, more blurry, where the image of the divine could look more like an animal than a superhuman.[9] The realms of human, animal, and divine morphed into one another. Each was entangled with the other; each helped shape how the others were imagined.[10]

Recognising this 'entanglement' has become easier because, if the last generation witnessed a 'spatial turn', it is equally plausible to speak now of an 'animal turn'. Since Edward E. Evans-Pritchard's identification of the bovine idiom in his studies of the Dinka and Nuer, there has been a growing awareness among anthropologists and philosophers that the human/animal relationship is fundamental to our sense of self.[11] Roderick Campbell has recently observed that 'definitions of animality are by implication definitions of humanity'.[12] A similar line of thought runs through the work of major thinkers such as Giorgio Agamben and Tim Ingold.[13] At its most radical, this 'animal turn' has led to the claim that 'the human–animal distinction can no longer and ought no longer to be maintained'.[14] At an ethical level, this may well be the case, in the same way that biological race is an outmoded concept. Yet, just as race is still a powerful weapon in political discourse, so, too, the belief that animals and humans are fundamentally somehow distinct remains firmly embedded in popular thinking. The recent trend towards declaring pet owners 'guardians' signals an evolving relationship but it is not a sign that we can yet speak of humans and animals interchangeably.[15]

It is a philosophical shift that, the politics of animal liberation aside, has proved productive in a number of areas. For example, Jacques Cauvin and other prehistorians at the Maison de l'Orient have made the case that the coming to consciousness of the human species was largely effected through the imaginative confrontation of humans and animals, especially those animals that humans hunt or those animals by whom humans were hunted.[16] From the beginning of settled life, ritual space in places such as Çatalhöyük and Göbekli Tepe attest to the insistent presence of animals in shaping human identities.[17] This is what makes the hybrid *Löwenmensch* (Figure 1.1) so striking: not that it stands at the head of a long tradition of figural art, but that by hybridising human and animal it foregrounds the question 'What makes a lion and a human what they are?' Subsequently, during the Neolithic, domestication would profoundly shift human/animal relations, but it is now rarely interpreted as a simple narrative of human dominance and is most often viewed as a symbiotic relationship. We owe animals our sense of humanity, and, consequently, classifying them is one of the earliest mental operations preserved in the literature of Mesopotamia.[18]

In the study of the Greeks, the investigation of animality in relation to humans and gods has largely followed two trajectories. An older line of enquiry concerned the animal avatars of Greek gods revealed by their epithets: 'Athena the owl', 'ox-eyed' Hera, Apollo Lykeios, and so forth.[19] Investigations of this phenomenon have tended to downplay the animality of the Olympian gods (but see this volume, Chapter 5). Athena simply *appears* to be an owl, as if described in some hyper-vivid metaphor, to explain the way she suddenly disappears into the rafters. Similarly, Hera's bovine associations are put down to her connection to the pastures and fecundity associated with the grazing herd.[20] In this line of argument the Greek gods are not genuinely theriomorphic. A god may momentarily take on the form of some other creature, but in Maurizio Bettini's words, 'il ne se transforme pas en cette autre entité'.[21] In some readings these appearances are no more than a relic of an earlier substrate. Robert Luyster, for example, asserts that Athena's 'incarnation in (or at the least, accompaniment by) [the owl] displays once again her character as Mistress of the Dead'.[22] Her essence is as a goddess of death, which is evoked by the owl, which may be a temporary incarnation of the goddess. This contingent and uncertain animality makes the Greek gods different from the Egyptian gods whose animality is unavoidable, persistent, and undeniable (see this volume, Chapter 9). (It is worth noting, in this respect, that some early 20th-century scholars dismissed Pausanias' account of a horse-headed Black Demeter; the periegete had been duped by local storytellers.[23])

The second line of enquiry has focused on the prominence of animals in the Greek imagination, particularly expressed in the Greeks' powerful devotion to

Figure 1.1 The Lion-man (*Löwenmensch*) from the Stadel cave in Hohlenstein in the Lone Valley (Germany), ca. 35,000–40,000 BP
Image: D. Hollmann, Wikimedia Commons, CC BY-SA 4.0 (open access)

sacrifice (on which see also, in detail, this volume, Chapter 8).[24] Why do the Greeks in endless variation and repetition offer sacrifices of domesticated animals to their gods? Although the 'Paris School' of Jean-Pierre Vernant and Marcel Detienne has offered a striking structuralist reading that sees animals serving as a principal mediator between the Greeks and their gods, it was Walter Burkert, more than anyone else, who framed the question in terms of historical processes. For Burkert, the answer was that, as hunters, we established modes of action and thinking over thousands of years. This resulted in a fundamentally tripartite system: we kill animals, but by offering them to the gods, we sacralise these murders.[25] Thus, humans and animals are actually only two legs of the tripod. Where we are and where our animals are, so, too, are our gods.

This is an extraordinarily satisfying picture of a coherent religious system. As an explanation, it is totalising, and thereby explains the ubiquity of sacrifice. It is also historicising, and therefore avoids the criticism often levelled at structuralism for its lack of historical specificity. It resonates with many modern Western historians who, raised within a Judeo-Christian milieu, are habituated to religious systems that display a similar blend of elements. The stories of Exodus, the Pascal lamb, and Christ's sacrifice, for example, all map easily on to a paradigm according to which animals are the medium by which we communicate with (and to some degree seek to control) the divine.

Yet, there are elements of both lines of enquiry – the purely metaphorical animality of the Greek gods and the hunter–gatherer origins of sacrifice – that miss the mark. For example, despite their overwhelmingly human appearance, the Greek gods never shake off their animal avatars; nor can the persistent habit of conceiving of the gods as somehow animalistic be explained away by appealing to an outdated evolutionary model – Athena Hippia, Poseidon Hippius, Dionysus, bull-horned or bull faced, and Apollo Lykeios are as much a part of the way the gods were experienced as were their anthropomorphic avatars.[26]

Sympathetic magic, for example, encouraged bringing the gods closer into human proximity by rendering the divine and mysterious into something familiar in the shape of an animal (see this volume, Chapter 12): piglets, evoking the genitals of Demeter, rendered her fecundity into something tangible. The animals were hurled into pits, and the fertiliser created from their rotting carcasses, the ancient equivalent of 'blood and bone' favoured by modern gardeners, was then hauled up by the goddess's attendants, the 'Bailers'.[27] Similarly, the *hieros gamos* that took place at the Boukoleion was not, despite Carl Kerenyi's arguments, a 'vestige of the old stratum of Dionysian religion' but a contemporary practice of Aristotle's own day.[28] The archon Basileus coupled with the Basilinna in order to guarantee the fecundity of the entire community. This was not a metaphorical performance; it was one that depended on deploying the animality of the god in order to access divine power on the community's behalf.[29]

Studies of sacrifice, too, though long a staple of studies of Greek religion, may have misconstrued the role of human/animal relations in framing the encounter with the divine. It is not from the aeons of human existence spent hunting and gathering that we developed sacrifice as a mode of communication with the divine. In fact, the indigenous people of Australia who were entirely hunter–gatherer communities before contact with Europeans in the late 18th century, though immersed in rituals, have no practices that correspond in any way to sacrifice. Instead, as Jonathan Z. Smith has pointed out, sacrifice is much more likely to have arisen in the millennia following domestication, when humans began to live in closer proximity to the herds they raised.[30] It is to our pastoral milieu that we should look to understand the prevalence of sacrifice in premodern societies. In fact, one can develop Smith's observation a good deal further. For example, unlike a wild herd, in which there may be a hierarchy of males, the domesticated herd is manipulated at every turn; the pastoralist controls the breeding of the herd, relying on a single bull or ram and often culling the other males as they reach maturity. Aside from making good alimentary sense, guaranteeing a steady supply of animal protein, this is a strategy of herd management that regularises culling the herd according to a sacred calendar consonant with seasonal conditions. The exploitation of the herd or flock as a resource is thereby rationalised. Sacralising the process as a sacrifice underscores its social significance and recasts the business of killing as a socially acceptable and necessary act.

Yet, even such a reading of sacrifice, where human, animal, and divine intersect, runs the risk of viewing the animal as no more than the medium for communication between the human and the divine. This would be to miss a critical feature of Greek religion: namely, that the categories of animal, human, and divine are not fixed but bleed into one another. If Dionysus is at one moment a louche easterner, a moment later he may be a wild bull or lion capable of transforming before our eyes, as Pentheus learns to his cost. Similarly, the many animal incarnations of Proteus are dangerous, as he transforms into a lion, a serpent, a leopard, and a bear, but Menelaus and his men hold on until the god grows weary and is compelled to reveal the truth.[31] It is the potential breakdown of barriers between human, animal, and divine that constantly lurks at the edge of our experience. From Kallisto and Io to Tereus and Acteon, the imaginative world of the Greeks is full of stories of gods and mortals transforming and being transformed as deception, punishment, or release.[32]

Key to this movement between the different categories is the proximity between each group. Domestication breaks down the distance between animals and humans. Where previously animals were glimpsed, smelled, and stalked at a distance carefully calibrated by human hunters (or avoided by human prey – even our original relationship to animals was contingent, depending on whether we were hunter and hunted), pastoralists are immersed in the daily presence of their animals, surrounded by the sights and smells of the cattle, sheep, goats, and pigs that are now brought into the close proximity of corral, pen, or farmyard.[33] And this shifting relationship with the animal world was understood to be profoundly significant: Enkidu's discovery of sex leads to his entry into human society, but his integration into the human world is marked by the rejection he suffers at the hands of his animal companions.[34] We may wish, like Dr Dolittle, to talk like the animals and learn their languages, but there is a gap between us. Can it be bridged?

Is there a way back to Eden?[35] Not really, because despite the existence of parrots and other talking animals, collectively these creatures are *ta aloga*, 'without reason or speech'. This is a fundamental divide, surmountable only in a fantasy such as Hicks's vision of early Philadelphia (see Figure 1.2).[36] In the real world, the lion does not lie down with the lamb. Even less likely is a perfect communion between human and animal. According to Theophrastus,

Figure 1.2 Edward Hicks, *The Peaceable Kingdom*, ca. 1834
National Gallery of Art, Washington, D.C., 1980.62.15 (open access)

Alcmaeon interpreted the distinction as the difference between perception and understanding:

Ἀλκμαίων μὲν πρῶτον ἀφορίζει τὴν πρὸς τὰ ζῷα διαφοράν. ἄνθρωπον γάρ φησι τῶν ἄλλων διαφέρειν ὅτι μόνος ξυνίησι, τὰ δ᾽ ἄλλα αἰσθάνεται μὲν οὐ ξυνίησι δέ, ὡς ἕτερον ὂν τὸ φρονεῖν καὶ αἰσθάνεσθαι.

Alcmaeon begins by determining the difference with regard to animals. For he says that a human being differs from the others because he is the only one that understands, while the others perceive but do not understand, since he considers that thinking and perceiving differ from one another.[37]

This was not the last word on the matter. Democritus, for example, was prepared to allow animals a share of reason, according to Porphyry.[38] But, in general, the similarities and differences that allowed animals and humans to be compared, such as modes of conception, qualities like speed and strength, and characteristics such as skin, teeth, and nails, showed two things: first, that we are closer to animals than to plants; but, second, that we were often in competition with animals for our survival.

This is a theme developed by Plato in his recapitulation of the rise of civilisation, outlined in the *Protagoras*.[39] For Plato, animals are the creatures upon whom Epimetheus squandered all the characteristics, attributes, and powers that he failed to share with humans. As a result, and as a compensation, Prometheus stole fiery *technē*, from which humans derive the means of surviving and flourishing, including articulate speech. We are used to reading the story of Prometheus as that of a culture hero and recognising that his theft from the gods set us on the path to civilisation 'since humankind has a share in the divine portion' (ἐπειδὴ δὲ ὁ ἄνθρωπος θείας μετέσχε μοίρας), but sometimes forgotten is that it is our weakness in relation to the animal kingdom that is compensated for by our being brought closer to the divine realm. Indeed, the primeval state imagined by Plato was one in which our natural inferiority to animals when attacked led the gods to intervene: once we had formed cities for our survival, the gods sent Hermes to teach humans how civil society should operate.[40] And just as Epimetheus distributes attributes to animals, Zeus distributes shares to men and gods alike. We were cheated by a second-rate imitation of Zeus, and compensated (eventually) by the real one. Nevertheless, our elevation came at a cost, exacted daily from Prometheus, reminding us that in the triangulation of human, animal, and divine, we must pay a price for our proximity to the gods by sacrificing some of the animals we now control.

This is not the only way that the three groups interact. For some of the Presocratics, such as Empedocles, the spirit ascends through what G. S. Kirk, J. E. Raven, and M. Schofield called 'ever higher realms of creation (plant, beasts, man) undergo[ing] the best form of incarnation possible within each, and finally regain[ing] his original status as a god'.[41] In such a schema, the movement upwards was based on a separation between the classes of beings. This corresponds to what are sometimes referred to as 'conceptual domains', defined by Robert Wuthnow as 'ontological categories that allow us to classify information under meaningful headings such as person, animal, or plant'.[42] But the lines were not so clearly drawn for everyone. Pythagoras' anecdote that he had heard his friend's voice in a dog's bark demonstrates that soul was not limited by these categories nor restricted to one of them. Aristotle, too, observed that it was difficult to determine the line of demarcation between something lifeless and an animal life. There was, he said, a continuous *metabasis* from plant to animal.[43] Aristotle's more fluid understanding of the relation between animals and humans reflects a dissatisfaction with Empedocles' rigid schema not unlike the way few people today would endorse the Cartesian notion of animals as mere *automata*.

Thanks to the proximity of humans and animals, and their undeniable intelligence (however construed), speculation regarding animal nature became a way of asking what it meant to be human. Circe's transformation of Odysseus' men into animals was an especially appropriate story to exploit to this end. Like Tiresias experiencing sex as a man and a woman, Odysseus' crew could be imagined to have a consciousness of their different states of being, both as humans and as animals (see Figure 1.3).

In the kylix, the hybrid creatures have begun their transformation but some, such as the figure taking the cup from Circe, appear to be trying to

Figure 1.3 Circe giving a potion to Odysseus' men: black figure kylix, ca. 550–525 BCE
   Museum of Fine Arts, Boston, 99.518 (public domain)
   Courtesy of the Museum of Fine Arts, Boston

communicate. The space between the figures is filled with letters that represent their attempts at speech, but what is shown is nonsensical: being theriocephalic, they can no longer produce human speech. This conceit was picked up by Plutarch, who reports an interview between Odysseus and one of the transformed men, Gryllus. His name, 'Grunter', calls attention to the first obstacle to the inquiry: pigs do not talk (at least not comprehensibly to humans).[44] The solution is to have Circe use more magic to make him capable of human speech. The satire, an early antecedent of Jonathan Swift's Houyhnhnms in *Gulliver's Travels* and perhaps even the dystopian fantasy of *The Planet of the Apes*, reveals how easily we can imagine an interior animal life not unlike our own. Gryllus argues that all the elements that we take pride in as distinctive markers of our humanity – nobility, courage, defence of our young, temperance, chastity – can be easily matched by animals. Take courage, for example. Unlike men, who resort to deceit and fraud to defeat their enemies, animals are paragons of virtue, he says.

ἀλλὰ τῶν γε θηρίων τοὺς πρὸς ἄλληλα καὶ πρὸς ὑμᾶς ἀγῶνας ὁρᾷς ὡς ἄδολοι καὶ ἄτεχνοι καὶ μετ᾽ ἐμφανοῦς γυμνοῦ τε τοῦ θαρρεῖν πρὸς ἀληθινῆς ἀλκῆς ποιοῦνται τὰς ἀμύνα.

Wild beasts, however, you will observe, are guileless and artless in their struggles, whether against one another or against you, and conduct their battles with unmistakably naked courage under the impulse of genuine valour.[45]

Similarly, if Penelope is praiseworthy for chastely waiting for Odysseus, a crow could laugh her to scorn. Being widowed, it will stay faithful to its partner for nine generations of men, and being unsusceptible to the illusions of fame or wealth – guileless, artless, and indomitable, in Gryllus' words – animals display a purer heart:

τὰ δὲ θηρία παντάπασιν ἀβάτους καὶ ἀνεπιμίκτους ἔχοντα τοῖς ἐπεισάκτοις πάθεσι τὰς ψυχὰς καὶ τοῖς βίοις πόρρω τῆς κενῆς δόξης ὥσπερ θαλάσσης ἀπῳκισμένα·

But beasts have souls completely inaccessible and closed to these adventitious passions and live their lives as free from empty illusions as though they dwelt far from the sea.[46]

When Odysseus challenges the notion that even sheep and asses have reason, Gryllus observes that just as one man may be clever and another an idiot, so, too, one animal's dullness is balanced by another's cleverness. Repeatedly, the fantasy, despite its satirical surface, invites the reader to confront the problem of the animal's similarity to the human. If Plutarch's Grunter and Swift's Houyhnhnms are odd, it is because what they say and do is so recognisably human. And since the shadow of the divine is present in all human affairs, a more human-like animal also presents a theological problem. Odysseus' last response to Gryllus expresses the anxiety that arises when we recognise that the boundaries between the human, animal, and divine are not stable. He asks,

Ἀλλ' ὅρα, Γρύλλε, μὴ δεινὸν ᾖ καὶ βίαιον ἀπολιπεῖν λόγον οἷς οὐκ ἐγγίνεται θεοῦ νόησις.

But consider, Gryllus: is it not a fearful piece of violence to grant reason to creatures that have no inherent knowledge of God?[47]

Perhaps even more disturbing than imagining rational, talking animals is the idea that some gods might be closer to animals than to the (usually) anthropomorphic Olympians: that is, that the categories of divine and animal might elide completely in some circumstances. Associated with Demeter Melaina is the worship of the Erinyes, who, far from existing only on the outskirts of civilisation in primitive Arcadia, were also given a home in Athens, where they were worshipped as the Dread Goddesses. Their disturbing animality is integral to their role as bloodthirsty avenging spirits in Aeschylus' *Eumenides*, a play profoundly concerned with human and divine relations, specifically in relation to justice. They are sleeping when the chorus first appears in the play, and are roused by the ghost of Clytaemnestra. Their appearance is the subject of a detailed description as the priestess sets the scene:

πρόσθεν δὲ τἀνδρὸς τοῦδε θαυμαστὸς λόχος
εὕδει γυναικῶν ἐν θρόνοισιν ἥμενος.

οὗτοι γυναῖκας, ἀλλὰ Γοργόνας λέγω,
οὐδ᾽ αὖτε Γοργείοισιν εἰκάσω τύποις.
εἶδόν ποτ᾽ ἤδη Φινέως γεγραμμένας
δεῖπνον φερούσας· ἄπτεροί γε μὴν ἰδεῖν
αὗται, μέλαιναι δ᾽ ἐς τὸ πᾶν βδελύκτροποι·
ῥέγκουσι δ᾽ οὐ πλατοῖσι φυσιάμασιν·
ἐκ δ᾽ ὀμμάτων λείβουσι δυσφιλῆ λίβα·
καὶ κόσμος οὔτε πρὸς θεῶν ἀγάλματα
φέρειν δίκαιος οὔτ᾽ ἐς ἀνθρώπων στέγας.
τὸ φῦλον οὐκ ὄπωπα τῆσδ᾽ ὁμιλίας
οὐδ᾽ ἥτις αἶα τοῦτ᾽ ἐπεύχεται γένος
τρέφουσ᾽ ἀνατεὶ μὴ μεταστένειν πόνον.

Before this man an extraordinary band of women slept, seated on thrones. No! Not women, but rather Gorgons I call them; and yet I cannot compare them to forms of Gorgons either. Once before I saw some creatures in a painting, carrying off the feast of Phineus; but these are wingless (featherless?) in appearance, black, altogether disgusting; they snore with repulsive breaths, they drip from their eyes hateful drops; their attire is not fit to bring either before the statues of the gods or into the homes of men. I have never seen the tribe that produced this company, nor the land that boasts of rearing this brood with impunity and does not grieve for its labor afterwards.[48]

They are a band of women, but not women; Gorgons, but then again not like gorgons. The priestess once saw a painting of the Harpies that snatched away Phineus' food, immediately calling to mind great winged beasts. These, however, are *apteroi* and *melainai*, which Peter G. Maxwell-Stuart has shown here means featherless, rather than wingless, and dark. Apollo also warns them to quit his shrine lest he shoot them and force them to vomit up the gobs of blood they have swallowed:

ἔξω, κελεύω, τῶνδε δωμάτων τάχος
χωρεῖτ᾽, ἀπαλλάσσεσθε μαντικῶν μυχῶν,
μὴ καὶ λαβοῦσα πτηνὸν ἀργηστὴν ὄφιν,
χρυσηλάτου θώμιγγος ἐξορμώμενον,
ἀνῆς ὑπ᾽ ἄλγους μέλαν᾽ ἀπ᾽ ἀνθρώπων ἀφρόν,
ἐμοῦσα θρόμβους οὓς ἀφείλκυσας φόνου.
οὔτοι δόμοισι τοῖσδε χρίμπτεσθαι πρέπει.

Out, I order you! Go away from this house at once, leave my prophetic sanctuary, so that you may not be struck by a winged glistening snake shot forth from a golden bow-string, and painfully release black foam, vomiting the clots of blood you have drained from mortals.[49]

Elsewhere, they are mistaken for old women or aged children, and, as with the descriptions of them as gorgon-like, they seem to have vaguely human faces that are crinkled and ugly. Maxwell-Stuart scoured the clues offered by Aeschylus' text to advance the argument that they were envisaged as resembling bats.[50] The visual component here is clearly very significant since audiences would have seen the Erinyes on stage before they speak, and the clues offered by Aeschylus give a sense not only of how they should be imagined in the mind's eye but how they appeared on stage. The impact of the priestess's words and Apollo's speech leaves no doubt: they were a truly horrifying spectacle. This monstrosity is then developed in a series of animal images. When Clytaemnestra's ghost describes them as we first encounter them sprawled asleep, she likens them to a pack of hunting dogs on the trail of the prey:

> ὄναρ διώκεις θῆρα, κλαγγαίνεις δ᾽ ἅπερ
> κύων μέριμναν οὔποτ᾽ ἐκλείπων πόνου.

> In a dream you are hunting your prey, and are barking like a dog that never leaves off its keenness for the work.[51]

The description suggests a kind of dumbshow in which the Furies are like a pack of sleeping dogs. The comparison with hunting dogs, baying and barking while chasing their prey, is, of course, apt since they are hunting Orestes, but the emphatic *onar* is striking: they are pursuing Orestes in their dreams, while we witness them twitching and yipping like sleeping dogs. And the Furies, as they wake, employ the same images to describe their situation. Their prey has slipped though the nets, they cry, and so they pursue him, quite literally using the traces of blood left by his murderous act to track him, vowing to drink his blood and make him a bloodless victim, drained, but not ritually slaughtered as a proper sacrificial victim:

> οὐδ᾽ ἀντιφωνεῖς, ἀλλ᾽ ἀποπτύεις λόγους,
> ἐμοὶ τραφείς τε καὶ καθιερωμένος
> καὶ ζῶν με δαίσεις οὐδὲ πρὸς βωμῷ σφαγείς.

> You do not answer, but scorn my words, you who are fattened and consecrated to me? Living, you will be my feast, not slain at an altar.[52]

Here, the hunting images lead easily into evocations of sacrifice, with Orestes transitioning from prey to victim, and the Furies from hunting pack to gruesome perversions of sacrificial priests. But, as suitable as the hunting and sacrificial imagery may be, the play is shot through with other animal references that keep destabilising how we read the Furies. They are stung by fear, as if they were horses in the traces subject to the charioteer's whip.[53] Clytaemnestra's ghost likens them to a dragon whose strength has been sapped by sleep and care.[54] In a particularly gruesome passage, Apollo describes the Furies as attending the dismemberment and disembowelling of victims as if they were torturers or executioners before saying:

πᾶς δ᾽ ὑφηγεῖται τρόπος
μορφῆς. λέοντος ἄντρον αἱματορρόφου
οἰκεῖν τοιαύτας εἰκός, οὐ χρηστηρίοις
ἐν τοῖσδε πλησίοισι τρίβεσθαι μύσος.
χωρεῖτ᾽ ἄνευ βοτῆρος αἰπολούμεναι.
ποίμνης τοιαύτης δ᾽ οὔτις εὐφιλὴς θεῶν.

The whole fashion of your form sets it forth. Creatures like you should live in the den of a blood-drinking lion, and not inflict pollution on all near you in this oracular shrine. Be gone, you goats without a herdsman! No god loves such a flock.[55]

So, they are, by turns, hunting dogs chasing their quarry, bloodsuckers prolonging the death of the sacrificial animal, a sleeping dragon, lions dripping with blood, whose surroundings are like the charnel house around a lion's den, and a herd of goats without a herdsman, so disgusting that they are spurned by the gods.

In addition to the shifting visual metaphors that make the goddesses into various animals, there is an aural component to the evocation of the Erinyes that also emphasises their animality. When the Eumenides are introduced, their first sounds are described as a *mugmos*, and soon after they utter an *ōgmos*. Since the 19th century, there has been a great deal of discussion about these terms, which are contained in the stage directions. The modern consensus has been that they cried 'Mu! Mu!' and 'Oh, Oh!' and that either Aeschylus or an early copyist replaced the direct speech with a stage direction. There is less consensus regarding the meaning and significance of these cries. LSJ defines *mugmos* as an 'utterance of the sound μὺ μῦ ("mu/mū"), moaning, whimpering (v. μύζω)', citing this passage in the *Eumenides*. The entry for the verb μύζω ('muzō') says, 'make the sound μὺ μῦ ("mu/mū"), mutter, moan', with, once again, references to the *Eumenides*. There is a distinct air of circularity surrounding these explanations. The moaning and whimpering are appropriate for sleeping dogs, to be sure, but perhaps we can go further than citing the Eumenides' cries to explain the stage directions (and vice versa). If we begin from the premise that the key is not *mu*– but *mug*– or *muk*– (not a stretch, since both are stop consonants, one (k) unvoiced, the other (g) voiced), we find a plausible explanation for the Erinyes' cries in μυκάομαι ('*mukaomai*') – to low, bellow, roar. Not only is this verb found in a variety of sources, including Homer, Aeschylus, Euripides, and even Aristophanes, but it is also consistently used to evoke the bellowing of cattle or similar sounds: the clapping of thunder, the reverberation of a drum, or the ringing sound of a shield. Perhaps most striking is a disturbing passage in the *Odyssey* in which Odysseus' men profane the Cattle of the Sun and the meat 'bellows' on the spits.[56] Like the various monsters in Hesiod's *Theogony*, the Erinyes defy clear classification. What lies beneath is not simply the opposite of human, not simply 'animal'; it is endlessly shifting in appearance and sound. Even Olympian gods like Apollo and Athena, as well as the ghost of the very human Clytaemnestra, struggle to convey the true awfulness of the Semnai Theai.

Could the Furies be both hunters and animals destined for sacrifice? Ann Lebeck has argued that in the play the 'fate of victim and avenger fuse'.[57] And Stefan Dolgert has recently tried to extend that reading by suggesting that the Erinyes 'must first become victims in order to become Eumenides'.[58] The language of the play is designed to give us auditory cues that prompt the audience to anticipate the sacrifice of the Erinyes. Their *mugmos* and *ōgmos*, in fact, are not the sounds of either whimpering hounds or baying hunters on the scent, but the lowing and bellowing of animals before an altar awaiting sacrifice. It was the experience of preparing herds of animals for butchery, as on the Acropolis at the Panathenaia, that supplied the Athenians with a rich soundscape of sacrifice evoked by Aeschylus.[59] In suggesting the sacrifice of the Erinyes, Aeschylus delves deep into the paradoxes of justice: the principle of blood guilt must be tempered by discourse, debate, and deliberation. The Eumenides will be appeased by Athena, but, ultimately, human society will be able to survive only if the Erinyes are themselves sacrificed. The animal must be sacrificed to make the emergence of the divine possible.

We began with a triad of human, animal, and divine. The difficulty of interpreting Greek religious thinking and practice using these categories is that, as we have seen, they are not fixed but fold recursively upon each other. It would, nevertheless, be a mistake to assert blithely that the categories were meaningless. Clearly, at most times, Zeus is imagined as the father of gods and men, a sky god capable of wielding thunderbolts. Similarly, if Athena were not his daughter, were not armed, were not the warrior–protectress of Athens and the mentor of Odysseus, it would be impossible to say anything about her that would make sense to the Greeks. If nothing else, the *Homeric Hymns* confirm that, at some basic level, the Greek gods are primarily anthropomorphic.[60] Yet there is this constant threat, or at least possibility, that Zeus will assume the shape of a bull or shower of gold. Dionysus may be a beautiful young man, but, in an instant, he may become a succession of terrifying creatures causing his would-be kidnappers to leap into the sea and be themselves transformed (Figure 1.4).

What are we to make of these threats, which invariably involve transformation into some manner of animal? Three elements seem to recur in episodes of transformation, closely related to Walter F. Otto's conception of numinous experience: an element of unpredictability, feelings of awe, and the close proximity of humans to animals and, if our rituals are efficacious, the divine.[61] The elements of unpredictability and awe are consonant with the human experience of the *mysterium tremendum*, but the third factor, proximity, suggests an overlooked feature of the Greek experience of the divine. Recent studies have drawn attention to concepts such as embodied and situated cognition to emphasise the ways that our cognitive systems cannot be divorced from our sensory participation in the world.[62] Our knowledge is shaped and expressed through our lived, sensory experiences. It is our proximity to animals as we raise them, as we control their breeding, as we decide if, how, and when they die that, in premodern societies, makes animals an integral component in our

Figure 1.4 The metamorphosis of the Tyrrhenian pirates by Dionysus: Etruscan black
      figure hydria, ca. 510–500 BCE
      Toledo Museum of Art, Toledo, 1982.134 (public domain)
      Courtesy of the Museum of Art, Toledo

experience of the world and our construction of divinity. In our interactions
with our domesticated animals, we are gods. If the Greek gods meet in council
and feast as they deliberate on the fate of men, how are they not doing what
we do in relation to our herds and flocks? Our pastoral experiences taught us
how to imagine the gods. Yet the animal encounter – mute and ever present –
is also disturbing. Every shepherd is also a killer.[63]

If we are gods to our animals, they are also our most direct link to the gods,
through divination, an institution that, in Sarah Iles Johnston's words, 'often plays
the buffer, standing between the world as humans experience it on an everyday
basis, and other worlds that threaten to impinge upon it in deleterious ways'.[64]
The animal, by its flight, its utterance, or its entrails, offers a sign of divine will (see
this volume, Chapter 9). It supplies an indication of how we should avert threats
and act in accordance with divine will. These signs are sensory, apprehended by
sight, by hearing, or by touch, yet they cannot speak directly to us; their meaning
is filtered through intermediaries who offer interpretation.

Accordingly, the proximity of animals to us offers us a way to communicate
with the gods while also calling attention to the semantic bubble surrounding
us, the limitations of speech. Hence, in the *Iliad*, Helenus seems capable of
understanding the deliberations of Apollo and Athena, who watch the battlefield as two vultures in an oak tree, and then conveys their divine advice to
Hector (although this does not prevent Hector from rejecting the omen of

birdflight when the advice of Polydamas does not suit him).[65] As John Dillery has shown, the formal apparatus of oracular sanctuaries was complemented by the widespread existence of *manteis, chrēsmologoi*, and other independent diviners of varying degrees of reputation and reliability.[66] The thought-world of the Greeks was rich with animal-focused experiences that served to make the gods as proximate to humans as were the animals. Theophrastus' Superstitious Man just knew that if a mouse had gnawed through his grain sack that it *meant* something. Even if the exegetes said it meant he should sew up the bag, he would still try to expiate the omen through sacrifice.[67]

For this reason, animals were central to the operation of major oracular cults. There is still much uncertainty over the exact ways the great shrines operated, but evidence for Dodona, to take a site that has been the focus of much recent study, points to the 'entanglement' of human, animal, and divine. In the first place, as an oracle, Dodona served as a place for the communication between human and divine, but unlike a place such as the oracle of Trophonius at Lebadeia, where the consultant experienced a terrifying vision or auditory experience, the oracular mode at Dodona may be described as noetic. By posing questions in human language with the expectation that they would receive answers, the seekers of divine guidance engaged in a form of active intellection that reframed conundrums, doubts, and uncertainties as specific enquiries to which there were definite answers. 'Should they use Diorios the soul-raiser?' 'For Xenon about his eye. Is the disease from a goddess or not?' 'Will I win my court case?' These are all questions that arise from dilemmas experienced by the questioner, and relayed to Zeus Naios as if he were, by turns, a doctor, financial advisor, and spiritual director.[68] He is an interlocutor felt to be close at hand, and can be expected to give a definitive answer.

Yet, the oracle of Dodona also persistently cast the exchange between the human and the divine in a natural setting that divorced speech and rationality from the communication. The oracle communicated through the rustling of leaves of a great oak tree, interpreted, it seems from the earliest descriptions in Homer, by priests – Selloi or Helloi – who had unwashed feet and slept on the ground, suggesting that their holiness and mantic powers derived from a physical connection to the earth.[69] By Herodotus' day, the human face of the oracle was identified with women known as 'Doves'. The various stories told about them also reveal that oracular events required more than mere human speech. The foundation story for the Dodonian 'Dove' was that two doves had been released from Egyptian Thebes and one had landed in an oak tree at Dodona, where it spoke with a human voice. It commanded the Dodonians to found an oracle of Zeus.[70]

Even rationalising accounts played with the same elements. Herodotus offers the explanation that 'dove' was merely the Thresprotian word for an old woman, used to describe a Theban priestess who had been kidnapped and ended up at Dodona where she founded the oracle of Zeus. According to Herodotus, the priestesses at the oracle were called 'Doves' by the people of Dodona because they were foreigners and when they spoke they sounded like birds. In his account, when these foreign women had finally learned enough

Greek to become intelligible they were said to speak with a human voice, whereas, before that, when they spoke no Greek, they simply sounded like birds. It is unclear whether one can reconcile all of the snippets of information we have regarding Dodona to produce a single coherent account of the oracle's operation, but there is a motif running through the sources: Dodona operated in two different registers – a human, logocentric register that was necessary if humans were to communicate with gods, and an animal register that was essential if these communications were to be deemed authoritative. It is their proximity to the human and, yet, the unbridgeable gap between the animal and the human that together permit the animal to leap straight to the divine.[71]

Similarly, animals often played conspicuous roles in conveying messages from the divine to the human: the king of the Molossians had a pet monkey that knocked over the urn in which lots were held when the Spartans consulted Dodona before Leuktra. The priestess interpreted this as a sign of the impending disaster.[72] Other instances of animals interceding decisively took place outside of the setting or oracular consultations. The Corcyrians experienced the odd phenomenon of a bull that kept walking down to the water's edge until they realised he was signalling the passing of a massive school of tuna fish, which they then successfully and profitably harvested.[73] They commemorated the act by erecting a statue to the bull at Delphi, thereby suggesting that they recognised it had been communicating a message from the gods to them. Animals might also need to be placated: the Phliasians made supplicatory offerings to a bronze goat that they covered with gold because the rising of the constellation of Capricorn coincided with the bad weather that threatened their vines.[74] Even quite banal episodes suggested that animals could be regarded as sufficiently significant for their presence to be noticed. Pausanias explains how Mycalessus got its name as follows:

ἑξῆς δὲ πόλεων ἐρείπιά ἐστιν Ἅρματος καὶ Μυκαλησσοῦ: καὶ τῇ μὲν τὸ ὄνομα ἐγένετο ἀφανισθέντος, ὡς οἱ Ταναγραῖοί φασιν, ἐνταῦθα Ἀμφιαράῳ τοῦ ἅρματος καὶ οὐχ ὅπου λέγουσιν οἱ Θηβαῖοι· Μυκαλησσὸν δὲ ὁμολογοῦσιν ὀνομασθῆναι, διότι ἡ βοῦς ἐνταῦθα ἐμυκήσατο ἡ Κάδμον καὶ τὸν σὺν αὐτῷ στρατὸν ἄγουσα ἐς Θήβας.

Adjoining are the ruins of the cities Harma (Chariot) and Mycalessus. The former got its name, according to the people of Tanagra, because the chariot of Amphiaraus disappeared here, and not where the Thebans say it did. Both peoples agree that Mycalessus was so named because the cow lowed (*emykēsato*) here that was guiding Cadmus and his host to Thebes.[75]

In each of these instances, the animal conveyed a message from the gods to humans, bypassing the logocentric modes on which humans rely. If mystics have had to navigate the paradox of rendering into human understanding an apophatic experience of the divine that is by definition beyond speech, the role of animals in the Greek experience of the divine seems similar.[76] That which is divine and cannot be rendered into our speech can nonetheless be suggested by the animal, whose intelligence can be easily controlled by the god to express divine will. It is apparent, therefore, that animals were critical to the Greek understanding of the divine. In both cases a paradox was at play: just as the human experience of the animal involved both familiarity and yet the suggestion of a chasm of speech and understanding that could scarcely be bridged, so, too, the divine was, by turns, like us yet forever different. All three were enmeshed with each other.

Notes

1 Schrödinger 1935a.
2 Schrödinger 1935b; Einstein *et al.* 1935. For a useful summary of current approaches to 'entanglement' in quantum mechanics, see Horodecki *et al.* 2009: 868.
3 For discussions of Arcadian cult and the peculiarities of Demeter cult in the region, see Bérard 1894 and Dietrich 1962: 129–148. The work of Madelein Jost remains fundamental to all discussions of Arcadian cult. See, for example, Jost 1985 and 1992.
4 Paus. 8.42.4 (here and below trans. Jones and Omerod).
5 Wace 1934: 108 describes them as 'a frieze of dancing figures, either of men with beast heads or beasts aping human attitudes'. Dickins and Kourouniotis 1906–1907: 393 are more confident, stating: 'It should be carefully noted that the figures are beasts in human clothes, not human beings with animal heads.'
6 Dickins and Kourouniotis 1906–1907: 393–395.
7 Paus. 8.25.5.
8 Detienne 1971.
9 Xenoph. Fr. 11 (DK).
10 On theriomorphism in Arcadian cult, see Krappe 1932.
11 Evans-Pritchard 1934, 1940, 1953.
12 Campbell 2015.
13 Agamben 2004: 14 postulates that Aristotle's distinction in the *De an.* 413a–b between 'the inanimate' and 'the ensouled' 'constitutes in every sense a fundamental event for western science', which makes possible Bichat's physiology, according to which humans are characterised both by organic life (circulation, respiration, excretion, and other automatic or unconscious functions) and by animal life, which is defined by its relations to the external world. Bichat's double human nature depends on but also undercuts the separation of human and animal. See also Tim Ingold's introductory essay and the various contributions to Ingold 1988 as well as Ingold 2007.
14 Calarco 2008: 3. For many, the logical culmination of this approach is summed up by Singer 1989. For a selection of essays addressing the human–animal relationship in a variety of contemporary contexts, see Kalof and Montgomery 2011.
15 Fellenstein 2011.
16 Cauvin 1994. See also Helmer *et al.* 2004: 143–163.
17 For Göbekli Tepe, see Clare *et al.* 2018. For Çatalhöyük, see Hodder 2006. For an interpretation of the animal scenes from Çatalhöyük as mimetic, see Girard 2015: 226, who observes, 'The explanation brought by mimetic theory to these pictures would suggest that there was probably internal disorder and violence inside this society; and the hunt, or at least the ritualized collective killing of these animals, was a measure invented to give back unity to the group. This procedure allowed the group to shift the violence internal to the community onto an external agent, which was ritually and collectively killed.'

18 See the various Babylonian and Sumerian bird and animal lists collected by Lewis and Llewellyn-Jones 2018: 8–16.
19 For 'owl-eyed Athena', see Luyster 1965: 133–163. For 'ox-eyed Hera', see Beck 1986: 480–488, and O'Brien 1990: 105–125 and 1993. For Apollo Lykeios, see Gershenson 1991.
20 Burkert 1985.
21 Bettini 2017: 26.
22 Luyster 1965: 153.
23 See, e.g., Wilamowitz-Moellendorff 1931: 403. See also Dietrich 1962: 130.
24 To attempt to reference every major treatment of Greek sacrifice would be fool-hardy, and theories of sacrifice are not the major theme of this chapter. I therefore restrict myself to some of the most important and recent contributions: Rudhardt and Reverdin 1981; Ekroth 2014; Naiden 2013; and Hitch and Rutherford 2017. See also this volume, Chapter 8 (with further bibliography).
25 For seminal works of the Paris School, see Detienne and Vernant 1978 and 1989. For Burkert's Paleolithic hunting thesis, which itself drew on earlier anthropological studies, see Burkert 1972.
26 For Athena Hippia and Poseidon Hippius, see Detienne 1971. Dionysus bull-horned (ταυρόκερως): Eur. *Bacch.* 100. Bull-headed (ταυρόκρανος): Eur. *Bacch.* 1378. Bull-faced (ταυρωπός): Orph. H. 29.4.
27 On Demeter's piglets, see Griffith 2016.
28 Kerényi 1976: 309.
29 On the location and rites conducted at the Boukoleion, see Arist. [*Ath. Pol.*] 3.5: 'ἀλλ᾽ ὁ μὲν βασιλεὺς εἶχετὸ νῦν καλούμενον Βουκόλιον, πλησίον τοῦ πρυτανείου (σημεῖον δέ: ἔτι καὶ νῦν γὰρ τῆς τοῦ βασιλέως γυναικὸς ἡ σύμμειξις ἐνταῦθα γίγνεται τῷ Διονύσῳ καὶ ὁ γάμος).' Northeast of the Acropolis, between the Roman Agora and the reported location of the Prytaneion, a relief depicting a bull was saved from destruction by Pittakis when the church of Ag. Konstantinos Saïta was demolished in 1851. Stephen Miller notes that the Boukoleion was situated in this vicinity (Arist. [*Ath. Pol.*] 3.5) and suggests that the bull relief was from the Boukoleion. See Miller 1970. For full discussion, see Luce 1998.
30 Smith 1987: 191–205.
31 Hom. *Od.* 4.455–462.
32 Forbes Irving 1992. Metamorphosis, however, is distinct from monstrosity. Monsters serve a very different function. See Baglioni 2017.
33 It need hardly be said that I am describing a premodern state. For a rumination on the ways we have removed the smells, sights, and sounds of our herds from our lives, see Witmore 2015.
34 Sallaberger 2008.
35 On the Edenic vision of Hicks, see Ford 1998 and Weekley 1999. Hicks painted more than 60 versions of the scene, inspired by Isaiah 11:6–8. The figures on the left of the painting are William Penn and the Lenni Lenape indigenous people with whom Penn supposedly signed the Great Treaty of 1682. See Newman 2012.
36 For the significance of the distinction between animals and humans based on the capacity to speak, see Heath 2005.
37 Alcmaeon D11 = Theophr. *Sens.* 25 (trans. Laks and Most).
38 Porph. *Abst.* 3.6.7.
39 Pl. *Prt.* 320d–322a.
40 A similar narrative of civilisation's origins born of our weakness in the face of threats from the animal kingdom is found in Diod. Sic. 1.8.1–9.
41 Kirk *et al.* 1983: 317. For applications of the schema, see Empedocles F. 351, 355, and 356. It is beyond the scope of this chapter to address but it should be recognised that both Presocratic and Aristotelian thought assigned plants a place within the class of *empsycha*. See Zatta 2016: 112–118.

42 Wuthnow 2007: 344.
43 Arist. *Hist an*. 7.1. (588b11).
44 For a useful summary of recent work on Gryllus, see Herchenroeder 2008. On the implications of the dialogue with respect to human and animal consciousness, see Konstan 2012.
45 Plut. *Mor*. 987c (here and below trans. Cherniss and Helmbold).
46 Plut. *Mor*. 989c.
47 Plut. *Mor*. 992e.
48 Aesch. *Eum*. 46–59 (here and below trans. Smyth).
49 Aesch. *Eum*. 179–185.
50 Maxwell-Stuart 1973: 81–84. Heath 2005: 241 refers to this version of 'vampire Erinyes'.
51 Aesch. *Eum*. 131–132.
52 Aesch. *Eum*. 304–305.
53 Aesch. *Eum*. 155–161.
54 Aesch. *Eum*. 128.
55 Aesch. *Eum*. 192–197.
56 Hom. *Od*. 12.395. Used to evoke cattle lowing or bellowing, *Il*. 18.580, 21.237 and *Od*. 10.413; a calf, Theoc. *Idylls* 16.37; Heracles in agony, Eur., *Hercules furens* 870 and Ar. *Ran*. 562; the creaking of the gates of heaven, *Il*. 5.749; thunder, Ar. *Nub*. 292; a drum, *Anth. Pal*. 6.220.11 (Diosc.); the ringing of a struck shield, *Il*. 20.260; and the sound made by meat from the Cattle of the Sun bellowing upon the spit, Hom. *Od*. 12.395. Note also μῡκηδόν ('*mūkēdon*'), adv. *with bellowings*, Poet. in POxy. 864.22.
57 Lebeck 1971.
58 Dolgert 2012.
59 The sensory dimensions of ancient sacrifice have only recently attracted attention. A stimulating study is Weddle 2013. For a discussion of the offal and excrement created by large-scale sacrifice, see McInerney 2014.
60 See, for example, *Hom. Hymn* 1.1–10 (the birth of Dionysus); *Hom. Hymn* 2.65–70 (Persephone, born from Demeter, who calls her 'sweet scion of my body'); *Hom. Hymn* 3.13–18 (Leto giving birth to Apollo and Artemis on Delos); *Hom. Hymn* 4.10–15 (Maia giving birth to the precocious Hermes); *Hom. Hymn* 5.22–25 (Hestia as the first- and last-born child of Cronus, having been first born and last disgorged). The figuring of the Olympian gods as superhuman, yet still modelled on the human, is perhaps the dominant theme of the *Homeric Hymns*.
61 Otto 1920.
62 See Wuthnow 2007. The notion of embodied cognition is particularly associated with the work of Thomas Csordas. See, for example, Csordas 2004. For an instance of this approach applied to the interpretation of a recent religious phenomenon, see Ulland 2012.
63 Marcel Detienne has explored this ambiguity in relation to the Greek gods. See Detienne 1986 and 1998.
64 Johnston 2005: 21–22
65 Hom *Il*. 7.23–62. Hector rejecting the omens: Hom. *Il*. 12.240.
66 Dillery 2005.
67 Theophr. *Char*. 16.5–6.
68 For Dodona, see Eidinow 2007 and Parker 2016. The latter is very helpful for his treatment of the uneven excavation and publication history of the Dodona tablets. In 2007 Eidinow estimated there were 1400 tablets, whereas Parker notes that by 2013 the number of published tablets had increased to over 4000, with Méndez Dosuna 2008: 53 suggesting the entire corpus of questions and responses numbered approximately 8000!
69 Hom. *Il*. 16.220–35.

70 Hdt 2.55. For recent treatment of Dodona's foundation legends, see Piccinini 2017: 123–131.
71 Baudrillard 1994: 129 recognises the anxiety that may by induced by humans' proximity to animals, noting '[b]estiality, and its principle of uncertainty, must be killed in animals'.
72 Kallisthenes *FGrH* 124 F22 a and b. For a discussion, see Eidinow 2007: 70.
73 Paus. 10.9.3–4.
74 Paus. 2.13.6.
75 Paus. 9.19.4.
76 The paradox of using language to describe the ineffable is the subject of Augustine's famous observation (*De doctrina Christiana* 1.6): 'God should not be said to be ineffable, for when this is said, something is said. And a contradiction in terms is created, since if that is ineffable which cannot be spoken, then that is not ineffable which is called ineffable.'

Bibliography

Agamben, G. (2004) *The Open. Man and Animal*, trans. K. Attell. Stanford, Calif.
Baglioni, I. (2017) *Echidna e suoi discendenti. Studio sulle entità mostruose della Teogonia esiodea*. Rome.
Baudrillard, J. (1994) 'The animals: territory and metamorphoses', in *Simulacra and Simulation*, trans. S. F. Galser. Ann Arbor, Mich., 129–142.
Beck, W. (1986) 'Choice and context: metrical doublets for Hera', *American Journal of Philology* 107, 480–488.
Bérard, V. (1894) *De l'origine des cultes arcadiens. Essai de méthode en mythologie grecque*. Paris.
Bettini, M. (2017) 'Visibilité, invisibilité et identité des dieux', in G. Pirnoti and C. Bonnet (eds.) *Les Dieux d'Homère. Polythéisme et poésie en Grèce ancienne*. Liège, 21–42.
Burkert, W. (1972) *Homo Necans. Interpretationen altgriechischer Opferriten und Mythen*. Berlin.
Burkert, W. (1985) *Greek Religion. Archaic and Classical*, trans. J. Raffan. Cambridge (German orig. 1977).
Calarco, M. (2008) *Zoographies. The Question of the Animal from Heidegger to Derrida*. New York, N.Y.
Campbell, R. (2015) 'Animal, human, god: pathways of Shang animality and divinity', in B. S. Arbuckle and S. A. McCarty (eds.) *Animals and Inequality in the Ancient World*. Boulder, Colo., 251–273.
Cauvin, J. (1994) *Naissance des divinités, Naissance de l'agriculture. La révolution des symboles au Néolithique*. Paris.
Clare, L. *et al.* (2018) 'Establishing identities in the Proto-Neolithic: "history making" at Göbekli Tepe from the late tenth millennium BCE', in I. Hodder (ed.) *Religion, History, and Place in the Origin of Settled Life*. Boulder, Colo., 115–136.
Csordas, T. (2004) 'Asymptote of the ineffable: embodiment, alterity, and the theory of religion', *Current Anthropology* 45, 163–176.
Detienne, M. (1971) 'Athena and the mastery of the horse', *History of Religions* 11, 161–184.
Detienne, M. (1986) 'L'Apollon meurtrier et les crimes de sang', *Quaderni Urbinati di Cultura Classica*, New Series 22, 7–17.
Detienne, M. (1998) *Apollon. Le Couteau à la main. Une approche expérimentale du polythéisme grec*. Paris.
Detienne, M. and J.-P. Vernant (1978) *Cunning Intelligence in Greek Culture and Society*, trans. J. Lloyd. Hassocks (French orig. 1974).

Detienne, M. and J.-P. Vernant (1989) *The Cuisine of Sacrifice among the Greeks*, trans. P. Wissing. Chicago, Ill. (French orig. 1979).

Dickins, G. and K. Kourouniotis (1906–1907) 'Damophon of Messene: II', *Annual of the British School at Athens* 13, 357–404.

Dietrich, B. C. (1962) 'Demeter, Erinys, Artemis', *Hermes* 90, 129–148.

Dillery, J. (2005) 'Chresmologues and manteis: independent diviners and the problem of authority', in S. I. Johnston and P. T. Struck (eds.) *Mantikê. Studies in Ancient Divination*. Leiden, 167–232.

Dolgert, S. (2012) 'Sacrificing justice: the Oresteia and the masks of consent', *Political Theory* 40, 263–289.

Eidinow, E. (2007) *Oracles, Curses and Risk among the Ancient Greeks*. Oxford.

Einstein A., B. Podolsky and N. Rosen (1935) 'Can quantum-mechanical description of physical reality be considered complete?', *Physical Review* 47, 777–780.

Ekroth, G. (2014) 'Animal sacrifice in antiquity', in G. L. Campbell (ed.) *The Oxford Handbook of Animals in Classical Thought and Life*. Oxford, 324–354.

Evans-Pritchard, E. E. (1934) 'Imagery in Ngok Dinka cattle-names', *Bulletin of the School of Oriental Studies* 7, 623–628.

Evans-Pritchard, E. E. (1940) *The Nuer*. Oxford.

Evans-Pritchard, E. E. (1953) 'The sacrificial role of cattle among the Nuer', *Africa* 23, 181–198.

Fellenstein, S. (2011) 'Pet owner or guardian', *Fetch dvm360*: http://veterinarynews.dvm 360.com/pet-owner-or-guardian (retrieved 1 January 2011).

Forbes Irving, P. M. C. (1992) *Metamorphosis in Greek Myths*. Oxford.

Ford, A. (1998) *Edward Hicks. Painter of the Peaceable Kingdom*. Philadelphia, Pa.

Gershenson, D. (1991) *Apollo the Wolf-God*. McLean, Va.

Girard, R. (2015) 'Animal scapegoating at Çatalhöyük', in P. Antonello and P. Gifford (eds.) *How We Became Human. Mimetic Theory and the Science of Evolutionary Origins*. Michigan, 217–231.

Griffith, R. D. (2016) 'Cannibal Demeter (Pind. Ol. 1.52) and the Thesmophoria pigs', *Classical Journal* 111, 129–139.

Heath, J. (2005) *The Talking Greeks. Speech, Animals, and the Other in Homer, Aeschylus, and Plato*. Cambridge.

Helmer, D., L. Gourichon and D. Stordeur (2004) 'À l'aube de la domestication animale. Imaginaire et symbolisme animal dans les premières sociétés néolithiques du nord du proche-Orient', *Anthropozoologica* 39, 143–163.

Herchenroeder, L. (2008) Τί γὰρ τοῦτο πρὸς τὸν λόγον: Plutarch's Gryllus and so-called "Grylloi"', *American Journal of Philology* 129, 347–379.

Hitch, S. and I. Rutherford (eds.) (2017) *Animal Sacrifice in the Ancient Greek World*. Cambridge.

Hodder, I. (2006) *The Leopard's Tale. Revealing the Mysteries of Çatalhöyük*. London.

Horodecki, R. *et al.* (2009) 'Quantum entanglement', *Review of Modern Physics* 81, 865–942.

Ingold, T. (2007) *Lines. A Brief History*. London.

Ingold, T. (ed.) (1988) *What is an Animal?* London.

Johnston, S. I. (2005) 'Introduction', in S. I. Johnston and P. T. Struck (eds.) *Mantikê. Studies in Ancient Divination*. Leiden, 1–28.

Jost, M. (1985) *Sanctuaires et culte d'Arcadie*. Paris.

Jost, M. (1992) 'Mystery cults in Arcadia', in M. Cosmopoulos (ed.) *Greek Mysteries. The Archaeology of Ancient Greek Secret Cults*. London, 143–168.

Kalof, L. and G. M. Montgomery (eds.) (2011) *Making Animal Meaning*. East Lansing, Mich.

Kerényi, K. (1976) *Dionysos. Archetypal Image of Indestructible Life*, trans, R. Mannheim. Princeton, N.J. (German orig. 1961).

Kirk, G. S., J. E. Raven and M. Schofield (1983) *The Presocratic Philosophers*. 2nd edn. Cambridge.

Konstan, D. (2012) 'A pig convicts itself of unreason: the implicit argument of Plutarch's Gryllus', in N. Almazova *et al.* (eds.) *Variante Loquella. Festschrift Alexander Gavrilov*. St. Petersburg, 371–385.

Krappe, A. H. (1932) ''EPINYΣ', *Rheinisches Museum für Philologie* 81, 305–320.

Lebeck, A. (1971) *The Oresteia. A Study in Language and Structure*. Cambridge, Mass.

Lewis, S. and L. Llewellyn-Jones (eds.) (2018) *The Culture of Animals in Antiquity*. London.

Luce, J.-M. (1998) 'Thésée, le synoecisme et l'agora d'Athènes', *Revue Archéologique* 1, 3–31.

Luyster, R. (1965) 'Symbolic elements in the cult of Athena', *History of Religions* 5, 133–163.

Maxwell-Stuart, P. G. (1973) 'The appearance of Aeschylus' Erinyes', *Greece and Rome* 20, 81–84.

McInerney, J. (2014) 'Bouphonia: killing cattle on the Acropolis', in A. Gardiesen and C. Chandezon (eds.) *Équidés et bovidés de la Méditerranée Antique. Rites et combats, jeux et savoirs*. Lattes, 113–124.

Méndez Dosuna, J. (2008) 'Novedades en el oráculo de Dodona: a propósito de une reciente monografía de Éric Lhôte', *Minerva* 21, 51–79.

Miller, S. (1970) 'Old discoveries from old Athens', *Hesperia* 39, 223–231.

Naiden, F. (2013) *Smoke Signals for the Gods. Ancient Greek Sacrifice from the Archaic through the Roman Periods*. Oxford.

Newman, A. (2012) *On Records. Delaware Indians, Colonists, and the Media of History and Memory*. Lincoln, Neb.

O'Brien, J. V. (1990) 'Homer's savage Hera', *Classical Journal* 86, 105–125.

O'Brien, J. V. (1993) *The Transformation of Hera. A Study of Ritual, Hero and the Goddess in the Iliad*. Lanham, Md.

Otto, R. (1920) *Das Heilige. Über das Irrationale in der Idee des Göttlichen und sein Verhältnis zum Rationalen*. Breslau.

Parker, R. (2016) 'Seeking advice from Zeus at Dodona', *Greece and Rome* 63, 61–90.

Piccinini, J. (2017) *The Shrine of Dodona in the Archaic and Classical Ages*. Macerata.

Rudhardt, J. and O. Reverdin (eds.) (1981) *Le Sacrifice dans l'Antiquité*. Vandoeuvres.

Sallaberger, W. (2008) *Das Gilgamesch-Epos. Mythos, Werk und Tradition*. Munich.

Schrödinger, E. (1935a) 'Die gegenwärtige Situation in der Quantenmechanik', *Naturwissenschaften* 23, 807–812.

Schrödinger, E. (1935b) 'Discussion of probability relations between separated systems', *Mathematical Proceedings of the Cambridge Philosophical Society* 31, 555–563.

Singer, P. (1989) 'All animals are equal', in T. Regan and P. Singer (eds.) *Animal Rights and Human Obligations*. Englewood Cliffs, N.J., 148–162.

Smith, J. Z. (1987) 'The domestication of sacrifice', in R. G. Hamerton-Kelley (ed.) *Violent Origins: Walter Burkert, René Girard & Jonathan Z. Smith on Ritual Killing and Cultural Formation*. Stanford, Calif., 191–205.

Ulland, D. (2012) 'Embodied spirituality', *Archiv für Religionspsychologie/Archive for the Psychology of Religion* 34, 83–104.

Wace, A. J. P. (1934) 'The veil of Despoina', *American Journal of Archaeology* 38, 107–111.

Weddle, C. (2013) 'The sensory experience of blood sacrifice in the Roman imperial cult', in J. Day (ed.) *Making Senses of the Past. Toward a Sensory Archaeology*. Carbondale, Ill., 137–159.

Weekley, C. (1999) *The Kingdoms of Edward Hicks*. Williamsburg, Va.

Wilamowitz-Moellendorff, U. von (1931) *Der Glaube der Hellenen*. Vol. 1. Berlin.

Witmore, C. (2015) 'Bovine urbanism: the ecological corpulence of bos urbanus', in B. Clarke (ed.) *Earth, Life, and System. Evolution and Ecology on a Gaian Planet*. New York, N.Y., 225–249.

Wuthnow, R. (2007) 'Cognition and religion', *Sociology of Religion* 68, 341–360.

Zatta, C. (2016) 'Plants' interconnected lives: from Ovid's myths to Presocratic thought and beyond', *Arion* 24, 101–126.

2 Sources for the study of animals in ancient Greek religion

I. S. Gilhus

Introduction

The study of animals in ancient Greek religion is dependent on a broad range of sources. The categories of sources raise conceptual and methodological issues and have through time invited various interpretations. The study of animals has over the course of a century moved from a predominance of textual and in the main literary sources to include other textual genres (such as epigraphy) as well as non-textual sources (such as iconography and material relicts). Since the 1970s, zooarchaeology – the study of animal remains – has offered additional information.

The study is further dependent on general perspectives on animals. While the context of research in the 19th and the first half of the 20th century was industrialised societies with animal husbandry and animals used for transportation, contemporary research is influenced by environmental concerns and life in post-industrial and urbanised societies where companion animals are broadly speaking the most accessible non-human animals. These influences have contributed to a rethinking of human/animal relations and a wish to see humans within their animal contexts – the so-called 'animal turn', which has also reached the study of religion.[1] While two loci of interest in the study of Greek religion have been sacrifice on the one hand and animals in symbols, metaphors, and metamorphoses on the other, a new focus is the broader interaction between animals and humans. According to a recent invitation, we 'should thus consider ancient societies not solely as human organisations but as rich ecological webs inhabited by many species together'.[2] This invitation presupposes a new view on the traditional sources. Furthermore, there is a challenge to include sources related to magic, astrology, and divination, which to only a small degree have been considered in the study of animals in Greek religion (see, in detail, this volume, Chapters 9 and 12).

This chapter discusses the types of sources available for the study of the role of animals in ancient Greek religion and compares their scope and value. Animals include a wide range of species. Some have multiple roles in religious narratives and practices, serving instrumental purposes and forming part of social and symbolic relationships with humans and postulated superhuman beings. The latter category includes gods, ghosts, demons, apparitions, etc. What do the sources say about the instrumental use of animals in ritual contexts? How do they present symbolic relations, social connections, and interactions between gods, humans, and animals? What does a multi-source approach to Greek religion mean for the interpretation of divine/human/animal relations? How do the sources respond to the 'animal turn'? In this chapter, I will present the various categories of sources, discuss their values, and show the benefits of consulting multiple sources. Overall, it constitutes an invitation to redirect the glance and become more aware of the emotional content of the sources and the variety of animal species within them.

Categories of sources

Sources include texts, material objects, images, and zooarchaeological material. Each of these categories contains several subgroups. Textual sources include inscriptions, literary sources – for example, epics, comedies, tragedies, novels, fables, poetry, hymns, and proverbs – magical texts, divinatory formulae, natural history, and philosophy. Material sources include temples, altars, ritual objects, such as statues, votive offerings, amulets, small personal items, such as jewellery, and coins. 'Art' includes mural images, votive reliefs, mosaics, and pots. Zooarchaeological sources are faunal remains, such as animals included in human burials or buried separately, and bones from places where animals were sacrificed. In addition, there is the comparative evidence from other cultures, both ancient and modern, and the possibility of checking the veracity of the ancient sources on sacrifice through experimental tests (see below).

Different categories of sources reflect different aspects of the cultural and religious presence of animals in the ancient world.[3] The sources differ in how representative they are, and not least what they represent and what purpose and agenda they pursue. Votive reliefs favour depictions of well-tended and calm animals in the stage before they are sacrificed (see also this volume, Chapter 8); magical papyri sometimes describe the mutilation of small animals to serve the purpose of the magician. Literary texts present narratives about animals and their interactions with humans and gods, reflecting ideas, fantasies, and emotions, and are sources for human imagination (see this volume, Chapter 4).

The various literary genres take different positions towards animals. In comedies, the natural hierarchy between animals, humans, and gods is turned on its head when the birds in Aristophanes' comedy of the same name are attributed with a better claim to divinity than the Olympian gods.[4] Animals have significant roles in comedies: for example, in the choruses of birds, frogs, and wasps. The latter frequently have human characteristics, and humans appear as animals.[5] A predominantly human world is depicted in Attic tragedy, but animals are present in sacrifices, which is a prominent theme.[6] Tragic representations of sacrifice stress the killing, tending to deviate from the sacrificial norm, and a close connection is made between animal and human sacrifices.[7] The blurring of the distinction between sacrifice and murder means that tragedies are a problematic source of information about animal sacrifice, because they give a distorted picture.[8]

In addition to their focus on sacrifice, tragedies include rich animal imagery and metaphors. Chiara Thumiger argues that 'animals appear more clearly and strongly in tragedy than any other genre in the ancient world'.[9] According to Thumiger, tragedies create a middle ground between animals and humans because generic words for animals are used to characterise human beings and because human emotions are animalised. The motif of animals eating human bodies recurs, and the prophetic function of animals appears as omens and narrative elements.[10]

A further consideration is that, since authors belonged to an elite, their texts do not necessarily reflect what moved ordinary people. The ancient authors pursued different interests and played with cultural stereotypes, meaning that the result should not always be taken at face value.

The Cyclades yields a treasure of animal votives, while the archaeological sources from Minoan and Mycenaean Greece reveal societies and religion where cattle played a major role. As with the animals of the Cycladic votives, it is not possible to interpret the religious function and meaning of cattle in any detail because narrative sources are lacking. However, consulting comparative sources may make the picture clearer. Jeremy McInerney has made a productive comparative analysis combining data from archaeological material, texts from later periods, and contemporary anthropological material.[11] The archaeological sources reveal that the 'bovine idiom' was pervasive, while the broader source material from later times shows that this idiom continued to be part of Greek religion in archaic and classical times and constitutes what McInerney characterises as a 'bovine register'.[12] As a third group of sources, McInerney has consulted comparative material from contemporary cattle-rearing cultures, especially in Africa. This African material helps to show the pervasiveness of the bovine idiom in such cultures throughout history. McInerney's research demonstrates how this comparative source material can illuminate the roles of animals in ancient Greece.

Cross-cultural and comparative studies of divine/human/animal relations based on sources from the ancient Mediterranean cultures and the Near East open up yet broader perspectives. Sian Lewis and Lloyd Llewellyn-Jones have pointed in this direction. Their sourcebook, *The Culture of Animals in Antiquity*,[13] includes both Greek sources and texts from other ancient cultures in the Mediterranean and the Middle East. It also treats the human species alongside other animals.

Specific studies have shown the usefulness of comparing ancient ritual practices involving animals with those of other cultures. One example is the burning of an oxtail in sacrifice. According to Gunnel Ekroth, this rite might have been imported from the Middle East, since it was an Israelite sacrificial ritual before becoming part of ancient Greek sacrifice.[14] This is a genealogical comparison between sources from different cultures based on the presupposition that there is a historical connection between them, while the comparison with the aforementioned African material was cross-cultural and analogical.[15] Both genealogical and analogical comparisons extend the source material and help to illuminate the Greek material. Christian apologetic material also includes information about animals in Greek religion, though usually seen from a critical or hostile perspective.[16]

Iconographic sources frequently depict animals, sometimes as part of an iconographical programme.[17] According to Folkert van Straten, in painted pots and votive reliefs depicting sacrifice, most 'iconographical components can be incorporated in a series of pictures that are similar, but never identical.'[18] This means that it is possible to say something general about sacrifice and the sacrificial animals based on these iconographic sources.

Paintings may further refer to divine actors and well-known myths. One example appears on an Attic hydria that shows a youth leading a sheep to an altar. An ox stands to one side of the altar and a large owl stands on top of it (see Figure 2.1).

The depiction of two of the most common sacrificial animals points to the pre-kill phase of sacrifice, while the owl symbolises the recipient of the sacrifice – the goddess Athena. The animals are depicted in two modes: realistically,

Figure 2.1 Black figure hydria featuring a sacrificial scene, ca. 480 BCE
Gustavianum, Uppsala University Museum, L CC PDM 1.0 (public domain)
Courtesy of the Uppsala University Museum

as sacrificial animals; and symbolically, with the owl as a stand-in for the goddess. Gods depicted as animals are common (see this volume, Chapter 5): for instance, Zeus Meilichios is depicted on votive reliefs as a huge serpent attended by worshippers.[19] What did it mean to worship a god in animal form? More enigmatic still is the serpent on a Laconian black figure cup.[20] The painting refers to a well-known myth: it depicts Odysseus' men running up to the Cyclops Polyphemus to blind him.[21] A decorative fish beneath the motif of the blinding and an equally decorative serpent above it complete the painting. Susan Woodford suggests that the fish alludes to Odysseus' sea voyages, but what about the serpent?[22] Is it just a decorative element, similar to animals appearing in the borders of textiles, or does it refer to something specific? How was it perceived?

Sources can disagree with one another and speak at cross purposes. One example is the ratio of sacrificial animals, which varied in sacrificial calendars, images on pots, and votive reliefs. Van Straten has shown that if we include calendars, cattle constitute 3.5 per cent of all sacrificial animals; based on the votive reliefs, they account for 7.9 per cent; and according to painted pots, 54.8 per cent.[23] He explains the variations by highlighting the different perspectives of the three categories combined with the cost of each type of animal. Calendars list communal sacrifices, the votive reliefs show personal sacrifices, and the painted pots reflect more festive occasions. Thus, cattle – the most expensive and esteemed category of animal – dominate the last category.[24] The discrepancy between the sources is explained by their different origins and interests.

In addition to literary, epigraphic, and iconographic sources, zooarchaeological material from cult places, burials, and rubbish heaps has been studied systematically since the 1970s. This material sheds light on animals, human diets, and sacrificial practices. The bone material has generated a lot of optimism: this osteological evidence 'promises to revolutionise our understanding of sacrificial victims and the way they were treated after death'.[25] Recently, there have been calls to study the social dimension in the zooarchaeological material as well as 'to regard the animals found in archaeological contexts as members of the community, part of the social fabric of the ancient society'.[26] Julia Kindt has encouraged classical scholars 'to make more of the enormous comparative material the ethnobiological literature provides'.[27] How the Greek material will stand up to the scrutiny and challenge of documenting the social and religious dimensions of ancient cultures remains to be seen.

Sacrifice and the benefits of multiple sources

Sacrifice has always been a main focus of interest in the study of ancient Greek religion (see, in detail, this volume, Chapter 8), and rightly so: Greek religion was sacrificial. The ritual slaughtering of animals was the key religious act, and sacrifice was communal and highly prestigious.[28] Since the three categories of beings – gods, humans, and animals – were brought together in the ritual, sacrifice has been the main reference for interpreting the relationship between them: humans sacrificed, animals were sacrificed, and gods received the sacrifices. Animals are seen as the medium between gods and humans, as victims and objects.

Research on blood sacrifice has broadened its scope from the use mainly of texts to consulting multiple sources, with zooarchaeology and animal remains the most recent successful additions. The inclusion of new categories of sources into the picture of the role of animals in ancient Greek religion increases knowledge by filling lacunae and correcting earlier mistakes as well as pointing to local variations and changes occurring over time.[29] Some sources are still neglected, however. Fred Naiden points to models of sacrificial animals made from different materials (metal, terracotta, wood) that commemorate a sacrifice already made, or symbolise a promise to make one, or replace a sacrifice.[30] Together with the range of primary sources considered, the perspectives broaden too. Multi-source approaches tend to be more alert to differences in time and space. Research on ancient Greek religion has produced extensive knowledge about how sacrifices were performed and the relations between animals, humans, and gods in the ritual setting. This research has also pointed

Figure 2.2 Mixing bowl (bell krater) depicting a sacrifice, ca. 425 BCE
Museum of Fine Arts, Boston, 95.24 (public domain)
Courtesy of the Museum of Fine Arts, Boston

to a lack of sources for some aspects of ancient Greek blood sacrifice, especially with regard to its practical details.[31]

Visual and epigraphic sources are more normative than literary sources in how they depict sacrifices.[32] They are therefore also more representative of what actually took place. Sacrificial calendars are a case in point: such calendars offer accurate information about what type of animal was sacrificed in public rituals and when the sacrifice was made.[33] This focus, however, does not mean that literary sources are necessarily distant from historical practices. They can explain, supplement, or correct impressions given by other sources. One example is the presumed decline of sacrifice in late antiquity (on which, see this volume, Chapter 8). In his analysis of four Greek novels from the first and second centuries CE, Jan Bremmer has shown that 'in all four novels a rich variety of people offers sacrifices: neighbours, town people, whole towns and islands, an embassy, a king and an army. Basically, there is no group that does not sacrifice.'[34] Sacrifice is not questioned, and its community aspect is stressed.[35] The novels reflect that animal sacrifice was still important for people coming together and enjoying their meals.

The veracity of sources pertaining to sacrifice has been tested with experiments. Michael H. Jameson performed a pioneering study in his backyard by burning an oxtail to see if it would behave as textual and iconographical sources on sacrifice describe.[36] The experiment confirmed the information provided: the tail rose in the fire, which, according to the ancient evidence, was a good omen. Since Jameson's oxtail study, other practical aspects of sacrifice have also been tested experimentally.[37]

Together with texts and iconography, the zooarchaeological material has offered new insights, especially about alimentary blood sacrifice (*thysia*), where some of the bones and the meat were offered to the gods, and the rest was boiled or grilled and eaten by the participants. There is sometimes a discrepancy between the information derived from textual evidence and that provided by ritual remains.[38] When the osteological material points in a different direction from the sources, 'the latter usually dictate part of an official script, whereas faunal remains reveal the chaos of actual practice'.[39] Osteological material, for instance, reveals that the range of species used for ritual purposes was much wider than what one may think based on the literary sources.[40]

Marine animals are a case in point. Sacrifices of fish are present in literary and iconographic sources, but they play only a marginal role. However, excavations in sanctuaries paint a different picture.[41] Fish remains from the Kommos sanctuary of southern Crete suggest that several kinds of sea animals were part of the ritual.[42] The same applies to the sanctuary of Poseidon in Kalaureia on Poros, where remains of at least 18 species of fish have been found.[43] More curious still is the large cache of seashells in a temple on Kythnos in the Cyclades, especially in the *adyton*, the inner room of the temple.[44] Tatiana Theodoropoulou poses interesting questions about these shells and their former occupants. Were they sacrifices? Did they accompany other offerings? Were they part of ritual meals? Were they accumulations of votive gifts? Who was worshipped in the temple and why were the seashells secondarily disposed in its inner space? The remains of fish and other marine animals continue to challenge researchers. According to Ekroth, the 'role of fish within religion is far from established'.[45] Remains of sea animals invite researchers to continue to expand their views of sacrifice and rituals involving animals. The zooarchaeological material has tended to stimulate small-scale research and case studies rather than grand theories. This is different from studies of sacrifice, where the results have frequently been generalised and sometimes universalised.

Generally speaking, the sources say more about what happened during sacrifice and what the actors did than what the rituals meant. Research on Greek religion, however, has been mainly preoccupied with the meaning of sacrifice.[46] Because sacrifice loomed large in the interpretation of animal/human/god relations, the dominant approach has been to view animals as instruments applied for human purpose and to a great degree as victims. A recent more relational approach to animals is informed by phenomenology and intersubjectivity. What characterises this approach to the ancient sources?

Redirecting the gaze

In *Human and Animal in Ancient Greece. Empathy and Encounter in Classical Literature*,[47] Tua Korhonen and Erika Ruonakoski interpret an iconic statue, the *Moschophorus* ('calf-bearer'), which dates from around 560 BCE (see Figure 2.3). The statue shows a young man (*kouros*) with a calf on his shoulders. It is productive to follow the direction of Korhonen and Ruonakoski's interpretation in a wider context of sacrifice. The focus is the intersubjectivity between human and non-human animals and the empathy of ancient people with animals. The authors make a successful attempt to modify the impression of a strong Greek anthropocentrism. According to them, the *kouros* represents either Apollo or the person who paid for the statue. The young man is shown with the traditional 'archaic smile', while the calf is both more lifelike and more expressive. At least seen with the modern eye, the calf reflects submissiveness.[48] The authors presume that the statue is cultic. It depicts the man or god in a formal and traditional position, while the calf, soon to be sacrificed, expresses vitality.

Korhonen and Ruonakoski ask whether the ancient beholder felt sympathy for the calf. Did it even arouse pity?[49] These are obvious questions raised by the posture of the animal. While it is difficult to answer on behalf of the ancients, the authors' questions are a strong argument for redirecting the gaze of the researcher. If we, for instance, look more closely at pre-kill scenes on painted pots and votive reliefs, we notice that in several cases the sacrificial animal is being kept still and tended by a youth, a woman, or a child.[50] There seems to be trust and a mutual bond between the humans and the sheep, goats, oxen, or pigs. Preserved votive reliefs show only pre-kill scenes, while painted pots also include a few (4.5 per cent) kill and many (40 per cent) post-kill scenes, which means that killing is underrepresented.[51] The painted pots show mostly pre-kill scenes with animals, usually depicted as calm and happy, though

Figure 2.3 The *Moschophoros* ('calf-bearer') from the Athenian Acropolis, ca. 560 BCE
    Acropolis Museum, Athens, Wikimedia Commons, CC BY-SA 4.0 (open access)
    Courtesy of the Acropolis Museum, Athens

there are also examples of them being more forcefully held. Marks from rings
in altars show that sacrificial animals were sometimes tied. Painted pots waver
between representing an ideal and giving a realistic description. They reflect a
view of the animals that is very much in line with farming cultures with their
domesticated animals.

Human and domesticated non-human animals engage in social relations.
How these relations were experienced and conceived of in ancient Greece
obviously differed from species to species, be it between humans on the one
hand and an ox, a sheep, or a pig on the other. The main point, however, is
that domesticated animals were ideally treated with respect and care up to the
moment they were slaughtered and turned into things – blood, meat, bone,
and fleece.[52] Some interpreters present the slaughtering as a betrayal and posit
that the participants in sacrifice played their parts in a 'comedy of innocence'

(*Unschuldskomödie*), to quote Karl Meuli's famous characteristic.[53] A basic mechanism in farming societies is the switch from friendliness towards an animal to 'othering' it at the moment of slaughter. When paintings of pre-kill scenes give glimpses of the social relations between humans and non-human animals before this 'othering' takes place, they indicate that there was room to treat animals with empathy even in the sacrificial context.

In some cases, it is possible to study divine/human/animal relations in more depth. McInerney's study of the meanings and functions of cattle has already been mentioned.[54] Another example of an in-depth study is Christiana Franco's examination of dogs in relation to humans, *Shamelessness. The Canine and the Feminine in Ancient Greece.* [55] Franco raises the introductory question 'Why does Hermes give Pandora the mind of a dog?' and draws on a wealth of primary sources to demonstrate what can be achieved by means of a sophisticated and theoretically informed reading of sources paired with a cross-cultural model. She treats the sources as raw material and looks for recurring phenomena. Because of the large quantity of texts about dogs, this proves to be fruitful.[56] Focusing on wide diffusion and long duration, Franco detects a complex tapestry of meanings and functions of dogs in Greek culture: they are at once humanity's best friend and the butt of abusive language.

'Redirecting the gaze' also involves becoming more acutely aware of the emotional content of both texts and images. David Morgan has invited a study of visual culture that stresses the emotional potential of images:

> Material culture, and visual culture as a subdivision of it, is not principally the expression of ideas and doctrines, but rather the cultural production, circulation, and reception of felt-knowledge. This means that images and their uses should be examined for the ways in which they help to create forms of sympathy, empathy, antipathy, and apathy – feeling with, feeling into or as, feeling against or other than, and feeling not at all.[57]

This approach can be transferred to the study of ancient Greek iconography. To redirect the gaze onto the ancient sources means to be more open to the emotional aspects of the divine/human/animal relationship and to the interactions between animals and humans.

As the sacrificial ox was so important in Greek culture, other animals have tended to stand in its shadow. Because sacrifice has been the dominant institution for describing relations between gods, humans, and animals, less focus has been directed to divinatory practices and magical sources (see this volume, Chapters 9 and 12, respectively).[58] In animal sacrifice, the animal changes status: from an actor in its own right to a victim that is devoid of agency. It connects gods and humans. In bird divination, the relationship between the categories of gods, humans, and animals is different: the birds are controlled by the gods, they move under the sky, out of reach, and humans merely 'read' the messages their movements and sounds convey. In magic, animals and animal parts are manipulated by humans for certain defined and stated purposes. Magic is dependent on a special knowledge about nature and how it works. Ghosts and demons, more than gods, are frequently part of the magical procedures.

The magical and divinatory sources feature a considerable variety of species.[59] One of the most limiting approaches to a study of non-human animals is to treat them as a single, homogeneous category. Redirecting the gaze also implies seeing the diversity of species present in the ancient sources and realising that these species were invested with multiple functions and meanings.

Birds are a case in point when it comes to variety. Jeremy Mynott has recently pointed to the number of known avian species in ancient Greece and their multiple functions and meanings.[60] These winged creatures had a basic religious significance because of their use in divination. This is reflected in the term for 'bird,' *ornis*, which also means 'omen', and shows that etymology connects birds tightly to systems of divination.[61] Birds were used in augury and perceived as messengers between gods and humans (see this volume, Chapter 9). Specific species belonged to specific gods and goddesses. In other words, the eagles and falcons, owls and doves of ancient Greece were part of a different conceptualisation of the world from ours; the modern interpreter of ancient sources should always keep this in mind. According to Mynott, in reading the ancient authors, 'we tend to move between experiences of happy recognition and deep puzzlement'.[62] When it comes to birds, larger differences between ancient and modern lifestyles matter: we usually overlook the fact that the ancient soundscapes had much fewer mechanical noises and that more sound came from the natural world than is the case today, including birdsong.[63] Physical surroundings and circumstances should be taken into account whenever ancient sources are studied.

In a different vein, curses and erotic spells show that birds and small animals functioning as effigies were manipulated, mutilated, and tortured for magical purposes (see this volume, Chapter 12).[64] A cursory glance at magical sources indicates that both birds and puppies were sometimes treated cruelly and in an extremely instrumental way. One example is a love-charm where a wryneck was tied by its legs and wings to the four spokes of a wheel, which continuously revolved while an incantation was spoken.[65] The taxonomic and magical reasoning behind the use of the various species of animals in magical texts has been successfully explored.[66] However, these sources have been little studied in relation to the broader interaction between animals, humans, and gods and the conception of the various species of animals they reflect.

Another dimension of magical literature is the tendency towards hybridisation, where evil and ugly superhuman beings are conceived as mixtures of humans and animals. Different sorts of animals produce different meanings. Child-killing demons combine conceptions of childless women with animals or parts of animals such as birds of prey, horses, wolves, and asses.[67] The interaction of non-human, human, and superhuman beings in the magical sources has generally received less scholarly attention than metamorphosis and hybridisation in the literary sources.

Human self-expansion turns animals into humans, or humans into animals, and is one aspect of human/animal relations. It is defined as 'the capacity to integrate, to some extent, another individual's resources, perspectives, and characteristics into the self-concept'.[68] In Greece, some gods and other super-human beings, such as centaurs, satyrs, and sirens, were imagined as hybrids – combinations of humans and animals. Sometimes they entirely take on animal shape. Are they symbolic entities or something more? Do iconography and literature give the same impression? One recent example of the exploration of composite creatures is Emma Aston's *Mixanthrôpoi: Animal–Human Hybrid Deities*. [69] Aston accesses literary and iconographic sources and also includes cross-cultural material, especially from Egypt and the Near East. Her book is one more example of a successful combination of sources. How is metamorphosis described in the various categories of sources? For instance, in the fifth century BCE there was a shift in the conception of metamorphosis from external to internal transformation, and this shift is evident both in literary texts and on painted pots.[70]

The consensus has been that animals in ancient Greek religion did not represent gods but that they were rather divine attributes or epithets.[71] How-ever, some of the things that are taken for granted need to be revisited. When votive reliefs depict Athena as an owl or Zeus in the form of a huge serpent, how were they experienced by the believers? Was the enigmatic serpent con-ceived of in line with theological rationalisations, or did it arouse feelings and reactions more directly dependent on its serpentine qualities? When Athena was depicted in the form of an owl, how did people react to the bird? Did they see it just as a pictographic sign for Athena or as something else? These are not easy questions to answer but posing them may lead to attempts to understand the messages these images convey. This presupposes being more aware of the presence of animals and of the emotional content of the images, and taking seriously the independent function of images in relation to texts, in line with Othmar Keel's assertion of 'the right of images to be seen'.[72]

Conclusion

The purpose that animals serve in relation to gods and humans varies according to context. As a result, the triangular symbolic relationships between gods, humans, and animals enacted in ancient Greek magic and religion differ. In sacrifices, animals are a means for humans to communicate with the gods, and the dead animal is turned into food for gods and humans. In magic, the status and worth of the animal are normally lower than in sacrifices: the animal is treated instrumentally, cruelly, and as an object; and the magical procedure involves ghosts and demons, not gods. In divination, birds are closely con-nected to gods as their messengers.

The ancient sources available for the study of the role of animals in ancient Greek religion are complex and multilayered. Different categories of sources and genres illuminate different aspects of the relationships between gods, humans, and animals. They range from the normative to the descriptive, from being founded on facts to giving free rein to the imagination. They offer glimpses of a rich and dynamic world and reflect development and changes over time. Language skills have been regarded as a *sine qua non* in the study of ancient Greek culture and religion. However, other skills have also proved to be useful: in addition to philology, the available sources invite various types of expertise in fields such as iconography, archaeology, and osteology, to mention just a few of the relevant fields. In the humanities, individual research has been most common, but multidisciplinary teamwork is a prerequisite for more complex and complete interpretations of the ancient sources.

Sources are dependent on their interpreters. We are the ones who make sense of them and make them speak. Our interpretations depend on what we look for and on the questions we pose, but also on our own worldviews and outlooks as researchers. Are animals treated 'as the Other, or as the Same', as outgroup or intergroup, as subjects or objects, by the ancients, by moderns?[73] Generally speaking, animals interact with humans and have agency. The interaction is obvious in some sources but under-communicated in others, and, where it is present, it is not always reflected upon.

Notes

1 Cf. Schwartz 2017: 225; Waldau and Patton 2006.
2 Lewis and Llewellyn-Jones 2018: 1.
3 There is an imbalance in the categories of surviving sources: due to the materials used, some have a lower survival rate than others. As many temples in Greece and statues of gods (*xoana*) were made of wood, most of them have gone. Likewise, most public art, such as paintings, has been lost. Painted pots, on the other hand, have survived in great numbers. See Arafat and Morgan 1998.
4 Ar. *Av.* 695–703.
5 Cf. Miles 2017.
6 Cf. Korhonen and Ruonakoski 2017: 44; Naiden 2015: 37, 76–81.
7 Cf. Henrichs 2012. In Euripides' *Iphigenia at Aulis*, Agamemnon sacrifices his daughter Iphigenia. Another example is Sophocles' *Electra*, in which by 'killing sheep to commemorate the killing of her husband, Clytemnestra draws a ritual analogy between animal sacrifice and murder' (Henrichs 2012: 185 and 181–182, referring to Soph. *El.* 266–281).
8 Cf. Henrichs 2012: 192–194.
9 Thumiger 2014: 84.
10 Thumiger 2014.
11 McInerney 2010.
12 McInerney 2010: 4.
13 Lewis and Llewellyn-Jones 2018.
14 Ekroth 2017: 28–29.
15 Cf. Freiberger 2018: 7.
16 Cf. Gilhus 2008: 227–244; Kindt 2012: 7, 179–186.
17 Alastair Harden 2014: 24 points out that the 'art of the ancient Mediterranean is replete with images of animals, and much Classical art features animals prominently, but there are few modern scholarly works that seem to analyse the semiotics of the depicted animals'.
18 Straten 1995: 6.
19 Parker 2011: 68–69. Meilichios was an ancient chthonic deity eventually subsumed by Zeus.

20 Woodford 2003: 40.
21 Laconian black figure cup: Woodford 2003: 40.
22 Woodford 2003: 40.
23 Sheep accounted for 57 per cent and pigs 20.8 per cent in the calendars; on the painted pots, there were 11.3 per cent sheep and 12.2 per cent pigs. The votive reliefs included 9.9 per cent sheep and 43.8 per cent pigs. See van Straten 1995: 170–186.
24 Straten 1995: 170–186.
25 Hitch *et al.* 2017: 4.
26 Ruscillo 2014: 2.
27 Kindt 2017: 222.
28 Cf. Ando 2012: 195, who disagrees; but see also Bremmer 2018: 224.
29 Cf. Ekroth 2017: 17.
30 Naiden 2015: 122–128.
31 Ekroth 2008: 259.
32 Cf. Hitch *et al.* 2017: 10.
33 Five Attic sacrificial calendars have been preserved: those of Thorikos, Erchia, the Marathonian Tetrapolis, the *genos* of the Salaminioi, and the fragmentary Athenian sacrificial calendar included in the law code. See van Straten 1995: 171–173.
34 Bremmer 2018: 221.
35 Bremmer 2018: 221–222.
36 Jameson describes this experiment in Jameson 1966; cf. Jameson 1986.
37 Forstenpointner 2003: 210–211; Ekroth 2017: 23–29.
38 Theodoropoulou 2013: 197.
39 Hitch *et al.* 2017: 10.
40 Carboni 2016: 257.
41 Carboni 2016; Mylona 2003; Ekroth 2017: 18.
42 Daniela Lefèvre-Novaro 2010: 49 connects the sacrifice of fish to a practice associated with the cult of Atargatis in Syria.
43 Ekroth 2017: 18.
44 Theodoropoulou 2013.
45 Ekroth 2017: 18.
46 The research on sacrifice has moved from making a connection between hunting and slaughtering – as evident in Burkert 1983 – to seeing sacrifice as a part of farmer culture (cf. Lincoln 2012; Graf 2012). The farmer perspective, including communal dining, was developed especially by Jean-Pierre Vernant and Marcel Detienne (Detienne and Vernant 1989). The so-called 'Hesiodic model' relied heavily on textual sources and was structuralist and synchronic (cf. Georgoudi 2010: 95). Their arguments have been criticised, lately by F. S. Naiden, who has moved the stress away from animal sacrifice and meat and focused especially on how 'sacrifices affect the gods' (Naiden 2015: 129; cf. also Lincoln 2012; Graf 2012).
47 Korhonen and Ruonakoski 2017.
48 Korhonen and Ruonakoski 2017: 54.
49 Korhonen and Ruonakoski 2017: 54–55.
50 Images are found in van Straten 1995.
51 Straten 1995: 186–192.
52 McInerney 2010; cf. Børresen 1997: 50.
53 Karl Meuli 1946 used a comparative source material – for instance, bear hunting among Siberians and other northern people – and pointed to similarities between hunting rituals and Greek sacrifice. According to Meuli, there are numerous parallels (see Meuli 1946: 261). One of the more prominent is that blame is removed from the killers. For instance, when a goat was sacrificed to Hera in Corinth, the knife was hidden, but the goat dug it out with its feet and was blamed for its own death. Meuli characterises those in charge of the sacrifice as 'similar artists of innocence' ('*Unschuldskünstler*') to the Arctic bear hunters (Meuli 1946: 267). The term 'comedy

of innocence' ('*Unschuldskomödie*') was coined for such sacrificial procedures (cf. Meuli 1946: 273) and Meuli uses it explicitly to characterise the bouphonia ('ox-slaying') in Athens (Meuli 1946: 276). Walter Burkert built on Meuli's work and returns repeatedly to the term '*Unschuldskomödie*' in Burkert 1983.

54 McInerney 2010.
55 Franco 2014; cf. also Trantalidou 2006.
56 Franco 2014: 164–166.
57 Morgan 2012: 147.
58 The evidence for bird omens includes literary sources, such as Homer and Aeschylus, a systematic collection of bird omens (Posidipp. *Oĩoskopika*), and depictions, for instance on pots (see Dillon 2016: 139–177). Magical sources are literary accounts, curse tablets, amulets, and papyrus recipes, such as the collection of *PGM*. See also Ogden 2009 and 2014.
59 Examples of animals in the magic sources are bats, chameleons, puppies, hyenas, fish, snakes, frogs, and birds. See Faraone 1999: 65–67; Ogden 2014: 295–302. In divination, the most significant birds were eagles, ravens, crows, and owls, but numerous other species are also mentioned in the literature (cf. Mynott 2018: 255; Dillon 2016: 139–177). In astrology, more than half of the constellations, including seven of the twelve zodiac constellations (Aries, Taurus, Cancer, Leo, Scorpius, Capricornus, and Pisces), represent animals.
60 Among the many merits of Mynott's book is an appendix titled 'Some Bird Lists from Ancient Sources', in which he compares the 75 bird species that appear in Aristophanes' works with a list of depictions of birds from Pompeii (Mynott 2018: 363–367).
61 Mynott 2018: vii.
62 Mynott 2018: vii.
63 Mynott 2018: 43–63.
64 Faraone 1999: 65–69.
65 There is a reference to this magical practice in Pind. *Pyth.* 213–219; see Ogden 2014: 295–296.
66 Faraone 1993 and 1999; Gordon 2010.
67 Sarah Iles Johnston points out that the choice of these animals is connected to nocturnal raptors being swift and usually silent. Even if the horse has frequently positive connotations, it is also associated with violence and the dark; the wolf is a predator; while the ass shape of the demon Empousa evokes the seductive and destructive power that this child-killing demon could hold over young men (Johnston 2001: 375–378).
68 Amiot *et al.* 2016: 557, with reference to Aron *et al.* 1991.
69 Aston 2011.
70 Rothwell 2016: 492; Alexandridis 2009.
71 E.g. Trantalidou 2006: 96; cf. Gilhus 2008: 105–107; Korhonen and Ruonakoski 2017: 90–91.
72 Keel 1992; cf. Harden 2014.
73 Other or Same: Gordon 2010: 249. Outgroup or intergroup: Amiot *et al.* 2016: 557.

Bibliography

Alexandridis, A. (2009) 'Shifting species: animal and human bodies in Attic vase paintings of the 6th and 5th centuries BC', in T. Fögen and M. M. Lee (eds.) *Bodies and Boundaries in Graeco-Roman Antiquity*. Berlin, 261–281.
Amiot, C., B. Brock, and P. Martehns (2016) 'People and companion animals: it takes two to tango', *BioScience* 66: 552–560.

Ando, C. (2012) *Imperial Rome AD 193–284. The Critical Century*. Edinburgh.

Arafat, K. and C. Morgan (1998) 'Architecture and other visual arts', in P. Cartledge (ed.) *The Cambridge Illustrated History of Ancient Greece*. Cambridge, 250–287.

Aron, A. *et al.* (1991) 'Close relationships as including other in the self', *Journal of Personality and Social Psychology* 60, 241–253.

Aston, E. (2011) *Mixanthrôpoi. Animal–Human Hybrid Deities in Greek Religion*. Liège.

Børresen, B. (1997) 'Er respekt for livet forenlig med jegerufølsomhet?', *Samtiden* 5/6, 47–53.

Bremmer, J. N. (2018) 'Transformations and decline of sacrifice in imperial Rome and late antiquity', in M. Blömer and B. Eckhardt (eds.) *Transformationen paganer Religion in der Kaiserzeit*. Berlin, 215–256.

Burkert, W. (1983) *Homo Necans. The Anthropology of Ancient Greek Sacrificial Ritual and Myth*, trans. P. Bing. Berkeley, Calif. (German orig. 1972).

Carboni, R. (2016) 'Unusual sacrificial victims: fish and their value in the context of sacrifices', in P. A. Johnston, A. Mastrocinque, and S. Papaioannou (eds.) *Animals in Greek and Roman Religion and Myth*. Newcastle, 255–279.

Detienne, M. and J.-P. Vernant (eds.) (1989) *The Cuisine of Sacrifice among the Greeks*, trans. P. Wissing. Chicago, Ill. (French orig. 1979).

Dillon, M. (2016) *Omens and Oracles. Divination in Ancient Greece*. London.

Ekroth, G. (2008) 'Meat, man and god: on the division of the animal victim at Greek sacrifices', in M. Jameson (ed.) *Mikros Ieromnemon. Meletes eis Mnemen*. Athens, 259–290.

Ekroth, G. (2017) 'Bare bones: zooarchaeology and sacrifice', in S. Hitch and I. Rutherford (eds.) *Animal Sacrifice in the Ancient Greek World*. Cambridge, 15–47.

Faraone, C. A. (1993) 'Molten wax, spilt wine and mutilated animals: sympathetic magic in Near Eastern and early Greek oath ceremonies', *Journal of Hellenistic Studies* 113, 60–80.

Faraone, C. A. (1999) *Ancient Greek Love Magic*. Cambridge, Mass.

Forstenpointner, G. (2003) 'Promethean legacy: investigations into the procedure of "Olympian" sacrifice', in E. Kotjabopoulou *et al.* (eds.) *Zooarchaeology in Greece. Recent Advances*. London, 203–211.

Franco, C. (2014) *Shameless. The Canine and the Feminine in Ancient Greece*. Berkeley, Calif.

Freiberger, O. (2018) 'Elements of a comparative methodology in the study of religion', *Religions* 9 (38), doi:10.3390/rel9020038.

Georgoudi, S. (2010) 'Sacrifices to the gods', in J. N. Bremmer and A. Erskine (eds.) *The Gods of Ancient Greece. Identities and Transformations*. Edinburgh, 92–105.

Gilhus, I. S. (2008) *Animals, Gods and Humans. Changing Attitudes to Animals in Greek, Roman and Early Christian Ideas*. London.

Gordon, R. (2010) 'Magian lessons in natural history: unique animals in Graeco-Roman natural magic', in J. Dijkstra, J. Kroesen, and Y. Kuiper (eds.) *Myths, Martyrs, and Modernity*. Leiden, 249–269.

Graf, F. (2012) 'One generation after Burkert and Girard: where are the great theories?', in C. A. Faraone and F. S. Naiden (eds.) *Greek and Roman Animal Sacrifice. Ancient Victims, Modern Observers*. Cambridge, 32–52.

Harden, A. (2014) 'Animals in classical art', in G. L. Campbell (ed.) *The Oxford Handbook of Animals in Classical Thought and Life*. Oxford, 24–60.

Henrichs, A. (2012) 'Animal sacrifice in Greek tragedy: ritual, metaphor, problematizations', in C. A. Faraone and F. S. Naiden (eds.) *Greek and Roman Animal Sacrifice. Ancient Victims, Modern Observers*. Cambridge, 180–194.

Hitch, S., F. Naiden, and I. Rutherford (2017) 'Introduction', in S. Hitch and I. Rutherford (eds.) *Animal Sacrifice in the Ancient Greek World*. Cambridge, 1–11.

Hitch, S. and I. Rutherford (eds.) (2017) *Animal Sacrifice in the Ancient Greek World*. Cambridge.

Jameson, M. H. (1966) 'The omen of the oxtail', *Scientific American* 214, 54.

Jameson, M. H. (1986) 'Sophocles, Antigone 1005–1022. An illustration', in M. Cropp, E. Fantham, and S. E. Scully (eds.) *Greek Tragedy and its Legacy. Essays Presented to D. J. Conacher*. Calgary, 59–65.

Johnston, S. I. (2001) 'Defining the dreadful: remarks on the Greek child-killing demon', in M. Meyer and P. Mirecki (eds.) *Ancient Magic and Ritual Power*. Leiden, 361–387.

Keel, O. (1992) *Das Recht der Bilder gesehen zu werden. Drei Fallstudien zur Methode der Interpretation altorientalischer Bilder*. Göttingen.

Kindt, J. (2012) *Rethinking Greek Religion*. Cambridge.

Kindt, J. (2017) 'Capturing the ancient animal: human/animal studies and the Classics', *Journal of Hellenic Studies* 137, 213–225.

Korhonen, T. and E. Ruonakoski (2017) *Human and Animal in Ancient Greece. Empathy and Encounter in Classical Literature*. London.

Lefèvre-Novaro, D. (2010) 'Les Sacrifices de poisson dans les sanctuaires Grecs de l'Âge du Fer', *Kernos* 23, 37–52.

Lewis, S. and L. Llewellyn-Jones (2018) *The Culture of Animals in Antiquity. A Sourcebook with Commentaries*. London.

Lincoln, B. (2012) 'From Bergaigne to Meuli: how animal sacrifice became a hot topic', in C. A. Faraone and F. S. Naiden (eds.) *Greek and Roman Animal Sacrifice. Ancient Victims, Modern Observers*. Cambridge, 13–32.

McInerney, J. (2010) *The Cattle of the Sun. Cows and Culture in the World of the Ancient Greeks*. Princeton, N.J.

Meuli, K. (1946) 'Griechische Opferbräuche', in O. Gigon and K. Meuli (eds.) *Phyllobolia. Festschrift Peter von der Mühll zum 60. Geburtstag am 1. August 1945*. Basel, 185–288.

Miles, S. (2017) 'Cultured animals and wild humans? Talking with the animals in Aristophanes' Wasps', in T. Fögen and E. Thomas (eds.) *Interactions between Animals and Humans in Graeco-Roman Antiquity*. Berlin, 205–232.

Morgan, D. (2012) *The Embodied Eye. Religious Visual Culture and the Social Life of Feelings*. Berkeley, Calif.

Mylona, D. (2003) 'Archaeological fish remains in Greece: general trends of the research and a gazetteer of sites', in E. Kotjabopoulou *et al.* (eds.) *Zooarchaeology in Greece. Recent Advances*. London, 193–200.

Mynott, J. (2018) *Birds in the Ancient World*. Oxford.

Naiden, F. S. (2015) *Smoke Signals for the Gods. Ancient Greek Sacrifice from the Archaic through Roman Periods*. New York, N.Y.

Ogden, D. (2009) *Magic, Witchcraft and Ghosts in the Greek and Roman World. A Sourcebook*. London.

Ogden, D. (2014) 'Animal magic', in G. L. Campbell (ed.) *The Oxford Handbook of Animals in Classical Thought and Life*. Oxford, 294–309.

Parker, R. (2005) *Polytheism and Society in Athens*. Oxford.

Parker, R. (2011) *On Greek Religion*. Ithaca, N.Y.

Pütz, B. (2014) 'Good to laugh with: animals in comedy', in G. L. Campbell (ed.) *The Oxford Handbook of Animals in Classical Thought and Life*. Oxford, 61–72.

Rothwell, K. S., Jr. (2016) 'The language of animal metamorphosis in Greek mythology', in P. A. Johnston, A. Mastrocinque, and S. Papaioannou (eds.) *Animals in Greek and Roman Religion and Myth*. Newcastle, 479–494.

Ruscillo, D. (2014) 'Review of Nerissa Russell, Social Zooarchaeology. Humans and Animals in Prehistory', *American Journal of Archaeology* 118, 1–4.

Schwartz, G. M. (2017) 'The archaeological study of sacrifice', *Annual Review of Anthropology* 46, 223–240.

Straten, F. T. van (1995) *Hiera Kala. Images of Animal Sacrifice in Archaic and Classical Greece*. Leiden.

Theodoropoulou, T. (2013) 'The sea in the temple: shells, fish and corals from the sanctuary of the ancient town of Kythnos and other marine stories of cult', in G. Ekroth and J. Wallensten (eds.) *Bones, Behaviour and Belief*. Stockholm, 197–222.

Thumiger, C. (2014) 'Animals in tragedy', in G. L. Campbell (ed.) *The Oxford Handbook of Animals in Classical Thought and Life*. Oxford, 84–98.

Trantalidou, K. (2006) 'Companions from the oldest times: dogs in ancient Greek literature, iconography and osteological testimony', in L. M. Snyder and E. A. Moore (eds.) *Dogs and People in Social, Working, Economic or Symbolic Interaction*. Oxford, 96–119.

Waldau, P. and K. Patton (eds.) (2006) *A Communion of Subjects. Animals in Religion, Science, and Ethics*. New York, N.Y.

Woodford, S. (2003) *Images of Myth in Classical Antiquity*. Cambridge.

3 Approaches

The animal in the study of ancient Greek religion

E. Kearns

Since it seems likely that humans are the only animals to reflect on their relationships with other species, the question of human/animal engagement has a perennial fascination not limited to any particular age. However, the growth of the animal rights movement in the last quarter of the 20th century gave a new impetus to the subject, suggesting a more focused approach informed by a clearer understanding of the range of possible human/animal relations. At the same time, cultural history was coming of age, and an early, major example of its application to the field was Keith Thomas's *Man and the Natural World*.[1] As is often the case, it took classical studies a decade or two to catch up (Richard Sorabji's more philosophically oriented work *Animal Minds and Human Morals* appeared precisely ten years later, in 1993), but after the turn of the millennium the pace accelerated, and from around 2005 onwards numerous monographs and edited volumes appeared tackling the subject from varying perspectives. Julia Kindt discussed some of the more important (mostly English) texts in a 2017 review article that examined the trend thematically.[2] Animals in religion were not forgotten, with works on gods in animal form and metamorphosis on the one hand and some useful – if brief – general surveys on the other, but the area remained relatively unexplored in comparison with philosophical or economic aspects.[3]

This is perhaps strange, because one conspicuous and much-discussed feature of ancient religion – sacrifice – is very much concerned with animals, and they have far more than incidental importance in at least some of the competing theories of sacrifice. The deficiency may be due to the fact that attention in the field of ancient Greek religion had started to shift away from sacrifice as the paradigmatic cult action (and indeed from cult action altogether). The focus was now on the gods themselves as the recipients of cult, and on the human mentalities of their worshippers.[4] Yet, there is a great deal more to animals in ancient Greek religion than simply sacrifice, however important that may remain. If we try to pull together work on Greek religion that has a bearing on animals, we find a plethora of approaches. Some have favoured an evolutionary perspective, whether that meant finding explanations in the supposed views of animals and the divine held by 'primitive' people or more radically in sociobiology, where certain behaviours of other animals are at the root of human modalities. Other approaches are more synchronic, but may see the animal as anything from an instrument in human/divine communication to part of a symbolic language used in understanding the world. A review of the interpretations in the more important trends in the study of Greek religion will make this clear.

A brief history

The so-called 'Cambridge ritualists' were among the first to apply anything like a coherent methodology to the study of ancient Greek religion. Jane Harrison, Gilbert Murray, Francis Cornford, and Arthur Bernard Cook had some major differences in interests and approaches, but they shared a belief in the primacy of ritual over myth, an interest in the 'primitive' origins of cult (the hypothetical first stage of Murray's *Five Stages of Greek Religion*), and the conviction that such origins explained a good deal about the developed forms of cult and myth.[5] Their concepts of early forms of religion in Greece were informed by contemporary anthropological theory, and their debt to *The Golden Bough* (1890) is obvious, particularly in the emphasis on the death and rebirth of vegetation deities, which in Harrison's hands were all incarnations of a postulated *eniautos-daimōn* or year spirit. Another important influence was William Robertson Smith, whose *Lectures on the Religion of the Semites* (1889) propounded the theory of sacrificial communion: the tribe was bound together by sharing in the killing and eating of its totemic animal, which was in turn closely linked to (perhaps even identical with) the tribal god. Totemism in general, a concept derived in part from the study of Amerindian peoples, in part from research into Australian Indigenous groups, was much in vogue as a catch-all theory of 'primitive religion'.[6] The idea that clan solidarity expressed through a 'totemic sacrament' can be discerned behind Greek religious practice permeates the writings of this group, and gives special importance to animals in their accounts of the origins of cult and myth. Sacrifice, therefore, was not originally conceived of as a gift of a lower to a higher being, but as something altogether different. Cook, for instance, writing about the peculiar Athenian festival of the Dipolieia, later to assume a central importance in the theories of Karl Meuli and Walter Burkert (see below), declared:

> The ox throughout is treated as divine … [There was] solemn communion of those who together devoured the sacred flesh and so … absorbed into their own bodies the very substance and virtues of the divine beast … We cannot but conclude that the ox of the Dipolieia … was the embodiment of Zeus Polieus himself – slain that he might live again in younger and more vigorous form.[7]

Similarly Harrison, in a chapter entitled 'Totemism, sacrament and sacrifice', linked somewhat obscure traditions of *ōmophagia* (eating raw flesh) with communal meals in which a sacred animal is solemnly consumed and its *mana* absorbed by the participants, and with Greek gods in more or less animal form.[8]

Gods in animal form, whether in stories of metamorphosis, such as those of Zeus becoming a bull or a swan, or in more cultic contexts, including the snake-form of Zeus Meilichios or the *Agathos Daimōn*, or Dionysus addressed as 'worthy bull' in the hymn of the Elean women preserved by Plutarch, were therefore of much interest to the ritualists as pointing to an earlier period in which the focus of religiosity was the totemic animal.[9] The same applied to the simple association of god and animal – Athena and the owl, Hera and the cow, for instance, where the epithets *glaukōpis* ('owl-eyed') and *boōpis* ('cow-eyed') clearly indicated a distant past where Athena really was an owl and Hera a cow. Cook wrote a lengthy article on 'Animal worship in the Mycenaean age'.[10] In *Themis*, Harrison traced the evolution of the Olympians and the later history of Greek religion from an early stage, where the difference between human and animal was not fully conceptualised, to the developed system of the classical period and beyond, in which the human form of the gods was such a distinctive feature.[11] In her view, strongly contrasting with Murray's, this was not a net gain: 'The ram-headed Knum of the Egyptians is to the mystic more religious than any of the beautiful divine humanities of the Greek.'[12] The presence of animals in the Greek religious system, whether as sacrificial victim or otherwise associated with a god, was therefore a pointer to a more ancient and perhaps more interesting phase in the development of religion, certainly a phase which in a sense supplied the solution to the many problems posed by the cults and myths of historical times.

A central plank toppled from the ritualists' edifice with the growing realisation that a unified concept of totemism, applicable to all or most 'primitive' peoples, is less than useful. Vegetation spirits and year spirits fell from favour. Animals could not be written out of ancient Greek religion, but they no longer had the importance they had enjoyed previously and there was no unified theory to account for their role. Most mid-20th-century writing on the subject, typified by the pre-eminent figure of Martin Nilsson, was considerably more cautious than that of Harrison and her associates. An important exception, at least as far as animal sacrifice was concerned, was the work of Meuli, whose theory, first published in 1946, linked Greek sacrificial practice with the hunting customs of Siberian nomads.[13] Though his ethnographic data have been questioned, Meuli observed that Central Asian hunters appeared to regret the slaughter of animals and to carry out rituals designed to compensate the animal for its death, playing out a 'comedy of innocence' in which they disclaimed responsibility for the killing.[14] He saw this as indicative of a very ancient pattern of thought that could be discerned in some features of Greek sacrificial ritual, such as the placing of skulls in sanctuaries, and above all in the bouphonia ('ox murder') enacted at the Athenian festival of the Dipolieia, which, as we have seen, also interested the Cambridge ritualists. In this very unusual sacrifice, a ploughing ox (not normally killed for sacrificial purposes) was slaughtered after eating grains and cakes placed on the altar of Zeus Polieus. After the slaughterer fled in apparent panic, an elaborate trial of the instruments used in the killing was staged and the victim's body was 'reconstituted' by stuffing its skin and yoking it to a plough. Meuli concluded that the origins of Greek sacrifice lay in the Palaeolithic past, and that human/animal relations, specifically feelings of guilt caused by killing for food, were at the heart of the development of religious forms.

Meuli's ideas were taken up and amplified by Walter Burkert in his hugely influential *Homo Necans*. [15] Burkert laid further emphasis on human aggression, drawing on the work of Konrad Lorenz, and in his scheme animal sacrifice, with its roots still in hunting custom, is in effect controlled aggression, directed towards other species, rather than fellow-humans, and contained in strictly ritualised form. A sense of unease, shock, and even guilt remained at the kill. Somewhat like Harrison's primitives, Burkert's Palaeolithic hunters saw likenesses between themselves and other mammals, so that even while lines were strictly drawn between killing humans in acts of outright aggression and killing animals for food in the hunt, a sense of transgression remained at the latter and left its traces in the ritual of sacrifice. [16] Animal sacrifice remained at the centre of Greek religion for Burkert, but his theoretical framework went beyond man-the-hunter and his relations with animals. Even in his theory of sacrifice, he travelled further from classical Greece than Meuli's Siberian shamans in looking to the period when proto-humans first moved from a largely vegetarian diet to become predators on a large scale. On a wider canvas, he extended his use of evolutionary biology to the pre-human past. In *Creation of the Sacred*, a work concerned with all 'early' religions, not merely Greek religion, he traced the idea of gods in an elevated sacred realm to the tendency of dominant primates to occupy treetops, and the anointing of sacred stones to animal 'marking'. [17] Here there is no longer a firm distinction between human and animal, and it is no longer the place of the animal in human religion that is significant so much as animal behaviour itself providing the key to the development of religious behaviour and mentalities.

Not unlike those of the Cambridge ritualists, Burkert's theories are concerned with origins rather than the illumination of religion in a specific cultural context. The other great force in the later 20th-century study of Greek religion, the 'Paris School' (Jean-Pierre Vernant, Pierre Vidal-Naquet, Marcel Detienne, Nicole Loraux, and others) adopted an entirely different approach. These scholars, too, used various insights and methodology from outside the disciplines of ancient history or classical philology, but their chief debt was to the structuralist anthropology of Claude Lévi-Strauss. Consequently, far from focusing on the origins of religion in the distant past, their work privileged synchronic over diachronic analysis even within Greek culture and history. Vernant and Detienne, especially, were interested in animal sacrifice giving vivid expression to the distinction between humans and gods on the one hand, and humans and animals on the other. Sacrifice itself, like the cooking of food, was a civilised practice that differentiated humans from beasts that eat their food raw and without ceremony, as well as assigning each member of the triad of animals, humans, and gods its proper place. Animals allow humans to communicate with gods, but as tools in the process of sacrifice, they are hierarchically below the humans who initiate the process. This hierarchy extended beyond the sacrificial context and was of the utmost importance in establishing the human position in the world.[18] Although some influential understandings of ritual have tended to downplay a symbolic aspect and often decouple the standardised performance of religious actions from a fixed meaning, it is apparent that this should be a fruitful approach, though hardly exhausting the significance of animals in Greek religion.[19]

Both the Paris School and the interests and theories of Burkert remain influential, even though they have been critiqued and perhaps overtaken by other approaches. More recent overarching trends in Greek religious studies have had relatively little to say about animals. By definition, the 'polis religion' model, in all its variants, is concerned with human organisation, and for the most part non-human species appear in its schemes only incidentally.[20] An important partial exception may be the investigation of observances such as the *arkteia* at Brauron, where the participants are sometimes named after, and play the part of, some kind of animal. When these rituals are identified as initiatory or maturation rites, the animal is often taken to represent more generally the realm of the wild, the uncivilised, which the young 'animal' must leave in order to attain the status of an adult member of the community. Such interpretations clearly owe a great deal to the structuralism of the Paris School, and it is no coincidence that Christiane Sourvinou-Inwood, who was both strongly influenced by structuralism and one of the most prominent advocates of the polis religion viewpoint, wrote extensively on both the social structure and the links between girls, animals, and the city.[21]

A very different trend has been the increasing application of cognitive approaches to the subject, especially in the 21st century. Frameworks of this type stress the role of brain function in the creation of religious thought and action, and since the human brain is not completely unlike the brains of other animals, especially primates, there is some potential overlap here with the sociobiological theory used by Burkert to explain Greek religious practice. However, there is some way to go in exploring this interface, and despite interest in the phenomenon of divine anthropomorphism, much remains to be done to bring cognitive theory to bear on the developed human understanding of the animal as it appears in the religious context.[22]

A few works that less obviously form part of the major interpretative trends have still made useful contributions to our understanding of the place of animals in the religion of the Greeks. The 1970s and 1980s produced the syntheses of, respectively, Liliane Bodson and Jean Prieur, neither of which fits easily into any of the main patterns of interpretation outlined above.[23] Both authors, in fact, approached the subject more from the 'animals' than the 'religion' side. On the subject of animal sacrifice, again, much important work stands independently of the grand theories, notably studies on the types and quantities of animals sacrificed (by Michael H. Jameson, Vincent J. Rosivach, Gunnel Ekroth, and others), on visual representations of sacrifice (by Folkert van Straten and, from under the umbrella of the Paris School, Jean-Louis Durand), and on possible meanings encoded in sacrificial variables (by Ekroth, again, and articles in numerous collected volumes).[24] Far less has been done on other aspects of animals in Greek religion, but we should note the work of Françoise Frontisi-Ducroux and Richard Buxton on myths of metamorphosis, of Emma Aston on mythical animal hybrids, and of Georgia Petridou on animal forms in epiphany.[25]

Moving forward

The last two decades, it has been remarked, have seen a move away from grand theories in the study of ancient religion, even while the contributions to our understanding made by their authors remain recognised.[26] Similarly with the new interest in animals in the ancient world: during the same period, there has been something of an explosion of works investigating the subject, yet, although most of these studies are influenced by current methodologies and abut on wider concerns, it is difficult to trace predominating trends, beyond the use of animals in human self-definition, and even that is not a universal concern.[27] What, then, should be the way forward at the intersection of these two subjects?

The contents of the present volume, as well as other work on the subject, suggest that we could think of the study of animals in Greek religion as falling roughly into two categories. First, there are questions concerning the place of animals in the religious imagination. In this category we may place everything concerning the threefold relationship between gods, humans, and animals, whether the boundaries between these groups are seen to be maintained, blurred, or even radically shifted. This will include not only less explicit material concerned with animals in general but everything to do with individual species in their relation to myth, cult, and the conceptualisation of the divine. Animals in myth, and mythical metamorphosis into animals, fall within this category, as do representations of deities in partly or wholly animal shape, but these far from exhaust the approach. Second, there are the various ways in which animals are relevant to the interactions between human and divine that are generally considered as constituting religious practice: sacrifice, obviously, but also, as is evident throughout this volume, divination, healing, and magic. Yet, it is clear that these two categories abut on and blend into each other at every turn. If animals are good to think with, what is thought about them will have an effect on what is done with them; and what is done with them, being construed as normative, will likewise have an effect on the way they are thought about. Thus, as we have already seen, for Vernant, Detienne, and others, the hierarchy of gods, humans, and animals that they discern in Greek thought is expressed not only in abstract reflection or even in unreflective acceptance of 'the way things are', but especially in sacrifice, in which animals are the material that facilitates communication between humans and gods, the middle and upper members of the triad.[28] Again, we might assume that the mythical possibility of metamorphosis, the transformation of anthropomorphic gods or indeed humans into animal shape, belongs firmly in the first category of thinking rather than doing. But surely it cannot be considered separately from the 'actual' transformation into animals that occurs in some forms of ritual mimesis, the most famous being the 'bear-ritual', *arkteia*, practised by female children at Brauron in Attica.[29]

Therefore, even while we acknowledge the usefulness of the distinction between the different directions in which our research may lead, corresponding roughly to the second and third parts of the present volume, it is important to keep in mind that the most fruitful results may come about in each case through remembering the other branch.

Thinking

Let us begin, then, by looking at animals in thought, within more or less religious contexts. What have the major trends in interpreting the religious systems of the Greeks contributed so far, and where might we expect the next steps to take us?

A good deal of ritualist theory now seems dated, and of more interest as a subject of study in its own right rather than for any light it might shed on the ancient Greek world. Nonetheless, the evolutionary perspective it shares with Meuli and Burkert is significant in that both accord an important place in the formation of religious systems to human relations with animals. Much in Meuli's and Burkert's theories of sacrifice has been convincingly challenged; even the centrality of animal sacrifice itself has not gone uncontested.[30] But if a close link between early hunting customs and Greek sacrificial ritual has become more difficult to maintain, or at least to consider as key, the idea that interaction with animals, whether in a predator or prey relationship, through the process of domestication or through simple observation, has somehow been formative in religion is likely to remain in play. It is undoubtedly also the case that much in Greek religious practice (including sacrifice) dates back to distant pre-Greek origins, whether Proto-Indo-European or Mediterranean, and we should expect the conditions of life lived in close proximity to, and dependent on, animals to be reflected in actions originating in these periods. When and if attention turns to the relationship between developed Greek practice and the distant past, we may expect human/animal relations to return to the spotlight.

Early taxonomies may also be relevant. Though the scholars of the Paris School generally avoided speculation on origins, it is reasonable to suppose that some of the patterns they discerned in Greek (and other) thought might be a good deal older. But wherever we wish to situate the origins of such patterns in human world-views, the structuralist contribution to our understanding of Greek views of animals remains of fundamental importance: the position of animals and the position of gods can be fully understood only with reference to each other. But just as the classic forms of structuralism have fallen out of favour more generally, in the study of ancient societies and religions the preferred models have moved away from relatively fixed patterns and towards an emphasis on fluidity and slippage, with increased recognition that overlapping and even contradictory forms of abstract understanding can coexist. This seems to make better sense of the totality of the material available to us. From the human perspective, animals, though like us in some ways, are also conspicuously 'other'. The same, of course, is true of gods, which leaves the way open for both a partial modelling of inferred gods on observed and experienced animals (reflected in theriomorphic deities and the denotation of certain animals as sacred) and the structuralist, three-term hierarchy in which humans are placed between higher gods and lower animals.

While the hierarchy is thus a crucially important insight, there were many other ways in which the relationship between gods and animals (and humans) was conceptualised. Several strands suggest that gods might in some way, or in some cases, be closely related to animals without the mediating presence of humans, or that the boundaries of the three categories are fluid. We might begin by thinking of deities in animal or partly animal form, for although the Greeks were very conscious of the fact that their own deities were typically anthropomorphic, the likes of 'the ram-headed Knum' were not absent from their awareness. Frequently, indeed, they thought of theriomorphic deities as a specifically non-Greek – usually Egyptian – phenomenon, which might provoke widely divergent responses. Yet, several of the gods they themselves worshipped were in whole or part animal form. The renowned oracular god Zeus Ammon, with his ram's horns, might be a partly Hellenised version of a Libyan and Egyptian deity, but the widely worshipped Zeus Meilichios, often depicted as a snake, was entirely Greek.[31] Serpentine, too, are the *Agathos Daimōn*, the Elean Sosipolis, and the Attic hero Cecrops, whose body ends in a snake's tail; Dionysus may be addressed, and appear, as a bull; while Arcadian cult and myth are rich in theriomorphic deities, including Pan, who eventually became widely diffused across the Greek world.[32] However, it must be said that these are exceptions to the way divinity usually appears, and the Greeks were quite right to see that the characteristic form of their gods was anthropomorphic.

Moreover, the animal or part-animal forms are not just numerically inferior to gods conceived in human form; they also tend to characterise deities who are in other ways less central, perhaps less 'Olympian' or less Panhellenic. Other Greeks perceived Arcadia as a strange and primitive place, inhabited by acorn-eaters, and even rumoured to be the location of human sacrifice.[33] It was scarcely surprising, then, that its myths told of Poseidon and Demeter in horse form, or that its inhabitants worshipped a goddess with a fish's tail or horse's head.[34] Cecrops and Sosipolis were important locally, as were river-gods with their part-bull form, but their significance was tied up with that local situation and could be transferred elsewhere only in exceptional circumstances.[35] Zeus Meilichios, at least in Attica, was the recipient of untypical cult, something which in the semantics of divinity always marks out a god as somehow different from the norm, at least for the occasion of the offering.[36] Even Dionysus, a frequent shape-shifter (see this volume, Chapter 7), though an Olympian and usually considered one of the Twelve Gods, is frequently seen as somehow divergent, one who transgresses norms and boundaries. Theriomorphic deities are certainly not always minor gods (though it is true that a hybrid animal form is commonly found among marginal mythical creatures, such as centaurs and satyrs).[37] Gods and heroes with animal or part-animal form may be extremely important in the local view, or indeed in any specific ritual context, yet they are seldom central to a concept of the divine.

The temporary transformation of gods in myth is clearly to be distinguished from their permanent representation in cult in wholly or partly animal form, yet the two phenomena are interconnected. Scholars rightly link the Arcadian mythic and cultic animal forms of deities, where there is a substantial coincidence of themes.[38] Here, zoomorphic forms can play into the perennial debate on the relationship between myth and ritual, but mythical metamorphoses such as the well-known bull and swan forms of Zeus seem to have little, if any, connection with cult, and more work is clearly needed on their rationale. How do animal forms relate to other types of metamorphosis – Zeus as a shower of gold, for instance, or as Alkmene's husband? It is noteworthy that many of the animal metamorphoses of the gods are connected with erotic pursuit, whether the shape change is that of the pursuer, the pursued, or both. But there are obvious exceptions even to this, such as the lion metamorphosis of Dionysus or the dolphin shape of Apollo in their respective *Homeric Hymns*.[39] At present, we seem to have more questions than answers in this area.

Different, again, are the associations of certain deities with particular animals, yet here it is perhaps easier to see a connection between a god's favourite animal and that god's possible identification with (or at least representation as) the same animal. Athena has many different links with birds, so it seems that there should be some connection between her fondness for owls and her appearance as a vulture or a swallow in Homer.[40] Similarly, Poseidon is universally associated with horses, and in Arcadian myth actually becomes one.[41] However, not all divine associations work in this way. In a somewhat obscure myth, Artemis becomes a doe, but she is far more often associated with shooting deer, and a better-known myth relates her substitution of a sacrificial deer for her victim Iphigeneia.[42] Similarly, it is her votary Kallisto, not herself, whom she transforms into a bear, and when young girls 'become bears' in her worship at Brauron, there is nothing to suggest that they are imitating the goddess.[43] Bears, deer, and, indeed, other animals may be intimately linked with Artemis, but she seldom adopts their form.

If individual gods vary in their relationships with animals, individual animal species display important variables in their relations with the divine. In other words, animals are, rather obviously, not only an undifferentiated group of beings in a triangular relationship with humans and gods but often better understood by distinguishing them from one another. Some species appear to be more significant in religious contexts than others. For instance, snakes and horses often appear in connection with the gods, whereas lizards and donkeys, though not completely absent, are much less prominent.[44] The more obviously significant animals have received some attention, but more remains to be done.[45] The interrelationships among different animals in religious and mythical contexts could be explored, as was done, for instance, by Wendy Doniger-O'Flaherty in an Indian setting.[46] In particular, the distinction between wild and domesticated, which is highly significant if not entirely straightforward in relation to sacrifice, might yield interesting results if extended to other areas.

So far we have been dealing with myth and imagination (with some overlap into cultic presentation), areas that tend to utilise 'intuitive' modes of thinking. Those who represent these areas of thought to us do not fully expound their thinking — that is left to the modern investigator. But 'reflective' modes of thought are also relevant to animals and religion.[47] Especially in later times, there is a good deal of reflection on the place of animals beside humans and gods, and on their role in relations between the two, not all of which fit easily into the three-term hierarchical model. We may think of the Neoplatonist Porphyry's treatise on abstention from animal food, in which he draws on the work of Aristotle's pupil Theophrastus to demonstrate that the killing of animals is incompatible with true human piety towards the gods, or of the Emperor Julian's discussion of the rationale of animal sacrifice in his *Hymn to the Mother of the Gods*, which is replete with details such as the reason why (in Julian's view) pigs should not be sacrificed. These and other works have been the subject of much interesting recent discussion.[48]

But the most radical tradition has undoubtedly early origins. Much of early Pythagoreanism is obscure, but it must be considered in any discussion of animals in Greek religion, not only for the negative point that the vegetarianism frequently attributed to the sect made animal sacrifice difficult or impossible but also because its overlaps with 'Orphism' (another problematic category) give it a strongly religious colouring.[49] That Pythagorean observances were perceived to be closely related to those of the Orphics is clear from Herodotus, who speaks of things (possibly rituals or writings) 'called Orphic and Bacchic, but actually Egyptian and Pythagorean'.[50] Both groups seem to have been concerned with observing an austere lifestyle, viewed in connection with some kind of better fate for the soul after death. For the Pythagoreans, at least, this seems in turn to have been linked to 'metempsychosis' — the progress of the soul through many different bodies, including those of animals, which itself urges the avoidance of meat-eating.

This idea and its consequences are seen most plainly in the allied thought of Empedocles, who famously presents a gruesome picture of sacrifice in which a father slaughters an animal without knowing that the beast is actually his dead son. It is through analogous bloodshed, among other crimes, that *daimones* (perhaps the original form of any soul) become outcast from their divine state; and, conversely, by avoiding this sort of wrongdoing, it is possible to move up the reincarnatory ladder and, presumably, eventually escape further rebirth.[51] There is, then, a hierarchy of beings in which humans are clearly placed between gods and other forms of life (souls may transmigrate into vegetable as well as animal forms — Empedocles himself remembered his bush form), since 'at the end' (just before they regain divine status) souls are born as 'seers, bards, healers and princes', the most exalted in human life. But since each individual travels through the whole series, from plant to god, the division is more apparent than real. Presumably, every human has been an animal at some point in the past; and every animal has been or will be a human. There is a kinship between all living beings, a shared identity even, since the categories 'human', 'animal', and 'plant' are only forms assumed at different stages by *daimones* whose essence is divine.

Ideas of this general sort probably showed a good deal of internal variation, and later writers debated whether the early Pythagoreans were necessarily and invariably vegetarian, but the evidence of Euripides indicates that in the last third of the fifth century BCE adherence to 'Orpheus' was associated with a vegetarian diet, and both came to mind when faced with someone whose life was apparently marked by unusual purity.[52] Metempsychosis, especially involving animal bodies, was a counter-intuitive idea in relation to more established ways of thinking about the human/animal relationship, often attracting suspicion and mockery, and, except perhaps in parts of southern Italy, it never became mainstream. But it was a *thinkable* idea (one that held some attraction for Plato, for instance), and to that extent it is a highly significant modifier of the structuralist three-term hierarchy.

Doing

Thus far we have largely considered more or less overt conceptualisations of animals in relation to gods (or gods in relation to animals), ranging from mythical tradition to philosophical speculation. However, as we have seen, there is no absolute boundary between the relationship thus conceived and the relationship as it is implied in religious practice. Both in the intuitive thought-systems surrounding cult and in contexts more detached from cult actions, we find multifarious versions of the triad of humans, animals, and gods, a common factor being that the three terms are almost always recognised as fundamental.[53]

As we have seen, the basic pattern of sacrifice fits the hierarchical, three-term model very well. The gods, as the recipients of the gift, are clearly on the highest rung. Equally, the humans who offer the sacrifice are clearly above the materials that allow them to make it, the animals – the agent and the instrument, respectively. Yet, other important religious practices, notably divination (and a form of divination is itself also a part of sacrifice), seem to fit less well (see below). Even in sacrifice, some aspects might seem less amenable to interpretation through this filter. Although there are exceptions, the animal victim is usually of the same gender as the divine recipient, suggesting some sort of homology, as is often evident between deity and priest, too. There can be further similarities, such as the frequent choice of dark-coloured animals for chthonic or underworld deities. The pattern is not unlike the (usually non-sacrificial) association between a deity and his/her favourite animal, as discussed above. We can see this most clearly by contrasting the sacrificial modalities of other cultures, which often imply a different sort of relationship between god and victim. Thus, in Egyptian sacrifice, the animal offered may represent either the eye of Horus, stolen by Seth and returned in sacrifice, or the enemy of the god, in which case it is the killing rather than the gift that is predominant.[54] Similarly, in modern Hindu practice, when animals are sacrificed to the Goddess in her various aspects, they are always male and often viewed as analogous to the buffalo demon killed by Durga in the most important of the Goddess myths.[55] In a Greek setting, the victim as the god's enemy does appear in some (perhaps late) mythological explanations of particular sacrifices, but on the whole in Greek sacrifice the offered animal appears rather as a delightful gift, often ornamented to look beautiful and, when cooked, providing delicious food and the pleasant savour of smoke that the gods appreciate so much. In this context, the selection of specific features (sex, colour, age, and so on) seems to imply that certain qualities please the deity in question and may (but need not) have some correspondence with his or her own qualities.

On the other hand, sacrificial animals are not seen as individuals, merely as examples of a particular type, whereas the other two partners in sacrifice are clearly individualised. For instance, 'the Athenians' or 'the demesmen of Thorikos' make an offering to Athena or Apollo, but the offering will be 'a perfect cow' or 'a young sheep', not 'Triphyllis who belongs to Kallistratos' or 'Oulios from Polemon's flock'. Sacrifices to a group of Twelve Gods, variously constituted, are well known, but sacrifices to 'all the gods' are quite rare. Rather, a sacrifice is usually made to a particular divinity by either an individual or a specific group on behalf of the group members (family, city, subdivision of the city, and so forth). Animals have no individual identity; they are 'interchangeable parts of larger whole, indistinct non-persons'.[56] Korshi Dosoo's point is crucial to the relationship of the three terms in sacrifice, but viewed in this way the model is asymmetrical: humans are more like gods than they are like animals. However, the three-term hierarchy remains a particularly useful tool in connection with this most prestigious religious practice.

Divination is another ritual practice whose importance can scarcely be overstated. Among its many forms, which include both spontaneous and solicited predictions and advice, animals are conspicuous; one has only to think of omens derived from birds in flight or from the internal organs of sacrificed animals. In some ways, divination could be seen as inverting the pattern of sacrifice. If in sacrifice humans as the agent use animals as a means of establishing communication with gods through gift-giving, in divination it is the gods who use animals as an instrument for communication with humans. This is especially clear in the case of omens sent spontaneously, without human solicitation, but even when humans set out to obtain information through established means of *manteia*, it is the gods whose action is most significant.

Here too, then, animals as instruments would occupy the lowest rung of the three. But this is not the only way to look at the role of animals in divination. It could also be the case that as conveyors of divine knowledge and will, animals (or some animals) are in some respects closer to gods than are humans. Birds may be especially significant here, as physically, too, they occupy an intermediate space between gods and humans, and can move from the domain of one to that of the other. For some, animals might themselves on occasion have special knowledge, shared with the gods, from which humans are excluded. Yet another viewpoint might stress precisely the *unknowingness* of animals as the factor that enables them to act as conduits for divine communication. Viewed in this way, the role of the behaviour of animals would be analogous to the taking of omens from 'chance' human behaviour, such as sneezing and words spoken without awareness of their hidden meaning (cledonomancy). Both humans and animals perform actions that are either involuntary or undertaken with a purpose that has nothing to do with divination, but an interpreter who is attuned to the divinatory process can discern the gods' purpose in such apparently random acts. So, despite the conspicuous position that animals occupy in the discerning and interpretation of omens, we should remember that they occupy only one part of a larger system of signs. Nonetheless, there is surely much that the use of animals in divination can tell us about Greek views of the natural world, as well as the study of religion.

Healing cults comprise another area where gods use animals to approach human beings, but here – even more than in divination – the animals appear to have something of the divine about them. The Epidaurian *iamata* (inscribed accounts of miraculous healing consequent on visits to Asclepius' sanctuary in Epidaurus) contain many examples of animals (snakes, dogs, geese) performing apparently simple actions that result in the curing of illnesses (see this volume, Chapter 11). In one case, a man is healed by a snake's lick, but he dreams of being healed by a handsome youth.[57] Something similar is depicted visually in the well-known dedication of Archinos to the Attic-Boeotian healing hero Amphiaraus (see this volume, Figure 11.3): Archinos both sleeps while a snake heals him and stands while a bearded man, presumably the hero, attends to his shoulder, with the second scenario suggesting Archinos' dream experience. Therefore, in some sense, the snake is identical with the deity, or at the very least used by the deity more as agent than as instrument. A sacrifice prescription from the Asclepieion in Pireus treats 'dogs' analogously to gods or heroes, ordaining for them an offering of three *popana* (cakes), which was standard for the deities associated with Asclepius. We cannot be sure that the inscription refers to living dogs present in the sanctuary, but such a conclusion is at least feasible, since dogs were certainly active in the sanctuary at Epidaurus.[58] Whatever may be meant in practice, a close conceptual link is clearly suggested between dogs and the realm of the divine. Although animals are not involved in all cases of sacred healing, there is evidently a strong expectation that certain species may have significant roles to play. In the dynamics of these cases, as in other religious practice, animals form a medium of communication between divine and human; but if we are to think of a three-term hierarchy, it would appear that animals, rather than humans, occupy the middle term here, too.

Of course, these forms of religious practice do not exhaust the areas where animals or their representations had roles to play. In magical actions, far from the animal acting as some sort of mediator between divine and human, one aim may be to reduce the human (the individuals or group against whom the ritual is performed) to animalistic status (see this volume, Chapter 12). On the other hand, the sacred ploughing rituals of Attica and perhaps elsewhere articulate a sort of partnership between human and animal (the ploughing ox) in performing the actions necessary to benefit from the divine gift of agriculture. There is some connection here with the shock expressed at the 'murder' of the ox in the bouphonia (see, p. 61).[59] Dedications representing animals (see this volume, Chapter 10), relics of a form of religious activity at least as basic and common as sacrifice, can have many meanings, not always recoverable with certainty; they need not always commemorate animal sacrifice. The same may be true of cakes and sweetmeats formed into animal shapes and offered to a deity.[60]

Conclusion

What is perhaps most striking in this review is the remarkable diversity in the roles of animals within the continuum of Greek religious practice and thought. While sacrifice and deities in partly or fully zoomorphic form spring immediately to mind when we think of animals and religion, we have seen that mythology is rich in other types of animal representations, that reflective thought on the divine frequently makes use of animals, and that their cultic functions are far from limited to that of sacrificial victim. We should beware of seeking out unitary explanations of animals in these linked but different areas, since these will inevitably oversimplify a complex phenomenon, or perhaps a cluster of phenomena with often blurred and uncertain edges. One important finding from recent work is that the place of animals in Greek religion cannot be fully explored solely from within the Greek domain: a wider remit is needed. From prehistory (the practices of early hunters, the domestication of animals, the origins of sacrifice) to cross-cultural influences in historical and near-historical times (Hittite and other Near Eastern religious ritual, the use of animals in magic) to confrontation and dialogue (Greek responses to Egyptian theriomorphic divinities), at every turn the Greek world of classical antiquity abuts on its neighbours in space and time. Similarly, non-human animals in Greek religion cannot be considered in isolation from other living beings, or even inanimate objects or concepts: both individually and collectively, they form part of a symbolic language, relating mainly to the natural world, which is deployed across the domain of religious imagination and activity and beyond.

This understanding is in line with developments elsewhere in classical studies, but it may seem disappointingly vague in contrast with the grand theories that flourished in at least some areas of the study of Greek religion until relatively recently. So, where might we go from here? Cognitive science is shaping up as a useful tool in our understanding of Greek religion, and we might expect it to inform more approaches to the religious role of animals. Perhaps the future will bring further ambitious, large-scale systems that we cannot yet imagine to bear on the study of Greek religion. But for the present, we should appreciate the exciting, wide perspectives and open-endedness that are apparent in the burgeoning interest in this corner of the subject.

Notes

1 Thomas 1983.
2 Sorabji 1993; Kindt 2017.
3 E.g. Aston 2011; Buxton 2009; the relevant chapters in Campbell 2014 and John-ston *et al.* 2016.
4 See, for instance, Harrison 2002 (and the author's subsequent publications); Brem-mer and Erskine 2010; Versnel 2011; Kindt 2012; Eidinow *et al.* 2016. This period has also seen increasing numbers of more specialised studies informed by allied approaches, though it should be noted that there is a great deal of diversity within both these and the more general works mentioned.
5 Murray 1925 was originally published in 1912, with four stages rather than five.
6 It was, for instance, a formative idea in Émile Durkheim's theory of religion, and Durkheim was another important influence on the Cambridge ritualists.
7 Cook 1912–1940, vol. 3: 605–606.
8 Harrison 1927: 118–157.
9 Zeus Meilichios: see below. On the Elean hymn, see Plut. *Mor.* 299a–b.
10 Cook 1894.
11 Cf. Harrison 1922: 257–258: 'Before he has himself clearly realised his own humanity – the line that marks him off from other animals, he makes his divinities sometimes wholly animal, sometimes of mixed, monstrous shapes.'
12 Harrison 1922: 258; cf. Harrison 1927: 114. On Harrison's preference for the 'pri-mitive', and for animal forms over human in religion, see Schlesier 1991: 203–207.
13 Meuli 1946.
14 Smith 1982: 53–65 argues that Meuli misplaced his rituals geographically and in any case was unjustified in retrojecting similar practices to Palaeolithic times. Graf 2012 succinctly summarises the arguments and suggests that sacrifice may be linked more plausibly with Neolithic domestication of animals.
15 Burkert 1972.
16 Burkert 1983: esp. 1–58. Cf. a late statement in Burkert 2013. Girard's rather dif-ferent take on religion and violence has been less influential on classical scholars and has less to do with relations between humans and animals.
17 Burkert 1996.
18 'Between beasts and gods' is the subtitle of Vernant 1972, though the remit is wider. The idea is developed slightly differently in Detienne 1972 and Vidal-Naquet 1975.
19 Downplaying 'meaning' is an approach pioneered by Staal 1979 and taken up by cognitivists, including Liénard and Boyer 2006. See also Ullucci 2015: 390–394.
20 As seen most clearly in the work of Louis Gernet, Louise Bruit-Zaidman and Pau-line Schmitt-Pantel, Christiane Sourvinou-Inwood, and Robert Parker, all of whom are described and evaluated in Kindt 2012: 12–35.
21 Sourvinou-Inwood 1988a, 1988b, 1990 and a posthumous work on girls and ani-mals to be edited by Emma Aston.
22 On cognitive approaches to anthropomorphism, see Larson 2016: 67–73. Kindt 2019 has some suggestive remarks on zoomorphism.
23 Bodson 1978; Prieur 1988.
24 Among others: Detienne and Vernant 1979; Durand 1979; Jameson 1988; Rosivach 1994; Straten 1995; Ekroth 2002, 2008; Hägg and Alroth 2005; Georgoudi *et al.* 2005; Pirenne-Delforge and Prescendi 2011; Ekroth and Wallensten 2013; Klöck-ner 2017; Hitch and Rutherford 2017.
25 Frontisi-Ducroux 2003; Buxton 2009; Aston 2011; Petridou 2015.
26 See, for instance, Lincoln 2012; Graf 2012; Ullucci 2015.
27 See the review of recent work on animals in classical studies in Kindt 2017.

28 In Sperber's terminology, adopted by Larson, 'intuitive beliefs/cognition' can be
    determined as much by cultural as by natural environment. See Sperber 1997;
    Larson 2016: 11–15.
29 See the very useful treatment and further references in Parker 2005: 229–248.
30 E.g. Ando 2012; Naiden 2013.
31 At least as far as the Greeks were concerned: Jameson *et al.* 1993: 92, 139–141
    revive in a modified form the idea of Cook 1912–1940, vol. 2: 1125–1129 and
    others that Meilichios really derives from the Phoenician deity Milik/Moloch,
    though with some hesitation. Cf. Lalonde 2006: 45–46.
32 Mitropoulou 1977; Gourmelen 2004; Jost 2005. For Dionysus as bull, see note 9,
    (Elean hymn).
33 E.g. Hdt. 1.66.2; [Pl.] *Minos* 315c. For a later period, see Balériaux 2017.
34 Paus. 8.41.5–6, 8.42.1–4.
35 'Achelous' was an exception, viewed as the archetypal river-god and present, for
    instance, in the sanctuary at Neon Phaleron founded by Xenokrateia. See *IG* II^2 4547.
36 Thuc. 1.126.6.
37 Treated alongside more major figures in Aston 2011.
38 See, for instance, Jost 2005.
39 *Hom. Hymn* 7.44–5, 3.399–401.
40 Hom. *Il.* 7.59–61, *Od.* 22.239–240.
41 Paus. 8.25.5–7.
42 Artemis as a doe: Apollod. 1.4.7.
43 Similarly, her priestess at Kyrene is called 'bear', but this does not imply that Arte-
    mis, too, is a bear.
44 Demeter transforms Askalabos into a lizard: Ant. Lib. 24. Donkeys are linked to
    Priapos in Ov. *Fast.* 1.391–440, 6.319–348, and Hyg. *Poet. astr.* 2.23, no doubt
    drawing on earlier Greek sources.
45 See, e.g., Küster 1913; Mitropoulou 1977 on snakes.
46 Horses and cattle: Doniger-O'Flaherty 1980: 239–280.
47 For the distinction, see the very clear exposition in Larson 2016: 11–15, using
    Sperber 1997.
48 Porph. *Abst.* 2; Julian. *Or.* 5.177b–c. On Julian and sacrifice, see Gilhus 2006: 138–
    147; Knipe 2017.
49 A valuable discussion on orphism can be found in Parker 1995. Edmonds 2013
    champions a sceptical approach reminiscent of the older work of Linforth.
50 Hdt. 2.81.2. Some manuscripts omit the words Βακχικοῖσι, ἐοῦσι δὲ Αἰγυπτίοισι
    καὶ, leaving simply 'called Orphic and Pythagorean'; cf. Ion of Chios.
51 Emp. frr. 115, 137 (sacrifice), 139, 146–147 DK (= 128, 11, 124, 136–137 Inwood).
52 Eur. *Hipp.* 952–954.
53 The system of Empedocles is markedly less triadic, in that plants as well as animals
    are incorporated, and within each group there are important distinctions: laurels and
    lions are each top in their respective categories (Emp. fr. 127, with its context in
    Ael. *NA* 2.7), prophets and princes (etc.) among humans (Emp. fr. 146).
54 Rutherford 2017: 254–259.
55 Fuller 1992: 83–85, 117–119.
56 This way of thinking is, of course, not distinctively ancient. For instance, the same
    viewpoint is expressed in a remark attributed to Philip, Duke of Edinburgh: 'the
    grouse are in no danger at all from people who shoot grouse'.
57 LiDonnici 1995: A17.
58 Pireus inscription: *IG* II^2 4962.
59 Three sacred ploughings in Attica: Plut. *Mor.*144a; see Humphreys 2018: 643–645.
60 Kearns 1994.

Bibliography

Ando, C. (2012) 'Afterword', in C. Faraone and F. Naiden (eds.) *Greek and Roman Animal Sacrifice. Ancient Victims, Modern Observers.* Cambridge, 195–199.

Aston, E. (2011) *Mixanthrôpoi. Animal–Human Hybrid Deities in Greek Religion.* Liège.

Balériaux, J. (2017) 'Pausanias' Arcadia between conservatism and innovation', in G. Hawes (ed.) *Myths on the Map. The Storied Landscapes of Ancient Greece.* Oxford, 141–158.

Bodson, L. (1978) *Hiera zōia. Contribution à l'étude de la place de l'animal dans la religion grecque.* Brussels.

Bremmer, J. N. and A. Erskine (eds.) (2010) *The Gods of Ancient Greece. Identities and Transformations.* Edinburgh.

Burkert, W. (1972) *Homo Necans. Interpretationen Altgriechischer Opferriten und Mythen.* Berlin.

Burkert, W. (1983) *Homo Necans. The Anthropology of Ancient Greek Sacrificial Ritual and Myth,* trans. P. Bing. Berkeley, Calif.

Burkert, W. (1996) *Creation of the Sacred. Tracks of Biology in Early Religions.* Cambridge, Mass.

Burkert, W. (2013) 'Sacrificial violence: a problem in ancient religions', in M. Juergensmeyer, M. Kitts, and M. Jerryson (eds.) *The Oxford Handbook of Religion and Violence.* Oxford, 437–451.

Buxton, R. (2009) *Forms of Astonishment. Greek Myths of Metamorphosis.* Oxford.

Campbell, G. L. (ed.) (2014) *The Oxford Handbook of Animals in Classical Thought and Life.* Oxford.

Cook, A. B. (1894) 'Animal worship in the Mycenaean age', *Journal of Hellenic Studies* 14, 81–169.

Cook, A. B. (1912–1940) *Zeus. A Study in Ancient Religion.* Cambridge.

Detienne, M. (1972) 'Entre bêtes et dieux', *Nouvelle revue de psychanalyse* 6, 231–246 (Eng. trans. in Gordon, R. L. (ed.) (1981) *Myth, Religion and Society. Structuralist Essays by M. Detienne, L. Gernet, J-P. Vernant and P. Vidal-Naquet.* Cambridge, 215–228).

Detienne, M. and J.-P. Vernant (eds.) (1979) *La cuisine du sacrifice en pays grec.* Paris.

Doniger-O'Flaherty, W. (1980) *Women, Androgynes, and Other Mythical Beasts.* Chicago, Ill.

Durand, J.-L. (1979) 'Bêtes grecques: propositions pour un topologique des corps à manger', in M. Detienne and J.-P. Vernant (eds.) *La Cuisine du sacrifice en pays grec.* Paris, 133–165.

Edmonds, R. G.III (2013) *Redefining Ancient Orphism. A Study in Greek Religion.* Cambridge.

Eidinow, E., J. Kindt, and R. Osborne (eds.) (2016) *Theologies of Ancient Greek Religion.* Cambridge.

Ekroth, G. (2002) *The Sacrificial Rituals of Greek Hero-cults in the Archaic to the Early Hellenistic Periods.* Liège.

Ekroth, G. (2008) 'Meat, man, god: on the division of the animal victim at Greek sacrifices', in A. P. Matthaiou and I. Polinskaya (eds.) *Μικρός ιερομνήμων. Μελέτες εις μνήμην Michael H. Jameson.* Athens, 259–290.

Ekroth, G. and J. Wallensten (eds.) (2013) *Bones, Behaviour and Belief. The Zooarchaeological Evidence as a Source for Ritual Practice in Ancient Greece and Beyond.* Stockholm.

Faraone, C. and F. Naiden (eds.) (2012) *Greek and Roman Animal Sacrifice. Ancient Victims, Modern Observers.* Cambridge.

Frontisi-Ducroux, F. (2003) *L'Homme-cerf et la femme-araignée. Figures grecques de la métamorphose.* Paris.

Fuller, C. J. (1992) *The Camphor Flame. Popular Hinduism and Society in India*. Princeton, N.J.

Georgoudi, S., R. Koch Piettre, and F. Schmidt (eds.) (2005) *La Cuisine et l'autel. Les sacrifices en question dans les sociétés de la Méditerranée ancienne*. Turnhout.

Gilhus, I. S. (2006) *Animals, Gods and Humans. Changing Attitudes to Animals in Greek, Roman and Early Christian Ideas*. London.

Girard, R. (1972) *La Violence et le sacré*. Paris.

Gourmelen, L. (2004) *Kekrops, le Roi-Serpent. Imaginaire athénien, représentations de l'humain et de l'animalité en Grèce ancienne*. Paris.

Graf, F. (2012) 'One generation after Burkert and Girard: where are the grand theories?', in C. Faraone and F. Naiden (eds.) *Greek and Roman Animal Sacrifice. Ancient Victims, Modern Observers*. Cambridge, 32–51.

Hägg, R. and B. Alroth (eds.) (2005) *Greek Sacrificial Ritual, Olympian and Chthonian*. Stockholm.

Harrison, J. E. (1922) *Prolegomena to the Study of Greek Religion*. 3rd edn. Cambridge (orig. published in 1903).

Harrison, J. E. (1927) *Themis: A Study of the Social Origins of Greek Religion*. 2nd edn. Cambridge (orig. published in 1912).

Harrison, T. (2002) *Divinity and History. The Religion of Herodotus*. Oxford.

Hitch, S. and I. Rutherford (eds.) (2017) *Animal Sacrifice in the Ancient Greek World*. Cambridge.

Humphreys, S. C. (2018) *Kinship in Ancient Athens. An Anthropological Analysis*. Vol. 1. Oxford.

Jameson, M. H. (1988) 'Sacrifice and animal husbandry in Classical Greece', in C. R. Whittaker (ed.) *Pastoral Economies in Classical Antiquity*. Cambridge, 87–119 (repr. in Jameson, M. (2014) *Cults and Rites in Ancient Greece. Essays on Religion and Society*, ed. A. B. Stallsmith. Cambridge, 198–231).

Jameson, M. H., D. R. Jordan, and R. D. Kotansky (1993) *A Lex Sacra from Selinous*. Durham, N.C.

Johnston, P. A., A. Mastrocinque, and S. Papaioannou (2016) *Animals in Greek and Roman Religion and Myth*. Newcastle-upon-Tyne.

Jost, M. (2005) 'Bêtes, hommes et dieux dans la religion arcadienne', in E. Østby (ed.) *Ancient Arcadia. Papers from the Third International Seminar on Ancient Arcadia, Held in the Norwegian Institute at Athens, 7–10 May 2002*. Athens, 93–104.

Kearns, E. (1994) 'Cakes in Greek sacrifice regulations', in R. Hägg (ed.) *Ancient Greek Cult Practice from the Epigraphical Evidence*. Stockholm, 65–70.

Kindt, J. (2012) *Rethinking Greek Religion*. Cambridge.

Kindt, J. (2017) 'Capturing the ancient animal: human/animal studies and the Classics', *Journal of Hellenic Studies* 137, 213–225.

Kindt, J. (2019) 'Animals in ancient Greek religion: divine zoomorphism and the anthropomorphic divine body', in T. S. Scheer (ed.) *Natur – Mythos – Religion im antiken Griechenland*. Stuttgart, 155–170.

Klöckner, A. (2017) 'Visualising veneration: images of animal sacrifice on Greek votive reliefs', in S. Hitch and I. Rutherford (eds.) *Animal Sacrifice in the Ancient Greek World*. Cambridge, 200–222.

Knipe, S. (2017) 'A quiet slaughter? Julian and the etiquette of public sacrifice', in S. Hitch and I. Rutherford (eds.) *Animal Sacrifice in the Ancient Greek World*. Cambridge, 267–283.

Küster, E. (1913) *Die Schlange in der griechischen Kunst und Religion*. Gießen.

Lalonde, G. V. (2006) *Horos Dios. An Athenian Shrine and Cult of Zeus*. Leiden.

Larson, J. (2016) *Understanding Greek Religion. A Cognitive Approach.* London.

LiDonnici, L. R. (1995) *The Epidaurian Miracle Inscriptions. Text, Translation and Commentary.* Atlanta, Ga.

Liénard, P. and P. Boyer (2006) 'Whence collective rituals? A cultural selection model of ritualized behavior', *American Anthropologist* 108, 814–827.

Lincoln, B. (2012) 'From Bergaigne to Meuli: how animal sacrifice became a hot topic', in C. Faraone and F. Naiden (eds.) *Greek and Roman Animal Sacrifice. Ancient Victims, Modern Observers.* Cambridge, 13–31.

McInerney, J. (2014) 'Bouphonia: killing cattle on the Acropolis', in A. Gardeisen and C. Chandezon (eds.) *Equidés et bovidés de la Méditerranée antique. Rites et combats: jeux et savoirs.* Lattes.

Meuli, K. (1946) 'Griechische Opferbräuche', in *Phyllobolia für Peter von der Mühll zum 60. Geburtstag am 1. August 1945.* Basel, 185–288.

Mitropoulou, E. (1977) *Deities and Heroes in the Form of Snakes.* Athens.

Murray, G. (1925) *Five Stages of Greek Religion. Studies Based on a Course of Lectures Delivered in April 1912 at Columbia University.* Oxford (rev. version of *Four Stages of Greek Religion.* New York, N.Y. 1912).

Naiden, F. S. (2013) *Smoke Signals for the Gods. Ancient Greek Sacrifice from the Archaic through Roman periods.* New York, N.Y.

Parker, R. (1995) 'Early Orphism', in A. Powell (ed.) *The Greek World.* London, 483–510.

Parker, R. (2005) *Polytheism and Society at Athens.* Oxford.

Petridou, G. (2015) *Divine Epiphany in Greek Literature and Culture.* Oxford.

Pirenne-Delforge, V. and F. Prescendi (2011) *'Nourrir les dieux?' Sacrifice et representations du divin.* Liège.

Prieur, J. (1988) *Les Animaux sacrés dans l'antiquité. Art et religion du monde méditerranéen.* Rennes.

Rosivach, V. J. (1994) *The System of Public Sacrifice in Fourth-Century Athens.* Atlanta, Ga.

Rutherford, I. (2017) 'The reception of Egyptian animal sacrifice in Greek writers: ethnic stereotyping or transcultural discourse?', in S. Hitch and I. Rutherford (eds.) *Animal Sacrifice in the Ancient Greek World.* Cambridge, 253–266.

Schlesier, R. (1991) 'Prolegomena to Jane Harrison's interpretation of ancient Greek religion', in W. M. Calder III (ed.) *The Cambridge Ritualists Reconsidered.* Atlanta, Ga., 185–226.

Smith, J. Z. (1982) *Imagining Religion. From Babylon to Jonestown.* Chicago, Ill.

Smith, W. R. (1889) *Lectures on the Religion of the Semites. First Series, the Fundamental Institutions.* Edinburgh.

Sorabji, R. (1993) *Animal Minds and Human Morals. The Origins of the Western Debate.* Ithaca.

Sourvinou-Inwood, C. (1988a) 'Further aspects of polis religion', *AION (Archeol)* 10, 259–274. (Reprinted in R. Buxton (ed.) (2000) *Oxford Readings in Greek Religion.* Oxford, 38–55)

Sourvinou-Inwood, C. (1988b) *Studies in Girls' Transitions. Aspects of the Arkteia and Age Representation in Attic Iconography.* Athens.

Sourvinou-Inwood, C. (1990) 'What is polis religion?', in O. Murray and S. Price (eds.) *The Greek City.* Oxford, 295–232.

Sperber, D. (1997) 'Intuitive and reflective beliefs', *Mind and Language* 12, 67–83.

Staal, F. (1979) 'The meaninglessness of ritual', *Numen* 26, 2–22.

Straten, F. T. van (1995) *Hierà Kalá. Images of Animal Sacrifice in Archaic and Classical Greece.* Leiden.

Thomas, K. (1983) *Man and the Natural World. Changing Attitudes in England, 1500–1800.* London.

Ullucci, D. (2015) 'Sacrifice in the ancient Mediterranean: recent and current research', *Currents in Biblical Research* 13, 388–439.

Vernant, J.-P. (1972) 'Introduction', in M. Detienne (ed.) *Les Jardins d'Adonis. La mythologie des aromates en Grèce*. Paris, 141–176 (repr. in Vernant, J.-P. (1974) *Mythe et société en Grèce ancienne*. Paris, 141–176).

Versnel, H. S. (2011) *Coping with the Gods. Wayward Readings in Greek Theology*. Leiden.

Vidal-Naquet, P. (1975) 'Bêtes, hommes et dieux chez les Grecs', in L. Poliakov (ed.) *Hommes et bêtes. Entretiens sur le racisme*. Paris, 129–142.

Part 2

Representations

4 Gods and heroes, humans and animals in ancient Greek myth

H. Willey

Introduction

Animals loom large in mythical accounts of relations between gods and humans. They are cast in a complex array of roles as myths repeatedly provide contexts in which to challenge and explore any straightforward hierarchy or neat boundaries between the categories of human, animal, and divine. We find animals as aids and opponents, models of behaviour, sacrificial offerings, and messengers to men from the gods, yet we also find them enjoying special relationships with the gods parallel or even superior to those enjoyed by humans. This, too, prompts reflection on what it is to be human. Are humans inherently superior to animals in this triangular relationship (albeit sometimes in danger of descending to their level)? Or are humans and animals on an equal footing in the eyes of the gods, and is it only privileged individuals, whether human or animal, who attain a higher status?

Myths frequently deal with extremes, and my interest here is chiefly in the exceptional. I will explore the diverse ways in which animals help to frame not just the human condition in general but the distinctiveness of special individuals or of individuals at exceptional moments. To this end, I offer two primary test cases. The first examines some of the ways in which animals help to define what it is to be a hero. We take as our focus the relationship between Achilles, the archetypal hero, and his no less special horse Xanthus as they engage in conversation within a narrative that plays extensively with the boundaries between men, beasts, and gods. In this context, I explore what questions the comparison and interaction between Achilles and Xanthus raise about the similarities or differences between humans and animals, and the nature of their relationships with the divine.

If the hero pushes human existence and identity to its limits, what happens when 'normal' humans step outside the boundaries of normal human society? Here we turn to our second test case – foundation narratives – which, in charting the disintegration and creation of human societies, the creation of new communities out of periods of chaos or turmoil, offer an especially rich source to explore this question. Through oracles and other forms of divine guidance, the relationship between men and gods is a prominent feature of foundation stories. In this context, too, animals – in their roles as guides, signposts, and hindrances – prove a productive way of thinking through this relationship and exploring the process by which a group proves itself worthy of claiming possession of new territory, or an individual distinguishes himself as *oikist* and so worthy of cult. In both test cases, then, we will consider how myths negotiate through animals questions of the identity of humans and their relations with the divine, but also of animal agency in its own right.[1]

Locating the hero: between the bestial and the divine

We begin with the hero. What role do animals play in myths that delineate or blur the boundaries between man and god?

It has long been noted that in Greek literature extremes of human behaviour and experience are often explored through appeal to the bestial. Men and women whose behaviour, emotions, or experiences push them beyond the normal limits of the human or beyond the norms of human society are frequently characterised as animalistic. They may be compared to animals through similes or, in more extreme circumstances, assume animal form through metamorphosis.[2] For Aristotle, famously, those who live beyond society are either beasts or gods.[3] In Sophocles' fragmentary *Tereus*, it is beyond the confines of the city, on the road from Athens to Thrace, that Tereus brutally rapes and disfigures Philomela.[4] De-civilised and then de-humanised, Philomela re-enters human society deprived of her voice, forced, like an animal, to explore non-verbal forms of communication to inform her sister of Tereus' crimes. Incensed, Procne murders her own child and forces her husband to engage in cannibalism, which, for Hesiod, ultimately distinguished beasts from men.[5] As Tereus pursues the sisters, a god intervenes and transforms the trio into birds. Tereus takes the form of the hoopoe, 'bold in his full panoply', bearing the mark of the son he consumed ('he shall show two forms from a single womb, the young one's and his own') and maintaining the hatred that characterised the end of his human life, while retreating forever beyond the limits of society.[6] His anger, his hatred, and his heinous act of cannibalism are all redirected and encapsulated in his avian form. Similarly, Procne, transformed into a nightingale – renowned, above all, for its sorrowful lament – is utterly consumed by, and made coterminous with, her grief.[7]

On Laurent Gourmelen's reading, the Tereus and Procne myth represents a regression towards animality. It is a cautionary tale about the disorder that results from introducing barbarian blood into the family line, a disorder that is cast as a return to a primitive world, lacking in proper differentiation between men and beasts.[8] No doubt there is truth in this, but this sort of boundary crossing *in extremis* not only confronts us with degradation and descent into the bestial but, at the same time, with the capacity to transcend typical human limitations in extraordinary ways. True, in one fragment of the *Tereus*, usually held to derive from a *deus ex machina*, human protagonists are characterised as lacking in *nous*, which might be felt to showcase their degradation.[9] Another fragment, though, perhaps from the chorus, cautions mortal *physis* to think mortal thoughts, recognising Zeus as the only steward of what will come.[10] The latter phrase suggests a warning against hybristic attempts to *exceed* human limitations.[11] Taking Aristotle's thought in a different direction, then, proximity to beasts may be a marker not just of alienation from human society but also of approximation towards the divine. As Chiara Thumiger notes, in Greek poetry, maenads in the grips of Dionysiac possession come close to the beasts with whom they associate, a '[f]amiliarity' and 'identification with animals' that marks their 'participation in the sphere of the divine and supernatural'.[12] We find here a notion, paralleled in other contexts, that beings who enjoy a higher than normal proximity and affinity to the natural world can *in this regard* imitate and approximate the gods.[13]

Achilles provides a particularly striking example. In the most sustained treatment of the topic, John Heath characterises Achilles of the later books of the *Iliad* as a man 'at his most bestial ... on the edge of humanity', someone who 'simultaneously transcends human nature and degrades it'.[14] As Heath and others have shown, Achilles becomes increasingly inhuman in his behaviour and decreasingly integrated into human society. Animals play an important role in his characterisation. If sacrifice and feasting mark proper relations within a community and between a human community and its animals and gods, Achilles stubbornly denies their importance. Desiring only to enter battle, he shows little appetite for participating in the feast or the oath and prayer which Agamemnon intends to perform over a sacrificial boar.[15] The animal similes, a staple of Homeric poetry, that are applied to Achilles become more frequent and more involved. As Achilles faces off against Aeneas in Book 20, we find a lengthy comparison between the *menos* driving Achilles and that which drives a ravening lion. Achilles' isolation from human society is emphasised as the lion is pitched against a gathered community.[16] Like Achilles, at first the lion stays detached from the fight, becoming involved only when a member of the opposing crowd injures him. Once he has entered the fray, his bloodlust and fury lead him on indiscriminately towards the destruction of either himself or one of the throng.[17]

As Achilles becomes more bestial, he also approximates more closely the gods, most strikingly when Athena sates his hunger with nectar and ambrosia.[18] It is in this context, as the boundaries between man, beast, and god become increasingly blurred, that we find Achilles engaging in conversation with his horse, Xanthus.[19] What is at stake in this exchange?

As Heath observes, it is not unusual in Homer for a hero to address his horse, but for the horse to reply as Xanthus does is indeed exceptional behaviour.[20] Outside fable, talking animals are a rarity.[21] Indeed, among Greek reflections on what separates men from animals, the ability to speak was prominent.[22] Thus, for Xanthus to be made *audēenta* – in possession of a human voice – is striking.[23] If part of what makes Achilles exceptional is that he is more beast-like than other humans, Xanthus is special because he possesses the human capacity for speech. For Tom Hawkins, drawing on the work of Thorsten

Fögen, talking animals are nothing short of a 'category crisis that demands explanation'.[24] That explanation comes, in this instance, in the form of divine intervention: it is Hera who has bestowed on Xanthus the capacity for speech.

There has been some debate among scholars as to whether Xanthus' speech is a temporary benefaction from Hera, bestowed at this very moment and removed by the Erinyes as soon as he has uttered Achilles' fate, or a more permanent feature of the horse's identity.[25] On the former interpretation, the key feature of Xanthus' speech is usually held to be the prophecy it allows him to utter. Here, Xanthus represents an unusual twist on a well-established tradition in which animals serve as messengers from the gods.[26] Xanthus' words are directly preceded by the mention of Hera, associating the speech that follows with the goddess and lending it her authority.[27] For Hawkins, Xanthus, as a talking animal (akin to others in Greek literature), has an 'other-worldly authority' that surpasses the speech of humans, making him a suitable vehicle for oracular pronouncements.[28] Regardless of whether this derives from a connection to a Golden Age before sharp divisions between humans and animals were established (as Hawkins argues), Xanthus' 'other-worldly authority' is indeed pronounced through the framing references to Hera and the Erinyes. The oddity of a talking horse and the need for a divine explanation remind us of the gods' involvement in a way a prophecy delivered by a human seer would not.

But what does the interlude achieve? The information Xanthus delivers serves no discernible plot need. Achilles expresses no surprise at the horse's behaviour but does question the need for his insight since the hero himself is well aware that he is destined to die.[29] Xanthus' words do not change Achilles' attitude or intended behaviour. Heath places the Erinyes' intervention to stop Xanthus' *audē* in the context of the blurring of boundaries between animals and men that characterises Achilles' portrayal at this point in the poem. In accordance with an ancient scholiast, who attributes the Erinyes' intervention to their role as 'overseers of things contrary to nature', Heath describes the speech of an animal as 'an offense to universal order' and 'a threat to the ordinances of nature'.[30] Thus, we might see Xanthus' curtailed speech as an object lesson in proper boundaries and, with the intervention of the Erinyes, a further warning about the dangers of Achilles' current trajectory. To behave in a manner that too far exceeds the limits of the human or the animal might invite divine action.

Jenny Strauss Clay's influential reading of Hesiod's catalogue of monsters provides a helpful point of comparison here. Clay explores the way this 'incestuous, interbred, and ultimately sterile tribe' challenges the ordered world of Hesiod's cosmos.[31] Monstrous hybrids like Echidna and Typhon blur the boundaries between species and between the categories of men, beasts, and gods. As monsters, they are '[b]y definition … anomalous' and, like talking horses, they defy attempts at classification.[32] Echidna, half snake, half maiden, 'resembles neither mortal men nor the immortal gods', while Typhon's many heads utter variously such sounds 'so that the gods could understand' as well as the cries of bellowing bulls, roaring lions, fawning puppies, and hissing snakes.[33] For Clay, even those creatures that are seemingly unexceptional in their morphology (if not their parentage, strength, or longevity), such as the Nemean lion, challenge the proper hierarchy between men and beasts in the havoc they inflict on human communities.[34] On her reading, the monsters offer both an example of what a world not organised under the principles of Zeus' hegemony might look like and an assertion of Zeus' control. Zeus neutralises or utilises the power of these monsters, underlining the legitimacy and security of his reign.[35] Most of them are dispatched by another race of hybrids, the heroes – products of the reign of Zeus and, thus, sanctioned agents of his rule – while Cerberus, for instance, becomes guardian of the underworld and thus 'enforces the clear distinction between gods and mortals'.[36] The normativity and authority of Zeus' rule is thus reflected and achieved, in part, through the treatment of hybrids.

As Clay notes, the parallel hybridity of the race of heroes is emphatic. The characterisation of Heracles, in his capacity as slayer of the Lernaean Hydra, is a particularly striking case in point: he is both 'son of Zeus' and 'Amphitryoniades'.[37] To emphasise the parallelism further, I note that the Hydra here has a similarly dual heritage. Not only is she herself a monstrous hybrid, child of the monstrous hybrids Echidna and Typhon, but, like Heracles, she was reared not by her parents but by white-armed Hera. As the heroes illustrate, hybridity or the blurring of boundaries is not simply or inherently a good or a bad thing. Though often unnerving and eliciting divine correction, it can represent extraordinary powers (as with Achilles and Xanthus) or even claims for authority. Alongside gods themselves of mixed form, we might point to culture heroes like Cecrops and Herodotus' Scythian echidna, whose serpentine halves emphasise their connection (and so claim) to the lands in which the Athenians and Scythians, respectively, are founded. A scholium to Aristophanes' *Wealth* attributes the conception of Cecrops as 'of double nature' to his role in founding the social practice of marriage, bringing the two halves of the species – men and women – together into a single unit.[38]

To return to Xanthus, his exceptional outburst might be thought to reflect the status or divine favour enjoyed by Achilles. As E. L. Harrison explains, the simple fact that Achilles possesses the immortal horses Balius and Xanthus sets him above his peers.[39] By receiving such a striking form of prophecy and possessing a *talking* immortal horse, then, the hero's exceptionality and favour in the eyes of the gods are emphasised. A contrast may be found in the *Odyssey* scene in which Polyphemus, blind and defeated, laments that his beloved ram cannot tell him where Odysseus is hiding.[40] For Heath, Polyphemus' desire to converse with the animal represents another way in which the Cyclops fails to distinguish between men and beasts (just as he consumes men as if animals).[41] While, as Heath suggests, this may indeed reveal a mentality at odds with that of Homer's audience, it is noteworthy that there is no actual blurring of categories here. Polyphemus may eat men but, even among the Cyclopes, animals are not of the same mind as men. Polyphemus wants to enjoy a special relationship with his animals that goes beyond the norm but, unlike Achilles, he cannot do so.[42]

Notably, the horses' lament at Patroclus' death is also markedly human: Balius and Xanthus weep and defile their manes.[43] For Hayden Pelliccia, the horses' lament might plausibly be interpreted as an early example of the trope that, when a great person dies, even the animals (and sometimes even the trees, rocks, and so on) mourn their passing.[44] Famous here is the case of Orpheus, who was able to calm animals (and move even plants and rocks) with his music. The ability to encourage such boundary-crossing behaviour is a marker of Orpheus' superhuman abilities, as is his success in persuading the gods of the underworld to relinquish his wife, thus (temporarily) conquering death itself. Finally, in death, he is, in some traditions, established as an oracle – facilitating communication between gods and men.[45] In this tradition, too, the capacity to challenge usual human limitations is entwined with the capacity to disrupt the ordinary limitations of animals and other 'natural' things – limitations that usually distinguish them from men. In later sources, Orpheus' death was said to have moved the animals, rivers, plants, and rocks to lament. Most striking is Ovid's poignant account of 'mournful birds, stricken animals … forest trees [that] cast down their leaves, tonsured in grief, and rivers too … swollen with their tears', while Pausanias records the Thracian claim that nightingales nesting on Orpheus' grave 'sing more sweetly and more loudly than others' and the claim of the people of Dium that, when his murderers sought to wash their hands of his blood in the Baphyra, the river sank below the ground in protest.[46]

The horses' reaction to Patroclus' death undoubtedly reflects his status. Nonetheless, Patroclus' personal relationship with the horses and their characterisation as exceptional beings elsewhere in the poem differentiate their grief from that of a local population of nightingales or the various natural phenomena that mourn Orpheus' demise. Finally, then, we ought to think about Xanthus as an agent and character in his own right and not only in relation to the characterisation of men. All the positions explored above that explain the significance of Xanthus' speech in the poem have their value: the superior gods are the source of prophecies and can make animals talk, and, by stopping them, might seek to highlight such behaviour as disordered and needing correction; Achilles is characterised as special by the superior status of his horse and as recipient of this prophecy, and is shown as detached from human interaction by his interaction with an animal. However, to reduce Xanthus to any of these roles is to deny him a special status that is significant for thinking about divine/human/animal relations in the context of Greek religion. On any reading, Xanthus himself is exceptional, and there are good reasons to choose him as the vehicle for this prophecy or recipient of this voice. The son of a divinity (like Achilles) and a harpy (surpassing Achilles, whose father is mortal), Xanthus is immortal, not fated to die like his doomed owner.[47] He is an agent with a distinct identity and clear emotional responses who enjoys a special relationship with the divine as well as a special relationship with Achilles and Patroclus. So, alongside his prophecy concerning Achilles' fate, Xanthus articulates a defence of his and Balius' role in Patroclus' death: the fault lies not with them but with Apollo, who gave glory to Hector.[48] Though, as many have noted, animals in

Homer may share many of the emotional responses and motivations of heroes, the sense of affront here is remarkably complex and well rounded, and the level of detailed reflection on interpersonal relations unusual.[49]

The parable of Balaam's donkey provides an instructive parallel.[50] Here we find another equine creature granted the power of speech by a divinity ('God opened the donkey's mouth') to defend itself against an unjust charge and punishment and to convey a divine message.[51] The donkey, seeing an angel in its path, has three times refused to go where Balaam leads and three times been beaten for its disobedience. Given the opportunity to speak, the donkey appeals to his past relationship with Balaam and his past credentials as a good steed. It is then that, just as he gave the donkey a voice, God gives Balaam sight and allows him to perceive the angel's presence. The angel praises the donkey, stating that, had it not stopped Balaam from taking the path opposed by God, the angel would have killed Balaam but spared his donkey.

We see here a similarity in the treatment of Balaam and his donkey: each receives a gift (true sight or speech) that raises him above the usual limitations of man or beast. Yet, as might be claimed for Xanthus, this passage also raises the possibility of a relationship and understanding between beast and god independent of – and indeed (temporarily) superior to – that between man and god. Like Balaam and his donkey, the parallels between Xanthus and Achilles are pronounced. Each with divine lineage and each exceptional among his kind (in part by being more human-like than other horses or more beast-like than other humans), each receives a benefit from the gods (speech on the one hand; insight into his own fate and support for his heroic efforts on the other). These similarities allow Xanthus to serve as a model for Achilles in his relationship with the gods. If Xanthus' gift is temporary, ended by the Erinyes, Achilles' exceptional achievements will also have their limit.

The idea that humans are exceptional among animals, particularly in their relations with the gods, is expressed in a number of Greek sources and much explored in scholarship.[52] Yet, texts that challenge this position, or present animals as independent agents capable of their own relationships with the gods, do much to enrich our understanding of the role of animals in myths that explore the relationship between men and gods.[53] For Porphyry (third century CE), myths in which gods adopt animal form, sire immortal animals, or are nursed by them demonstrate an esteem for animals that his contemporaries no longer shared.[54] Among the stories he relates is Aristodocus' visit to Apollo's oracle at Didyma, as recorded by Herodotus (see also this volume, Chapter 9).[55] Seeking advice on whether to surrender a suppliant to his enemies, Aristodocus receives an affirmative response. He then goes around the temple, dislodging the sparrows and other birds that are nesting there. A voice rises up from the inner temple, berating him for daring to despoil the temple of its suppliants. Pointing out the god's double standard in protecting his own suppliants while encouraging men to abandon theirs, Aristodocus is informed that Apollo responded in this way only to hasten the Cymeans' destruction for impiety for even raising the question. In this story, both Aristodocus and the god treat as comparable the human and avian suppliants. If Aristodocus wished to make a comparative point about the relative worth of human, as opposed to animal, lives, this is not made explicit.[56] Rather, what is emphasised is the relationship of each to the god and the protection this ensures. Removing the birds from the sanctuary makes Aristodocus the 'most unholy of men' (*anosiōtate anthrōpōn*), while refusing the suppliant will bring punishment upon the Cymeans for their impious action (*asebēsantes*).

The *parodos* that opens the *Agamemnon* offers another example. The powerful simile of the eagles that have lost their young describes how one of the mighty gods sends an Erinys in response to their shrill-screaming birdsong lament to avenge those resident in his realm.[57] Heath remarks that 'the chorus is … humanizing the birds, for we would not expect the gods to be concerned with justice within the animal kingdom, much less to send a Fury to avenge them.'[58] It is undoubtedly true that the eagles' response is described in human terms, as Heath explores, but the birds are also characterised as close to the gods.[59] They live among them (*metoikōn*), occupying the heights (*hypatoi*), a term picked up a few lines later as a way of describing the gods (*hypatos … ē tis Apollōn*).[60]

Such stories make us wonder about the myriad ways in which animals can enjoy a relationship with the gods in a manner that is not merely independent of human worship but on a par with it.

Entering the wilderness: foundation narratives

We have seen how, beyond the norms of human existence or the boundaries of 'normal' human society, the relationship between humans, animals, and gods may shift. Foundation narratives are interesting in this respect, since the act of foundation requires the creation of a new political entity out of either chaos or the disintegration of a prior social and/or political structure.[61] What does it mean for men to navigate this reintegration? Once again, this is a context in which we find the divine/human/animal relationship on prominent display and in a variety of formulations. What role do animals play in this moment of crisis and glory, of special favour shown to a colonising group or to an exceptional *oikist*, who ends as something more than mortal, in defining what it means to be human or to be a human community? From animals used to mark out or characterise the appropriate spot for a foundation or as guides to it, described or positioned by the gods, to animals with special relations to the gods as obstacles for would-be colonists to overcome and animals cast as welcoming locals, the furred, feathered, and scaly are frequent actors in foundation stories.

A central feature of many foundation narratives, as Carol Dougherty has explored, is the riddling oracle (see also this volume, Chapter 9).[62] What role do animals play in these stories? Riddling oracles inform would-be colonists where or how to find a site to settle in a way that is, on the surface, either confusing or nonsensical. Such oracles frequently present the future sites of colonisation as what Dougherty calls 'impossible landscapes'.[63] Animals contribute to these landscapes by engaging in apparently unnatural behaviour, serving as unexpected guides, or, through puns, confusing the categories of human, animal, and inanimate object. These riddles therefore present the colonial site as unfamiliar, foreign, and suitable to have a Greek ordering principle set upon it.[64] The act of interpretation, of solving the riddle, is thus placed centre-stage to 'mimic on a linguistic level the act of foundation itself'.[65] It, like colonisation, is challenging and so reflects positively on the *oikist* or group of Greek colonists who successfully solve the riddle.[66] As Irad Malkin emphasises, the *oikist*, receiving signs and instructions from Delphi, 'became for the colonists what Apollo was for the *oikist*: an expounder (*exēgētēs*)'.[67] The prominence of animals in Greek divinatory practice, the reading of their movements and behaviours as signs from the gods, makes them particularly suitable in such a context of exegesis whereby men come to understand divine words. With their greater perceived connection to the land and environment, they allow for exploration of man's relationship to a place and shift the focus away from inter-human interaction. Furthermore, animals are themselves actors or even protagonists in these stories, prompting reflection on their relationship with the gods involved.

Let us consider one version of the story of the foundation of Tarentum. Diodorus Siculus reports that Phalanthus and the Epeunactae, after a failed coup at Sparta, sent envoys to Delphi to ask if they might settle the territory of Sicyon.[68] The god vetoed this plan but did offer an alternative:

καλόν τοι τὸ μεταξὺ Κορίνθου καὶ Σικυῶνος
ἀλλ᾽ οὐκ οἰκήσεις οὐδ᾽ εἰ παγχάλκεος εἴης.
Σατύριον φράζου σὺ Τάραντός τ᾽ἀγλαὸν ὕδωρ
καὶ λιμένα σκαιὸν ταὶ ὅπου τράγος ἁλμυρὸν οἶδμα
ἀμφαγαπᾷ τέγγων ἄκρον πολιοῖο γενείου
ἔνθα Τάραντα ποιοῦ ἐπὶ Σατυρίου βεβαῶτα.

Fair is the plain between Corinth and Sicyon;
But not a home for you, even if you were clad
All in bronze. Look to Satyrion
And Taras' gleaming flood, the harbour on
The left, and where the goat loves
The briny sea, wetting the tip
Of his grey beard. There build Tarentum
Mounted upon Satyrion.[69]

The would-be colonists are denied the familiar and relatively close-at-hand spot they had desired – even in a fantasy world where they were all-of-bronze, Sicyon would be beyond their grasp – and offered instead a fantasy world where goats love to drink salt water. As Dionysius of Halicarnassus reports, the impossibility collapses when we grasp that the 'goat' (*tragos*) shares its name with a wild fig tree.[70] The colonists encounter such a specimen on landing and, after seeing that it was draped with a vine that trailed into the sea, founded Tarentum (named for the river).

Setting aside for a moment the puzzle of the brine-enamoured goat and its resolution, what sort of an environment is conjured here? This is a world described without explicit appeal to men but with positive potential for human habitation. In contrast to the image of Sicyon conjured by the appeal to men all-of-bronze, the appeal to natural features of the landscape and the (alleged) animal inhabitants presents this spot as a blank slate to be readily obtained.[71] We might compare the *Odyssey*'s famous goat island, an ideal settlement if only the Cyclopes had the technology to reach it by sea.[72] A near Golden Age idyll, goat island has all the amenities a Greek settler could desire: 'meadows by the shores of the grey sea' and 'a harbour giving safe anchorage'.[73] It also has no men:

οὔτ᾽ ἄρα ποίμνησιν καταΐσχεται οὔτ᾽ ἀρότοισιν,
ἀλλ᾽ ἥ γ᾽ ἄσπαρτος καὶ ἀνήροτος ἤματα πάντα
ἀνδρῶν χηρεύει, βόσκει δέ τε μηκάδας αἶγας.

It is rich neither in flocks, nor in cornfields,
but unsown and unploughed perpetually
it is empty of men, but feeds the bleating goats.[74]

Animals and other features of the natural world, then, in contrast to men and existing settlements, might suggest (however imaginatively) a blank slate. The imagery suggests at one and the same time that the location is both inhabitable and uninhabited. As in Homer, the emphasis in Diodorus' oracle is on the point of disembarkation, the seashore, highlighting the potential of the spot for future travel and trade opportunities, while remaining in a neutral space, 'outside the structural world of the polis'.[75] Goats, traditionally denizens of the mountainous regions outside poleis, are tended by men, but by men whose task takes them beyond the limits of the community.[76] Both the seashore and the suggestion of a potential for goat-herding put us in mind of activities at the physical and conceptual edges of human communities.[77] This liminality that contains both the absence of a current community and the potential for one is emblematic of the experience of colonists and the colonial enterprise.

We might compare Creophylus' foundation story of the Ephesians, in which an oracle instructs the colonists to 'found a city in a place a fish would show them and to which a wild boar would lead the way'.[78] When some fishermen were having lunch, a fish, struck by an ember, jumped out of the fire and set alight some scrub. The fire drove out a wild boar who was struck down by a javelin, and the would-be Ephesians settled the spot. Here the resolution of the riddle is marked by human intervention – the fish and the boar mark the spot through the human activities of fishing, cooking over fire, and hunting. Not only do the men solve the riddle by interpreting these events in its light, but it is human action that clarifies relations between men and wild animals: the guides come to be understood as food and prey. To commemorate these events, the colonists found temples celebrating Artemis and Apollo, highlighting these two sides of human endeavour – hunting and exegesis.

Nonnus' account of Tyre's foundation provides a particularly cinematic example of a pre-colonial impossible landscape.[79] Here Melquart/Heracles informs a group of autochthonous men that if they construct a vessel and turn wherever their mind draws them, they will come upon two floating rocks. One of these will be topped by an olive tree, surrounded but not consumed by flame, perched upon by an eagle, and writhed around by a snake. Just as the flame fails to burn the tree, so the snake and eagle coexist in a state of unnatural harmony. A well-made bowl completes the scene. The men are instructed to capture the eagle (which, it transpires, offers itself up willingly) and to sacrifice it to the gods, Poseidon, Zeus, and the blessed. The act of sacrifice will end the island's wandering, fixing it upon immovable foundations, a perfect site for the city's foundation. The muddled paraphernalia of sacrifice (fire, vessel, victim) is reordered and the chaos subsides. Sacrifice here marks the foundation of a new colony but also the (re-)establishment of the natural order, including proper relations between men, gods, and animals (on sacrifice, see also this volume, Chapter 8).

Through these examples, then, we see the varied ways in which the animals of impossible landscapes can encourage reflection on the roles of, and relationships between, men and gods in the act of foundation.

Returning to Tarentum, if the Taras and Satyrion of Diodorus' verses echo the proto-colonial site of Homer's *Odyssey*, the idyll is complicated by the riddling element of the oracle. As Dougherty notes, the blurring of the 'customary distinctions between flora and fauna' is embellished by the details provided in Dionysius' explanation. The tendrils of the vine mimic the goat's beard as they dip into the sea.[80] The confusion of categories goes further. The animal and non-animal are brought together in the goat's love affair with the sea, and further conflation may be implied by the use of the epic genitive *polioio*, used here of the goat's beard, but a common attribute of the sea in Homer.[81] The humanising characterisation of the goat as 'in love' (*amphagapaî*) and with a grizzled beard may be further suggested by the name of the region – Satyrion – which brings to mind those most famous bearded half-breeds, the satyrs. If goat island is home to nymphs, are we here in the land of satyrs? We might find here a further hint that this is a place on the margins of the Greek world and an appropriate location to restage or explore the emergence of culture and civilisation from the natural world.[82]

The fictionality of this image of the land as an uninhabited blank slate is flagged by the alternative Pythian oracle that Diodorus relates: 'Σατύριόν τοι ἔδωκα Τάραντά τε πίονα δῆμον|οἰκῆσαι καὶ πῆματ' Ἰαπύγεσσι γενέσθαι' ('I give to you Satyrion and the fat land of Taras, too, there to live, and to be a bane to the Iapygians').[83] The 'fat' land and the local people will prove as easy for the colonists to benefit from as goats on the mountainside, but undeniably there are men here. In the case of Ephesus, too, in contrast to Creophylus' account of a boar and a fish, Strabo has the Athenian prince Androclus, son of Codrus, found the city after driving away the local inhabitants.[84] Animals, then, may be used to explore the relationship of would-be colonists to a new land in place of narratives, or realities, that pit these colonists against the men who already claim such land as their home. Animals can be used to express either the happy acceptance of the colonists into their new territory or their struggles to claim it.[85] Rather than being welcomed by or conquering a native population, the colonists may be imagined as accepted by wild beasts or as subduing them.

The foundation of Thebes provides an obvious example. Cadmus, having located the site of his future city, plans to perform a sacrifice to Athena to mark the foundation but is prevented from doing so by a great *drakōn* that guards the local spring.[86] As we have seen, snakes can prove a powerful symbol for autochthonous claims to a region, so, when Cadmus dispatches the serpent, he reinforces his claim to the site. In Apollodorus' account of the foundation of Phthiotis, too, we find Athamas asserting his worthiness and claim to the region through his interaction with the local wildlife, but here in a rather less combative manner. An oracle bid him not to slay a local scourge on the community, but 'to settle in a place where he should be received as a guest by wild beasts'.[87] Athamas does so when, on reaching Thessaly, he startles some wolves away from the sheep they are consuming. By scaring off the wolves, Athamas promises protection to future flocks and, through his subsequent marriage to Themisto (a name that connotes lawfulness and divine approval), inserts civilised order in place of wildness and confusion. A final, illustrative example of the ways the gods, via oracles, were held to use animals to explore and sanction the connection of founders to sites is found in Strabo's account of the foundation of Chrysa. He recounts an early tradition (attributed to Callinus of Ephesus of the mid-seventh century BCE) in which the would-be founders receive an oracle bidding them to stay on the spot where the earth-born (*hoi gēgeneis*) should attack them.[88] The attack materialises near Hamaxitus when a great multitude of field-mice swarm out of the ground at night and consume all the leather in the men's weapons and equipment. Here, again, the mice provide a way of thinking through the sort of conflict that colonists would often encounter. Described as *gēgeneis*, they are autochthonous inhabitants of a sort, but cast disparagingly as a rustic multitude (*plēthos arouraiōn*).[89] While this language humanises them, the mice also burst forth like flowers blooming (*exanthēsan*), further confusing 'natural' categories. These category-blurring rodents invert the usual criteria of failure and success. The attack by the 'autochthons' is not successfully repelled, yet it signals the future success of the colonial enterprise. In sharp contrast to an imagined need to be 'all-of-bronze', here, with the divine sanction the oracle provides, a colony is founded as weapons are set aside.

To return a final time to Tarentum, Diodorus' second oracle, as we have seen, similarly downplays the need for the Epeunactae to display martial strength in order to settle the promised land. Yet, this more straightforward oracle is interesting, too, in that it also removes the need for the would-be colonists to display any skills in exegesis. Contrary to the frequent emphasis on the powers of interpretation, which lend the *oikist* or colonising group authority, highlighted by Dougherty, here the Epeunactae announce themselves unable to understand the puzzling oracle they receive and are offered a simplified version. The emphasis is not on human intelligence (or physical strength) but on the god's benefaction in supplying the land.[90] In another riddling example, which again 'blurs the customary distinctions between plant and animal life', Plutarch records the oracle Opus received before he settled Ozolian Locris.[91] The god instructed him 'to found a city where he should happen to be bitten by a wooden dog (*kynos xulinēs*)'.[92] He stepped on a dog-briar and, in the enforced period of recuperation, explored the local area, founding multiple cities. Though one can imagine a narrative in which Opus understands that the oracle has been fulfilled and so engages in the act of foundation, this is not pronounced in Plutarch's account. Plutarch follows up the story by enquiring why the Locrians are called Ozolian. Deriving Ozolian from *ozein* ('to smell'), a number of explanations are proffered: because the bodies of Nessus (the centaur) or Python washed up there to rot; because they wear fleeces and goatskins and spend their time with goats; or because the country is full of sweet-smelling flowers. In these stories, then, interpretation is not always key, and, indeed, successful interpretation does not always dispel the oddity that lingers and continues to typify the colonists' existence on the edges of the Greek world: Ozolian Locris continues to be potentially a world where men mingle with goats, or hybrid monsters wash up on the beach to rot.[93]

We might compare, finally, the account of Scythia's foundation that Herodotus attributes to the Pontic Greeks.[94] Heracles, driving the horses of Geryon, comes to the future site of Scythia. As he sleeps, divine fortune spirits away the animals. Searching for them, Heracles comes to a wild wood, wherein he finds a cave containing a *mixoparthenos*, a double-formed echidna.[95] Revealing that she has his mares, the creature refuses to return them unless Heracles has sex with her. Heracles assents, and three sons are born. Heracles instructs the woman how to determine which of her sons should rule the country, and departs after leaving the necessary equipment for a proper Greek trial of strength (a bow to draw and a belt to wear). Thus, the Scythian race is founded. It is undeniable that this story plays with the narratives of Heracles, slayer of beasts and monsters, and of the sorts of monsters that were slain by his ilk.[96] Heracles, fresh from killing Geryon, cloaks himself in his lion-skin – the very pelt he claimed from the Nemean lion, offspring of Hesiod's Echidna. Like the latter creature, which guards Erima, Herodotus' snake-woman dwells in a cave far from men and gods. Her world, prior to Heracles' arrival, is similarly desolate and uninhabited.[97] While, elsewhere, Heracles kills such creatures, here he beds one and creates a race descended from a hybrid hero and a hybrid monster. As we have seen, the echidna brings positive associations in this story: her close relationship with the earth expresses the claim of an autochthonous people to their land and, though more controlled than the monsters of Hesiod's catalogue, she shares in their fecundity. Here again, the mixed-up oddity of this world is not resolved but embraced. Herodotus' Pontic Greeks use this oddity as a way to characterise the current race of Scythians.

Alongside impossible landscapes as a way of conveying the journey that needs to take place from the familiar into the strange (until that strangeness is transformed back into the familiar), the journey itself may be played up as a marker of this same strangeness. Here animals play a role as guides for would-be colonists, usually on the advice of an oracle.[98] For Claudia Zatta, animals as 'beings of the natural world' are appropriate guides for humans as they seek to create new landscapes out of wilderness.[99] Thus, they do not serve just as markers of a non-civilised world but as appropriate guides for its navigation. Zatta explores particularly how the departure from the known world to a fresh new environment may be emphasised in the need to adopt 'disorienting' animal modes of movement.[100] If animal guides might encourage their followers to behave like animals (as Zatta argues), animals might also be cast in the role of *oikist*. Pausanias recounts the story of Aigeira, which was renamed in honour of the goats that helped to save the city (previously Hyperesia) from invading Sicyonians by convincing them that the city's army was twice its actual size.[101] On the spot where 'the most beautiful goat which led the others' laid down, they founded a shrine to Artemis Agrotera since they believed the inspiration for the trick had come from the goddess.[102] Here, we are confronted with an exceptional and superior animal, worthy, like Xanthus, of its role in the goddess' intervention. Through the renaming of the city, selection of the site for a new sanctuary, and description of the leading goat, the animals play a role akin to the *oikist* in other foundation narratives.[103]

Some stories create further slippage in relation to the identity of the guide: is it the god or the animal they dispatch? Pausanias' account of the foundation of Boeae plays with the nature of the deity's involvement.[104] An oracle informs the would-be colonists (expelled from their respective cities) that Artemis will show them where to settle. When they reach the shore, a hare appears to them (*epiphainetai*), which they view as their guide (*hēgemona*) on their way. Diving into a myrtle tree, the travellers take this as the appropriate spot and found a city, worshipping down to this day the myrtle tree and calling Artemis 'Saviour'.[105] As Zatta notes, the seashore is not an obvious habitat for hares.[106] This oddity, in addition to the oracle, was clearly sufficient to merit the conclusion that the goddess' hand was at work in the hare's appearance.[107] The verb *epiphainetai*, though certainly not necessitating an epiphanic interpretation, is at least suggestive in context and in combination with the epithet Soteira.[108] Gods could, of course, adopt an animal form to interact with mortals. In a foundation context, Philostratus tells how, when the Athenians set out to colonise Ionia, they were guided by the Muses in the form of bees.[109] Therefore, we might wonder if, when the hare dives (*kataduntos*) into the tree to which the citizens later offer worship, the goddess was perceived as manifested in both forms.[110] Here, then, in another, rather different, case of blurred categories, we find a narrative that explores the relationship between the animal, the environment, and the god, as the colonists seek to relate themselves to all three.

Conclusion

We have seen in this chapter some of the diverse ways in which animals are significant alongside gods as a way of thinking about what it means to be human and what it means to be exceptional. We have explored stories conveying the ability to communicate with or influence the behaviour of animals and to follow and understand their movements. We have also encountered humans confronting and resolving the disorder animal behaviour can signal, or else making a home within it. We saw men adopting animal behaviour and characteristics in extraordinary – and sometimes threatening – ways. In all these cases, those in close proximity to animals can set themselves apart from other men. Alongside such exceptional men, we have also considered the ways in which animals might be thought to engage independently in relations with the gods and so, in turn, allow for further reflection on the nature of divine/human interaction. Especially in foundation myths, we found animals serving as vehicles for divine communication, as ways of characterising a place (as fertile, remote, or confused), and as agents with their own manner of movement, communication, and relation to the gods. They can act as signs, guides, instruments, or else manifestations of the divine and the natural environment itself. In both our test cases, we have seen how animals can be used in order to think through relations between humans, their gods, their societies, and their environments but also as objects of preoccupation and interest in their own right. In approaching the divine, animals prove useful both to think with and to think about. We encounter them as full-blooded agents and characters as well as symbols and vehicles for reflection.

Notes

1   See Bodson 1975: vii: 'les animaux ne sont pas, dans la religion grecque, des acteurs moins importants que les hommes et les dieux'.
2   Animal similes: e.g. Clarke 1995; Lonsdale 1990; Heath 1999. Metamorphosis: Thumiger 2014; Forbes Irving 1990.
3   Arist. *Pol.* 1.2 1253a28–30.
4   Discussions of the play and its relation to other versions of the myth: Forbes Irving 1990: 99–107; Fitzpatrick 2001; Coo 2013.
5   Hes. *Op.* 276–280.
6   Soph. *Ter.* Fr. 581: θρασὺν ... ἐν παντευχίᾳ; δύο γὰρ οὖν μορφὰς φανεῖ παιδός τε χαὐτοῦ νηδύος μιᾶς ἄπο (trans. Lloyd-Jones).
7   The sorrow of the nightingale's song: e.g. Ar. *Av.* 210–222; Pl. *Phd.* 85a.
8   Gourmelen 2005: 413.
9   Soph. *Ter.* F589 l.1.
10   Soph. *Ter.* F590; for the human condition, cf. F591.
11   For the same thought: Pind. *Isthm.* 5.16; Epicharm. DK 23 B20. Cf. Arist. *Eth. Nic.* 10.7 1177b31–1178a3.
12   Thumiger 2014: 388.
13   We might compare Hippolytus' ill-conceived attempt to live an Artemisian existence or the Cyclopes' special relation to the gods in Homer.
14   Heath 2005: 124, 126. The ways in which Achilles is super- and sub-human and generally transgressive in his power, emotions, and behaviour have been much discussed. See, e.g., Muellner 1996; Clarke 1995: 53–59; King 1987: 13–28.
15   Hom. *Il.* 19.198–214.
16   Hom. *Il.* 20.166: ἀγρόμενοι πᾶς δῆμος.

96   H. Willey

17   Hom. *Il.* 20.172–3. On the extreme anthropomorphising of this simile, see King 1987: 22–24 and Heath 2005: 139.
18   Hom. *Il.* 19.352–354. See Heath 2005: 128.
19   Hom. *Il.* 19.399–423.
20   Heath 2005: 39.
21   For a discussion of the conceits of fable and the play on the similarity and difference between humans and talking animals, see Lefkowitz 2014. As noted by Johnston 1992: 86, the caveat that we are under-informed about the broader context of the epic cycle is important. Yet, the broader tradition of talking animals she reconstructs is inevitably highly speculative (so Pelliccia 1995: 106–107).
22   On the question of animal speech, see, e.g., Sorabji 1993. Heath makes a convincing broader case for speech as an important status marker both within the human community and beyond it, comparing human speech to the speech/sounds of animals, the gods, and the dead (Heath 2005: 52–56 and 57–61, respectively). On animal communication, see Fögen 2003, 2007; Hawkins 2017.
23   For a discussion of the semantic range of *audē* in epic, see Clay 1974: 131; Ford 1992: 173–178, followed by Heath 2005: 54–61.
24   Hawkins 2017: 1.
25   Speaking as a one-off event: Pelliccia 1995: 105–108; Heath 2005: 40; Heath 1999: 42; Xanthus as more generally a talking horse: Johnston 1992, followed by Hawkins 2017: 3. The text is not decisive either way but, given the neat mirroring between Hera's grant of speech and the Erinyes' action to end *this* speech, the benefaction is more likely a one-off event.
26   Pelliccia places Xanthus alongside other animals given speech for the purpose of prophecy. See Pelliccia 1995: 107, followed by Heath 2005: 40. Cf. Pl. *Phd.* 84e–85b for swans given the gift of prophecy because they are sacred to Apollo, and Pl. *Phdr.* 258e–259d for cicadas as intermediaries between the Muses and their human devotees.
27   Hom. *Il.* 19.407.
28   Hawkins 2017: 2–5 (quotation at 2), drawing on Gera 2003: 18–67.
29   Hom. *Il.* 19.420–423.
30   Schol. *ad* 19.418: ἐπίσκοποι γάρ εἰσι τῶν παρὰ φύσιν; Heath 2005: 40; cf. Edwards 1991 *ad loc.* and Johnston 1992: 90–91, n. 16 for previous scholarship. Johnston is right to highlight the anachronism of the Erinyes as policers of the *natural* order but, without appealing to a later category of nature, it is still possible to see some truth in the idea that the Erinyes' action restores ordinary, perhaps even normative, boundaries that Xanthus disrupts.
31   Clay 1993: 115. See also Clay 2003: 150–174.
32   Clay 1993: 106.
33   Hes. *Theog.* 295–296: οὐδὲν ἐοικὸς | θνητοῖς ἀνθρώποις οὐδ᾽ ἀθανάτοισι θεοῖσιν; 823–35: ὥστε θεοῖσι συνιέμεν.
34   Clay 1993: 112. For continuity between monstrous animals and their hybrid relations, see Ogden 2013: 68, 148.
35   Clay 1993: 107; cf. Lonsdale 1979: 156.
36   Clay 1993: 113, 110.
37   Hes. *Theog.* 314–317; Clay 1993: 111. The hybridity of heroes: Brelich 1958: 297; Clay 2003: 161; and, particularly of Heracles, Silk 1985: 6–8. Cf. Ogden 2013: 215–246 for the use of mirroring in descriptions of hero/monster battles.
38   Part-animal gods: Aston 2011. Cecrops: schol. *ad* Ar. *Plut.* 773; Philoch. *FGrH* 328 F94; Cic. *Leg.* 2.63 with Gourmelen 2005; Ogden 2013: 259–263, Ogden 2009: 114–116; Aston 2011: 379–380. The Scythian echidna: Hdt. 4.9–10 with Hartog 1988: 22–27; Visintin 1997; Ogden 2013: 188; Ustinova 1999: 87–93 (for alternate versions of her story). Dowden 1992: 86–87 explores further the connection between snakes and autochthony.

39 Harrison 1991.
40 Hom. *Od.* 9.447–457.
41 Heath 2005: 82; cf. Gera 2003: 13–14.
42 On this passage: Gera 2003: 13–15 (noting the contrast between Xanthus as divine horse and Polyphemus' ram as favourite pet); Heath 2005: 79–84; Fögen 2007: 66–67.
43 Hom. *Il.* 17.426–440. For Johnston 1992: 87–88 the divine steeds' behaviour is differentiated from that of the mortal (Pedasos) by the choice of vocabulary (*klaion* versus *makōn*).
44 Pelliccia 1995: 106–107.
45 Charming animals, often together with trees and/or rocks: Simon. Fr. 567 (Campbell); Paus. 9.30.4; Eur. *Bacch.* 561–564; Diod. Sic. 4.25.2–3 Conon *FGrH* 26 F1. 45. Charming Hades and/or Persephone: Eur. *Alc.* 357–359; Diod. Sic. 4.25.4; cf. Apollod. 1.3.2. Prophecy: Philostr. *Her.* 28.8, *VA* 4.14. See Watson 2013 for earlier (fifth-century) evidence for this tradition.
46 Ov. *Met.* 11.44–49 (trans. Melville); Paus. 9.30.6: ἥδιον καὶ μεῖζόν τι ᾄδειν.
47 Hom. *Il.* 16.148–154.
48 Hom. *Il.* 19.411–417; cf. Heath 2005: 50–51 for Xanthus' 'self-defensiveness, pride, and indisputable logic'.
49 Clarke 1995: 146: 'Homer's beasts have the same emotional and cognitive apparatus as men.' Cf. Heath's (2005: 42 and 50, n. 3) summary of past scholarship on the (lack of) difference between animals and men in Homer. Contrast with, e.g., Renehan 1981: 254–256 for the view that Homer and Hesiod contain evidence for man's perceived exceptionalism.
50 Numbers 22:21–39.
51 Numbers 22:28: הָאָתוֹן פִּי אֶת יְהוָה וַיִּפְתַּח.
52 On the question of human (non-)uniqueness, see, e.g., Renehan 1981; Sorabji 1993; Newmeyer 2003; Osborne 2007.
53 For the diversity of views, see Newmeyer's (2003: 113, n. 5) neat summary: 'almost every claim of human uniqueness is countered by one ancient authority or another at some point'.
54 Porph. *Abst.* 3.16.4–5, 17.1–2.
55 Hdt. 1.159; Porph. *Abst.* 3.16.1.
56 Contrast, e.g., the parable of the sparrow at Matthew 10:28–30.
57 Aesch. *Ag.* 49–59.
58 Heath 2005: 26, following Rose 1958 *ad* 59. Heath discusses the collapsing of distinctions between human and animal as a key theme in the play.
59 See Heath 1999: 19, 23–25.
60 Aesch. *Ag.* 57, 50, 55.
61 Colonies preceded symbolically by 'une période de chaos': Vian 1963: 80–82.
62 Dougherty 1992 and 1993: 45–60.
63 Dougherty 1992: 34.
64 Dougherty 1992: 37, 43–44.
65 Dougherty 1992: 43.
66 Dougherty 1992: 36.
67 Malkin 1987: 5, drawing on Plut. *Mor.* 407f–408a.
68 Diod. Sic. 8.21.
69 Trans. adapted from Dougherty 1992.
70 Dion. Hal. 19.1.
71 Cf. MacSweeney 2013: 144 on Creophylus' account of the future site of Ephesus: 'an empty *terra nullius*, seemingly inhabited only by animals'; and Zatta 2016: 228 on colonial sites as 'virgin territory'. Donà 2003: 36 notes that the presence of animals, particularly domestic ones, may be 'un pegno di futura prosperità'.
72 Hom. *Od.* 9.116–158. See, e.g., Bakker 2016: 60, with n. 15 for past scholarship.

73   Hom. *Od.* 9.132: λειμῶνες ἁλὸς πολιοῖο παρ'; 136: λιμὴν εὔορμος.
74   Hom. *Od.* 9. 122–124.
75   Petridou 2016: 197. See also Montiglio 2005: 7–23.
76   Goats as representative of 'marginal space': Guettel Cole 2000: 479; Viscardi 2016: 116.
77   Cf. the discussion of activities 'perceived as being in between' in Petridou 2016: 197.
78   Athen. 8.361c–e = Creophylus *FGrH* 417 F1. As Dougherty 1992: 40 notes, neither animal is a natural guide so, again, the oracle has a riddling feel.
79   Nonnus *Dion.* 40.428–534.
80   Dougherty 1992: 35.
81   As in the description of goat island at Hom. *Od.* 9.132.
82   On the connection between satyrs and cultural inventions: Seaford 1976, 1984: 36–37, 41–42; and Lämmle 2013: 371–380.
83   Diod. Sic. 8.21.3 (trans. adapted from Oldfather).
84   Strab. 14.1.3. Creophylus also hints at difficulties in settling the area when he states that this is the colonists' second attempt.
85   See, e.g., Buxton 1994: 189–190 (drawing on Vian 1963) for a discussion of this dynamic.
86   The Cadmus legend: Vian 1963; Ogden 2013: 48–54, 181–183. After the *drakōn's* death, the violence that is so often a feature of colonisation continues to play out through the infighting of the Spartoi who are sown from its teeth.
87   Apollod. 1.9.2: κατοικεῖν ἐν ᾦπερ ἂν τόπῳ ὑπὸ ζῴων ἀγρίων ξενισθῇ.
88   Strab. 13.1.48.
89   See Gourmelen 2005: 24–31 for a discussion of the term *gēgenēs* in relation to Cecrops.
90   Cf. the emphasis on the god's role in Nonnus' Tyre foundation story (in giving instructions, Melquart 'indulg[es his] mood of founding cities' (φιλόκτιτον ἦθος; D. 40.504–506, trans. Rouse)) – unsurprising, given that the god himself is narrating the tale.
91   Dougherty 1992: 35; Plut. *Mor.* 294d–f.
92   κτίζειν πόλιν ὅπουπερ ἂν τύχῃ δηχθεὶς ὑπὸ κυνὸς ξυλίνης, trans. Dougherty 1992.
93   Cf. Thucydides' (1.5) characterisation of the Locrians through their outdated habits of piracy and carrying arms.
94   Hdt. 4.8–10. See n. 38. above.
95   We see how lost herds, like animal guides (on which more below), may prompt new human discoveries or experiences and serve as vehicles of divine guidance.
96   Heracles' marked and varied association with animals: Burkert 1985: 209; Clay 1993: 112; Bonnet *et al.* 1998.
97   Hdt. 4.8.1: ἐς γῆν ταύτην ἐοῦσαν ἐρήμην; Visintin 1997: 209–210.
98   Animal guides: Frazer 1898 *ad* 10.6.2; Vian 1963: 76–79; Zatta 2016; and, outside Greece, Donà 2003.
99   Zatta 2016: 228.
100 Zatta 2016: 233. Melquart's instruction to the founders of Tyre to construct a boat and steer a winding course, turning wherever their mind draws them (Nonnus *Dion.* 40.465), shows that men, in a new environment, are as apt to meander without perceived purpose as are animals elsewhere.
101 Paus. 7.26.1–4.
102 For a discussion of the episode, see Viscardi 2016: 122.
103 Cf. Paus. 10.33.9–11 for Amphicleia in Phocis renamed Ophiteia ('Snake City') after a snake performs a valiant deed. See Ogden 2013: 163, n. 96.
104 Paus. 3.22.11–12.
105 Hunt 2016: 79–81 explores whether the tree was worshipped *in addition to* Artemis Soteira or *as* Artemis/as representative of her.
106 Zatta 2016: 236.

107 Hares enjoyed a special relationship with Artemis: Xen. *Cyn.* 5.14; cf. Callim. *Dian.* 2; Philostr. *Imag.* 1.28.6. For archaeological evidence, see Bevan 1985: 187–189.
108 For the language of epiphany and salvation discussed in a different context, see Slater 1988: 126–128. Seashores as prime 'epiphanic landscapes': Petridou 2016: 196–197.
109 Philostr. *Imag.* 2.8.6.
110 Pausanias (3.23.7) uses the same verb in close proximity to our passage when a snake disappears into the earth and marks out another spot for foundation and cultic activity. See Petridou 2016: 72–73 for divine bodies 'abbreviated … and represented by the bodies' of animals and plants; cf. 92–93 for the blurred distinction between animals as *pars pro toto* representatives of the divine and actual zoomorphic manifestations.

Bibliography

Aston, E. (2011) *Mixanthrōpoi. Animal-Human Hybrid Deities in Greek Religion.* Liège.
Bakker, E. (2016) *The Meaning of Meat and the Structure of the Odyssey.* Cambridge.
Bevan, E. (1985) 'Representations of animals in sanctuaries of Artemis and of other Olympian deities'. Ph.D. diss., Edinburgh University.
Bodson, L. (1975) *Hiera zôia. Contribution à l'étude de la place de l'animal dans la religion grecque ancienne.* Brussels.
Bonnet, C., C. Jourdain-Annequin, and V. Pirenne-Delforge (1998) *Le Bestiaire d'Héraklès. IIIᵉ rencontre héracléenne.* Liège.
Brelich, A. (1958) *Gli eroi greci. Un problema storico-religioso.* Rome.
Burkert, W. (1985) *Greek Religion*, trans. J. Raffan. Cambridge, Mass.
Buxton, R. (1994) *Imaginary Greece. The Contexts of Mythology.* Cambridge.
Clarke, M. (1995) 'Between lions and men: images of the hero in the *Iliad*', *Greek, Roman and Byzantine Studies* 36, 137–159.
Clay, J. (1974) 'Demas and Aude: the nature of divine transformation in Homer', *Hermes* 102, 129–136.
Clay, J. (1993) 'The generation of monsters in Hesiod', *Classical Philology* 88, 105–116.
Clay, J. (2003) *Hesiod's Cosmos.* Cambridge.
Coo, L. (2013) 'A tale of two sisters: studies in Sophocles' *Tereus*', *Transactions of the American Philological Association* 143, 347–382.
Donà, C. (2003) *Per le vie dell'altro mondo: l'animale guida e il mito del viaggio.* Cantanzaro.
Dougherty, C. (1992) 'When rain falls from the clear blue sky: riddles and colonization Oracles', *Classical Antiquity* 11, 28–44.
Dougherty, C. (1993) *The Poetics of Colonization. From City to Text in Archaic Greece.* Oxford.
Dowden, K. (1992) *The Uses of Greek Mythology.* London.
Edwards, M. (1991) *The Iliad. A Commentary.* Cambridge.
Fitzpatrick, D. (2001) 'Sophocles' *Tereus*', *Classical Quarterly* 51, 90–101.
Fögen, T. (2003) 'Animal communication', in G. L. Campbell (ed.) *The Oxford Handbook of Animals in Classical Thought and Life.* Oxford, 216–233.
Fögen, T. (2007) 'Antike Zeugnisse zu Kommunikationsformen von Tieren', *Antike und Abendland* 53, 39–75.
Forbes Irving, P. M. C. (1990) *Metamorphosis in Greek Myths.* Oxford.
Ford, A. L. (1992) *Homer. The Poetry of the Past.* Ithaca, N.Y.
Frazer, J. G. (1898) *Pausanias's Description of Greece.* London.

Gera, D. L. (2003) *Ancient Greek Ideas on Speech, Language and Civilization*. Oxford.

Gourmelen, L. (2005) *Kékrops, le Roi-Serpent. Imaginaire athénien, représentations de l'humain et de l'animalité en Grèce ancienne*. Paris.

Guettel Cole, S. (2000) 'Landscapes of Artemis', *The Classical World* 93, 471–481.

Harrison, E. L. (1991) 'Homeric wonder-horses', *Hermes* 119, 252–254.

Hartog, F. (1988) *The Mirror of Herodotus. The Representation of the Other in the Writing of History*, trans. J. Lloyd. Berkeley, Calif.

Hawkins, T. (2017) 'Eloquent *alogia*: animal narrators in ancient Greek literature', *Humanities* 6(37), 1–15.

Heath, J. (1999) 'Disentangling the beast: humans and other animals in Aeschylus' *Oresteia*', *Journal of Hellenic Studies* 119, 17–47.

Heath, J. (2005) *The Talking Greeks. Speech, Animals, and the Other in Homer, Aeschylus, and Plato*. Cambridge.

Hunt, A. (2016) *Reviving Roman Religion. Sacred Trees in the Roman World*. Cambridge.

Johnston, S. I. (1992) 'Xanthus, Hera and the Erinyes (*Iliad* 19.400–418)', *Transactions of the American Philological Association* 122, 85–98.

Jones, W. H. S. and H. A. Ormerod (1926) *Pausanias, Description of Greece, Volume II: Books 3–5*. Cambridge, Mass.

King, K. C. (1987) *Achilles. Paradigms of the War Hero from Homer to the Middle Ages*. Berkeley, Calif.

Lämmle, R. (2013) *Poetik des Satyrspiels*. Heidelberg.

Lefkowitz, J. (2014) 'Aesop and animal fable', in G. L. Campbell (ed.) *The Oxford Handbook of Animals in Classical Thought and Life*. Oxford, 1–20.

Lonsdale, S. (1979) 'Attitudes towards animals in ancient Greece', *Greece and Rome* 26, 146–159.

Lonsdale, S. (1990) *Creatures of Speech. Lion, Herding and Hunting Similes in the Iliad*. Stuttgart.

MacSweeney, N. (2013) *Foundation Myths and Politics in Ancient Ionia*. Cambridge.

Malkin, I. (1987) *Religion and Colonization in Ancient Greece*. Leiden.

Montiglio, S. (2005) *Wandering in Ancient Greek Culture*. Chicago, Ill.

Muellner, L. (1996) *The Anger of Achilles. Mēnis in Greek Epic*. Ithaca, N.Y.

Newmeyer, S. (2003) 'Paws to reflect: ancients and moderns on the religious sensibilities of animals', *Quaderni Urbinati di Cultura Classica* 75, 111–129.

Ogden, D. (2009) 'Bastardy and fatherlessness in ancient Greece', in S. Hübner (ed.) *Growing up Fatherless in Antiquity*. Cambridge, 105–119.

Ogden, D. (2013) *Drakōn. Dragon Myth and Serpent Cult in the Greek and Roman Worlds*. Oxford.

Osborne, C. (2007) *Dumb Beasts and Dead Philosophers. Humanity and the Humane in Ancient Philosophy and Literature*. Oxford.

Pelliccia, H. (1995) *Mind, Body, and Speech in Homer and Pindar*. Göttingen.

Petridou, G. (2016) *Divine Epiphany in Greek Literature and Culture*. Oxford.

Renehan, R. (1981) 'The Greek anthropocentric view of man', *Harvard Studies in Classical Philology* 85, 239–259.

Rose, H. J. (1958) *A Commentary on the Surviving Plays of Aeschylus*. Amsterdam.

Schmidt, M. (1972) 'Ein neues Zeugnis zum Mythos vom Orpheushaupt', *Antike Kunst* 15, 128–137.

Seaford, R. (1976) 'On the origins of Satyric drama', *Maia* 28, 209–221.

Seaford, R. (1984) *Euripides, Cyclops*. Oxford.

Silk, M. (1985) 'Heracles and Greek tragedy', *Greece and Rome* 32, 1–22.

Slater, W. (1988) 'The epiphany of Demosthenes', *Phoenix* 42, 126–130.

Sorabji, R. (1993) *Animal Minds and Human Morals. The Origins of the Western Debate.* Ithaca, N.Y.

Thumiger, C. (2014) 'Metamorphosis: human into animal', in G. L. Campbell (ed.) *The Oxford Handbook of Animals in Classical Thought and Life.* Oxford, 384–413.

Ustinova, Y. (1999) *The Supreme Gods of the Bosporan Kingdom. Celestial Aphrodite and the Most High God.* Leiden.

Vian, F. (1963) *Les Origines de Thebes. Cadmos et les Spartes.* Paris.

Viscardi, G. (2016) 'Constructing humans, symbolising the gods: the cultural value of the goat in Greek religion', in P. Johnston, A. Mastrocinque, and S. Papaioannou (eds.) *Animals in Greek and Roman Religion and Myth.* Newcastle, 115–140.

Visintin, M. (1997) 'Di Echidna, e di altre femmine anguiformi', *Mètis* 12, 205–221.

Watson, S. B. (2013) 'Muses of Lesbos or (Aeschylean) muses of Pieria? Orpheus' head on a fifth-century hydria', *Greek, Roman, and Byzantine Studies* 53, 441–460.

Zatta, C. (2016) 'Flying geese, wandering cows: how animal movement orients human space in Greek myth', in P. Johnston, A. Mastrocinque, and S. Papaioannou (eds.) *Animals in Greek and Roman Religion and Myth.* Newcastle, 227–236.

5 The theriomorphism of the major Greek gods[1]

J. N. Bremmer

Introduction

Around the time I started work on this contribution, I came across a newspaper article about a schism in the Party for the Animals, one of many political parties in the Dutch parliament.[2] It seems the Netherlands is in the vanguard, in that no other country had such a party before its foundation in 2006. I am interested less in the party's political platform than the fact that it gained enough followers to earn a seat in the Dutch parliament. Such an event is only one sign of a changing attitude towards animals in the West, observable in social-media reactions to big-game hunting and, more subtly, the increasing protection of animal well-being through legal measures. These developments demonstrate that human attitudes towards animals are not fixed but subject to cultural, economic, and political changes. This transformation started in the West in the early modern period but is clearly accelerating in our own era, albeit at different speeds at different times.[3] There are undoubtedly a number of reasons for this development, chief among which is the realisation that our DNA and behaviour differ little from those of the great primates.[4] This change has also reached the study of the ancient world, as evidenced by the proliferation of works on animals and their relationships with humans.[5]

Perhaps not surprisingly, the new attention paid to animals has also seen a return to the problem of the theriomorphic shapes of Greek divinities and their metamorphosis into animals. To gain a better understanding of this development and its results, I will look first at what scholars had to say about gods in animal shape in the 20th century, proceed with recent work in the 21st, take a closer look at the theriomorphic shapes (horses and bulls) of some great gods, and end with a few conclusions.

Because it would be impossible to treat such a subject in detail in a single chapter, I will not discuss permanent hybrid gods or supernatural beings, such as Pan, satyrs, or centaurs. This has recently been done comprehensively.[6] I am interested here particularly in the temporary changes and permanent theriomorphic states of the great gods and their backgrounds. These have been the focus of considerable interest and research over the past decade, as have the Greek gods themselves.[7] A full study would have to look at the entire body of evidence of every single great divinity, which could easily comprise an entire book. My aim here is more modest. I highlight some of the changes in approach to those theriomorphic moments and states since 1900, but I also intend to illustrate the problems and varied contexts connected with the theriomorphism of the major gods and goddesses. These have not always been properly considered; here, perhaps, some progress may be made.

The 20th century

The modern study of ancient Greek divine theriomorphism dates to 1900, when the Dutch scholar Marinus Willem de Visser (1875–1930) obtained his doctorate at the University of Leiden with a dissertation, written in Latin, on the non-human shapes of the Greek gods, in which he duly collected virtually all of the relevant material concerning the worship of stones, trees, and animals.[8] The subject was clearly of the moment, as his thesis was reviewed widely by eminent scholars. Leading historians of folklore, Greek religion, anthropology, and sociology – such as the German Eduard Hugo Meyer (1837–1908), the French scholars Salomon Reinach (1858–1932) and Marcel Mauss (1872–1950), and Robert Marett (1866–1943) and Lewis Farnell (1856–1934) from the United Kingdom – all praised de Visser's industry and solid scholarship.[9] However, some, including Mauss, questioned his use of the then-current hermeneutical tools of animism and totemism in order to explain his texts.[10] Although his obituary stressed (perhaps rather harshly) de Visser's mediocrity as a philologist and his lack of originality, he had taken such criticism in his stride. The updated German edition of his book reflects this, with its fewer references to contemporary theories and a more careful and reticent style.[11] He did, however, stick to his notion that the rise of divine anthropomorphism scaled back the worship of non-human divine shapes, such as theriomorphic divinities. We shall return to this idea below. After publishing these books, de Visser changed careers, training as an interpreter with the Dutch Embassy in Tokyo and finishing up as the Chair of Japanese Studies at Leiden.

Strangely, his books are not mentioned in the next extensive discussion of Greek animal worship by Ulrich von Wilamowitz-Moellendorff (1848–1931), arguably the greatest Hellenist of modern times.[12] The first volume of his final book, a history of Greek religion, is wholly dedicated to the older gods until Homer, but its scheme of pre-Hellenic, old-Hellenic, and Homeric gods was rendered obsolete by the decipherment of Linear B. It is remarkable how much attention Wilamowitz pays to the theriomorphic shapes of the Greek gods in his discussion.[13] He starts with avian epiphanies in Homer. Although much discussed and doubted, it should by now be clear that Homer indeed represents divinities such as Athena and Apollo as morphing into birds, usually on their departure.[14] There is a well-known example in the *Odyssey*, where Homer narrates the departure of Athena from Pylos as follows:

ὣς ἄρα φωνήσασ' ἀπέβη γλαυκῶπις Ἀθήνη
φήνῃ εἰδομένη· θάμβος δ' ἕλε πάντας Ἀχαιούς.
θαύμαζεν δ' ὁ γεραιός, ὅπως ἴδεν ὀφθαλμοῖσι·.

So saying, owl-eyed Athena went away
likening herself to a vulture, and astonishment took hold of all Achaeans
watching,
and the old man [Nestor] was amazed, as he saw it with his eyes.[15]

Scholars have often wrestled with this passage, but Wilamowitz was too good a philologist not to accept the metamorphosis. However, he notes, probably with some satisfaction, that Ionian epic (i.e., Homer) had risen above the ancestral belief in this respect, even though the Greek mainland and the majority of the Ionian people might still have believed in gods as birds. He also observes that gods rarely appear in thalassic or cetacean form, with the exception of Apollo as a dolphin in his *Homeric Hymn*.[16]

Wilamowitz does not offer any ideas about the origin of the bird metamorphosis. Although it is possible to see here an influence of bird epiphanies in Minoan and/or Mycenaean art, it is perhaps more likely that this is one more example of the influence of the ancient Near East.[17] In a Hittite narrative, *Elkunirsa and Ashertu*, which derives from a west Semitic source, the goddess Anat-Astarte became an owl and perched on the wall to spy on the god El and his wife Ashertu. Afterwards she 'flew off like a bird across the desert' to warn her brother Baal, who had spurned the advances of El's wife.[18] The story thus contains the Old Testament motif of Joseph and Potiphar's wife, which is also part of the Bellerophon myth, another with various Anatolian motifs.[19] Influence from this or similar myths seems possible.

Regarding mammals, Wilamowitz points to the myth of the Aloadai, two monstrous brothers who wanted to storm Olympus. Artemis changed herself into a deer, and when the brothers tried to shoot her, they killed each other instead. As suggested by its parallels with giants and Titans, the myth is old, which is also supported by its appearance on a red-figure fifth-century BCE Athenian krater.[20] The metamorphosis must also be connected to other associations of Artemis with deer, such as her epithets Elaphia(ia) ('of the deer') and Elaphebolos ('deer-shooting'), which gave its name to the Elaphebolia festivals in Athens and Hyampolis as well as the Ionian month of Elaphebolion in Athens and Iasos.[21] Athenians sacrificed 'deer cakes' (made of spelt, honey, and sesame) and possibly even whole deer to Artemis during their festival.[22] The same connection is visible in the myth of Iphigeneia, in which Artemis replaces the heroine with a deer on the altar, and in the many vase paintings of the goddess with deer.[23]

It is unsurprising that Wilamowitz does not comment on the connections between Artemis and bears, because our epigraphical and archaeological evidence has increased substantially since his time. Essentially, we now have four areas where we find Artemis associated with bears: Cyrene, Arcadia, Sparta, and

Attica. In Cyrene, brides and pregnant women went to the local priestess of Artemis, who was called *arkos* in the fourth century BCE.[24] The Arcadians related that, while bathing with her nymphs, Artemis discovered that the nymph Kallisto was pregnant and, in anger, turned her into a bear.[25] In Sparta, the sanctuary of Artemis Orthia produced several bear figurines in the archaic period, although bulls, horses, and lions were found, too, which makes it unclear whether the bear here signifies Artemis.[26] Our most interesting finds, though, are in Artemis' sanctuary in Brauron, where we know from the literary evidence that Athenian girls called *arktoi* ('bears') performed an initiation ritual during the Brauronia, a quadrennial festival of Artemis. Moreover, the decorations on black figure *kratēriskoi* – small goblets dating from the late sixth and fifth centuries BCE – reveal that these young girls competed in races under the supervision of a man and a woman, both wearing bear masks.[27]

The combined evidence of Cyrene, Arcadia, and Brauron strongly suggests a connection between Artemis, the bear, and the coming of age of girls, even without our knowing that Artemis herself was represented in ursine form. The meaning of the bear in this context had already attracted the attention of Johann Jakob Bachofen (1815–1887), author of *Das Mutterrecht* (1861).[28] Robert Parker suggests that the hunter's experience of the bear, with its concomitant terrors and guilts – a very Burkertian approach – is the link to Artemis.[29] Perhaps it is. Be that as it may, the rich symbolism of the bear in northern folklore suggests there is more to the creature than merely as prey for hunters.[30] Obviously, the connection goes back a long time, and we have no early material to help us understand its significance.

Wilamowitz concludes his survey with divinities in equine form, a subject to which we will return shortly. His explanation of the animal shape of divinities is typically romantic: meeting a large animal in the forest must have been an uncanny experience. 'That was not a bear but a god!' This reasoning is of little use with regard to Athena's appearance as a swallow or Leukothea's as a seagull, yet Wilamowitz still attempts to corroborate his theory by relating his own epiphany with Pan. While riding a horse in Arcadia, a bucolic area of Greece, he saw a goat in a tree.[31] Evidently, this is not very helpful, so we turn to our next scholar.

We enter a different world with the publication of the first volume of the history of Greek religion by Martin P. Nilsson (1874–1967) in 1941, which marked the start of the author's domination of this area of study during the middle third of the 20th century.[32] Nilsson refers to de Visser merely for the material and notes that the gods were often represented in theriomorphic shape, particularly the less important ones.[33] Overall, he is rather sceptical about the worship of theriomorphic gods and rejects the explanation of totemism, yet he does give a few examples.[34] An intriguing one is the worship of Zeus in various serpentine forms, such as Zeus Meilichios and Zeus Ktesios.[35] The association of these gods with the household and its wealth suggests that these forms go far back in history, and a connection with well-attested house snakes is plausible.[36] We might add that it is probable that these anguiform (snake-shaped) gods may even have influenced the conception of the healing hero/god Asclepius as a snake, given that he was invoked for physical well-being (see this volume, Chapter 13).[37] Elsewhere in his book Nilsson suggests that Poseidon was represented as both a horse and a bull.[38] He also briefly discusses the bird epiphany of Athena and suggests a Minoan background.[39] Compared to Wilamowitz, though, Nilsson is clearly less inclined to theriomorphic gods, and he categorically states that there is no real evidence for an animal cult in ancient Greece.[40]

This scepticism grew in the last decades of the 20th century. For instance, in his famous 1986 essay on the body of the gods, Jean-Pierre Vernant (1914–2007) gives no credence to possible theriomorphic shapes of divinities.[41] The case is slightly different in the history of Greek religion written by Walter Burkert (1931–2015), which replaced Nilsson's text as the authoritative handbook in the final years of the century because it was seen as more concise, better written, and more up-to-date; moreover, it was translated into English in 1985.[42] Given Burkert's fascination with sacrifice, he unsurprisingly sees it as key to the association between gods and animals.[43] This might be one aspect of divine theriomorphism but hardly the sole or even the most likely one, as we shall see below.

The 21st century

The situation has changed dramatically in the current century with the appearance of several studies offering new perspectives on Greek religion from Henk Versnel and Robert Parker, even though neither discusses the connection between gods and animals in their recent books.[44] The first to open new vistas – in a study of Greek myths of metamorphosis – was Richard Buxton.[45] From his discussion, I note the following four points. First, unlike earlier scholars who concentrated on theriomorphism itself, Buxton focuses on the reactions of the human observers of theriomorphic epiphanies, as reported by the poets. He notes the importance of the Greek word *thambos* in these descriptions, which he renders as 'astonishment', yet the English word (which the *Oxford English Dictionary* defines as 'surprise' and 'amazement') does not convey the notion of fear that can also be part of *thambos*. [46] It is important to realise that Greeks did not experience theriomorphic epiphanies with mere astonishment, as we do in the case of an impressive trick by an illusionist. Indeed, such epiphanies could be profoundly unsettling events.

Second, Buxton accepts de Visser's division of the evidence for non-anthropomorphic representations of divinity in stones, trees, and animals, even as he points out fuzzy edges in the material.[47] But he rightly argues against de Visser's evolutionistic idea of a development from a belief in gods embodied in material phenomena to one principally of anthropomorphism and suggests that we should think instead of a coexistence of both modes of representation, even though Greek religion is predominantly anthropomorphic.[48] Third, Buxton notes that it is sometimes impossible to decide, on the basis of the text, whether it is a transformation or a comparison that is at stake. We should be wary of cutting the knot too hastily, which 'would reduce the subtle differentiations of the Homeric narrative to a flat homogeneity'.[49] Fourth, Buxton notes a difference between ritual and myth in connection with divine metamorphosis in which mythical narratives can express a sense of danger and promise not found in ritual.[50] These are important suggestions, and we will return to some of them.[51]

Like Buxton, Georgia Petridou is interested in metamorphosis, but in her case from the perspective of epiphany. She divides her material into three categories: avian, reptilian, and bovine epiphanies, the last of which we discuss below.[52] Strikingly, she is much more reluctant than earlier scholars to accept the reality of avian metamorphoses.[53] Certainly, there are cases where bird-like departure is a simile, as with Poseidon leaving 'as a hawk, swift of flight', but it is hard to see Athena and Apollo sitting on a tree branch in human form instead of 'like vultures', let alone Athena on a roof-beam.[54] We have evidence, as Petridou also notes, of the cult of Athena Aithuia ('seagull') in Megara, but also of a Megarian myth about the metamorphosis of Athena into a seagull to hide the primeval Athenian king Cecrops and bring him to Megara.[55] In any case, Athena's bird shape dovetails with her close association with the owl. Yet, despite the numerous representations of owls on their vases, we do not know exactly how Athenians interpreted the bird.[56] Did they see Athena herself in each and every owl on their ceramics? Would they have regarded the birds with religious awe? Or did these images merely remind them of the goddess? Whatever the case, while precise details elude us, there is a close connection between the goddess and this particular bird.

Petridou turns next to reptiles.[57] Again, she is cautious and in the case of Asclepius even wonders whether the Greeks saw his snake as a symbol of the god's presence, as fragments of his divine essence, or as his actual zoomorphic manifestation.[58] Although she concedes that there are arguments to support each case, she concludes that, for the devotees in Asclepius' temples, the snakes are 'signifiers of the divine presence'.[59]

The most recent and ambitious study of divine zoomorphism is by Julia Kindt, who concentrates her discussion on the problem of the theriomorphic divine body.[60] She poses the important question: 'What is the symbolic significance of the divine body imagined fully or partially as an animal body?'[61] She adduces several examples, taken from cult and the Roman era, to illustrate the ideas of the ancient Greeks about the suitability of an animal body for divinities, and rightly concludes that the Greeks drew on the animal body to represent their divinities in various ways.[62]

Importantly, Kindt observes that the 'animal form seems reserved for those aspects of divinity that lie beyond the human realm'; in other words, 'divine zoomorphism defamiliarises'.[63] Yet, the advantage of their theriomorphic shape is that they remain available for physical interaction. However, Kindt argues, it is not necessary for the gods to revert to their anthropomorphic shape to permit human-to-human interaction.[64] The admittedly exceptional case of Zeus and Leda is one example.[65] It is true, though, that the gods lose their individuality when transformed into animals.[66] Moreover, the temporary or permanent, whole or partly theriomorphic shape bridges the ultimately insurmountable boundary between humanity and animality. Hybrid divinities, such as Pan and Dionysus, per Kindt, represent an ontological monstrosity, even though I would not equate these two divinities in this manner, as Dionysus, unlike Pan, is always visually represented in anthropomorphic form.[67] In sum, the theriomorphic manifestations show that, for the Greeks, divine essence cannot be reduced to a single shape or form, or even a single order of being.[68]

Equine and bovine divine manifestations: Poseidon and Dionysus

Having looked at the various discussions of the 120 years, we now focus on horses and bulls, the two animals most associated with theriomorphic manifestations of the major gods. Wilamowitz calls the horse shape 'the most widespread and the most significant' (*'am verbreitetsten und bedeutsamsten'*) of the various forms.[69] Disappointingly, though, he provides very little Greek evidence for his thesis. His main example is Hippo from Euripides' drama *Wise Melanippe*, whom Zeus turned into a horse on the birth of her daughter Melanippe ('black mare').[70] Understandably, he also points to Euripides' description of the Theban twins Amphion and Zethos as 'white colts of Zeus' in *Antiope*, [71] a designation that that the pair share with the Dioscuri.[72] It is clear, though, that neither the twins nor the Dioscuri were worshipped as horses. Yet, the equine connection goes back to Indo-European times, as comparative evidence from Indian, Germanic, and Lithuanian traditions shows.[73] In all these cases, though, we find horse-riding twins – not horses, let alone gods, worshipped in the shape of horses. As a man of his totemistic era, Wilamowitz was too quick to see earlier theriomorphic manifestations of later anthropomorphic gods.

Wilamowitz is more convincing when he discusses Poseidon. Although he notes that this god sometimes appeared in horse shape, he does not elaborate. Yet, we have an interesting case in the Arcadian myth that Poseidon morphed into a stallion to mate with Demeter, thus begetting the first horse, Arion (or Erion). The Thessalians rationalised this myth by having their first horse, Skyphios, born from a blow from Poseidon's trident or his accidental ejaculation. The Arcadian myth must be very old – the horse appears on early local coins and the story has clear Indian parallels.[74] Similar equine mating is attested for Kronos and Philyra, the parents of the centaur Chiron (on which, see also this volume, Chapter 11).[75] This early myth clearly serves to explain the horse shape of the centaurs, but the motif of mating in equine form may stem from the Arcadian myth, which seems to be older. We might wonder whether Poseidon's Homeric epithet *kyanochaita* (literally 'dark-maned' – also applied to Boreas as a horse in the *Iliad*) originally derives from a description of a hippomorphic shape of Poseidon.[76] Given the myth of the man-eating horses of Diomedes, the Greeks were apparently very taken with the wild, nervous, and powerful nature of the horse.[77] We may well have to look in this direction for the connection of Poseidon and the horse. Only a powerful god like Poseidon could master such fierce animals, as is also attested by his frequent epithet Hippius ('of the horse'), but there is nothing to suggest that the Greeks originally worshipped him in horse shape.[78]

Nilsson, too, notes Poseidon's connections to the horse and observes that these were especially prominent in ancient mainland landscapes, but also that in Ionia he was particularly associated with the bull.[79] He cites as supporting evidence Poseidon's epithet Taureios ('of the bull'), the name Tauria for one of his festivals, and the fact that young wine pourers in Ephesos were called *tauroi* ('bulls').[80] Moreover, it was Poseidon who sent the bull that frightened the horses of Hippolytos in Euripides' drama, just as Poseidon sent the bull with which Pasiphae fell in love.[81] From these details, Nilsson concludes that Poseidon was represented, once upon a time, in 'horse and probably also in bull shape' ('*in Pferde- und wohl auch in Stiergestalt*').[82]

Of the two shapes, the bull is perhaps easier to understand. Yet, it is important to differentiate: not every 'divine' bull has the same meaning for his worshippers. Poseidon's association with the bull probably points to the sphere of war. Artemis Tauropolos ('bull-ranger') was the goddess of both the Macedonian army and the Diadochs. Surprisingly, this connection between Artemis and a bull has received very little attention so far, even though it is also attested on coins in Macedonia and other parts of Greece.[83] As Fritz Graf persuasively argues, the bull reflects men's associations, given that the ritual of Artemis Tauropolos in Halai shows a background in male initiation.[84] As Poseidon was linked to initiation and men's associations, the Poseidon/bull connection evokes indomitable force, which is obviously desirable in battle, just as ancient German and Celtic warriors wore bull helmets to draw on and project the bull's power.[85] It is well known that bulls can be very dangerous, an aspect of their nature that also figures in Greek mythology: witness the formidable Minotaur and the bronze, fire-breathing bulls yoked by Jason.[86] Similarly, the Greeks ascribed a whole or partial bull shape to some river gods, representing the violent force of waterways, especially in winter.[87]

Not surprisingly, both Wilamowitz and Nilsson briefly discuss the theriomorphic Dionysus, whereas, significantly, Burkert neglects to mention him.[88] Yet, if there is one god other than Zeus who is a shape-shifter, it is Dionysus. In his *Homeric Hymn*, he appears in the shape of a lion and a bear to frighten a band of unruly pirates, who jump overboard and are turned into dolphins – animals that often occur in a Dionysiac context.[89] In Euripides' *Bacchae*, he is invoked to appear as a bull, a snake, and a lion, but elsewhere in the play he appears – and is described or seen – as a bull.[90] Of these forms, the bull shape is clearly the most important and the only one that can also be found both in cult – that is, in statuary – and through his epithet Taurus ('bull').[91] The connection with the bull has often been discussed, and most scholars associate this connection with force and fertility.[92] This is a reasonable interpretation. Yet, a different aspect appears in an archaic hymn of the women in Elis:

Ἐλθεῖν, ἥρω Διόνυσε,
Ἀλείων ἐς ναὸν
ἁγνὸν σὺν Χαρίτεσσιν
ἐς ναὸν τῷ βοέῳ
ποδὶ θύων.'
'ἄξιε ταῦρε', 'ἄξιε ταῦρε'.

Come, Lord Dionysus,
to the holy temple of the Eleans,
with the Graces,
to the temple with bull
foot raging.
'Worthy bull', 'worthy bull'.[93]

This song is important in two respects, as it illustrates significant aspects of Dionysus' theriomorphic form. First, it clearly summons the god, as was traditional in such songs.[94] In other words, the women seek the epiphany of Dionysus. This epiphanic aspect of the god is an important part of his essence, as Albert Henrichs (1942–2017) stresses in some of his last articles.[95] Second, the epiphanic moment does not appear in the middle of nowhere but literally among Dionysus' worshippers. Rather than the whole body, the god's feet are the focus, which in itself is not unusual.[96] Nor are the feet singled out by chance. As scholars have long noted, they are a reference to the dancing of Dionysus amid his worshippers.[97] It is significant that the song summons Dionysus in bull form: surely the bull is the leader of the ecstatic maenadic 'herd', just as Dionysus is charmed 'by the dancing herds of even wild beasts'.[98]

At the end of his *Homeric Hymn*, Dionysus presents himself as follows: 'I am Dionysus the mighty roarer, whom Cadmus' daughter Semele gave birth to, having made love to Zeus.'[99] We might overlook this 'mighty roarer', but Pindar calls the god Eriboas ('loud-shouter').[100] Apparently, we are to think of a roaring lion or a bellowing bull, not a friendly, domesticated pet. It is in his epiphany, so characteristic of this god (see above), that he displays his terrifying might. The bull's bellowing and raging are symbolic of the ecstatic dancing of the maenads, which can eventually lead to mania and destruction, as in the *Bacchae*, but also in other Greek myths connected with Dionysus, such as those of the Minyads and the Proetids.[101]

This connection with bulls is also evident in Euripides' *Cretans*, which may have been performed in the 430s BCE.[102] Granted, the chorus are initiates of Zeus Idaios and refer to Zagreus and the Kouretes, but that may be seen as 'local colour'. Yet, the description of the rites is very Dionysiac, even including the *ōmophagia*. For us, it is interesting to see that the chorus mentions that they were first a *mystēs*, then a *boutēs* (presumably the same as a *boukolos*), and then a *bakchos*; later sources show that the *boukolos* was indeed a kind of mid-range Bacchic initiate.[103] In other words, there seems to be a strong connection here between the Dionysiac worshippers and the world of cows and oxen.

There is other evidence that the ecstatic worshippers of Dionysus imagined (sometimes even represented) themselves as members of a herd, which seems to be an archaic feature of Dionysiac worship.[104] In the very first mention of Dionysus in Greek literature, in Book Six of the *Iliad*, 'murderous Lycurgus' chases the god's nurses, presumably maenads, 'with an ox-goad', which makes sense when the worshippers are seen as the god's 'herd'.[105] This myth is clearly old, as it also occurs in Eumelus' *Europia*. [106] Consequently, the Dionysus/cow/oxen connection points to maenadic rituals dating from well before Homer.

In Aeschylus' *Edonians*, the (probably) maenadic ritual is described as follows: 'and the twang of strings resounds; and terrifying imitators of the voice of bulls bellow in response from somewhere out of sight'.[107] Macedonian women wear horns in imitation of Dionysus.[108] The god's bull shape, then, is part of a complicated interplay of myth and ritual that is not easily untangled. Yet here, too, we should remain alert to different contexts. Dionysus is never imagined as a bull on the thousands of Athenian symposiastic vase paintings in which he appears.[109] Apparently, it was in the epiphany among his dancing worshippers, not at the symposium, where the bull manifestation was thought to be at home.

Conclusions

What might we conclude from our discussions and recent insights regarding the theriomorphic shape of the great Greek gods? I would like to make five main observations.

First, it is not without reason that we have concentrated on the major Greek gods. There is clearly a difference between them and gods lower on the divine pecking order, such as Pan or local manifestations of Zeus like Zeus Meilichios, who was often represented, as we saw, in anguiform. In the case of the lesser gods, we can regularly note differences in comparison to the sanctuaries and rituals of the great gods. For instance, Zeus Meilichios usually has a sacred precinct instead of a proper temple; his worshippers are individuals or family groups rather than the whole of the community; and his sacrifices do not always fit the normal standard ritual but often consist of wineless sacrifices and victims burnt partially or whole.[110] In other words, a theriomorphic shape goes together with non-standard ritual features.

We can also see this clearly with another theriomorphic divinity. Pausanias tells us that, when travelling through Arcadia, he came to the sanctuary of Eurynome, not far from Phigalia, which was situated in a dense wood of cypresses and opened only once a year. Unfortunately for our traveller, he was not there at the time of the festival, but he heard from the Phigalians that 'golden chains bind the wooden statue that represents a woman until the hips but below that she is like a fish'.[111] Eurynome, so still the Phigalians, is the epithet of Artemis, but Pausanias himself cannot believe that the statue has anything to do with Artemis and, on the basis of the fish tail, interprets it as that of an oceanid mentioned in the *Iliad*. [112]

It is curious to find a fish-tailed goddess in the wooded mountains of Arcadia, and Nilsson persuasively surmised that the archaic statue must have looked like a herm tailing off at the end – and he has been followed by Fritz Graf.[113] The latter has shown that several statues of Artemis were bound and that these usually have an archaic or uncanny appearance. The associated myths often point to human sacrifice, and the rituals connected with these statues are nonstandard, such as the closure of their sanctuaries save for one day of the year, as in the case of Eurynome, and Saturnalia-like festivals.[114] The theriomorphic body of divinities, then, puts them in opposition to the anthropomorphic ones and is a signifier of their alterity, which is confirmed and supported by the nonstandard rituals connected with them. Surely, all divinities were different, but some were clearly more different than others.

Second, it is typical of recent investigations into divine theriomorphism that they do not differentiate much in time with regard to the evidence. Yet, there are diachronic aspects that we should consider. First, we know that when the proto-Greeks invaded the Greek mainland, they brought with them a body of myths and mythological motifs. These are not easy to reconstruct, but close parallels with the Indian tradition of the mating by Poseidon and Demeter in horse form strongly suggest that theriomorphic mating was one.[115] Although the influence of the ancient Near East cannot be excluded (see above), the same Indo-European background can perhaps be inferred in departures as birds. These have a close parallel in Norse mythology, where at the end of a riddle contest the god Óðin 'made off in the form of a falcon'; similarly, when stealing the skaldic mead from Suttung, he took the shape of an eagle and escaped.[116] Martin West, to whom I owe the first example, notes that not all Norse gods could fly, and the same observation can be made about ancient Greece.[117] Whereas, in Homer, Poseidon, Athena, and Apollo can take off as birds, this is never said of other great gods, such as Zeus and Hera. Were they too important to be imagined as small birds?

A second diachronic aspect is the historical development within Greek religion. One cannot escape the impression that the divine theriomorphic shape and moment belong to an older layer of Greek religion, even as that layer survives in numerous later texts and areas. The growing focus on humankind, started by the sophists, gradually widened the gap between humans and animals, and, in the course of time, divine theriomorphism developed into a literary motif rather than remaining a feature of living belief.[118] It is unimaginable that the famous sculptors of the late classical era would make theriomorphic statues of great gods, and in the Greek novel it is only peasants who believe in actual epiphany.[119] Admittedly, there is an exception to this rule. Even in the Roman Empire there was still room for new theriomorphic gods: witness Alexander of Abonuteichus' invention of the snake god Glycon (on Glycon, see also this volume, Chapter 11).[120] Yet, it is not happenstance that our main source is a satiric pamphlet by Lucian, who pokes fun at this theriomorphic new god, rather than a serious study of the deity and his prophet. Whereas earlier generations of scholars preferred to think of a kind of evolution from theriomorphism to anthropomorphism in the case of the gods, I suggest we should think of an internal development in Greek religion that, however, was never absolute. Anthropomorphic and theriomorphic shapes coexisted until the end of pagan religion.[121]

Third, in our material we can observe a difference between myth and cult. As Albert Henrichs observes, 'with few exceptions (e.g. Dionysus' bovine epiphanies), divine theriomorphism is a feature of myth rather than cult'.[122] It is indeed striking how few examples of divine zoomorphism we find in rituals or cultic statues, even though they are not absent, as we have seen. On the other hand, myth teems with examples of theriomorphic moments. It is obvious, of course, that theriomorphic shapes and moments – especially multiple ones – are much easier on the narrative level than on a cultic level. There is, for example, the well-known case of Thetis changing shape multiple times to escape a wedding with Peleus or, less familiar, the many metamorphoses of Nemesis and Metis to avoid sex with Zeus.[123]

However, we have to differentiate on the level of myth regarding the various divinities and occasions. Once again, we must first note that some divinities are more prone to theriomorphic shape-shifting than others. For reasons that are unclear, male deities, such as Zeus, Poseidon, and Dionysus, are more often attested as shape-shifters than the female Hera, Athena, Artemis, or Aphrodite.[124] In addition to this difference, we must note the variations in the reasons for the motif. Thus, Apollo's transformation into a dolphin (see above) is clearly aetiological in order to explain the god's epithet Delphinios.[125] However, there is another case of a theriomorphic Apollo. According to Callimachus, in his *Hymn to Apollo*, the god in the form of a raven led Battos and his followers to Cyrene.[126] Neither Pindar nor Herodotus mentions the bird, but Callimachus may well be relating an original detail of the Cyrenean foundation legend, since a fragment of a sixth-century Cyrenean krater contains a dedication to 'Apollo the Raven'.[127] As ravens also occur in other traditions about Libya, the presence of Apollo as a raven in the foundation myth seems likely – all the more so because the raven is Apollo's spy in Hesiod.[128]

In the case of Poseidon, we have seen his change into a stallion to approach Demeter, but, according to a fairly late myth, he also changed into a ram to mate with Theophane as a ewe, a union that produced the famous ram with the golden fleece that was sought by the Argonauts. This metamorphosis, though, looks like an imitation of his mating as a stallion.[129] It is different with Zeus, who often morphs into different animals.[130] We have already noted the case of Leda, but Zeus also changed into a swan to make love to Nemesis, transformed himself into a bull to abduct Europa, and became a snake to father Aratus and Alexander the Great.[131] Georgia Petridou has argued convincingly that such divine transformations point to the ontological differences between mortals and immortals. It was impossible for a divinity to have intercourse with a mortal in his or her original shape: when Zeus revealed himself to Semele in his full divine glory, the result was her instantaneous death.[132] The intercourse between Peleus and Thetis is the exception that confirms this rule, presumably because she is a lesser divinity. These erotic narratives about divine theriomorphism, then, call attention (albeit indirectly) to the fundamental differences between the mortal body and the immortal body.[133]

Dionysus, our final example, is more complicated. On the one hand, the successive transformations in his *Homeric Hymn* show his divine muscle. But this is also a frightening power. As we have connected the theriomorphic forms of some lower gods with their non-standard rituals (see above), we may connect Dionysus' terrifying appearance as a bull with the fact that on various Greek islands he was associated with murder and human sacrifice and worshipped under the less than complimentary epithets of Omestes ('eater of raw meat'), Omadios (which probably had a similar meaning), and Anthroporrhaistes ('man destroyer').[134] On Chios, he also had a statue that was bound (see above), while his festival, the Dionysia, displayed the characteristics of an *Ausnahmefest*. As Aelian mentions raging women on Chios, it is not a stretch to connect them with Dionysus Omestes.[135] In Macedonia, the god had the epithet Agrios ('savage'), and an important Dionysiac festival was called the Agrio(a)nia in Boeotia and on the Peloponnese, from where it was exported to many Greek colonies.[136] Myths about murder and dismemberment played an important role in this festival. Evidently, we find here an old layer in the history of the god.[137] For our purpose, it is enough to stress that Dionysus clearly had a dangerous, frightening side, which was probably linked to his form as a bull.

Fourth, whereas Christian theologians thought long and wrote much about the body of God, it is not easy to find what the Greeks thought about the bodies of their divinities, let alone the theriomorphic divine body.[138] As we have seen, scholars have had many different ideas in this respect. In his brief discussion, Burkert usefully distinguishes 'a god named, described, represented and worshipped in animal form, a real animal worshipped as a god, animal symbols and animal masks in the cult, and finally the consecrated animal destined for sacrifice'.[139] It should now be apparent that earlier discussions often failed in this process of differentiating – as, in a way, did Burkert himself.

It is evident that some great Greek gods were closely connected with animals. We can see it from their epithets, such as Poseidon Hippius, Dionysus Taurus, and Artemis Elaphia, discussed above. Yet, we can now also see that these epithets refer to different backgrounds: Poseidon was closely connected with the power of the horse, Dionysus was thought to appear to his worshippers as a bull, and Artemis' connection with a deer probably derives from her hunting. Of all the gods, Dionysus seems to be the most closely identified with his animal for his worshippers. It is also true that sacrifice played a role in this connection. For example, Dionysus Eriphius ('of the kid') was worshipped under that epithet in Metapontum and Sparta and derived it from receiving well-attested sacrifices of kids.[140] In the case of other divinities, the sacrificial associations are even clearer. Hera had the epithet Aigophagos ('goat-eating') in Sparta, and Dionysus the epithets Taurophagos ('bull-eating'), presumably because of bull sacrifices (even though bulls were sacrificed to many other gods, too), and Aigobolos ('goat-shooting') in Boeotian Potniai, presumably due to goat sacrifices.[141] Yet, against Burkert, we also see that these sacrificial animals do not determine the nature of the god, and in several places may well be typically local features of the divinities concerned.

Finally, the divine/human/animal schema figured prominently in the titles of structuralist studies of the Golden Age of the Paris *équipe* of Jean-Pierre Vernant.[142] In general, it must be said, these studies focus surprisingly little on animals and gods, rather, they concentrate on mortals and what makes them human. Still, the structure is clearly hierarchical: animals at the bottom and gods at the top. Indeed, as signifiers, animals work rather well in myths that attempt to clarify the place of humans in the world, with human metamorphoses into animals virtually always signifying some sort of degradation from the human ontological status. The reason for divine metamorphosis into animal form is less clear. Why did Zeus have to morph into a swan in order to have sex with Leda? Could he not have appeared as a young man? Evidently, the change into an animal entails a lessening of status, but does it mean that these kinds of myth stress the inferiority of the animals? This is not immediately obvious. Perhaps, in earlier times, the distance between the three elements of the divine/human/animal schema was less pronounced?[143]

In the end, we must conclude that the theriomorphism of the major Greek gods serves different functions and cannot be reduced to a single idea. Undoubtedly, in several cases, theriomorphism underscores the difference from the mortal body, but in others it magnifies the status of the god and enhances his frightening nature. Or, very differently, it helps explain the birth of the hybrid centaurs or the epithet Delphinios of Apollo. The bodies of the great gods of ancient Greece, be they anthropomorphic or theriomorphic, still pose many questions.

Notes

1 I am most grateful to Bob Fowler and Julia Kindt for comments, and to Maria Merkeling for help with the English translation of this chapter.
2 I limit myself in the notes to the most recent literature so as not to overload the chapter with references.
3 See the classic study of Thomas 1983.
4 As an example, I mention here several books of my compatriot, the primatologist and ethologist Frans de Waal: Waal 2009, 2013, 2019.
5 For a survey of recent work, see Kindt 2017, but note also the reflections of Lloyd 2011.
6 Aston 2011. On centaurs, see also Bremmer 2012.
7 Bremmer and Erskine 2010; Clauss *et al.* 2016; Pironti and Bonnet 2017; Gagné and Herrero de Jáuregui 2019.
8 De Visser 1900.
9 See the reviews by Mauss 1900: 279–280; Farnell 1901: 105–1077; Marett 1901: 326–328; Reinach 1901: 459–460; Meyer 1902: 33–34.
10 For a good modern analysis of these concepts, see Insoll 2011.
11 Duyvendak 1931: 164–173; deVisser 1903.
12 For Wilamowitz-Moellendorff and the gods, see Bremmer 2019b: 9–12.
13 Wilamowitz-Moellendorff (1931–1932): Vol. 1: 140–155.

14 Hom. *Il.* 7.17–22, 59–60, 15.237–238; Hom *Od.* 1.319–323, 5.351–353, 22.239–240.
15 Hom. *Od.* 3.371–373.
16 *Hom. Hymn Ap.* 399–400.
17 For Minoan/Mycenaean influence, see Carter 1995: 287–292.
18 Hoffner 1998: 91 (§5); see also West 1997: 185.
19 Hom. *Il.* 6.155–195, for the Anatolian background, see, most recently, Bachvarova 2016: 421–426.
20 Hyg. *Fab.* 28; Apollod. 1.7.4; schol. Pind. *Pyth.* 4.156a; Simon 1981.
21 Elaphia(ia): Str. 8.3.12; Paus. 6.22.10–11.
22 Artemis Elaphebolos: Sapph. F 44A.9; *Hom Hymn Art.* 2; Soph. *Trach.* 213; Plut. *Mor.* 966A; *BCH* 1883, 263 (Pamphylia); *Arch. Deltion* 2 (1916): 263–268 (Hyampolis); *SEG* 39.855 (Patmos), 43.399 (Thasos); 62.397 (Ulcinium). Festival: Plut. *Mor.* 244e, 660d; *IG* IX.1.90. Athens: Athenaeus 14.646e (cakes); *Anecd. Bekker* 1.249.7–9 (sacrifice), doubted by Parker 2005: 468, but deer were more often sacrificed than is normally realised; cf. Bremmer 2019b: 334, 377.
23 Kahil 1984; Bremmer 2019b: 382–383.
24 *SEG* 9.13.12, 9.72.98. For this famous sacred law, see Dobias-Lalou 2000: 297–309, corrected in *CGRN* 99 (http://cgrn.ulg.ac.be/file/99/; accessed 27 August 2019). *Arkos* is a variation of *arktos*, as nouns like *arkullos* ('bear cub') and names like Arkoleon ('Bear-Lion') demonstrate; cf. Masson 1990, vol. 2: 617–620; Dobias-Lalou 2000: 61; add to her linguistic and onomastic analysis: *IG* XIV.1302, 1308; Slater on Ar. Byz. F 174b.
25 For the myth of Kallisto and its many variants, see Dowden 1989: 182–191; McPhee 1990; Jost 1998: 231–234 and Jost 2005b; Arrigoni 2004.
26 Cf. Bevan 1987: 17–21; Léger 2017: 121.
27 See, especially, the many studies of Lily Kahil, such as Kahil 1977: 86–98, 1983, 1988: 799–813. For the ritual, see Parker 2005: 228–249 (with full bibliography) and Waldner 2000.
28 Bachofen 1863.
29 Parker 2005: 246.
30 Pentikäinen 2007.
31 Wilamowitz-Moellendorff 1931–1932: Vol. 1: 151.
32 On Nilsson, see Bremmer 2019b: 13–16 (with bibliography).
33 Nilsson 1955: 212–216 ('Der Tierkult').
34 Rejection of totemism: Nilsson 1955: 215–216.
35 Jaillard 2004: 871–893; Gourmelen 2012; Ogden 2013: 279–309, whose suggestion that the anguiform cult originated in the later fifth century is improbable. For the identification of the snakes, see Diggle 2004 on Theophr. *Char.* 16.4.
36 Cf. Nilsson 1955: 198, 214, 402–406.
37 Asclepius as snake: Ogden 2013: 310–317; Petridou 2015: 92–95, 184–186.
38 Nilsson 1955: 450.
39 Nilsson 1955: 349. This is also considered possible by Burkert 1985: 40, although he does not really commit himself.
40 Nilsson 1955: 213.
41 Vernant 1986.
42 Burkert 1977.
43 For Burkert and sacrifice, see Bremmer 2019b: 329–331. Sacrifice as key: Burkert 1977: 65–66.
44 Versnel 2011; Parker 2011: 64–102.
45 Buxton 2009.
46 Richardson 1993 on Hom. *Il.* 24.482–483 and *Hom. Hymn Dem.* 188–190; Bourdel 1974; Aubriot 1989; Semenzato 2015. *Thambos* as astonishment: Buxton 2009: 164–168.
47 Buxton 2009: 187.

48 Buxton 2009: 187–189.
49 Buxton 2009: 46. See also Buxton 2004.
50 Buxton 2009: 190.
51 Buxton 2009: 177–190.
52 Petridou 2015: 87–98.
53 Petridou 2015: 87–91.
54 Poseidon: Hom. *Il.* 13.62: αὐτὸς δ’ ὥς τ’ἴρηξ ὠκύπτερος ὦρτο πέτεσθαι, with Janko 1991 *ad loc.*, Hom. *Il.* 19.349–50, *Od.* 5.51. Athena and Apollo: *Il.* 7.17–22, 58–60. Athena on a roofbeam: Hom *Od.* 22.239–240. In general, see also Heubeck *et al.* 1988 on Hom. *Od.* 3.371–372.
55 Petridou 2015: 90, where she also compares Athena Boudeia, but her translation of the epithet as 'the gull- or the storm-bird maiden' is probably incorrect. See Hornblower 2015 on Lycophron 359. For the evidence, see Paus. 1.5.4, 46.6; Hesych. ε 2737. For Megarian mythmaking in competition with Athens, see Bremmer 2014: 176–177.
56 Shapiro 1993; Watson 1998; Kreuzer 2010.
57 Petridou 2015: 91–96.
58 For Asclepius and the snake, see, most recently, Renberg 2017: Vol. 1: 215–216 (with bibliography).
59 Petridou 2015: 93.
60 Kindt 2019.
61 Kindt 2019: 159.
62 Kindt 2019: 166.
63 Kindt 2019: 163 and 164, respectively.
64 Kindt 2019: 165.
65 For the myth, see Eur. *Hel.* 17–19; Isoc. 10.59; Hyg. *Fab.* 77 and *Poet. astr.* 2.8; Luc. *Dial. D.* 20.14, *Charidemus* 7; schol. Hom. *Od.* 11.298; Kahil and Icard-Gianolio 1992.
66 Kindt 2019: 165–166.
67 Kindt 2019: 167.
68 Kindt 2019: 169.
69 Wilamowitz-Moellendorff 1931–1932: Vol. 1: 148.
70 Wilamowitz-Moellendorff 1931–1932: Vol. 1: 149; Eur. F 481.14–16 Kannicht.
71 Wilamowitz-Moellendorff 1931–1932: Vol. 1: 149–150.
72 Amphion and Zethos: Eur. F 223.127 Kannicht; see also Pherecydes *FGrH* 3 F 124 = F 124 Fowler; Eur. *HF* 29–30, *Phoen.* 606; Hesych. δ 1929. Dioscuri: Pind. *Pyth.* 1.66.
73 West 2007: 146, 186–191.
74 A(E)rion: Antimachus F 33 Matthews; Call. F 652 Pfeiffer; Paus. 8.25.4–10 and 42.1; Apollod. 3.6.8; *POxy.* 61.4096 fr. 10, re-edited by Rossum-Steenbeek 1997: 290; Hesych. α 7267; schol. Lycophron 152; Krauskopf 1981. Skyphios: Hesych. ι 791; schol. Pind. *Pyth.* 4.246b; *Etym. Magnum* 473.42; Mili 2015: 237. India: Burkert 1979: 127; O'Flaherty 1980: 174–178.
75 *Titanomachy* F 10 Bernabé = 9 Davies = Eumelus F 12 West; Pherecydes *FGrH* 3 F 50 = 50 Fowler; Apoll. Rhod. 2.1232; Verg. G. 3.92–94, 550; Ov. *Met.* 6.126; Plin. *HN* 7.197; Apollod. 1.2.4.
76 Hom. *Il.* 20.224, cf. Janko 1991 on Hom. *Il.* 13.563.
77 Kurtz 1975.
78 For the epithet, see Bremmer 2019b: 22 (with bibliography).
79 Nilsson 1955: 449–450. Graf 1985: 171–172 also notes this difference between the mainland and Ionia. Its prominence in Arcadia suggests a really old cult.
80 Poseidon Taureios: Hes. *Sc.* 104; Hesych. τ 253. Tauria: Hesych. τ 248. Tauroi: Apollonius Soph. 156.16 Bekker; Ath. 10.425c; Hesych. τ 250.
81 Hippolytos: Istros *FGrH* 334 F 8. Pasiphae: Diod. Sic. 4.77.1–4; Apollod. 3.15.8.

82   Nilsson 1955: 450.
83   Kahil 1984: 674; Graf 1985: 415, n. 58; Paglialunga 2012.
84   For Artemis Tauropolos, Halai, and the 'bull warriors', see Graf 1985: 413–416; note also Parker 2005: 241–242 (relation between Brauron and Halai), 481; Fowler 2000–2013: Vol. 2: 72–73 (Athena Tauropolos); Kalogeropoulos 2010: 167–182; Kalogeropoulos 2013; McInerney 2015.
85   Poseidon: Graf 1985: 207–208; Bremmer 2019b: 23–24. 'Bull warriors' and their helmets: Wackernagel 1959: 222–244; Zawadzka 2009. Compare the famous boar-tusk helmet of Odysseus (Hom. *Il.* 10.260–271): most recently, Whitley 2013: 399–401; Mödlinger 2013: 391–412; and the rich medieval material in Höfler 1992: 87–107.
86   Minotaur: Fowler 2000–2013: Vol 2: 468–474 (with recent bibliography). Jason and the bulls: Pherecydes *FGrH* 3 F 30, 112 = F 30, 112 Fowler; Herodoros *FGrH* 31 F 52 = F 52 Fowler; Apoll. Rhod., *Arg.* III; Apollod. 1.9.23.
87   Bremmer 2019a: 97–99.
88   Wilamowitz-Moellendorff 1931–1932: Vol. 1: 147–148; Nilsson 1955: 156, 571; Burkert 1985: 161–167.
89   Dionysus: *Hom. Hymn Dion.* 44–48. Context: Csapo 2003; Beaulieu 2016; Lightfoot 2019: 481–491.
90   Eur. *Bacch.* 1017–1019 (bull, snake, and lion), 100, 618, 920–922 (bull).
91   Statues: Ath. 11.476a. Taurus Lycoph. 209; *SEG* 32.552.
92   For a full collection of evidence, see Farnell 1909: 97–98, 250–251, 284–285; Otto 1933: 153–155. Iconographical material: Bérard 1976: 61–78; Jaccottet 2003: Vol. 1: 102–103; Aston 2011: 127–132; Hornblower 2015 on Lycophron 209. The cult of Theos Tauros in Thespiae, which is often cited in the older literature, is actually linked to the Roman senatorial family of the Statilii Tauri; cf. Marchand 2013.
93   Plut. *Mor.* 299B. For text, translation, and commentary, see Furley and Bremer 2001: Vol. 1: 369–372; Vol. 2: 373–377, who unpersuasively interpret the bull as a sacrificial animal. See also Schlesier 2002.
94   Nisbet and Hubbard 1991 on Hor. *Carm.* 1.2.18; Austin and Olson 2004 on Ar. *Thesm.* 315–317.
95   Henrichs 2019a and 2019c.
96   Fraenkel 1957: 204, n. 4.
97   Scullion 1998: 101–104.
98   Leader: Eur. *Ba.* 1022–1023. Dancing herds: Pind. F 70b.22–3 Maehler.
99   *Hom. Hymn Dion.* 56–57.
100 Dionysus: *Hom. Hymn Dion* 36–37 West. Eriboas: Pind. F 75.10 Maehler.
101 Eur. *Bacch.* 748–749; Bremmer 2019b: 39–41 (with bibliography).
102 Eur. F 472.9–19 Kannicht; cf. Casadio 1990; Cropp *et al.* 1995: 58–60, 67–70; Bernabé 2004; Collard and Cropp 2008: 536–539 (with notes and bibliography).
103 For the *boukolos*, see also Eur. *Antiope* F 203 with Kannicht *ad loc.*; Cratinus, *Boukoloi* F 17–22. Initiate: *Orphic Hymns* 1.10, 31.7; Jaccottet 2003: Vol. 2: 182–190.
104 Lycophron 1238 with schol. *ad loc.*; Scullion 2001: 213–218.
105 Nurses: as persuasively argued by Fowler 2000–2013: Vol. 2: 372–373. Ox-goad: Hom. *Il.* 6.135–136: θεινόμεναι βουπλῆγι.
106 Eumelus, F 27 West; cf. West 2011: 380.
107 Aesch. F 57.8–11 Radt, trans. Sommerstein.
108 Lycoph. 1238 with schol. *ad loc.*
109 As noted by Heinemann 2016: 71.
110 Cf. Henrichs 2019b: 142–143.
111 Paus. 8.41.6: τῶν Φιγαλέων δ᾽ ἤκουσα ὡς χρυσαῖ τε τὸ ξόανον συνδέουσιν ἁλύσεις καὶ εἰκὼν γυναικὸς τὰ ἄχρι τῶν γλουτῶν, τὸ ἀπὸ τούτου δέ ἐστιν ἰχθύς.
112 Hom. *Il*.18.398.

113 Nilsson 1906: 230; Graf 1985: 85, n. 76.
114 Graf 1985: 81–96. See also Faraone 1992: 136–140; Icard-Gianolio 2004: 468–471; Eich 2011: 371–399; Boschung 2015: 281–305.
115 For the Indo-European heritage of horses and horse imagery in Greek epic and myth, see Platte 2017.
116 Falcon: *Hervarar saga* 10 *ad fin*. Skaldic mead: 'This myth is preserved fragmentary in *Hávamál*, st 104–110 and in the skaldic poem *Haustlöng*, but best in Snorri's *Edda, Skáldskaparmál* 57–58' (personal email communication, Olof Sundquist, 18 August 2019).
117 West 2007: 102–103.
118 See many contributions in Alexandridis *et al*. 2008.
119 Hägg 2004: 146.
120 The classic study of Glycon is Robert 1980: 393–421. For further bibliography, see Oesterheld 2008: 129–136; Petsalis-Diomidis 2010: 43–49; Bendlin 2011: 233.
121 Cf. Buxton 2009: 189–190.
122 Henrichs 2019b: 374, n. 55; cf.: 'Dionysus the great exception in ritual: he is anything and everything. We were all taught by structuralists to think that he is the god of opposites (however that works): perhaps it is better to say he is the god of metaphor!' (personal email communication, Bob Fowler, 30 August 2019).
123 Thetis: West 2013: 72. Nemesis: *Cypria* F 9 Bernabé = 7 Davies = 10 West. Metis: Apollod. 1.3.6.
124 I agree with Griffiths 1960 that the gods' flight to Egypt in animal shapes betrays Egyptian, presumably Alexandrian, influence, as the presence of the cat (Ovid) and the ibis (Plutarch) among those animals clearly shows; cf. Ov. *Met*. 5.325–331; Plut. *De Is. et Os*. 379e; Anton. Lib. 28: Apollod. 1.6.3; Lucian *Sacr*. 14.
125 Cf. Csapo 2003: 90; Polinskaya 2013: 222–223. For Apollo Delphinios, see Graf 1979, who notes that the precise meaning of Delphinios is unclear but almost certainly has nothing to do with dolphins.
126 Callim. *Hymn* 2.66.
127 *SEG* 44.1541, no. 1; cf. Parker 2017: 27.
128 Libya: Williams 1978: 64, who compares Heraclides Ponticus (rather Heraclides Lembus 17 Dilts) and Str. 17.1.43. Spy: Hesiod F 60 Merkelbach/West. Pindar's *skopos* in *Pyth*. 3.27 probably alludes to the story; cf. Young 1968: 37–38.
129 Ov. *Met*. 6.117; Hyg. *Fab*. 188.
130 Is it chance that Óðin is also famous for his shape-shifting, even if the manner of doing so is different? Cf. *Ynglinga saga* 7, trans. Lindow: 'Óðin could shift his appearance. When he did so his body would lie here as if he were asleep or dead; but he himself, in an instant, in the shape of a bird or animal, a fish or a serpent, went to distant countries on his or other men's errands. He was also able with mere words to extinguish fires, to calm the sea, and turn the winds any way he pleased.'
131 Nemesis: Isoc. 10.59; Hyg. *Poet. astr*. 2.8; Apollod. 3.107. Europa: Hesiod F 140 Merkelbach/West; Bacchyl. F 10 Maehler; Phrynichus *TrGF* 3 F 16; Lycoph. 1296–1311; Moschos, *Europa*; cf. Buxton 2009: 126–131; Robertson 1988. Aratus: Paus. 4.14.7–8. Alexander: Just. *Epit*. 11.11; Plut. *Alex*. 3.1–4; Paus. 4.14.7–8; Arr. *Anab*. 3.3.2.
132 Pind. *Ol*. 2.22–27; Eur. *Bacch*. 1–9; Apollod. 3.4.3.
133 Petridou 2015: 244.
134 For the latter epithet, see Georgoudi 2011.
135 Ael. *VH* 3.42.
136 Dionysus Agrius: *SEG* 48.748.IV.
137 See the detailed discussion in Graf 1985: 74–96; add Hellanicus F 160A Fowler (Dionysus Omestes on Lesbos); Henrichs 2019b: 46–56 (Themistocles' alleged human sacrifice as reported by Phaenias of Lesbos). Agrio(a)nia: Bremmer 2019b: 38–41.

138 Markschies 2016; but cf. Osborne 2011: 185–215.
139 Burkert 1985: 161–167.
140 Dionysus Eriphius: Apollod. *FGrH* 244 F 132; Hesych. ε 1000, 5906 (Meta-
     pontum); Herodian, *Peri orthographias* 3.2, p. 502 Lentz (Sparta). Kids: *CGRN* 21
     (Athens), 86 and 146 (Kos), 116 (Lindos).
141 Hera: Paus. 3.15.9. Dionysus Taurophagos: Soph. F 668 Radt; Hesych. τ 254.
     Dionysus Aigobolos: Paus. 9.8.1.
142 Vernant 1974: 141–176 (titled 'Entre bêtes et dieux', originally the introduction
     to Detienne (1972b)), followed by Detienne 1972a: 231–246 and Vidal-Naquet
     1975, with the latter's title perhaps inspired by F. A. Ossendowski's travelogue
     Bêtes, hommes et dieux: à travers la Mongolie interdite (1924).
143 For Arcadia, this is persuasively argued by Jost 2005a.

Bibliography

Alexandridis, A., M. Wild, and L. Winkler-Horaček (eds.) (2008) *Mensch und Tier in der
     Antike*. Wiesbaden.
Arrigoni, G. (2004) 'Un mito enigmatico: la Lyssa di Kallisto', in G. Sena Chiesa and E.
     A. Arslan (eds.) *Miti greci. Archeologia e pittura dalla Magna Grecia al collezionismo*.
     Milano, 236–238.
Aston, E. (2011) *Mixanthrôpoi. Animal–Human Hybrid Deities in Greek Religion*. Liège.
Aubriot, D. (1989) 'Remarques sur l'usage de θάμβος et des mots apparentés dans
     l'*Iliade*', *Orpheus* 10, 249–260.
Austin, C. and S. D. Olson (2004) *Aristophanes. Thesmophoriazusae. Edited with Introduc-
     tion and Commentary*. Oxford.
Bachofen, J. J. (1863) *Der Bär in den Religionen des Altertums*. Basel (new edn. in Bollinger, A.
     and K. Meuli (eds.) (2020) *J. J. Bachofen. Gesammelte Werke*. Vol. 5. Basel, 117–186).
Bachvarova, M. (2016) *From Hittite to Homer*. Cambridge.
Beaulieu, M.-C. (2016) 'The dolphin in classical mythology and religion', in P.A.
     Johnston, A. Mastrocinque, and S. Papaioannou (eds.) *Animals in Greek and Roman
     Religion and Myth*. Cambridge, 237–253.
Bendlin, A. (2011) 'On the uses and disadvantages of divination: oracles and their lit-
     erary representations in the time of the Second Sophistic', in J. North and S. Price
     (eds.) *The Religious History of the Roman Empire*. Oxford, 175–250.
Bérard, C. (1976) 'Axie taure', in *Mélanges d'histoire ancienne et d'archéologie, offerts à Paul
     Collart*. Lausanne, 61–78.
Bernabé, A. (2004) 'Un fragmento de Los Cretenses de Eurípides', in J. López Férez
     (ed.) *La tragedia griega en sus textos*. Madrid, 257–286.
Bevan, E. (1987) 'The goddess Artemis, and the dedication of bears in sanctuaries',
     Annual of the British School at Athens 82, 17–12.
Boschung, D. (2015) 'Unheimliche Statuen und ihre Bändigung', in D. Boschung and
     C. Vorster (eds.) *Leibhafte Kunst. Statuen und kulturelle Identität*. Paderborn, 281–305.
Bourdel, C. (1974) 'Τάρβος et θάμβος chez Homère', *Annales de la Faculté des Lettres et
     Sciences humaines de Nice* 21, 113–119.
Bremmer, J. N. (2012) 'Greek demons of the wilderness: the case of the centaurs', in L.
     Feldt (ed.) *Wilderness Mythologies*. Berlin, 25–53.
Bremmer, J. N. (2014) *Initiation into the Mysteries of the Ancient World*. Berlin.
Bremmer, J. N. (2019a) 'Rivers and river gods in ancient Greek religion and culture', in
     T. S. Scheer (ed.) *Nature – Myth – Religion in Ancient Greece*. Stuttgart, 89–112.

Bremmer, J. N. (2019b) *The World of Greek Religion and Mythology*. Tübingen.

Bremmer, J. N. and A. Erskine (eds.) (2010) *The Gods of Ancient Greece*. Edinburgh.

Burkert, W. (1977) *Griechische Religion der archaischen und klassischen Epoche*. Stuttgart.

Burkert, W. (1979) *Structure and History in Greek Mythology and Ritual*. Berkeley, Calif.

Burkert, W. (1985) *Greek Religion*, trans. J. Raffan. Oxford.

Buxton, R. (2004) 'Similes and other likenesses', in R. L. Fowler (ed.) *The Cambridge Companion to Homer*. Cambridge, 139–155.

Buxton, R. (2009) *Forms of Astonishment. Greek Myths of Metamorphosis*. Oxford.

Carter, J. B. (1995) 'Ancestor cult and the occasion of Homeric performance', in J. B. Carter and S. P. Morris (eds.) *The Ages of Homer*. Austin, Tex., 285–312.

Casadio, G. (1990) 'I *Cretesi* di Euripide a l'ascesi orfica', *Didattica del Classico* 2, 278–310.

Clauss, J. J., M. Cuypers, and A. Kahane (eds.) (2016) *The Gods of Greek Hexameter Poetry. From the Archaic Age to Late Antiquity and Beyond*. Stuttgart.

Collard, C. and M. Cropp (2008) *Euripides. Fragments I*. Cambridge.

Cropp, M., C. Collard, and K. H. Lee (1995) *Euripides. Selected Fragmentary Plays I*. Warminster.

Csapo, E. (2003) 'Dolphins of Dionysus', in E. Csapo and M. C. Miller (eds.) *Poetry, Theory, Praxis*. Oxford, 69–98.

Detienne, M. (1972a) 'Entre bêtes et dieux', *Nouvelle Revue de Psychoanalyse* 6, 231–246 (rev. in Detienne, M. (1977) *Dionysos mis à mort*. Paris, 133–160).

Detienne, M. (1972b) *Les Jardins d'Adonis: La mythologie des aromates en Grèce*. Paris.

Diggle, J. (2004) *Theophrastus. Characters. Edited with Introduction, Translation and Commentary*. Cambridge.

Dobias-Lalou, C. (2000) *Le Dialecte des inscriptions grecques de Cyrène*. Paris.

Dowden, K. (1989) *Death and the Maiden*. London.

Duyvendak, J. J. L. (1931) 'Levensbericht van Marinus Willem de Visser', *Jaarboek van de Maatschappij der Nederlandse Letterkunde*, 164–173.

Eich, P. (2011) *Gottesbild und Wahrnehmung. Studien zu Ambivalenzen früher griechischer Götterdarstellungen (ca. 800 v. Chr.–ca. 400 v. Chr.)*. Stuttgart.

Faraone, C. (1992) *Talismans and Trojan Horses. Guardian Statues in Ancient Greek Myth and Ritual*. Oxford.

Farnell, L. R. (1901) 'Review of M. W. de Visser, De Graecorum diis non referentibus speciem humanam (Diss. Leiden, 1900)', *Man* 1, 105–107.

Farnell, L. R. (1909) *The Cults of the Greek States*. Vol. 5. Oxford.

Fowler, R. L. (2000–2013) *Early Greek Mythography*. 2 vols. Oxford.

Fraenkel, E. (1957) *Horace*. Oxford.

Furley, W. D. and J. M. Bremer (2001) *Greek Hymns*. 2 vols. Tübingen.

Gagné, R. and M. Herrero de Jáuregui (eds.) (2019) *Les Dieux d'Homère II. Anthropomorphismes*. Liège.

Georgoudi, S. (2011) 'Sacrificing to Dionysos: regular and particular rituals', in R. Schlesier (ed.) *A Different God? Dionysos and Ancient Polytheism*. Berlin, 47–60.

Gourmelen, L. (2012) 'Le Serpent barbu: réalités, croyances et représentations. L'exemple de Zeus Meilichios à Athènes', *Anthropozoologica* 47, 323–343.

Graf, F. (1979) 'Apollo Delphinios', *Museum Helveticum* 36, 2–22.

Graf, F. (1985) *Nordionische Kulte*. Rome.

Griffiths, J. G. (1960) 'The flight of the gods before Typhon: an unrecognised myth', *Hermes* 88, 374–376.

Hägg, T. (2004) *Parthenope. Studies in Ancient Greek Fiction*. Copenhagen.

Heinemann, A. (2016) *Der Gott des Gelages. Dionysos, Satyrn und Mänaden auf attischem Trinkgeschirr des 5. Jahrhunderts v. Chr.* Berlin.

Henrichs, A. (2019a) 'Göttliche Präsenz als Differenz: Dionysos als epiphanischer Gott', in A. Henrichs (ed.) *Greek Myth and Religion. Collected Papers II*, ed. H. Yuns. Berlin, 453–466.

Henrichs, A. (2019b) *Greek Myth and Religion. Collected Papers II*, ed. H. Yunis. Berlin.

Henrichs, A. (2019c) 'The epiphanic moment: sight and insight in ancient Greek encounters with the divine', in A. Henrichs (ed.) *Greek Myth and Religion. Collected Papers II*, ed. H. Yuns. Berlin, 431–451.

Heubeck, A., S. West, and J. B. Hainsworth (1988) *A Commentary on Homer's Odyssey*, Vol. 1: *Introduction and Books i–viii*. Oxford.

Hoffner, H. A. (1998) *Hittite Myths*, ed. G. A. Beckman. Atlanta, Ga.

Höfler, O. (1992) *Kleine Schriften*. Hamburg.

Hornblower, S. (2015) *Lykophron. Alexandra. Greek Text, Translation, Commentary and Introduction*. Oxford.

Icard-Gianolio, N. (2004) 'Statues enchaînées', in *ThesCRA*. II, 468–471.

Insoll, T. (2011) 'Animism and totemism', in T. Insoll (ed.) *Oxford Handbook of the Archaeology of Ritual and Religion*. Oxford, 1004–1016.

Jaccottet, A.-F. (2003) *Choisir Dionysos*. 2 vols. Kilchberg.

Jaillard, D. (2004) '"Images" des dieux et pratiques rituelles dans les maisons grecques. L'exemple de Zeus Ktésios', *MEFRA* 116, 871–893.

Janko, R. (1991) *The Iliad. A Commentary*. Cambridge.

Jost, M. (1998) 'Versions locales et versions "panhelléniques" des mythes arcadiens chez Pausanias', *Kernos* S8, 227–240.

Jost, M. (2005a) 'Betes, hommes et dieux dans la religion arcadienne', in E. Østby (ed.) *Ancient Arcadia*. Athens, 93–104.

Jost, M. (2005b) 'Deux Mythes de métamorphose en animal et leurs interprétations: Lykaon et Kallisto', *Kernos* 18, 347–370.

Kahil, L. (1977) 'L'Artémis de Brauron: rites et mystère', *Antike Kunst* 20, 86–98.

Kahil, L. (1983) 'Mythological repertoire of Brauron', in W. G. Moon (ed.) *Ancient Greek Art and Iconography*. Madison, Wis., 231–244.

Kahil, L. (1984) 'Artemis', in *LIMC*. Vol. 2. 1, 671–674.

Kahil, L. (1988) 'Le Sanctuaire de Brauron et la religion Grecque', in *CRAI*, 799–813.

Kahil L. and N. Icard-Gianolio (1992) 'Leda', in *LIMC*. Vol. 4. 1, 231–246.

Kalogeropoulos, K. (2010) 'Die Entwicklung des attischen Artemis-Kultes anhand der Funde des Heiligtums der Artemis Tauropolos in Halai Araphenides (Loutsa)', in H. Lohmann and T. Mattern (eds.) *Attika. Archäologie einer zentralen Kulturlandschaft*. Wiesbaden, 167–182.

Kalogeropoulos, K. (2013) *Το ιερό της Αρτέμιδος Ταυροπόλου στις Αλές. Αραφηνίδες (Λούτσα)*. 2 vols. Athens.

Kannicht, R. (ed.) (2004) *Tragicorum Graecorum Fragmenta*, Vol. 5: *Euripides*. Göttingen.

Kindt, J. (2017) 'Capturing the ancient animal: human/animal studies and the classics', *Journal of Hellenic Studies* 137, 213–225.

Kindt, J. (2019) 'Animals in ancient Greek Religion: divine zoomorphism and the anthropomorphic divine body', in T. S. Scheer (ed.) *Nature – Myth – Religion in Ancient Greece*. Stuttgart, 155–170.

Krauskopf, I. (1981) 'Areion', in *LIMC*. Vol. 1. 1, 477–479.

Kreuzer, B. (2010) 'ἐν Ἀθήναις δε γλαῦκας. Eulen in der Bilderwelt Athens', *Jahreshefte des österreichischen archäologischen Instituts in Wien* 79, 119–178.

Kurtz, D. C. (1975) 'The man-eating horses of Diomedes in poetry and painting', *Journal of Hellenic Studies* 95, 171–172.

Léger, R. M. (2017) *Artemis and her Cult*. Oxford.

Lightfoot, J. (2019) 'Something to do with Dionysus? Dolphins and dithyramb in Pindar fragment 236 SM', *Classical Philology* 114, 481–491.

Lloyd, G. E. R. (2011) 'Humanity between gods and beasts? Ontologies in question', *Journal of the Royal Anthropological Institute* 17, 829–845 (repr. in Lloyd, G. E. R. (2012) *Being, Humanity, and Understanding*. Oxford, 8–30).

Marchand, F. (2013) 'The Statilii Tauri and the cult of the Theos Tauros at Thespiai', *Journal of Ancient History* 1, 145–169.

Marett, R. R. (1901) 'Review of M. W. de Visser, De Graecorum diis non referentibus speciem humanam (Ph.D. diss. Leiden, 1900)', *Classical Review* 15, 326–328.

Markschies, C. (2016) *Gottes Körper*. Munich.

Masson, O. (1990) *Onomastica graeca selecta*. 2 vols. Paris.

Mauss, M. (1900) 'Review of M. W. de Visser, De Graecorum diis non referentibus speciem humanam (Diss. Leiden, 1900)', *L'Année Sociologique* 5, 279–280.

McInerney, J. (2015) 'There will be blood: the cult of Artemis Tauropolos at Halai Araphenides', in K. Daly and L. A. Riccardi (eds.) *Cities Called Athens. Studies Honoring John McK. Camp II*. Lewisburg, Pa., 289–320.

McPhee, I. (1990) 'Kallisto', in *LIMC*. Vol. 5. 1, 940–944.

Meyer, E. H. (1902) 'Review of M. W. de Visser, De Graecorum diis non referentibus speciem humanam (Diss. Leiden, 1900)', *Indogermanische Forschungen* 13, 33–34.

Mili, M. (2015) *Religion and Society in Ancient Thessaly*. Oxford.

Mödlinger, M. (2013) 'From Greek boar's-tusk helmets to the first European metal helmets: new approaches on development and chronology', *Oxford Journal of Archaeology* 32, 391–412.

Moon, W. G. (ed.) (1983) *Ancient Greek Art and Iconography*. Madison, Wis.

Nilsson, M. P. (1906) *Griechische Feste*. Leipzig

Nilsson, M. P. (1955) *Geschichte der griechischen Religion I*. 2nd edn. Munich (orig. published 1941).

Nisbet, R. G. M. and M. Hubbard (1991) *A Commentary on Horace – Odes*. Oxford.

Oesterheld, C. (2008) *Göttliche Botschaften für zweifelnde Menschen*. Göttingen.

O'Flaherty, W. D. (1980) *Women, Androgynes, and Other Mythical Beasts*. Chicago, Ill.

Ogden, D. (2013) *Drakōn*. Oxford.

Osborne, R. (2011) *The History Written on the Classical Greek Body*. Cambridge.

Otto, W. F. (1933) *Dionysos*. Frankfurt.

Paglialunga, A. (2012) 'La conciliazione degli opposti. Il culto e il santuario di Artemide Tauropolos ad Anfipoli', in *Aristonothos. Scritti per il Mediterraneo* 6, 119–166.

Parker, R. (2005) *Polytheism and Society at Athens*. Oxford.

Parker, R. (2011) *On Greek Religion*. Ithaca, N.Y.

Parker, R. (2017) *Greek Gods Abroad. Names, Natures, and Transformations*. Oxford.

Pentikäinen, J. (2007) *Golden King of the Forest. The Lore of the Northern Bear*. Helsinki.

Petridou, G. (2015) *Divine Epiphany in Greek Literature & Culture*. Oxford.

Petsalis-Diomidis, A. (2010) *Truly beyond Wonders. Aelius Aristides and the Cult of Asklepios*. Oxford.

Pironti, G. and C. Bonnet (eds.) (2017) *Les Dieux d'Homère. Polythéisme et poésie en Grèce ancienne*. Liège.

Platte, R. (2017) *Equine Poetics*. Washington, D.C.

Polinskaya, I. (2013) *A Local History of Greek Polytheism. Gods, People and the Land of Aigina.* Leiden.

Reinach, S. (1901) 'Review of M. W. de Visser, De Graecorum diis non referentibus speciem humanam (Diss. Leiden, 1900)', *Revue Archéologique* 38, 459–460.

Renberg, G. H. (2017) *Where Dreams May Come. Incubation Sanctuaries in the Greco-Roman World.* 2 vols. Leiden.

Richardson, N. (1993) *The Iliad. A Commentary.* Vol. 6. Cambridge.

Robert, L. (1980) *A Travers l'Asie Mineure.* Paris.

Robertson, M. (1988) 'Europe I', in *LIMC.* Vol. 4. 1, 76–92.

Rossum-Steenbeek, M. van (1997) *Greek Readers' Digests? Studies on a Selection of Sub-literary Papyri.* Leiden.

Schlesier, R. (2002) 'Der Fuß des Dionysos: Zu PMG 871', in H. F. J. Horstmanshoff *et al.* (eds.) *Kykeon. Studies in Honour of H.S. Versnel.* Leiden, 161–191.

Scullion, S. (1998) 'Dionysos and Katharsis in Antigone', *Classical Antiquity* 17, 96–122.

Scullion, S. (2001) 'Dionysos at Elis', *Philologus* 145, 203–218.

Semenzato, C. (2015) 'Θάμβος: une frayeur étonnante. Parcours archaïque du VIIIe au Ve siècle avant J.-C.', in S. Coin-Longeray and D. Vallat (eds.) *Peurs antiques.* Saint-Etienne, 25–39.

Shapiro, H. A. (1993) 'From Athena's owl to the owl of Athens', in R. M. Rosen and J. Farrell (eds.) *Nomodeiktes. Studies in Honor of Martin Ostwald.* Ann Arbor, Mich., 213–224.

Simon, E. (1981) 'Aloadai', in *LIMC.* Vol. 1. 1, 570–572.

Thomas, K. (1983) *Man and the Natural World. Changing Attitudes in England 1500–1800.* Oxford.

Vernant, J.-P. (1974) *Mythe et société en grèce ancienne.* Paris.

Vernant, J.-P. (1986) 'Mortels et immortels: le corps divin', in C. Malamoud and J.-P. Vernant (eds.) *Corps des dieux.* Paris, 19–45 (Eng. trans. in Vernant, J.-P. (1991) *Mortals and Immortals. Collected Essays,* ed. F. Zeitlin. Princeton, N.J., 27–49).

Versnel, H. S. (2011) *Coping with the Gods.* Leiden.

Vidal-Naquet, P. (1975) 'Bêtes, hommes et dieux chez les Grecs', in L. Poliakov (ed.) *Hommes et bêtes. Entretiens sur le racisme.* Paris, 129–140 (repr. in Vernant, J.-P. and P. Vidal-Naquet (1992) *La Grèce ancienne 3. Rites de passage et transgressions.* Paris, 17–33).

Visser, M. W. de (1900) 'De Graecorum diis non referentibus speciem humanam'. Ph. D. diss., University of Leiden.

Visser, M. W. de (1903) *Die nicht menschengestaltigen Götter der Griechen.* Leiden.

Waal, F. de (2009) *The Age of Empathy. Nature's Lessons for a Kinder Society.* New York, N.Y.

Waal, F. de (2013) *The Bonobo and the Atheist. In Search of Humanism among the Primates.* New York.

Waal, F. de (2019) *Mama's Last Hug. Animal Emotions and What They Tell Us about Ourselves.* New York.

Wackernagel, H. W. (1959) *Altes Volkstum der Schweiz.* Basel.

Waldner, K. (2000) 'Kulträume von Frauen in Athen: Das Beispiel der Artemis Brauronia', in T. Späth and B. Wagner-Hasel (eds.) *Frauenwelten in der Antike.* Stuttgart, 53–81.

Watson, M. (1998) 'The owls of Athena: some comments on owl–skyphoi and their iconography', *Art Bulletin of Victoria* 39, 35–44.

West, M. L. (1997) *The East Face of Helicon.* Oxford.

West, M. L. (2007) *Indo-European Poetry and Myth.* Oxford.

West, M. L. (2011) *Hellenica I.* Oxford.

West, M. L. (2013) *The Epic Cycle.* Oxford.

Whitley, J. (2013) 'Homer's entangled objects: narrative, agency and personhood in and out of Iron Age texts', *Cambridge Archaeological Journal* 23, 395–416.

Wilamowitz-Moellendorff, U. von (1931–1932) *Der Glaube der Hellenen*. 2 vols. Berlin.

Williams, F. (1978) *Callimachus. Hymn to Apollo*. Oxford.

Young, D. C. (1968) *Three Odes of Pindar. A Literary Study of Pythian II, Pythian 3, and Olympian 7*. Leiden.

Zawadzka, A. (2009) 'Gallic horned helmets on Roman Republican coinage', *Archeologia. Rocznik Instytutu Archeologii i Etnologii Polskiej Akademii Nauk* 60, 35–43.

6 Greek anthropomorphism versus Egyptian zoomorphism[1]

Conceptual considerations in Greek thought and literature

J. Kindt

Introduction

From earliest times onwards, the ancient Greeks came into contact with other peoples – through travel, trade, colonisation, and warfare – who differed from themselves, notably in their religious beliefs and practices.[2] Inevitably, perhaps, such encounters resulted in the Greeks examining the nature of their own beliefs and practices and their engagement with the supernatural more generally. The ensuing conversation about the nature of the divine and the ways in which it is and is not accessible to humans resonates through Greco-Roman literature. It is included in the writings of authors as diverse as Herodotus, Diodorus Siculus, Strabo, and Tacitus.

Animals feature variously in this particular form of cross–cultural engagement.[3] Due to the centrality of animals within and across various religious practices (as examined in the other chapters of this book), cultural similarities and differences manifested themselves above all in their use for religious purposes. The difference between the anthropomorphism of the ancient Greek gods and other forms of divine representation in particular stood out and warranted commentary. Herodotus, for example, observes about Persian religion:

> ἀγάλματα μὲν καὶ νηοὺς καὶ βωμοὺς οὐκ ἐν νόμῳ ποιευμένους ἱδρύεσθαι, ἀλλὰ καὶ τοῖσι ποιεῦσι μωρίην ἐπιφέρουσι, ὡς μὲν ἐμοὶ δοκέειν, ὅτι οὐκ ἀνθρωποφυέας ἐνόμισαν τοὺς θεοὺς κατά περ οἱ Ἕλληνες εἶναι. οἱ δὲ νομίζουσι Διὶ μὲν ἐπὶ τὰ ὑψηλότατα τῶν ὀρέων ἀναβαίνοντες θυσίας ἔρδειν, τὸν κύκλον πάντα τοῦ οὐρανοῦ Δία καλέοντες.

> It is not their custom to make and set up statues and temples and altars, but those who make such they deem foolish, as I suppose, because they never believed the gods, as do the Greeks, to be in the likeness of men; but they call the whole circle of heaven Zeus, and to him they offer sacrifice on the highest peak of the mountains.[4]

The absence of statuary representations of deities in ancient Persia here prompts Herodotus to consider the broader differences between Greek and Persian religion.

Within the spectrum of different modes of imagining divinity, the zoo-morphism of the Egyptians constituted one of the most notable and con-sequential religious differences. The fully or partly theriomorphic representation of Egyptian deities stood in sharp contrast to Greek religious customs, which, on the whole, preferred the representation of the gods in human form.[5] It repre-sented a departure from the Greek conception that the human rather than the animal body was more suitable to the representation of divinity. This difference between Egyptian and Greek religion mattered even more because the former was not just any other religious tradition but one that the ancient Greeks them-selves considered to be closely related to their own.[6] Indeed, there is ample evidence to illustrate numerous crossovers and influences from each tradition to the other.[7]

This chapter explores the way in which the Greeks conceived of the full or partial zoomorphism of Egyptian deities. To this end, it considers three case studies – one from the transition of the archaic to the classical period (Her-odotus) and two from Roman Greece (Plutarch and Philostratus). The first two are considered regularly in scholarship on Greek perceptions of Egyptian reli-gion, whereas Philostratus features rarely, if ever, in such considerations. I take these to be instances of a larger Greek (and Roman) conversation about the modes of divine representation to have emerged from the comparative per-spective on Egyptian religion.[8] I show that in Greek thought and literature, the encounter with Egyptian zoomorphism prompted thinking about what is at stake in human representations of the gods and goddesses more generally. It inspired some Greek thinkers to raise, and to speak to, fundamental questions of theology.[9] Occasionally, it even led to critical reflection on the principles and practices of anthropomorphism as the preferred form of divine representa-tion in the ancient Greek and Roman worlds.

We start with a discussion of Egyptian religion in Herodotus' *Histories* as one of the earliest considerations of divine zoomorphism in extant Greek thought and literature. How do animals feature in the context of his views on Egyptian religion?

Egyptian zoomorphism as a cultural practice in Herodotus' *Histories*

The ancient Greek historian and ethnographer Herodotus (ca. 484–420 BCE) had a sustained interest in the religious beliefs and practices of non-Greek peoples.[10] In the course of his account of the cultures subjugated by the Persian Empire prior to the Greco-Persian Wars, he comments extensively on the customs of different peoples. In particular, dietary habits, marriage customs, and religious rituals are aspects of non-Greek culture to which Herodotus returns time and again to sketch a rich picture of cultural similarities and differences. In his work, these provide a foil against which the features of Hellenicity (Greekness) could emerge more clearly.[11]

The religious customs of Egypt in particular attracted his interest. Book Two of the *Histories* is full of information on the religious beliefs and practices of the ancient Egyptians – information that Herodotus claims to have derived through autopsy, written sources, and a number of local informants, chief among them priests.[12] Herodotus considered the ancient Egyptians to be particularly religious. His abstract observation – 'they are beyond measure religious, more than any other nation' (θεοσεβέες δὲ περισσῶς ἐόντες μάλιστα πάντων ἀνθρώπων) – is supported by detailed examples of how religious beliefs and practices played into different aspects of life in ancient Egypt.[13] So, to what is Herodotus referring here?

Egyptologists have long realised that animals played a particularly prominent role in the religion of the ancient Egyptians.[14] For example, numerous material artefacts attest to this prominence.[15] And yet, despite this rich source base, the real and symbolic relevance of animals has not yet been fully acknowledged in mainstream studies of Egyptian religion. As Dieter Kessler has pointed out, this is mostly due to the lack of a broad and comprehensive work that brings together and integrates recent developments in the field at large, most notably the emergence of personal religion and insights on the role of animals in Egyptian divinatory practices.[16] What has become clear, however, is that what we refer to summarily as Egyptian 'animal worship' ('Tierkult') actually encompassed a wide array of diverse ritual practices and the beliefs associated with them. These included the use of full or partly zoomorphic cult statues, the ritual use of specific animal species (or clusters of animals) in certain locations, their mummification, as well as numerous animal representations on stelae and standards.[17]

Therefore, Herodotus will have encountered numerous Egyptian animals and animal representations. And his interest in them retained a specifically cultural focus throughout. His account of the animals that the Egyptians hold sacred is a case in point.[18] As Herodotus explicitly states, he is unwilling to engage in speculation about the reasons why these animals are held sacred – which would have necessitated delving into Egyptian theology – but he is happy to describe the customs relating to them.[19] Mostly this takes the form of a series of short notes on the animals in question and the burial rituals associated with them. When Herodotus does go into more detail, his observations focus on the relevant cultural practices without explaining them. For example, he touches on a curious ritual during which townspeople shave off (part of) their children's hair while saying a vow.[20] The hair is then weighed and an equal amount in silver is paid to the guardian of the animal (which is sacred to the relevant deity) for its upkeep. Here, as elsewhere, Herodotus offers no explanation of the religious considerations that drive such practices; he merely records the ceremony.

As has been noted before, Herodotus' account of Egypt is shaped by two divergent tendencies. First, there is his desire to present the Egyptian way of life – including Egyptian religious customs – as a direct inversion of Greek culture. Second, there is a strong tendency to highlight similarities and continuities between Greece and Egypt, especially in terms of their respective religions.[21]

The first tendency becomes tangible in the religious examples Herodotus includes in his famous list of Egyptian inversions of Greek customs, which includes several examples from the realm of religion: 'No woman is dedicated to the service of any god or goddess; men are dedicated to all deities, male or female' (ἱρᾶται γυνὴ μὲν οὐδεμία οὔτε ἔρσενος θεοῦ οὔτε θηλέης, ἄνδρες δὲ πάντων τε καὶ πασέων);[22] 'Everywhere else, priests of the gods wear their hair long; in Egypt they are shaven' (οἱ ἱρέες τῶν θεῶν τῇ μὲν ἄλλῃ κομέουσι, ἐν Αἰγύπτῳ δὲ ξυρῶνται);[23] 'They use two kinds of writing; one is called sacred, the other common' (διφασίοισι δὲ γράμμασι χρέωνται, καὶ τὰ μὲν αὐτῶν ἱρὰ τὰ δὲ δημοτικὰ καλέεται).[24] These examples form part of what François Hartog has called 'the mirror of Herodotus' – his efforts to use cultural differences to reflect on the situation at home.[25]

Herodotus' second tendency – his assertion of the continuities and equivalences between Greek and Egyptian religion – frequently takes the form of an enquiry into origins.[26] It becomes tangible, for example, in his curious views on the Egyptian roots of the twelve primary (Olympian) deities – and their names – which became central to the Greek pantheon.[27] He states that 'the Egyptians (said they) first used the appellations of twelve gods (which the Greeks afterwards borrowed from them)' (δυώδεκά τε θεῶν ἐπωνυμίας ἔλεγον πρώτους Αἰγυπτίους νομίσαι καὶ Ἕλληνας παρὰ σφέων ἀναλαβεῖν).[28] Such ideas about religious diffusion mattered to Herodotus because they inform and sustain a larger aspect of his 'theology': his belief in the existence of a single divine pantheon overlooking the human world. This theology motivates, for example, his observation that the Egyptian goddess Isis is worshipped in ancient Greece as Demeter, and that the goddess whom the Egyptians know as Bubastis is known as Artemis to the Greeks.[29] In Herodotus' view, different peoples worshipped what was essentially a single set of gods.[30] Any variations were limited to the deities' names and the religious customs associated with their worship.

In the realm of divine representation, too, Herodotus acknowledges the primacy of the Egyptians, stating that 'it was they who first assigned to the several gods their altars and images and temples, and first carved figures in stone' (βωμούς τε καὶ ἀγάλματα καὶ νηοὺς θεοῖσι ἀπονεῖμαι σφέας πρώτους καὶ ζῷα ἐν λίθοισι ἐγγλύψαι).[31] Yet, if the Egyptians pioneered the material representation of divinity in images and carved figures, the Greeks later revised it to make it fit their own purposes. It was in this context that Herodotus made his famous statement about the origins of Greek views of divinity:

ἔνθεν δὲ ἐγένοντο ἕκαστος τῶν θεῶν, εἴτε αἰεὶ ἦσαν πάντες, ὁκοῖοί τε τινές τὰ εἴδεα, οὐκ ἠπιστέατο μέχρι οὗ πρώην τε καὶ χθὲς ὡς εἰπεῖν λόγῳ. Ἡσίοδον γὰρ καὶ Ὅμηρον ἡλικίην τετρακοσίοισι ἔτεσι δοκέω μευ πρεσβυτέρους γενέσθαι καὶ οὐ πλέοσι· οὗτοι δὲ εἰσι οἱ ποιήσαντες θεογονίην Ἕλλησι καὶ τοῖσι θεοῖσι τὰς ἐπωνυμίας δόντες καὶ τιμάς τε καὶ τέχνας διελόντες καὶ εἴδεα αὐτῶν σημήναντες.

But whence each of the gods came into being, or whether they had all forever existed, and what outward forms they had, the Greeks knew not till (so to say) a very little while ago; for I suppose that the time of Hesiod and Homer was not more than four hundred years before my own; and these are they who taught the Greeks of the descent of the gods, and gave to all their several names, and honours, and arts, and declared their outward forms.[32]

In other words, the Greeks gleaned their knowledge of the existence of twelve primary deities from the Egyptians, but it was the poets Homer and Hesiod who shaped the way in which these gods were imagined by their fellow-Greeks.

Such forays into the history of religions provide the background to the way in which the apparent zoomorphism of Egyptian deities features in Herodotus' account. The *Histories* include several zoomorphic or partly zoomorphic Egyptian deities. There is, for example, the prominent case of Apis, a divine bull whose death at the hands of the Egyptian king Cambyses provides an explanation for the king's own untimely death.[33] Yet, it is especially in the ethnographic sections of Book Two that zoomorphism is set in relation to ancient Greek religion.[34] Herodotus presents divine zoomorphism primarily as a cultural phenomenon.

A few examples. Herodotus asserts that the Egyptians sacrifice bulls and male calves but not cows because they are sacred to the goddess Isis. This observation is followed by a comment on her representation: 'For the images of Isis are in woman's form, horned like an ox, as the Greeks picture Io, and cows are held by far the most sacred of all beasts of the herd by all Egyptians alike' (τὸ γὰρ τῆς Ἴσιος ἄγαλμα ἐὸν γυναικήιον βούκερων ἐστὶ κατά περ Ἕλληνες τὴν Ἰοῦν γράφουσι, καὶ τὰς βοῦς τὰς θηλέας Αἰγύπτιοι πάντες ὁμοίως σέβονται προβάτων πάντων μάλιστα μακρῷ).[35] By pointing to the depiction of Io in Greek myth, Herodotus foregrounds cultural similarities between Greek and Egyptian religion over differences. Yet, in Greek myth, Io is human, not divine, which makes her unsuitable as an example of a correspondence between Greek and Egyptian beliefs. Herodotus neglects to mention this, and similarly ignores the fact that she is turned (by divine intervention) into a full-bodied cow. By focusing instead on the customs that sustain the worship of Isis in Egypt — the sacrificial rituals and connected taboos and the reference to sacred animals in Egypt more generally — Herodotus in effect offers a strictly cultural account for Isis' animal form that does not touch upon the (ultimately theological) question of how and whether the animal form is a suitable form of the goddess's divine essence.

In a later section, Herodotus attempts to account for the fact that the Thebans sacrifice goats but not sheep. The explanation he offers for this local peculiarity leads him again into the realm of mythology, this time by relating an account he claims to have heard from the Theban priests themselves. Apparently, Heracles wanted to behold Zeus in all his mighty glory — a dangerous endeavour that frequently ends in disaster. To make this possible without causing serious harm to Heracles, Zeus thought of a trick: he 'contrived a device, whereby he showed himself displaying the head and wearing the fleece of a ram, which he had flayed and beheaded' (τάδε τὸν Δία μηχανήσασθαι: ριὸν ἐκδείραντα προσχέσθαι τε τὴν κεφαλὴν ἀποταμόντα τοῦ κριοῦ καὶ ἐνδύντα τὸ νάκος οὕτω οἱ ἑωυτὸν ἐπιδέξαι).[36] The partly zoomorphic representation of Zeus in Egypt is explained here with the help of a myth that presents it as an artificial disguise fabricated by the god himself for the purpose of safely revealing himself to Heracles. Yet, what started as the deity's exceptional disguise is soon appropriated in human culture and passed on by way of cultural dissemination: 'It is from this that the Egyptian images of Zeus have a ram's head; and in this the Egyptians are imitated by the Ammonians'[37] (ἀπὸ τούτου κριοπρόσωπον τοῦ Διὸς τὤγαλμα ποιεῦσι Αἰγύπτιοι, ἀπὸ δὲ Αἰγυπτίων Ἀμμώνιοι). So the myth explains the Egyptian cultural practice of representing Zeus with a ram's head, a convention that the Ammonians (the inhabitants of the oasis of Siwa, which houses a famous oracle) subsequently adopt.[38]

In the case of another quasi-zoomorphic deity – Pan – Herodotus employs essentially the same strategy: once again, he foregrounds questions of culture over questions of theology. On the subject of Egyptian representations of this deity, he states: 'Now in their painting and sculpture the image of Pan is made as among the Greeks with the head and the legs of a goat' (γράφουσί τε δὴ καὶ γλύφουσι οἱ ζωγράφοι καὶ οἱ ἀγαλματοποιοὶ τοῦ Πανὸς τὤγαλμα κατά περ Ἕλληνες αἰγοπρόσωπον καὶ τραγοσκελέα).[39] Here, too, the part-animal form is highlighted as a feature that Egyptian religion shares with that of the ancient Greeks. It is not exclusive to the Egyptians. Yet, Herodotus still finds it necessary to emphasise that even the Egyptians did not consider Pan to be a goat, or even like a goat. He observes, 'not that he is deemed to be in truth such, or unlike to other gods' (οὔτι τοιοῦτον νομίζοντες εἶναί μιν ἀλλὰ ὁμοῖον τοῖσι ἄλλοισι θεοῖσι).[40] In other words, Pan's partial zoomorphism is a cultural convention that the ancient Greeks share with the Egyptians. It is not a statement of his divine essence, which is no different from the other (presumably non-zoomorphic) gods. The reasons underlying this peculiar form of representation, however, are swiftly declared out of bounds: 'but why they so present him I have no wish to say' (ὅτευ δὲ εἴνεκα τοιοῦτον γράφουσι αὐτόν, οὔ μοι ἥδιόν ἐστι λέγειν).[41] Herodotus abstains from asking why the Egyptians chose to represent Pan in this form, presumably because doing so would have entailed a discussion of 'religious principles' (*ta theia*) – a topic he is keen to avoid both here and elsewhere.[42] In this case, he saves himself from a discussion of how the Egyptians saw the nature of divinity reflected in animal form. Inevitably, such a discussion would have led him from customs to the thorny subject of the deeper religious principles that underpin divine zoomorphism.[43] Instead, he simply states that the Mendesians consider all goats to be sacred and that 'in the Egyptian language Mendes is the name both for the he-goat and for Pan' (καλέεται δὲ ὅ τε τράγος καὶ ὁ Πὰν Αἰγυπτιστὶ Μένδης).[44] He therefore extricates himself from the tricky theological question of divine zoomorphism (essentially a question of religious meaning and symbolism) and returns to the safer ground of culture, in particular cultural practices.

Ultimately, then, it appears that the way in which divine zoomorphism features in Herodotus' account of Egyptian religion reconciles his desire to present the cultural differences that separate the Egyptians from the Greeks, on the one hand, with his aim to maintain a unified divine pantheon, on the other. To this end, Herodotus presents the zoomorphism of the Egyptian deities as a cultural construct that is partly shared by the Greeks but ultimately unable to represent the real essence of the deities in question. Throughout his account of Egyptian culture and customs, he avoids a deeper (symbolical/theological) engagement with the principles and practices of Egyptian divine zoomorphism. The question whether the animal form is an adequate representation of a god's divine essence does not really feature in his description of Egyptian deities. It is alluded to in the statement that not even the Egyptians believe that Pan is actually a goat, but it is never discussed explicitly, let alone answered. As a result, Herodotus is able to present Egyptian divine zoomorphism as both a local cultural curiosity and as a point where the Greek and Egyptian religions intersect.

Animals as religious symbols in Plutarch's *On Isis and Osiris*

Our second case study, that of Plutarch (ca. 46–after 120 CE), shows that not all Greek thinkers shied away from addressing the underlying theological issues of divine zoomorphism. It provides another perspective on the origins and meaning of the zoomorphism of the Egyptian gods and enquires into their symbolic potential.

Plutarch's *On Isis and Osiris* (*De Iside et Osiride*) is one of the richest and most complex religious treatises that has come down to us from the ancient Greek world. As the title indicates, it revolves around a discussion of Isis, Osiris, and a number of other Egyptian deities, but Plutarch also extends his focus to include Greek and Egyptian notions of the relationships and correspondences between their respective religious traditions with the ultimate aim of exploring more general religious principles.[45] *On Isis and Osiris* is a comparative investigation of Egyptian and Greek religious beliefs and practices and the theologies and cosmologies underpinning them that explores the universal nature of the divine and its place in the cosmos.

Like Herodotus, Plutarch highlights the parallels and correspondences the Greeks and Egyptians saw between their respective religious traditions. Indeed, he does this to such an extent that he is sometimes thought to Hellenise the Egyptian gods.[46] He states that the Greeks came to identify Osiris with Dionysus, and that the Egyptians frequently refer to Isis as Athena.[47] Likewise, 'Amun' is simply an Egyptian name for Zeus.[48] Most of the time, such correspondences stand as mere cultural observations. Occasionally, however, they seem to extend into a larger theory of cultural transmission, such as in the (somewhat puzzling) claim that both Isis and Typhon are ultimately Greek words.[49] Is Plutarch suggesting here that the Egyptians used Greek names for some of their gods? Is he implying that the gods in question were worshipped by the Greeks first, and only later by the Egyptians? If so, this would invert Herodotus' views on the origins of the gods (see above). In a recent commentary on the text, J. Gwyn Griffiths takes this statement to mean that Plutarch thought that Isis' name 'could be etymologically explained as Greek'.[50] Whatever the case, it is clear that while it is not always possible to distinguish Plutarch's voice from those of his informants, here the author certainly expresses his own opinion, or at least a view he shares with his informants. He theorises different religious traditions with the ultimate aim of revealing the larger (philosophical and theological) principles behind them.

This is to say that Plutarch does not confine himself to merely reporting Egyptian religious beliefs and practices; unlike Herodotus, he does not just present Egyptian rituals as cultural curiosities.[51] Rather, he uses these rituals and the beliefs and theologies that sustain them as an entry point for an extensive discussion of their cultural meanings. The sphinxes that adorn many Egyptian shrines, for example, articulate an insight into Egyptian religion, namely 'that their religious teaching has in it an enigmatical sort of wisdom' (ὡς αἰνιγματώδη σοφίαν τῆς θεολογίας αὐτῶν ἐχούσης).[52] In a similar vein, he reports that some people believe that Isis represents the moon, so her statues bear horns as 'imitations of the crescent moon' (τῆς σελήνης ἀποφαίνοντες).[53] In Plutarch's account, religion is a symbolic medium that allows those who are well versed in it to make statements about the nature of the universe.

More often than not, this way of interpreting religion involves a rationalising of – and abstracting from – mythological tales about the gods. For example, when Plutarch elaborates on the Egyptian view that Isis is the moon, he relates that some people hold that Osiris either lived or reigned for 28 years. An explanation for this seemingly curious belief quickly follows: 'for that is the number of the moon's illuminations, and in that number of days does she complete her cycle' (τοσαῦτα γὰρ ἔστι φῶτα τῆς σελήνης καὶ τοσαύταις ἡμέραις τὸν αὐτῆς κύκλον ἐξελίσσει).[54] Theology and cosmology merge in such allegorical readings of religion. Elsewhere, local natural conditions form the basis of allegorical readings. In Plutarch's discussion of mythological tales relating to the exploits of Typhon, he states:

> Ἡ δὲ Τυφῶνος ἐπιβουλὴ καὶ τυραννὶς αὐχμοῦ δύναμις ἦν ἐπικρατήσαντος καὶ διαφορήσαντος τήν τε γεννῶσαν ὑγρότητα τὸν Νεῖλον καὶ αὔξουσαν. ἡ δὲ συνεργὸς αὐτοῦ βασιλὶς Αἰθιόπων αἰνίττεται πνοὰς νοτίους ἐξ Αἰθιοπίας.

> The insidious scheming and usurpation of Typhon, then, is the power of drought, which gains control and dissipates the moisture which is the source of the Nile and of its rising; and his coadjutor, the Queen of the Ethiopians, signifies allegorically the south winds from Ethiopia.[55]

Such readings are designed to cast a bright light on the capacity of religion to make sense of the universe in all its aspects. As Griffiths has pointed out, the allegorising and rationalising of Egyptian religion also allows Plutarch to make Egyptian beliefs cohere with Platonic philosophy.[56]

That Plutarch is a member of the 'Middle Platonist' philosophical tradition is evident throughout *On Isis and Osiris*. [57] It is implicit, for example, in the idea of a single, omniscient, supreme deity, as articulated at the very beginning of the text.[58] It is further evident in Plutarch's conception of *logos* as a single ordering principle behind the startling array of cultural representations of the divine.[59] And it informs his conception of Osiris as a being with an (immanent, temporal) body and a (transcendent, eternal) soul.[60] All these features are representative of the way in which Plutarch philosophises (and thereby, to some extent, Helle-nises) Egyptian religion.

The principles and practices of divine representation are central to this endeavour. They provide Plutarch with a pathway to move from mere description to interpretation. This is because the way in which the gods are represented in the human realm points to the symbolic meanings that humans attribute to them. Take, for example, a peculiar representation of Osiris that formed part of an Egyptian religious ceremony: 'The wood that they cut on the occasions called the "burials of Osiris" they fashion into a crescent-shaped coffer because of the fact that the moon, when it comes near the sun, becomes crescent-shaped and disappears from sight' (τὸ δὲ ξύλον ἐν ταῖς λεγομέναις Ὀσίριδος ταφαῖς τέμνοντες κατασκευάζουσι λάρνακα μηνοειδῆ διὰ τὸ τὴν σελήνην, ὅταν τῷ ἡλίῳ πλησιάζῃ, μηνοειδῆ γινομένην ἀποκρύπτεσθαι).[61] The representation of a specific deity here symbolises a particular transformation of the cosmos at a certain point in time.

So, how does all this affect the ways in which animals feature in Plutarch's work?

Well, he relates that some people in Egypt do not consume particular kinds of fish;[62] that the Egyptians consider the pig to be unclean;[63] that they inter certain animal species that were honoured in ancient Egypt; and that they hold the lion in high esteem, decorating shrines with lions' heads.[64] There are many further examples, but the point is already clear: animals feature prominently in Plutarch's account due to their centrality to various Egyptian beliefs and practices.

Moreover, symbolic readings abound with regard to animals. Material representations of a carved baby, an aged man, a hawk, a fish, and a hippopo-tamus in the vestibule of the temple of Athena at Saïs, for example, are promptly unpacked as representing universal principles:

τὸ μὲν γὰρ βρέφος γενέσεως σύμβολον, φθορᾶς δ' ὁ γέρων· ἱέρακι δὲ τὸν θεὸν φράζουσιν, ἰχθύι δὲ μῖσος, ὥσπερ εἴρηται, διὰ τὴν θάλατταν, ἵππῳ ποταμίῳ δ' ἀναίδειαν· λέγεται γὰρ ἀποκτείνας τὸν πατέρα τῇ μητρὶ βίᾳ μίγνυσθαι.

The babe is the symbol of coming into the world and the aged man the symbol of departing from it, and by a hawk they indicate God, by the fish hatred, as has already been said, because of the sea, and by the hippopo-tamus shamelessness; for it is said that he kills his sire and forces his mother to mate with him.[65]

Here, even though the meaning of the hippopotamus, at least, has a striking Oedipean ring, Plutarch reveals the cultural meanings behind such animal symbols. The animal form takes on an allegorical role: it points to certain aspects of the universe (such as birth and death, hatred and shamelessness) without, however, ever containing its entire nature.[66]

Elsewhere, it is the nature of the gods themselves that is represented through the animal form. For example, Plutarch explains that Anubis (as a representation of the horizon) is depicted as a dog. He explains further that the dog has the capacity to see clearly by both day and night. Egyptians use the canine form to bring out this faculty of the deity.[67] Similarly, Plutarch states that Osiris is frequently depicted as a hawk. Again, it is a particular faculty of the god that is represented in animal form: 'for this bird is surpassing in the keenness of its vision and the swiftness of its flight, and is wont to support itself with the minimum amount of food' (εὐτονίᾳ γὰρ ὄψεως ὑπερβάλλει καὶ πτήσεως ὀξύτητι καὶ διοικεῖν αὐτὸν ἐλαχίστῃ τροφῇ πέφυκε).[68] In the same vein, the crocodile is a suitable symbol for the representation of a god 'since he is the only creature without a tongue; for the divine has no need of a voice' (μόνος μὲν ἄγλωσσος ὤν. φωνῆς γὰρ ὁ θεῖος λόγος ἀπροσδεής ἐστι).[69] Dogs, hawks, and crocodiles are all suitable symbols for the representation of divinity because each of them has a particular aspect or faculty that selectively articulates certain aspects of divinity. Indeed, these examples suggest that it is the superhuman features of the Egyptian gods that find their representation in animal form. So, in contrast to the Greeks, who famously represented these faculties by giving their anthropomorphic gods what Jean-Pierre Vernant has termed a 'super-body' – one that is more perfect than the typical human body – the Egyptians, in Plutarch's account, employ the animal form to make essentially the same point.[70]

Sometimes, not just one but several animals are used to underscore a particular divine faculty, as in the case of a statue of Typhon at Hermopolis that is in the form of a hippopotamus with a hawk and a serpent on its back.[71] Plutarch's explanation for this curious representation again points to the symbolic: 'By the hippopotamus they mean to indicate Typhon, and by the hawk a power and rule, which Typhon strives to win by force, oftentimes without success, being confused by his wickedness and creating confusion' (τῷ μὲν ἵππῳ τὸν Τυφῶνα δεικνύντες, τῷ δ' ἱέρακι δύναμιν καὶ ἀρχήν, ἣν βίᾳ κτώμενος ὁ Τυφὼν πολλάκις οὐκ ἀνίεται ταραττόμενος ὑπὸ τῆς κακίας καὶ ταράττων).[72] Animal symbols, as this example shows, can take on complex forms. They can be stacked up (sometimes literally) to supplement each other with the ultimate purpose of creating a more intricate representation of divinity.

Plutarch, then, presents divine zoomorphism as a preferred form of divine representation among the Egyptians. Yet, he indicates that it was only one of several: for instance, he suggests that objects and abstract shapes were used for the same purpose.[73] Moreover, even human or partly human representations were not entirely unknown in ancient Egypt: 'Everywhere they point out statues of Osiris in human form of the ithyphallic type, on account of his creative and fostering power' (πανταχοῦ δὲ καὶ ἀνθρωπόμορφον Ὀσίριδος ἄγαλμα δεικνύουσιν ἐξορθιάζον τῷ αἰδοίῳ διὰ τὸ γόνιμον καὶ τὸ τρόφιμον).[74] Ratio-nalising explanations prevail for all these symbols. As a result, there is nothing particularly animal-like about the gods (nor, indeed, human–like). It is always a particular faculty or power that comes into the picture in their external repre-sentation. Plutarch himself refers to this as a 'force' (*dynamis*).[75]

Yet, notwithstanding the attention he gives to the fully or partly zoomorphic divine form, Plutarch is careful to point out the importance of not confusing the representation of divinity with the real thing. The distinction between a god and his or her representation is important, because Plutarch is keen to assert that any form of divine representation is merely symbolic. In his view, it is a mistake to conflate the image with the deity. He directs his warning first at the Greeks and their anthropomorphic representation of divinity: 'there are some among the Greeks who have not learned nor habituated themselves to speak of the bronze, the painted, and the stone effigies as statues of the gods and dedications in their honour, but they call them gods' (ὥσπερ Ἑλλήνων οἱ τὰ χαλκᾶ καὶ τὰ γραπτὰ καὶ λίθινα μὴ μαθόντες μηδ' ἐθισθέντες ἀγάλματα καὶ τιμὰς θεῶν ἀλλὰ θεοὺς καλεῖν).[76] A number of examples swiftly follow:

> εἶτα τολμῶντες λέγειν, ὅτι τὴν Ἀθηνᾶν Λαχάρης ἐξέδυσε, τὸν δ' Ἀπόλ-λωνα χρυσοῦς βοστρύχους ἔχοντα Διονύσιος ἀπέκειρεν δὲ Ζεὺς ὁ Καπε-τώλιος περὶ τὸν ἐμφύλιον πόλεμον ἐνεπρήσθη καὶ διεφθάρη, λανθάνουσι συνεφελκόμενοι καὶ παραδεχόμενοι δόξας πονηρὰς ἐπομένας τοῖς ὀνόμασιν.

> And then they have the effrontery to say that Lachares stripped Athena, that Dionysius sheared Apollo of the golden locks, and that Jupiter Capitolinus was burned and destroyed in the Civil War, and thus they unwittingly take over and accept the vicious opinions that are the concomitants of these names.[77]

Therefore, divine names matter because they frequently come with certain assumptions as to the natures of the divinities in question.

What starts as a criticism of a certain form of misguided anthropomorphism among the Greeks soon extends to the zoomorphism of the Egyptians:

> Τοῦτο δ' οὐχ ἥκιστα πεπόνθασιν Αἰγύπτιοι περὶ τὰ τιμώμενα τῶν ζῴων. Ἕλληνες μὲν γὰρ ἔν γε τούτοις λέγουσιν ὀρθῶς καὶ νομίζουσιν ἱερὸν Ἀφροδίτης ζῷον εἶναι τὴν περιστερὰν καὶ τὸν δράκοντα τῆς Ἀθηνᾶς καὶ τὸν κόρακα τοῦ Ἀπόλλωνος καὶ τὸν κύνα τῆς Ἀρτέμιδος ... Αἰγυπτίων δ' οἱ πολλοὶ θεραπεύοντες αὐτὰ τὰ ζῷα καὶ περιέποντες ὡς θεοὺς οὐ γέλω-τος μόνον οὐδὲ χλευασμοῦ καταπεπλήκασι τὰς ἱερουργίας, ἀλλὰ τοῦτο τῆς ἀβελτερίας ἐλάχιστόν ἐστι κακόν· δόξα δ' ἐμφύεται δεινὴ τοὺς μὲν ἀσθενεῖς καὶ ἀκάκους εἰς ἄκρατον ὑπερείπουσα τὴν δεισιδαιμονίαν, τοῖς δὲ δριμυτέροις καὶ θρασυτέροις εἰς ἀθέους ἐμπίπτουσα καὶ θηριώδεις λογισμούς.

This has been to no small degree the experience of the Egyptians in regard to those animals that are held in honour. In these matters the Greeks are correct in saying and believing that the dove is the sacred bird of Aphrodite, that the serpent is sacred to Athena, the raven to Apollo, and the dog to Artemis ... But the great majority of the Egyptians, in doing service to the animals themselves and in treating them as gods, have not only filled their sacred offices with ridicule and derision but this is the least of the evils connected with their silly practices. There is engendered a dangerous belief, which plunges the weak and innocent into sheer superstition, and in the case of the more cynical and bold, goes off into atheistic and brutish reasoning.[78]

This is to say that, although animals, thanks to their capacity to reveal certain aspects of the divine, can be sacred to certain deities, they themselves cannot – and should not – be taken to be divine. This observation is as close as Plutarch gets to a critique of divine zoomorphism. He acknowledges the capacity of the Egyptian modes of divine representation to bring out certain aspects of the deities by giving them animal form. He even finds equivalents in the Greeks' use of full or partial zoomorphism in certain representations of divinity.[79] Yet, he strongly dismisses the possibility that the animal form – or indeed any form of physical representation – can ever be anything more than a mere approximation. This applies equally to divine anthropomorphism and divine zoomorphism and culminates in the conclusion that 'the divine is no worse represented in these animals than in works of bronze and stone, which are alike subject to destruction and disfiguration, and by their nature are void of all perception and comprehension' (ὅθεν οὐ χεῖρον ἐν τούτοις εἰκάζεται τὸ θεῖον ἢ χαλκοῖς καὶ λιθίνοις δημιουργήμασιν, ἃ φθορὰς μὲν ὁμοίως δέχεται καὶ ἐπιχρώσεις, αἰσθήσεως δὲ πάσης φύσει καὶ συνέσεως ἐστέρηται).[80] In other words, no material artefact, no human form, and no animal form can fully capture the nature of the divine, which in many ways transcends such earthly representations.[81]

Overall, then, the zoomorphism of the Egyptian gods prompts Plutarch to consider the principles and practices of divine representation more generally. The allegorical reading of divine representation in the human realm allows him to conceive of the animal form as suitable for bringing out certain aspects of a deity, just as the human form is able to represent certain aspects of the gods. However, in his view, the capacity of both zoomorphism and anthropomorphism to represent a deity always remains only partial: it cannot fully represent the divine essence itself as this is neither (fully) human- nor animal-like.

The divine body as a human and animal body in Philostratus' *Life of Apollonius of Tyana*

As we have seen, while Herodotus avoids questions of theology in favour of a cultural account of divine zoomorphism, Plutarch sees an opening for the animal form to bring out certain aspects of divinity. Our third case study introduces a new angle. Here, we explore the most outspoken dismissal of the animal's suitability for divine representation as well as the most elaborate reflection on the mental processes at stake in human conceptions of divinity. And, again, we see questions about Greek divine anthropomorphism emerging in comparison with divine zoomorphism.

Philostratus' *Life of Apollonius of Tyana* is not one of the core sources in the analysis of Greek representations of Egyptian religion. In this text, which is perhaps best described as the sensationalistic biography of a vain but charismatic man, the zoomorphism of Egyptian gods features as an aside in a single short section.[82] Yet, this comprises a discussion of the kind of cognitive operations at work in divine representation – zoomorphic, anthropomorphic, or other. We shall therefore launch into how divine representation enters the picture in Philostratus' *Life*.

The text tells the story of one Apollonius – philosopher, sage, and self-proclaimed miracle worker – from the city of Tyana in Cappadocia.[83] He belonged to the ranks of holy men who roamed the ancient world in the first few centuries CE; another member of this group was Jesus of Nazareth.[84] At the time, these men played an important role by addressing a range of religious and spiritual needs to which traditional Greco-Roman religion failed to cater. They had to tread a fine line in negotiating their elevated position with the beliefs and structures of Greco-Roman religion, and they were not always successful. For instance, on one occasion, Apollonius was identified as a *goēs* ('magician'), although Philostratus volubly refutes this accusation. In the rest of his text, he relates in great detail the many ways in which the sage showcased his knowledge and expertise.

So, how does divine representation in general and divine zoomorphism in particular enter into the picture painted by Philostratus? In Book Six of the *Life*, the charismatic prophet meets up with Thespesion, a senior member of the Egyptian 'Naked Ones' sect, for the purpose of exchanging wisdom.[85] In the course of their conversation, Apollonius raises the question of why, with very few exceptions, the Egyptians devise gods in 'strange and ridiculous shapes' (ἄτοπα καὶ γελοῖα εἴδη), and continues: 'Why do I say few? Very few are represented as knowledgeable and in godlike form, while your other holy places appear to honour dumb, worthless animals rather than gods' (ὀλίγων γάρ; πάνυ μέντοι ὀλίγων, ἃ σοφῶς καὶ θεοειδῶς ἵδρυται, τὰ λοιπὰ δ' ὑμῶν ἱερὰ ζῴων ἀλόγων καὶ ἀδόξων τιμαὶ μᾶλλον ἢ θεῶν φαίνονται).[86] So, in Apollonius' view, the animal form is eminently unsuitable to serve as a mode of divine representation. Due to their inferior standing, animals cannot represent divinity. As a result, animal worship appears ridiculous to the Greek sage; indeed, he views it as a slur on the gods rather than an appraisal of their true nature.

Surprisingly, perhaps, Thespesion does not respond with a strong rebuttal but with a question: is Apollonius comparing the Egyptians' divine images with famous Greek representations of divinity, such as the Cnidian Aphrodite and the Zeus at Olympia – images that stand out even in the Greek context as particularly accomplished works of human craftsmanship?[87] The suggestion

here is that Apollonius is comparing two very different kinds of cultural production that do not enjoy the same level of significance in their respective
religions. Is it really fair to compare such outstanding works of human endeavour as the Olympian Zeus and the Cnidian Aphrodite with the Egyptians'
run-of-the-mill divine representations? In response, Apollonius is quick to
emphasise that he is making a more fundamental point: 'Not those merely ...
but in general I hold that the sculpture of other peoples aims at propriety, but
you mock divinity rather than worship it' (οὐ μόνον ... ἀλλὰ καὶ καθάπαξ τὴν
μὲν παρὰ τοῖς ἄλλοις ἀγαλματοποιΐαν ἅπτεσθαί φημι τοῦ προσήκοντος, ὑμᾶς
δὲ καταγελᾶν τοῦ θείου μᾶλλον ἢ νομίζειν αὐτό).[88] So, in Apollonius' view,
the Egyptian worship of animal gods is a farce, an abuse of the gods, rather than
a proper acknowledgement of the innate quality of divinity.

Unsurprisingly, perhaps, given the dismissive turn of the conversation, Thespesion is not amused. He tries to turn the tables on Apollonius by pointing out
an apparent weakness in the Greek concept of divine representation. Citing
two creators of famous divine statues in ancient Greece, he asks: 'Your Phidias ... your Praxiteles, they did not go up to heaven and make casts of the
gods' forms before turning them into art, did they? Was it not something else
that set them to work as sculptors?' (οἱ Φειδίαι δὲ ... καὶ οἱ Πραξιτέλεις μῶν
ἀνελθόντες ἐς οὐρανὸν καὶ ἀπομαξάμενοι τὰ τῶν θεῶν εἴδη τέχνην αὐτὰ
ἐποιοῦντο, ἢ ἕτερόν τι ἦν, ὃ ἐφίστη αὐτοὺς τῷ πλάττειν;).[89] With these questions, Thespesion effects a slight but consequential change of focus: he has
moved the conversation away from the most appropriate form for the depiction
of gods in the human sphere and on to the principles at work in crafting divine
images. The anthropomorphism of the Greek gods, he argues, is an illusion
because it creates an impression of what the gods are like despite the obvious
fact that no famous Greek sculptor ever set eyes on a deity.

Apollonius manages to find an elegant solution to Thespesion's conundrum.
First, he refers rather vaguely to that which guides the creation of divine images
as 'something related to wisdom' (καὶ μεστόν γε σοφίας πρᾶγμα), but he soon
offers a more precise description: 'Imagination created these objects... a more
skilful artist than Imitation. Imitation will create what it knows, but Imagination will also create what it does not know, conceiving it with reference to the
real' (φαντασία ... ταῦτα εἰργάσατο σοφωτέρα μιμήσεως δημιουργός· μίμησις
μὲν γὰρ δημιουργήσει, ὃ εἶδεν, φαντασία δὲ καὶ ὃ μὴ εἶδεν, ὑποθήσεται γὰρ
αὐτὸ πρὸς τὴν ἀναφορὰν τοῦ ὄντος).[90] In other words, imagination (*phantasia*) – rather than imitation (*mimēsis*) – allows artists to perceive the divine in
different ways and informs the way material representations of the gods articulate an understanding of what deities are like.

This observation is remarkable because it speaks to a number of questions
that are at the core of all divine representations in the human sphere, be they
ancient Greek, Egyptian, or other. How can we represent the supernatural?[91]
What is the relationship between the gods and their images? How can an
artefact crafted by a human being in this world bring out the otherworldly,
transcendent quality of a god?[92] It would, of course, be wrong to consider

Apollonius' answer as representing Greco-Roman religion more widely. Yet, it is astonishing to find this theological debate emerging from a comparative discussion of different forms of divine representation. By speaking to these issues, Apollonius is able to present himself as a theological expert.

Apollonius asserts that the relationship between gods and their images is not in any way mimetic but relies on the human capacity to grasp the nature of divinity through imagination, rather than the senses. With his answer to Thespesion's conundrum, the debate returns to its original focus: from a discussion of the principle that inspires the production of divine images to the most appropriate mode of divine representation in the human sphere. Because *phantasia* is at work in the creation (and viewing) of divine images, Apollonius takes the animal body to be fundamentally unsuitable for the purpose of divine representation as it evokes images and associations that do not capture the true nature of gods.

Nowhere is this spelled out more clearly than in Apollonius' final assertion of Greek anthropomorphism's superiority over Egyptian zoomorphism as a form of divine representation. He states:

> Δεῖ δέ που Διὸς μὲν ἐνθυμηθέντα εἶδος ὁρᾶν αὐτὸν ξὺν οὐρανῷ καὶ ὥραις καὶ ἄστροις, ὥσπερ ὁ Φειδίας τότε ὥρμησεν, Ἀθηνᾶν δὲ δημιουργήσειν μέλλοντα στρατόπεδα ἐννοεῖν καὶ μῆτιν καὶ τέχνας καὶ ὡς Διὸς αὐτοῦ ἀνέθορεν. εἰ δὲ ἱέρακα ἢ γλαῦκα ἢ λύκον ἢ κύνα ἐργασάμενος ἐς τὰ ἱερὰ φέροις ἀντὶ Ἑρμοῦ τε καὶ Ἀθηνᾶς καὶ Ἀπόλλωνος, τὰ μὲν θηρία καὶ τὰ ὄρνεα ζηλωτὰ δόξει τῶν εἰκόνων, οἱ δὲ θεοὶ παραπολὺ τῆς αὐτῶν δόξης ἐστήξουσιν.

> Doubtless if you envisage the shape of Zeus, you must see him together with the heaven, the seasons, and the planets, as Phidias ventured to do in his day. If you are planning to portray Athena, you must think of armies, intelligence, the arts, and how she sprang from Zeus himself. But if you create a hawk, an owl, a wolf, or a dog, and bring it into your holy places instead of Hermes, Athena, or Apollo, people will think animals and birds worth envying for their images, but the gods will fall far short of their own glory.[93]

Here, Apollonius advocates a strictly anthropomorphic conception of gods' bodies, as prevailed over large parts of ancient Greek religion (but see this volume, Chapter 5). This conception of the divine form was strongly grounded in Greek mythology and proved so powerful that it also informed the production of statuary in the ancient world – hence the nods to set attributes of particular gods in Greek myth and to Phidias as one of the most famous Greek sculptors of divine statues.[94] By contrast, Apollonius regards representing the divine in animal form not only as pointless and misguided but also as a denial of the gods' status.[95] It evokes associations and images that do not reflect the true glory of the divine.[96]

The relationship between divine image and deity has received considerable scholarly attention, with classical scholars discussing in detail the manifestation of divine qualities in the religious traditions of ancient Greece and Rome.[97] The examples from Plutarch and Philostratus indicate that similar questions were debated in the ancient world, too.

In the case of Apollonius, the answer is clear: divine anthropomorphism is superior to divine zoomorphism. Yet, not all Greek thinkers arrived at this conclusion. Some, such as Plutarch, understood – at least in theory – what divine zoomorphism had to offer on the theological plane. Others merely dismissed divine anthropomorphism in favour of more abstract representations of divinity. Yet others – notably the Greek philosophers Empedocles, Plato, and Aristotle, among others – took issue with the fact that humans imagined gods in human form.[98] Indeed, the conceptual weaknesses of anthropomorphism were discussed throughout the ancient world from as far back as Xenophanes' famous dictum 'if horses or oxen or lions had hands or could draw with their hands and accomplish such works as men, horses would draw the figures of the gods as similar to horses, and the oxen as similar to oxen, and they would make the bodies of the sort which each of them had' (ἀλλ᾽ εἰ χεῖρας ἔχον βόες ἵπποι τ᾽ ἠὲ λέοντες ἢ γράψαι χείρεσσι καὶ ἔργα τελεῖν ἅπερ ἄνδρες, ἵπποι μέν θ᾽ ἵπποισι βόες δέ τε βουσὶν ὁμοίας καί κε θεῶν ἰδέας ἔγραφον καὶ σώματ᾽ ἐποίουν τοιαῦθ᾽ οἷόν περ καὐτοὶ δέμας εἶχον ἕκαστοι).[99] This debate ultimately revolved around the very questions that informed Apollonius and Thespesion's discussion: what is the most appropriate way to represent the divine in the human sphere, and what principles and practices are at work in the creation of divine images? In their case, though, the conversation took on additional complexity by including a comparative dimension in which Egyptian divine zoomorphism was juxtaposed directly with ancient Greek divine anthropomorphism.

Conclusion

This chapter started with the observation that the Greek encounter with other religious traditions prompted engagement with larger questions of a theological nature. I proposed that the full or partial zoomorphism of Egyptian deities inspired Greek thinking about the principles and practices of divine representation in general and anthropomorphism as the prevailing form of divine representation in ancient Greece in particular. To this end, I considered three case studies in which divine zoomorphism features in a comparative context.

The three authors considered – Herodotus, Plutarch, and Philostratus – all speak to the same set of three questions. Why do the Egyptians represent their gods in full or partial animal form? What is at stake in representing the gods in the human world? And how does divine zoomorphism relate to the anthropomorphism of the Greek gods? Differences between them then emerge in the answers they propose.

In Herodotus' *Histories*, the full or partial theriomorphism of Egyptian deities is presented merely as a cultural curiosity rather than as a legitimate representation of divine essence. By contrast, in Plutarch's *On Isis and Osiris*, the animal form can symbolically articulate at least some features of divinity, analogous to anthropomorphism, which is similarly capable of representing aspects of the divine. Against this backdrop, Philostratus' *Life of Apollonius of Tyana* stands out as a text in which the principles and practices informing the production of divine images come into full focus. Here we find two holy men investigating the cognitive processes that inform the creation of divine images in the human sphere. In the course of their conversation, divine zoomorphism and divine anthropomorphism are both characterised as mere approximations of what the gods may be like rather than precise replications of their true essence.

Many more examples could have been presented, but the overall picture would not have changed. For instance, in his extended account of Egypt, Diodorus Siculus addresses the same questions and recounts three different reasons that the Egyptians offer for their worship of animals.[100] One of these is that they revere animals that are particularly useful to man, with respect to which Diodorus cites the typical representation of Anubis with a dog's head.[101] This calls to mind Herodotus in that it favours a cultural explanation.

As is often the case in ancient Greek religion, there seemed to be little interest in reaching a unified position on this or other equally weighty matters of theological concern. Rather, a spectrum of views continued to revolve around a core set of examples. Yet, some overlap is discernible in the work of the three authors studied here. For example, they all use the anthropomorphism of the Greek gods and goddesses as the backdrop for a discussion of divine representation in Egypt. And all three highlight the fact that the zoomorphism of the Egyptian gods is markedly different from the anthropomorphism of ancient Greek religion. By raising the question of divine representation in the context of another culture (Egypt), these authors create the necessary conceptual space not merely for an appreciation of the idiosyncrasies of Egyptian religion but also for a discussion of one of the core problems of ancient Greek religion.

Notes

1 I thank Richard Gordon for commenting on an earlier draft of this chapter.
2 On Greco/Roman/Egyptian cultural contacts in the ancient world, see Moyer 2011. See also Lloyd 1975–1988: Vol. 1: 1–60.
3 On the Greek gods in other ancient cultures, see Parker 2017.
4 Hdt. 1.131. (here and below trans. Godley, with changes).
5 But see Buxton 2010; Aston 2008; Kindt 2019 on the possibility of full or partial divine zoomorphism in ancient Greece as well as this volume, Chapter 5. On divine representations in the ancient world, see also Platt 2009; Gaifman 2010, 2012; Estienne *et al.* 2014. On Egyptian animal cults, see Fitzenreiter 2013.
6 Various ancient authors theorise on the relationship between Greek and Egyptian religion. See, e.g., Hdt. 2.50; Plut. *De Is. et Os.* 377d; Diod. Sic. 1.23.8–1.42.1. See Smelik and Hemelrijk 1984 and, in particular, Pfeiffer 2008 for detailed studies of how Egyptian animal cults feature in Greek and Roman texts.
7 Due to the relative proximity of the two cultures, both geographically and culturally, from early on in the history of the ancient world there was close contact,

exchange, and transfer of ideas. As a result, certain Egyptian deities, such as Isis, eventually made their way into the Greek world, where they came to be venerated alongside the traditional Greek gods (see, e.g., *IG* II.168). At the same time, there is ample evidence that Greeks inhabiting the cities of Egypt came to embrace divine zoomorphism in ways that reflect more broadly their adoption of Egyptian religious customs (see, in detail, Pfeiffer 2014). On the relationship between Greece and Egypt, see also Burkert 2004; Moyer 2011.

8 In addition to the authors and texts discussed in the case studies of this chapter, see, e.g., Cic. *Tusc.* 5.78, *Nat. D.* 1.101; Ath. 7.299f–300b; Strab. 17.1.19–28; Diod. Sic. 1.11.1–1.27.6; Cass. Dio 50.24.5–7; Ael. *NA* 1.101. For a comprehensive collection of all ancient sources touching upon Egyptian religion, see the multi-volume work by Hopfner 1922–1925.

9 Theology in the sense of thinking about the nature of the divine, see Eidinow, Kindt, and Osborne 2016.

10 Herodotus and religion: e.g. Gould 1994; Harrison 2000; Scullion 2006. Herodotus and Egyptian religion: Rutherford 2005; Moyer 2013.

11 On Herodotus' place in ancient Greek conceptions of Hellenicity, see Hall 2002: 189–190.

12 Priests as sources of knowledge on Egyptian religion: e.g. Hdt. 2.3, 2.99, 2.116. On the sources of Herodotus' account of Egypt, see Lloyd 1975–1988: Vol. 1: 77–140.

13 Hdt. 2.37.1. See also 2.37.4: 'One might call their religious obligations countless' (ἄλλας τε θρησκηίας ἐπιτελέουσι μυρίας ὡς εἰπεῖν λόγῳ).

14 See, e.g., Hopfner 1913 and Hornung 1967 for early but still relevant studies in this area.

15 For recent, extensively illustrated works, see, e.g., Houlihan 1996 and Germond 2001. For an older work with numerous examples from the Old Kingdom, see Smith 1946. And on animal mummies specifically, see Ikram 2005.

16 Kessler 2003: 33, n. 1. The situation is even more pressing now. Significant newer works on the role of animals in Egyptian religion include Kessler 1989 and Fitzenreiter 2013.

17 In addition, the role of animals in Egyptian cult underwent significant changes throughout the long history of ancient Egypt. This means that when drawing up a picture of the role of animals in Egyptian religion, a temporal differentiation is also necessary.

18 Hdt. 2.65–76. See also Lloyd 1975–1988: Vol. 2: 296–297.

19 Hdt. 2.65. On this passage, see also Lloyd 1975–1988: Vol. 2: 297; Harrison 2000: 182–183.

20 Hdt. 2.65.

21 On this point, see, e.g., Harrison 2000: 209 (with further literature).

22 Hdt 2.35. Lloyd 1975–1988: Vol. 2: 251 explains that this implies that 'no woman in Egypt performs the divine cult of any deity or occupied the pre-eminent rôle in worship which would make her equivalent to what he would call a ἱρείη in Greece'.

23 Hdt. 2.36. See Lloyd 1975–1988: Vol. 2: 152 for background.

24 Hdt. 2.36. The 'sacred writing' here is hieroglyphs; the 'common' one, Demotic. See, in detail, Lloyd 1975–1988: Vol. 2: 163, who notes that Herodotus omits Hieratic as a third script.

25 Hartog 2009.

26 The enquiry into origins is a common theme in the *Histories* that extends far beyond Herodotus' account of Egypt and the ethnographic section of his work to include historical events and even geography. On this point, see Kindt 2006: 34 (with further literature).

27   Hdt. 2.4. See also Lattimore 1939; Harrison 2000: 208–214, 251–264; Burkert
     2013. Burkert offers a plausible explanation for the apparent contradiction in the
     Histories between the observation that the Greek names for the gods are Egyptian
     in origin and their translatability into Greek. Pointing to ancient Greek language
     theory, he argues that Herodotus ultimately makes an ontological, not a lexico-
     graphical or etymological, statement. For a similar statement, see Hdt. 2.50–52.
28   Hdt. 2.4. For different interpretations of this statement, see Lloyd 1975–1988:
     Vol. 2: 28–29.
29   See Hdt. 2.59 and 2.137, respectively. For a comprehensive list of all Egyptian
     deities with their Greek equivalences mentioned in Herodotus, see Harrison 2000:
     210–211; Burkert 2013: 204.
30   The exceptions to this rule are discussed in Hdt. 1.2. See Harrison 2000: 214–220.
31   Hdt. 2.4.
32   Hdt. 2.53. See also the commentary on this passage by Lloyd 1975–1988: Vol. 2:
     esp. 249–251.
33   On Apis and Cambyses, see Hdt. 3.7. See also Munson 1991.
34   See below in detail.
35   Hdt. 2.41. On the figure of Io, see Dowden 1989: 117–146; Davidson 1991;
     Grimal 1996: 232.
36   Hdt. 2.42. On Herodotus' account of Heracles, see Harrison 2000: 220–221, who
     terms this 'the most "theological" section' of the *Histories*.
37   Hdt. 2.42.
38   For further ancient evidence on the Egyptian ram cults, see Lloyd 1975–1988:
     Vol. 2: 189–190.
39   Hdt. 2.46. See Lloyd 1975–1988: Vol. 2: 215 on the different stages in icono-
     graphical representations of Pan and Herodotus' place within them.
40   Hdt. 2.46.
41   Hdt. 2.46.
42   See Hdt. 2.3: 'Now, for the stories that I heard about the gods, I am not desirous
     to relate them, saving only the names of the deities; for I hold that no man knows
     about the gods more than another; and I will say no more about them than what I
     am constrained to say by the course of my history.'
43   On Herodotus' reluctance to discuss certain aspects of foreign religions, see Har-
     rison 2000: 182–207.
44   Hdt. 2.46.
45   On Isis and Osiris in Egyptian religion, see: Griffiths 1970: 33–74. Plutarch's
     sources: Griffiths 1970: 75–100. On Plutarch, Egypt, and Osiris in the Roman
     context, see, in particular, Brenk 2002.
46   On this tradition and Plutarch's views on Egyptian religion more generally, see, in
     detail, Griffiths 1970: 18–33, esp. 31–32 (on Plutarch's Hellenism).
47   Osiris and Dionysus: Plut. *De Is. et Os.* 13 (356b). Isis as Athena: Plut. *De Is. et
     Os.* 61 (376a). On Plutarch's Osiris, see also Brenk 2002.
48   Plut. *De Is. et Os.* 9 (354c).
49   Plut. *De Is. et Os.* 2 (351f).
50   Griffiths 1970: 257 also points to Plut. *De Is. et Os.* 60 (375c).
51   Cf. Herodotus' reports on the curious behaviour of Egyptian cats when they find
     a house on fire and the no less curious Egyptian rituals following the death of a
     cat (Hdt. 2.66). No explanation is offered for either.
52   Plut. *De Is. et Os.* 9 (354c) (here and below trans. Babbitt with changes).
53   Plut. *De Is. et Os.* 52 (372d).
54   Plut. *De Is. et Os.* 42 (368a).
55   Plut. *De Is. et Os.* 39 (366c).
56   Griffiths 1970: 32.

57 I follow here Dillon's detailed account of Plutarch's philosophical views in the context of Middle Platonism (Dillon 1996: 192–230). On Plutarch's Platonism, see also Boys-Stones 2001: 99–122; Frazier 2008.

58 Plut. *De Is. et. Os.* 1 (351c–d).

59 *Logos* as an ordering principle: Plut. *De Is. et Os.* 67 (377f–378a). See Griffiths 1970: 22–25. See also Dillon 1996: 200.

60 Duality of Osiris: Dillon 1996: 200 on Plut. *De Is. et Os.* 54 (373a–b).

61 Plut. *De Is. et Os.* 42 (368a).

62 Plut. *De Is. et Os.* 7 (353c–d).

63 Plut. *De Is. et Os.* 8 (353f).

64 Lions: Plut. *De Is. et Os.* 38 (366a).

65 Plut. *De Is. et Os.* 32 (363f–364a).

66 On allegorical readings in Plutarch, see Griffiths 1970: 100–101, 419–423 (on the use of allegory in Chapter 23 specifically). On the use of allegory in Pythagoreanism and Platonism, see Brisson 2004: 58–86, esp. 63–71 (on Plutarch), and Boys-Stones 2001: 109.

67 Plut. *De Is. et Os.* 44 (368e).

68 Plut. *De Is. et Os.* 51 (371e).

69 Plut. *De Is. et Os.* 75 (381b).

70 Vernant 1991.

71 Plut. *De Is. et Os.* 49 (371c).

72 Plut. *De Is. et Os.* 50 (371d–e).

73 E.g. Plut. *De Is. et Os.* 56 (373f –374a) on geometric shapes and numbers.

74 Plut. *De Is. et Os.* 51 (371f–372a). On full or partial anthropomorphism among the Egyptian gods, see Griffiths' commentary on this passage (Griffiths 1970: 494–495).

75 Plut. *De Is. et Os.* 65 (377d). See also Plut. *De Is. et Os.* 74 (381a).

76 Plut. *De Is. et Os.* 71 (379c–d).

77 Plut. *De Is. et Os.* 71 (379d).

78 Plut. *De Is. et Os.* 71 (379d–e). See Griffiths 1970: 542–544.

79 See, e.g., the comparative account of Egyptian representations of Osiris and Dionysus in Plut. *De Is. et Os.* 35 (364e–f).

80 Plut. *De Is. et Os.* 76 (382c).

81 A theological statement Plutarch makes elsewhere in the treatise (Plut. *De Is. et Os.* 59 (375b)) seems relevant here: 'The relations and forms and effluxes of the god abide in the heavens and in the stars; but those things that are distributed in susceptible elements, earth and sea and plants and animals, suffer dissolution and destruction and burial, and oftentimes again shine forth and appear again in their generations.'

82 Flinterman 1995: 1 refers to it as a '*vie romancée*'.

83 For a succinct account of the background of this text as well as its modern interpretation, see Nesselrath's introduction to Bäbler and Nesselrath 2016: 1–17.

84 On the figure of the holy man (*theios anēr*), see Anderson 1994; Toit 1997; and, most recently, MacMullen 2019.

85 Philostr. *VA* 6.18–22. On this passage, see also the brief commentary by Nesselrath 2016. Thespesios was actually not an Egyptian but an Ethiopian gymnosophist. Here, Plutarch makes him represent Egyptian religion and borrows the name Thespesios, the narrator of the myth of the tripartite soul, from his treatise *On the Delays of the Divine Vengeance* (*De sera numinis vindicta*).

86 Philostr. *VA* 6.19.1 (here and below trans. Jones with changes).

87 On the Cnidian Aphrodite and her representation in Philostratus' text, see Kindt 2012: 174–179.

88 Philostr. *VA* 6.19.2.

89 Philostr. *VA* 6.19.2.

90 Philostr. *VA* 6.19.2.

91   On Apollonius' views on anthropomorphism and divine representation, see also Bäbler 2016.
92   On this passage, see also Platt 2009.
93   Philostr. *VA* 6.19.3.
94   On Phidias and his divine statues, see Papini 2014.
95   On Egyptian zoomorphism, see, e.g., Hart 2005.
96   On the constant assumption of Greek cultural superiority in the *Vita Apollonii*, see Flinterman 1995: 89–91; but see also Abraham 2014 on the image of Greece in the cultural landscape created by Apollonius' travels.
97   See, e.g., Donohue 1988; Scheer 2000; Steiner 2001; Osborne 2011: 185–215; Gaifman 2012.
98   See, e.g., Plut. *Num.* 8.7; Pl. *Resp.* 380d with Buxton 2009: 183–184 and 234–236.
99   Xenoph. fr. 15 (Lesher)
100   Diodorus 1.86.1–89.3.
101   Diodorus 1.87.2.

Bibliography

Abraham, R. J. (2014) 'The geography of culture in Philostratus' *Life of Apollonius of Tyana*', *Classical Journal* 109, 465–480.

Aghion, I. (1994) *Héros et dieux de l'antiquité: guide iconographique*. Paris.

Alexandridis, A. (2008) 'Wenn Götter lieben, wenn Götter strafen: zur Ikonographie der Zoophilie im griechischen Mythos', in A. Alexandridis, M. Wild, and L. Winkler-Horaček (eds.) *Mensch und Tier in der Antike. Grenzziehung und Grenzüberschreitung*. Wiesbaden, 285–311.

Anderson, G. (1994) *Sage, Saint, and Sophist. Holy Men and Their Associates in the Early Roman Empire*. London.

Asheri, D., A. B. Lloyd, and A. Corcella (2007) *A Commentary on Herodotus Books I–IV*, ed. O. Murray and A. Moreno. Oxford.

Aston, E. (2008) 'Hybrid cult images in ancient Greece: animal, human, god', in A. Alexandridis, M. Wild, and L. Winkler-Horaček (eds.) *Mensch und Tier in der Antike. Grenzziehung und Grenzüberschreitung*. Wiesbaden, 481–502.

Aston, E. (2011) *Mixanthrôpoi. Animal–Human Hybrid Deities in Greek Religion*. Liège.

Bäbler, B. (2016) 'Wann ist ein Gott ein Gott? Apollonios über Anthropomorphismus und göttliche Präsenz in Kultstatuen', in B. Bäbler and H.-G. Nesselrath (eds.) *Philostrats Apollonius und seine Welt. Griechische und nichtgriechische Kunst und Religion in der 'Vita Apollonii'*. Berlin, 125–138.

Bäbler, B. and H.-G. Nesselrath (eds.) (2016) *Philostrats Apollonios und seine Welt. Griechische und nichtgriechische Kunst und Religion in der 'Vita Apollonii'*. Berlin.

Boys-Stones, G. R. (2001) *Post-Hellenistic Philosophy*. Oxford.

Brenk, F. (2002) 'Religion under Trajan: Plutarch's resurrection of Osiris', in P. Stadter and L. van der Stockt (eds.) *Sage and Emperor. Plutarch, Greek Intellectuals, and Roman Power in the Time of Trajan (98–117AD)*. Leuven, 72–92.

Brisson, L. (2004) *How Philosophers Saved Myths. Allegorical Interpretation and Classical Mythology*, trans. C. Tihanyi. Chicago, Ill.

Burkert, W. (2004) *Babylon, Memphis, Persepolis. Eastern Contexts of Greek Culture*. Cambridge, Mass.

Burkert, W. (2013) 'Herodotus on the names of the gods: polytheism as a historical problem', in R. V. Munson (ed.) *Oxford Reading in Classical Studies: Herodotus*. Vol. 2. Oxford, 198–209.

Buxton, R. (2009) *Forms of Astonishment. Greek Myths of Metamorphosis.* Oxford.

Buxton, R. (2010) 'Metamorphoses of gods into animals and humans', in J. Bremmer and A. Erskine (eds.) *The Gods of Ancient Greece. Identities and Transformations.* Edinburgh, 81–91.

Davidson, J. M. (1991) 'Myth and periphery', in D. C. Pozzi and J. M. Wickersham (eds.) *Myth and the Polis.* Ithaca, N.Y., 49–63.

Detienne, M. (1981) 'Between beasts and gods', in R. L. Gordon (ed.) *Myth, Religion and Society. Structuralist Essays by M. Detienne, L. Gernet, J.-P. Vernant and P. Vidal-Naquet.* Cambridge, 215–228.

Dillon, J. (1996) *The Middle Platonists: 80 BC to AD 220.* Rev. edn. with a new afterword. Ithaca, N.Y.

Donohue, A. A. (1988) *Xoana and the Origins of Greek Sculpture.* Atlanta, Ga.

Dowden, K. (1989) *Death and the Maiden. Girls' Initiation Rites in Greek Mythology.* London.

Eidinow, E., J. Kindt, and R. Osborne (eds.) (2016) *Theologies of Ancient Greek Religion.* Cambridge.

Estienne, S. *et al.* (eds.) (2014) *Figures de Dieux. Construire le divin en images.* Rennes.

Fitzenreiter, M. (ed.) (2013) *Tierkulte im pharaonischen Ägypten.* Munich.

Flinterman, J.-J. (1995) *Power, Paideia & Pythagoreanism. Greek Identity, Conceptions of the Relationship between Philosophers and Monarchs and Political Ideas in Philostratus' Life of Apollonius.* Amsterdam.

Frankfort, H. (1948) *Ancient Egyptian Religion. An Interpretation.* New York, N.Y.

Frazier, F. (2008) 'Philosophie et religion dans la pensée de Plutarque: Quelques réflexions autour des emplois du mot πίστις', *Études platoniciennes* 5, 41–61.

Gaifman, M. (2010) 'Aniconism and the notion of the "primitive" in Greek antiquity', in J. Mylonopoulos (ed.) *Divine Images and Human Imaginations in Ancient Greece and Rome.* Leiden, 63–86.

Gaifman, M. (2012) *Aniconism in Greek Antiquity.* Oxford.

Germond, P. (2001) *An Egyptian Bestiary. Animals in Life and Religion in the Land of the Pharaohs,* trans. B. Mellor. London.

Gilhus, I. S. (2006) *Animals, Gods, and Humans. Changing Attitudes to Animals in Greek, Roman and Early Christian Thought.* London.

Griffiths, J. G. (1970) *Plutarch's De Iside et Osiride. Edited with an Introduction, Translation and Commentary by J. G. Griffiths.* Cardiff.

Gould, J. (1994) 'Herodotus and Religion', in R. V. Munson (ed.) *Oxford Reading in Classical Studies: Herodotus.* Vol. 2. Oxford, 183–197.

Grimal, P. (1996) *The Dictionary of Classical Mythology,* trans. A. R. Maxwell-Hyslop. Oxford.

Hall, J. (2002) *Hellenicity. Between Ethnicity and Culture.* Chicago, Ill.

Harrison, T. (2000) *Divinity and History. The Religion of Herodotus.* Oxford.

Hart, G. (2005) *The Routledge Dictionary of Egyptian Gods and Goddesses.* London.

Hartog, F. (2009) *The Mirror of Herodotus. The Representation of the Other in the Writing of History.* Berkeley, Calif.

Hopfner, T. (1913) *Der Tierkult der alten Ägypter.* Wien.

Hopfner, T. (1922–1925) *Fontes Historiae Religionis Aegyptiacae.* 5 vols. Bonn.

Hornung, E. (1967) 'Die Bedeutung des Tieres im alten Ägypten', *Studium Generale* 20, 69–84.

Houlihan, P. F. (1996) *The Animal World of the Pharaohs.* London.

Ikram, S. (2005) *Divine Creatures. Animal Mummies in Ancient Egypt.* Cairo.

Immerwahr, H. R. (1966) *Form and Thought in Herodotus*. Cleveland, Oh.

Kessler, D. (1989) *Die heiligen Tiere und der König*. Wiesbaden.

Kessler, D. (2003) 'Tierische Missverständnisse: Grundsätzliches zu Fragen des Tierkultes', in M. Fitzenreiter (ed.) *Tierkulte im pharaonischen Ägypten und im Kulturvergleich*. London, 33–68.

Kindt, J. (2006) 'Delphic oracle stories and the beginning of historiography: Herodotus' Croesus *logos*', *Classical Philology* 101, 34–51.

Kindt, J. (2012) *Rethinking Greek Religion*. Cambridge.

Kindt, J. (2016) *Revisiting Delphi. Religion and Storytelling in Ancient Greece*. Cambridge.

Kindt, J. (2019) 'Animals in ancient Greek religion: divine zoomorphism and the anthropocentric divine body', in T. Scheer (ed.) *Nature, Myth, Religion in Ancient Greece*. Stuttgart, 155–170.

Lattimore, R. (1939) 'Herodotus and the names of the Egyptian gods', *Classical Philology* 34, 357–365.

Lesher, J. H. (ed.) (1992) *Xenophanes of Colophon. Fragments. A Text and Translation with a Commentary*. Toronto.

Lloyd, A. B. (1975–1988) *Herodotus Book II. Commentary*. 3 vols. Leiden.

MacMullen, R. (2019) 'The place of the holy man in the later Roman Empire', *Harvard Theological Review* 112, 1–32.

Moyer, I. (2011) *Egypt and the Limits of Hellenism*. Cambridge.

Moyer, I. (2013) 'Herodotus and the Egyptian mirage: the genealogies of the Theban priests', in R. V. Munson (ed.) *Oxford Reading in Classical Studies: Herodotus*. Vol. 2. Oxford, 292–320.

Munson, R. V. (1991) 'The madness of Cambyses', *Arethusa* 24, 43–65.

Nesselrath, H.-G. (2016) 'Vita Apollonii VI 19. Über die richtige Weise, Götter darzustellen', in B. Bäbler and H.-G. Nesselrath (eds.) *Philostrats Apollonios und seine Welt. Griechische und nichtgriechische Kunst und Religion in der 'Vita Apollonii'*. Berlin, 48–52.

Osborne, R. (2011) *The History Written on the Classical Body*. Cambridge.

Papini, M. (2014) *Fidia. L'uomo che scolpì gli dei*. Bari.

Parker, R. (2017) *Greek Gods Abroad. Names, Natures, and Transformations*. Oxford.

Pfeiffer, S. (2008) 'Der ägyptische Tierkult im Spiegel der griechisch-römischen Literatur', in A. Alexandridis, M. Wild, and L. Winkler-Horaček (eds.) *Mensch und Tier in der Antike. Grenzziehung und Grenzüberschreitung*. Wiesbaden, 373–393.

Pfeiffer, S. (2014) '"The snake, the crocodile and the cat": Die Griechen in Ägypten und die theriomorphen Götter des Landes', in F. Hoffmann and K. S. Schmidt (eds.) *Orient und Okzident in hellenistischer Zeit*. Würzburg, 215–244.

Platt, V. (2009) 'Virtual visions: phantasia and the perception of the divine in The Life of Apollonius of Tyana', in E. L. Bowie and J. Elsner (eds.) *Philostratus. The Life of a Sophist*. Cambridge, 13–154.

Platt, V. (2011) *Facing the Gods: Epiphany and Representation in Graeco-Roman Art, Literature and Religion*. Cambridge.

Rutherford, I. (2005) 'Down-stream to the cat goddess: Herodotus on Egyptian pilgrimage', in J. Elsner and I. Rutherford (eds.) *Pilgrimage in Graeco-Roman and Early Christian Antiquity. Seeing the Gods*. Oxford, 131–150.

Scheer, T. (2000) *Die Gottheit und ihr Bild. Untersuchungen zur Funktion griechischer Kultbilder in Religion und Politik*. Munich.

Scullion, S. (2006) 'Herodotus and Greek religion', in C. Dewald and J. Marincola (eds.) *The Cambridge Companion to Herodotus*. Cambridge, 192–208.

Smelik, K. A. D. and E. A. Hemelrijk (1984) '"Who knows not what monsters demented Egypt worships?" Opinions on Egyptian animal worship in antiquity as part of the ncient conception of Egypt', in *ANRW*. Vol. 2, 17.4, 1852–2000.

Smith, W. S. (1946) *A History of Egyptian Painting and Sculpture in the Old Kingdom.* London.

Steiner, D. T. (2001) *Images in Mind. Statues in Archaic and Classical Greek Literature and Thought.* Princeton, N.J.

Toit, D. S. du (1997) *Theios Anthropos. Zur Verwendung von θε ος ἄνθρωπος und sinn-verwandten Ausdrücken in der Literatur der Kaiserzeit.* Tübingen.

Vernant, J.-P. (1991) 'Mortals and immortals: the body of the divine', in F. Zeitlin (ed.). *Mortals and Immortals. Collected Essays Jean-Pierre Vernant.* Princeton, N.J., 27–49.

7 Philosophers on animals in ancient Greek religion

J. H. Collins II

Introduction

As this book shows, animals feature prominently in ancient Greek religion. Religious rituals and practices interpret the movements of animals, read their insides, sacrifice them for consumption and to honour divinity. Theological frameworks capture the natural order of things – not only the place of divinity and our obligations to it but the places of other creatures and aspects of the natural world that also require care and cultivation. And there are stories and songs that involve animals and beasts as otherworldly actors or that draw on animal behaviour in order to explore human capacities and relations. So it makes sense that animals should also feature heavily in the work of intellectuals bent on investigating, rationalising, criticising, supplementing, or even supplanting conventional religious beliefs and practices. These intellectuals target not only popular beliefs but also the positions of their own intellectual peers and rivals; and if their ultimate aims are protreptic, they also consider the personal religious views of the interlocutor at hand. Animals populate every corner of this rhetorical multiverse. And to make matters even more complicated, the religious views of these intellectuals never seem to constitute a separate system of practice, belief, and myth, but rather personal (or sometimes, in a very narrow sense, communal) variations of conventional religious beliefs and practices.[1] Even the philosophers can make no unequivocal claims of consistency of beliefs and practices, and would feel no pressure to do so given the relative absence of religious structure and authority.[2] In all of these twisting forays into conventional views and personal variations, animals assume different capacities, meanings, and relations, sometimes even among and within the works of a single thinker.

So, how do we begin to tell a story about philosophical views of animals in ancient Greek religion? In this chapter, I offer neither a comprehensive investigation of classical philosophical views on Greek religion nor a full account of classical philosophical understanding of animals and their natures.[3] Instead, I focus on the various ways that philosophical thinkers and practitioners rework the roles and natures of animals and beasts within conventional religious frameworks in order to suggest alternative cosmic orders. It will be helpful to draw a distinction between those intellectuals who make relatively direct and substantial challenges to Greek religious conventions (e.g. some Pythagoreans and Theophrastus) and those who disrupt religious conventions in an effort not to supplant them but to supplement and re-centre them with new ways of conceiving and being part of the cosmos (e.g. Socrates and Plato).[4] All of these approaches have profound implications for the place of humans in the cosmos and their obligations to other creatures who inhabit it with them. Animals are inserted into or reworked within religious contexts in order to develop our moral capacities and sense of kinship; in some instances, these transformations go a long way towards developing an intrinsic significance of animals (i.e., apart from what they might mean for humans), while at the same time narrowing the gap between human and animal experience. In these instances, self-care and care for animals can, at turns, become mutually entwined moral imperatives.

Sacrifice, vegetarianism, and the animal soul

I begin with the philosophical conceptualisations of animals that are most radical for the ancient Greek religious context. Richard Sorabji notes that 'eating and sacrifice were the two uses of animals most discussed in philosophical texts'.[5] It is to this central religious practice, and the nature of the animal within it, that I now turn.[6] It appears that some early elements of Pythagoreanism lie at the heart of this challenge. Yet, it is notoriously difficult to say which tenets belonged to the historical figure of the sixth century BCE and the so-called 'Pythagorean way of life' that his immediate followers observed, and which are part of Neophythagorean legend and debates dating from nearly a millennium later.[7] Still, the early satirical fragment of Xenophanes establishes that Pythagoras promoted not only a view that human souls may be reincarnated as animal souls and thus animals deserve both our compassion (*epoiktirai*) and our protection but also perhaps (if this is not pure ridicule) that something of the human capacity for speech (*logos*) carries over into, and may be recognised within, the voice (sc. *phthegma*) of an animal.[8] It is only a short step – if a step at all – from reincarnation to the natural kinship of humans and animals. Diogenes Laertius reports many generations later that Pythagoras forbade blood sacrifice and the murder and consumption of animals that share with humans the lot of having a soul.[9] Iamblichus, too, clarifies that Pythagoras forbade the most contemplative of philosophers from eating, harming, or sacrificing animals, and urged them to act entirely with justice by doing no wrong to 'kindred-creatures' (*tōn syngenōn zōōn*). A 'hereditary partnership' (*syngenikē hē metochē*) results from a communion of life and substance; all creatures are 'linked in a kind of brotherhood' (*hōsanei adelphotēti*).[10] These advanced initiates, as these passages of Iamblichus have it, honour and protect their material and psychical kinship with their cosmic partners and siblings.

Empedocles appears to initiate a far-ranging philosophical tradition of bloodless sacrifice in a Golden Age and subsequent pollution.[11] His position is grounded not only in the central tenet of reincarnation satirised by Xenophanes but also in a cosmology that has all past, present, and future life – trees, people, beasts, birds, fish, and gods – arise from ever-shifting combinations of the same four elements under the same forces of Strife and Love.[12] All creatures (and their environments) are made of the same elements under the influence of the same cosmic principles; in fact, they are always becoming one another. And all ancestral creatures appear to have understood this under the reign of Cypris, for in that time 'the altar was not drenched with the unmixed blood of bulls' (ταύρων δ' ἀκρήτοισι φόνοις οὐ δεύετο βωμός), and, similarly, 'All were tame and gentle to human beings/Wild beasts and birds, and benevolence blazed forth' (ἦσαν δὲ κτίλα πάντα καὶ ἀνθρώποισι προσηνῆ/θῆρές τ' οἰωνοί τε, φιλοφροσύνη τε δεδήει). To act without this benevolence – 'To rip out the life and to devour the noble limbs' – was the 'greatest pollution' (ἀλλὰ μύσος τοῦτ' ἔσκεν ἐν ἀνθρώποισι μέγιστον/θυμὸν ἀπορραίσαντας ἐέδμεναι ἠέα γυῖα).[13] Empedocles maintains that somewhere along the way a certain carelessness of mind (akēdeiēsi nooio) extinguished this benevolence and ushered in an age of murder and mutual destruction.[14] Having forgotten the cosmic principles of reincarnation and kinship of all living things, humans started to murder and devour their fellows. They wet their altars with unlawful blood, and thereby became aggrieved exiles from the divine and wanderers for 30,000 years.[15] This is even the fate of Empedocles himself, who yearns for purification from past pollution.[16] Like Pythagoras in Xenophanes' satire, but in deadly and ghastly seriousness, Empedocles, no longer careless, can hear the voices of his human kin in the cries of sacrificial beasts:

μορφὴν δ' ἀλλάξαντα πατὴρ φίλον υἱὸν ἀείρας
σφάζει ἐπευχόμενος μέγα νήπιος· οἱ δ' ἀπορεῦνται
λισσόμενον θύοντες· ὁ δ' αὖ νήκουστος ὁμοκλέων
σφάξας ἐν μεγάροισι κακὴν ἀλεγύνατο δαῖτα.
ὣς δ' αὔτως πατέρ' υἱὸς ἑλὼν καὶ μητέρα παῖδες
θυμὸν ἀπορραίσαντε φίλας κατὰ σάρκας ἔδουσιν.

The father, lifting up his own son who has changed shape,
Cuts his throat, with a prayer – fool that he is! The others are unable to understand
While they sacrifice the one begging; but he [sc. the father], deaf to the rebukes,
Has cut the throat and prepared an evil meal in his house.
In the same way, a son seizes his father and children their mother,
And ripping out their life they devour the flesh of their dear ones.[17]

The souls of loved ones beg and cry from the mouths of beasts as heedless families slaughter their recently departed kin. Horrifically, the human participants in the sacrifice play their customary ritual parts – lifting the victim, offering a prayer, cutting the throat, preparing and eating the meat – while not hearing or recognising (sc. aporeō) the one who really begs them to stop. Only

Empedocles and we hear and see, and in the larger framework also recognise the violence meted out to kin who are not immediate family. Ritual sacrifice and the consumption of meat have been exposed as gruesome crimes, the sentence for which is near-eternal vagrancy and pain.

A few generations later, the Peripatetic philosopher Theophrastus appears to have developed both the tenet of kinship and the burgeoning trope of Golden Age vegetarianism into analytic arguments against animal sacrifice and the consumption of meat.[18] These are preserved in Porphyry's *On Abstinence from Animal Food*, written more than half a millennium later.[19] It is difficult to tell where Theophrastus ends and Porphyry begins, but the former appears to offer a number of new arguments, including the following:

1   Animal sacrifice was an unlawful, unnatural, and very late deviation from the ancient conventions of sacrificial offering and subsistence.[20]
2   Famine, war, and other misfortunes drove some to neglect sacrifice and the sacred altogether, and others to human sacrifice. The consequence of both paths has been annihilation for some communities.[21]
3   Accidents, rage, or greed drove communities to substitute animal for human or first-fruit offerings.[22]
4   We do harm to animals when we sacrifice and consume them because we deprive them of soul – of clear intrinsic value (cf. *timiōtera*) – and we commit further wrong by offering to the gods something that was not ours to take.[23]
5   And, most importantly, the kinship (*oikeiotēs*) of humans and *all* animals results not from shared primary elements but from the sameness of skin, flesh, and fluids, along with psychical sameness:

πολὺ δὲ μᾶλλον τῷ τὰς ἐν αὐτοῖς ψυχὰς ἀδιαφόρους πεφυκέναι, λέγω δὴ ταῖς ἐπιθυμίαις καὶ ταῖς ὀργαῖς, ἔτι δὲ τοῖς λογισμοῖς, καὶ μάλιστα πάντων ταῖς αἰσθήσεσιν. ἀλλ' ὥσπερ τὰ σώματα, οὕτω καὶ τὰς ψυχὰς τὰ μὲν ἀπηκριβωμένας ἔχει τῶν ζῴων, τὰ δὲ ἧττον τοιαύτας, πᾶσί γε μὴν αὐτοῖς αἱ αὐταὶ πεφύκασιν ἀρχαί. δηλοῖ δὲ ἡ τῶν παθῶν οἰκειότης ... φρονοῦσι μὲν ἄπαντα φῦλα.

[T]he souls of animals are no different, I mean in appetites and desires, and also in reasoning and above all in perception. Just as with bodies, so with souls: some animals have brought them to perfection, others less so, but the principles are naturally the same in all. The kinship of passions also shows this ... [A]ll species have intelligence.[24]

Something of this last principle of kinship was felt (*aisthēseōs*) by everyone in the Golden Age when it 'ruled everything and no one killed any creature'.[25] Again, humans were more heedful and sensitive to the true nature of animals in the past; however, according to Theophrastus, the kinship they sensed was based not on a doctrine of reincarnation but on the commonality of mental capacities and states (i.e., of motivations and experiences and efforts to make sense of the world). When communities deprive animals of souls, they deprive them of all those capacities and states that we deem vital to our own condition.[26]

Sacrifice, uncertainty, and philosophy as service

Let us now turn from Theophrastus (and the late tradition that preserves his arguments) to Plato in order to explore a different strand of engagement with (animals in) religious conventions. As we shall see, Plato seems to accommodate some of the challenges outlined above, such as original kinship and shared cognitive capacities, but these are ultimately mitigated by a Socratic scepticism about theological frameworks and the value of any practice (religious or otherwise) without first understanding the correct intent. This uncertainty, as we will see later, opens up new possibilities for animals and our relation to them, especially within the broader cosmological context that includes divinity.

Several characters in the Platonic dialogues develop the trope of Golden Age vegetarianism in different contexts in order to highlight the tendency of the material world to corrupt human relationships with one another and with the natural and supernatural worlds over time.[27] The Eleatic Stranger tells the tale of an earlier time when Cronus held sway over the cosmos: humans – indeed, all living things – knew no pain or labour because divine spirits (*daimones*) tended to all their needs. Under the care of these spirits, no one was savage, nor did they eat each other, and there was no conflict.[28] They had no need of political constitutions or families, and gathered food from an abundance of wild fruits and plants.[29] Moreover, most interestingly, in their unceasing leisure, we could imagine that humans gathered in conversation (*dia logōn ... syngignesthai*) with one another and with animals to enquire (*pynthanomenoi*) whether any one possessed a capacity better suited to gather wisdom (*synagyrmon phronēseōs*).[30] But then Cronus and his *daimones* let go of the rudder and the cosmos, under its own allotted and innate desire, turned backwards, eventually bringing savagery to animals and resourcelessness, then technical inventiveness, to the bereft humans.[31] Previously, all animals had conspired in dialogue on philosophical capacities because divinity (and the earth under its dominion) took care of all their bodily needs (which were very few) and thereby provided them with lives of leisure. But in their new forlorn and degenerate state, humans and animals were forced to contend with lack, savagery, and forgetfulness, and the ancient philosophical gathering had long since dispersed. Daniel A. Dombrowski connects this Golden Age myth with the vegetarian diet of Socrates' ideal city, under the rule of golden stock (honest cakes of barley and wheat along with simple, even primitive, relishes and desserts, including acorns – a diet for peace and health), and the Athenian's account of how humans once abstained from eating and sacrificing animals on the grounds of impiety in order to suggest that Plato venerated the ideals of a mythic vegetarianism and bloodless sacrifice, even though he had to address greater, more pressing problems in the 'cave-like world around him'.[32]

This last point of ethical prioritisation taps into a far more complicated engagement with conventional religious beliefs and practices than we have seen thus far. These complications, as we shall see, lead to new possibilities for animals and divine/human/animal interactions. In brief, as Rick Benitez argues, while Plato, at turns, participates in an intellectual tradition that 'demythologises' gods into abstract metaphysical and meta-ethical principles, his chief characters often demonstrate a 'fervent piety' in religious conventions while also, and this is key, expressing a certain 'theological uncertainty' regarding things that are difficult to know.[33] For instance, when concluding his final myth about souls in the Underworld, Socrates explains, 'I think it is fitting and worth risking to believe – for the risk is a noble one – that this, or something like this, is true ... and a person should sort of sing it to himself like a ritual enchantment.'[34] Similarly, after a survey of traditional theologies and myths, Socrates also suggests that, 'due to our ignorance of the truth about antiquity, we liken [*aphomoiountes*] the false to the true as much as possible, and thus make it useful [*chrēsimon*]'.[35] This project of fashioning likenesses (or other likenesses of those likenesses) is useful and vital to the higher-priority project of self-examination, and bringing others to such examination – a priority that Plato makes religious.[36] Golden Age myths about human–animal kinship, vegetarian diets, and bloodless sacrifice are important to develop and explore only inasmuch as they help us understand something crucial about our own condition.

The prioritisation of philosophical self-examination over theological correctness in Plato's work would naturally extend from myth to ritual practice, too. Figures like Socrates and the Athenian of the *Laws* promote not only a belief in the gods but ritual veneration of them. Socrates delivers prayers and invocations, and arguably 'sacrifices' leisure, livelihood, and family in his devotion to Apollo.[37] Yet, these prayers have psychagogic functions for others, and his 'sacrifice' is fundamentally in the service of persuading citizens to care for virtue (*epimeleisthai aretēs*).[38] In a speech to the new colonists of Magnesia, the Athenian lays out the 'finest and truest doctrine':

ὡς τῷ μὲν ἀγαθῷ θύειν καὶ προσομιλεῖν ἀεὶ τοῖς θεοῖς εὐχαῖς καὶ ἀνα-θήμασιν καὶ συμπάσῃ θεραπείᾳ θεῶν κάλλιστον καὶ ἄριστον καὶ ἀνυσι-μώτατον πρὸς τὸν εὐδαίμονα βίον καὶ δὴ καὶ διαφερόντως πρέπον.

[F]or a good man to sacrifice to the gods and keep them constant company in his prayers and offerings and every kind of worship he can give them is pre-eminently the most fitting conduct, and the most noble and good and effective means to a happy life.[39]

The Athenian encourages the presentation of honours to the Olympians, gods of the state, *daimones*, heroes, ancestral gods, and living parents.[40] However, after delivering the speech, he explains that he hopes it will make the citizens 'supremely easy to persuade along the paths of virtue' (εὐπειθεστάτους πρὸς ἀρετὴν εἶναι), 'make them a trifle easier to handle, and so that much easier to teach' (σμικρὸν … εὐμενέστερον γιγνόμενον εὐμαθέστερον ἀπεργάσεται).[41] Prayer and sacrifice must ultimately serve philosophical ends; they may even sometimes serve as a screen for educating and improving souls.[42] Is it any wonder that Mark McPherran reduces ritual sacrifice and prayer to an 'epiphenomenon' of the supplicant's 'inner piety' and scarcely 'sufficient evidence that his soul is in a virtuous state'?[43] Anna Lännström takes this a step further when proposing that 'sacrifices impede our relationship with the gods since our continuing the sacrifices suggests that we have failed to understand what is important'.[44] Sacrifice becomes an 'optional manifestation of inner piety, important due to respect for the *nomoi*', but irrelevant to the condition of our souls, unless, of course, Apollo really cares.[45]

These passages indicate that Plato is far less interested in an ancestral kinship between humans and animals and the conventions of sacrifice, animal or otherwise, than he is in the cultivation of virtue. Yet, still, his characters devote an extraordinary amount of time to reflecting on, analogising, or fabulising animal capacities and behaviours. Indeed, animals abound in nearly every dialogue.[46] In the next section, I explore how Plato uses them to disrupt and re-centre conventional religious beliefs and practices.

Unstable ground, flying horses, and Sirenic cicadas

At the centre of this strategy of re-centring is a curious view of how a human soul enters the world, and how a city's institutions and citizens may best influence its development. In Plato's *Laws*, the Athenian proposes that humans initially sit somewhere between savagery and divinity:

> ἄνθρωπος δέ, ὥς φαμεν, ἥμερον, ὅμως μὴν παιδείας μὲν ὀρθῆς τυχὸν καὶ φύσεως εὐτυχοῦς, θειότατον ἡμερώτατόν τε ζῷον γίγνεσθαι φιλεῖ, μὴ ἱκανῶς δὲ ἢ μὴ καλῶς τραφὲν ἀγριώτατον, ὁπόσα φύει γῆ.

> Man is a 'tame' animal, as we put it, and of course if he enjoys a good education and happens to have the right natural disposition, he's apt to be a most heavenly and gentle creature; but his upbringing has only to be inadequate or misguided and he'll become the wildest animal on the face of the earth.[47]

Humans begin life not as wild and uncultivated animals, but with a tame nature. They then become either more tame (or even god-like) or wild, depending on their education and upbringing. A city's most important function is to steer a tame nature away from savagery and towards godliness, so this task demands the attention of the best all-round citizen. This model of the human condition is somewhat surprising, given the Athenian's later assertion that children must to be broken like horses:

> ὁ δὲ παῖς πάντων θηρίων ἐστὶ δυσμεταχειριστότατον· ὅσῳ γὰρ μάλιστα ἔχει πηγὴν τοῦ φρονεῖν μήπω κατηρτυμένην, ἐπίβουλον καὶ δριμὺ καὶ

ὑβριστότατον θηρίων γίγνεται. διὸ δὴ πολλοῖς αὐτὸ οἷον χαλινοῖς τισιν δεῖ δεσμεύειν...

Of all wild things, the child is the most unmanageable: an unusually powerful spring of reason, whose waters are not yet canalised in the right direction, makes him treacherous and sly, the most unruly animal there is. That's why he has to be curbed by a great many 'bridles', so to speak...[48]

In other words, children are not tame beasts, but the most obstinate and insolent of all creatures. And it appears that everyone – nurses and mothers, tutors and instructors, any passing citizen – should employ a bridle to redirect their intelligence (*phronēsis*) away from treachery and towards virtue and goodness. This critical protreptic role (sc. *trepōn pros tagathon*) of citizens and their highest institutions maintains at its core the view that the most dangerous threat any city faces is the animal element in or near its own children.[49]

So it is that we find Socrates and young Phaedrus reflecting on the state of the human soul. They stroll along the banks of the Ilisus, taking stock not only of aspects of the natural world – the trees, their shade and fragrance, the breeze and the freshness of the air, the clear stream, the grassy slope, the sweet song of cicadas – but also the stories of gods and mortals that are tied to these aspects and a nearby altar, figurines (*korōn*), and statues (*agalmatōn*) that are tied to the stories.[50] When Phaedrus asks Socrates whether he believes the traditional tale of Boreas abducting Orithuia, Socrates sends a shockwave through this mixed natural–cultural landscape that leaves virtually nothing unsettled and generates new tales of natural and supernatural beings. New gods, animals, and monsters swirl around the grove and even inside our protagonists, pulling them in every direction, as Socrates aims to direct Phaedrus away from a love of speeches and towards a love of wisdom.

Phaedrus and Socrates negotiate a path through places dedicated to mythical Athenian multiforms. There is high-flying Boreas, who 'morphed into a dark-maned stallion' and sired the 12 mares of the legendary Athenian king Erichthonios.[51] Then there is the sanctuary devoted to the chthonic river-god Achelous, portrayed as a bull-horned merman or centaur.[52] Among these multiforms, Socrates wonders aloud if he is 'a beast more complicated and savage than Typhon, or am I a tamer, simpler animal with a share in a divine and gentle nature?' (εἴτε τι θηρίον ὂν τυγχάνω Τυφῶνος πολυπλοκώτερον καὶ μᾶλλον ἐπιτεθυμμένον, εἴτε ἡμερώτερόν τε καὶ ἁπλούστερον ζῷον, θείας τινὸς καὶ ἀτύφου μοίρας φύσει μετέχον).[53] The surrounding faces and forms of the figurines, statues, and altar, along with their respective domains and Phaedrus' question, prompt Socrates to offer a puzzle – is he more or less typhonic than Typhon? – while he also insists that he has no time to make sense of the traditional tales of animal-gods and monsters. Typhon has a hundred snake heads flickering dark tongues, each of which gives voice to unutterable (*athesphaton*) sounds:

ἄλλοτε μὲν γὰρ
φθέγγονθ' ὥσ τε θεοῖσι συνιέμεν, ἄλλοτε δ' αὖτε
ταύρου ἐριβρύχεω, μένος ἀσχέτου, ὄσσαν ἀγαύρου,
ἄλλοτε δ' αὖτε λέοντος ἀναιδέα θυμὸν ἔχοντος,
ἄλλοτε δ' αὖ σκυλάκεσσιν ἐοικότα, θαύματ' ἀκοῦσαι,
ἄλλοτε δ' αὖ ῥοίζεσχ', ὑπὸ δ' ἤχεεν οὔρεα μακρά.

Sometimes they would utter sounds as though for the gods to understand, sometimes
The sound of a loud-bellowing, majestic bull, unstoppable in its strength,
At other times that of a lion, with ruthless spirit,
At other times like young dogs, a wonder to hear,
And at other times he hissed, and the high spots echoed from below.[54]

Stirred by traditional sacred multiforms in sacred civic spaces, Socrates has summoned not only a rushing flood (*erippei de ochlos*) of the Chimera, Hippocentaurs, Gorgons, and winged horses, but the most complex and tangled, most terrible multiform of all in order to determine what he himself is in comparison. Typhon, that 'marvel of miscegenation', becomes a matchless standard for the 'conspiracy of voices within a single human soul'.[55] The surge of animal-gods is mythopoetically turned into an occasion for self-examination. What sort of spirit do I possess? Is it animal, divine, or monstrous? Tangled or simple? Savage or gentle? Plato invites the reader to recognise how the strangeness (*atopiai*) of mixed forms in the sacred civic space cannot rival the strangeness (*atopōtatos*) of the philosopher or the strange (cf. *atopia*) amalgamations he finds inside himself.[56]

It would be easy to read the myth of the charioteer and his horses as a purely theoretical retreat from the world around Socrates and Phaedrus. After all, Socrates claims, 'Landscapes [*chōria*] and trees have nothing to teach me,' and his topics require speculation (sc. *eoiken*) if not supernatural talents.[57] But this myth, too, draws on the immediate surroundings. Socrates repurposes elements of the sanctuary space on the Ilisus to approximate the structure of a human soul, and qualities of the heavens and a place beyond. The grassy slope (*prosantei*) on which Socrates and Phaedrus lie becomes the slope (*pros anantes*) to the rim of heaven.[58] The grass under their heads becomes the metaphysical grassy pasturage (*nomē*) for the best part of the soul.[59] The lowest point of the river sanctuary, near the water, where Socrates and Phaedrus have made their home (which, again, is dedicated to Achelous) becomes the hearth of Hestia from which the train of gods ascends on *theōria*; Hestia appears to have shared altars with Achelous and Cephisus, whose river the Ilisus feeds.[60] Socrates and Phaedrus bend their heads back upon the grass to watch the procession ascend. It is tempting to wonder what roles the other surrounding statues might play in this myth. Might figurines of dancing Nymphs inspire us to think of chorality, for example of the ascending gods (sc. *chorou*) and the cicadas (sc. *chorō*) overhead?[61] Might the nearby mares of Boreas become the horses of the Olympian procession? Socrates disrupts the sanctuary of Achelous entirely, reverses the theoric direction, and redirects our gaze away from what is conventionally sacred at the water to what is philosophically sacred beyond the hill. The train of divine charioteers and their horses draw our attention away from the sacred civic space, from its grass and statues, towards something for which even the gods hunger.[62]

Socrates also draws our attention away from the sanctuary with other animals in other ways that re-centre and transform conventional cult practices. The cicadas are singing and conversing (*dialegomenoi*) over the sanctuary of Achelous, and looking down (*kathoran*) on our protagonists.[63] Socrates likens them to the Sirens, thereby transforming other aspects of the sanctuary, for Achelous was their father.[64] The Sirens are chthonic, too – virgin daughters of the earth – like cicadas.[65] In this chthonic sacred space, rather than material offerings to Achelous, Nymphs, or Sirens, we should offer aloft conversation – the music of a philosophical life.[66] When the race of cicadas came into being, the Muses gave them the gift (*geras*) of freedom from nourishment. When they die, they report back which mortals have honoured (*tima*) the Muses with music; those mortals, in turn, become dearer (*prosphilesterous*) to the gods.[67] Socrates turns the language of sacrifice and prayer into a new prestige economy. Hesiod's daimonic Golden Age generation knew the joys of feasts (*terpont' en thaliēsi*), and on their death they had the royal gift (*geras basilēion*) of dispensing wealth and serving as invisible wards of mortals.[68] But the daimonic cicadas forgo material things, and give no material reward. They are first linked to the Nymph/Siren constellation of the chthonic sanctuary, but they are transformed into Musical envoys. As humans, they overindulged – 'overwhelmed with pleasure' (*exeplagēsan hyph' hēdonēs*), like dissolute Sirens – but as more sober wards, they watch and report.[69] Socrates was 'overwhelmed' (*me ekplagēnai*) by Phaedrus' pleasure in speech – a kind of Bacchic frenzy – and is attempting to redirect that appetite to the music of philosophical dialogue.[70] He repurposes the surrounding trappings of conventional cult and the song of the cicadas for the activities of self-examination and care.

It is clear, then, that Plato's Socrates not only brings surrounding animals to bear on new but very human philosophical concerns; he also imbues them with very human qualities and capacities that either aid or hinder us in our approach to divinity. The cicadas were once humans with appetites for pleasure; they retain model capacities for dialogue and bearing witness, which make us dear to the gods. The charioteer's undisciplined horse at times neighs, but at other times insults (*eloidorēsen orgē*) and makes accusations (*kakizōn*) from a crude tongue (*kakēgoron glōttan*), and often has a word to say to the charioteer (*echei hoti legē*), all of which prevents our spiritual ascent.[71] These animals develop moral and intellectual capacities; they answer to philosophising agents. Here and elsewhere, human qualities in fabulised animals draw our attention to fundamental vulnerabilities and limits in human behaviour, which in turn highlights how extraordinarily difficult it would be for humans to approach the perfectly harmonious configurations of the divine. We have seen that other philosophers consider the psychical and intellectual capacities of animals fundamental to living the most godlike life possible. Some of these accounts go so far as to make the case for an intrinsic value of other creatures, while Socrates merely uses animals to reflect on himself and establish what sort of creature — savage or god-like — he truly is. But all of these tasks demand that humans think about animals when they think about how best to conceive of, and approach, the divine.

Feelings from and for kin

It strikes me that there are further substantial implications of these attempts to recognise animals as mediators between humans and the divine, implications that go far beyond the putative aims of supplementing or supplanting religious conventions, though they certainly touch on capacities like reverence and compassion that have roles to play in religion. We have been asked to imagine kinds of natural kinship that are now lost to us. Recall that in a primordial time of unceasing leisure, humans and animals gathered with one another in conversation and shared enquiry into whether anyone possessed a capacity better suited to gather wisdom.[72] All creatures possessed sufficient capacities of speech and enquiry to investigate which of them were most adept at collecting intelligence. In other words, all creatures shared capacities that afforded them the recognition of one another as reason-bearing, analytical fellows. Only when creatures can see and acknowledge intelligence and curiosity in themselves and one another can they embark on the shared enterprise of investigating the reach of their respective capacities. In this lost age, humans and animals regarded themselves and one another as fellow wisdom-gatherers.

We do not receive a full account of how the ancient philosophical gathering dispersed when Cronus let go of the cosmic rudder, when the other gods abandoned their posts and all things devolved. We do not hear exactly how each creature regressed. But we do learn that animals that had been by nature difficult to deal with (*chalepa*) became wild (*apagriōthentōn*), and humans were ravaged (*diērpazonto*) by them.[73] We do not hear which natural qualities had made some animals more difficult than others; whatever their qualities and difficulties, the ancient philosophical gathering had managed in spite of them. All of that changed, however, when the gods departed and the world grew forgetful (*lēthēs engignomenēs*). None of the old fellowship spoke with the others any more. In the great forgetting, just as the animals lost the capacity for speech, perhaps humans lost the capacity to recognise their other shared faculties. In this way, both humans and animals now encounter cruelty. The animals seize their old companions. Is this any wonder given that they have simply and suddenly lost the capacity to speak? Theophrastus argues that they are no different in appetites, desires, reasoning, and perception; all species have intelligence (*phronousi*).[74] Humans have forgotten something more critical to the ancient fellowship: the ability to see animals as capable of that fellowship; the capacity to recognise them as kin.[75]

If we add that the inner lives of animals are not just similar to ours, but, as Empedocles argues, the same as ours, our failure to recognise them is even more devastating. Now *we* are doing the seizing, the tearing apart. The outward shape of the son has changed into another creature, but the father lifts his own child, and sacrifices him while he begs, the child's voice having horrifically harmonised (sc. *homokleōn*) with that of the sacrificial animal.[76] As his child tries to speak in supplication (*lissomenon*), the father cuts his throat. Another son seizes (*helōn*) his father, rips out his life (*thymon aporraisante*), and 'gulps down the flesh of his family' (φίλας κατὰ σάρκας ἔδουσιν).[77] In this state, as unkowning fools, human beings are unable to recognise that the voice, flesh, and life-force of animals are the very same voice, flesh, and life-force of kin. They believe they are doing something that is religiously correct and reverent. But their actions – the slaughter of suppliants, the murder of family, cannibalism – could not be more irreverent. Family transformed into animals cannot make the ceremonial approach of supplication, cannot grasp the knees; and their pleas at the altar can sound a beseeching tone only inasmuch as their animal tongues allow. Yet, as Empedocles has it, there are reminders of sacred laws, of moral duties, of the need for compassion in those ineffable pleas – all that our family as animals can muster – all of which go unnoticed. The executioners, in turn, although they have the means to live just and reverent lives, courtesy of the poet, choose instead to drive further into pollution and blindness. They do not expect that they will soon be vulnerable to the same ignorance, voracity, and violent crimes, so they can show no compassion. They cannot act with reverence because they do not recognise their proper place in the cosmos. They destroy themselves because they neither see nor hear themselves in others.

It is worth noting how Empedocles, in another way, further unsettles the distinction between human and animal when he reminds us that all creatures are the results of accidents. There is nothing inevitable about our human status: we come haphazardly from the same mess as everything else. The first generation of primitive creatures emerged from the initial blending of elements: 'many heads sprang up without necks/Naked arms wandered about, bereft of shoulders/And eyes roamed about alone, deprived of brows' (ἧι πολλαὶ μὲν κόρσαι ἀναύχενες ἐβλάστησαν/γυμνοὶ δ' ἐπλάζοντο βραχίονες εὔνιδες ὤμων/ὄμματά τ' οἶ' ἐπλανᾶτο πενητεύοντα μετώπων).[78] According to Aëtius' account of Empedocles, autonomous heads, arms, and eyes wandered the earth as 'the first generations of animals and plants' (τὰς πρώτας γενέσεις τῶν ζῴων καὶ φυτῶν).[79] Then, under the influence of Love, these single-limbed, single-organed creatures randomly combined to form a second generation of complex creatures, some of which thrived while others perished:

πολλὰ μὲν ἀμφιπρόσωπα καὶ ἀμφίστερνα φύεσθαι,
βουγενῆ ἀνδρόπρωιρα, τὰ δ' ἔμπαλιν ἐξανατέλλειν
ἀνδροφυῆ βούκρανα, μεμειγμένα τῆι μὲν ἀπ' ἀνδρῶν
τῆι δὲ γυναικοφυῆ σκιεροῖς ἠσκημένα γυίοις.

> Many grew double of face and double of chest,
> Races of man-prowed cattle, while others sprang up inversely,
> Creatures of cattle-headed men, mixed here from men,
> There creatures of women fitted with shadowy genitals.[80]

Daimones are banished into a world of viable accidents. Empedocles himself was a boy, girl, bush, bird, and fish before he became a sage.[81] If cattle-headed men had survived, he might have been one of them, too. Some surviving accidents are more excellent, it seems, than others: lions are chief among the beasts, and laurels (by the criterion of beauty rather than functionality) are chief among the lovely-haired (*ēukomoisin*) trees.[82] Seers, hymn-singers, doctors, and leaders (*promoi*) are the acme of the human accident. But all of these – laurels, lions, leaders – are still accidents, occupied by fallen, polluted spirits.[83] As such, even they can make no claims to cosmic eccentricity. In fact, they have the wisdom to recall their occupation of, and thus kinship with, all of their other forms of life, and the insight to understand that other *daimones* also inhabit these accidental creatures. This insight makes them more a part of their surroundings than ever before, just as they near restoration to godhood.

   If all the creatures of the world are accidents, humans no less so, if they are inhabited by the same fallen spirits, if they possess and exercise similar appetites and intelligence and could potentially recognise one another as intelligence-bearing fellows, if humans suddenly felt vulnerable to the same ignorance and violence they visit on other creatures, how might our experience of the world change? I have already suggested how feelings of vulnerability might lead us to show compassion towards other creatures. We might also experience a deepening of those feelings of awe, respect, and shame that belong to the capacity of reverence.[84] For we have become aware of our obligations to creatures that, while relatively powerless, now share in our genealogy, intellectual capacities, and even past, intimate experiences of family and home. Animals might deserve reverence even without these revelations, simply on the grounds of powerlessness and our shared mortality. But the song of Empedocles flattens the cosmic hierarchy. *Daimones* inhabit the shells of all living things, and are themselves only degrees of pollution away from the hearth of pure immortals.[85] All the spirits of the world in this way draw close to one another. Theophrastus might have us show the respect that is due to creatures that think and desire and perceive in ways that are principally (sc. *archai*) the same; this regard might resemble that of an adult for a child. But Empedocles makes the life-force of all creatures and the gods themselves cosmic siblings. As the harmonising influence of Love climaxes, all these creatures are subsumed into the great god Sphairos. Indeed, it is conceivable that they even fuse into 'a single perfectly self-sufficient global organism, whose component limbs will function in perfect unison', much like simple single-limbed creatures merged into complex animals.[86] Self-care (purifying oneself) and care for other creatures (helping them on to paths of purification) become care for the global organism, in the face of which we must feel tremendous awe and, in light of our impurity, shame. What is lawful (*nomimon*) extends to the limits of this cosmic body.[87] This shared horizon demands recognition and the stewardship of the kindred vital force in all living things.

Notes

1 Cf. Kindt 2015: esp. 39–40, though there may be a fine line sometimes between variation and heresy, as we see, e.g., in the charge of belief in new divinities (Pl. *Ap.* 24b).

2 On 'polis religion' and regulation, see Sourvinou-Inwood 2000a and 2000b; Parker 2011; and Arist. *Pol.* 6.1322b25–30. But what of household religion (Boedecker 2008 and Faraone 2008), magic (Faraone and Obbink 1991), and *theōria* (Elsner and Rutherford 2005)? On the limits of the polis model, see Kindt 2009. For a theory of hybridity in belief and practice in more reified contexts, see Boyarin and Burrus 2005 and McGuire 2008.

3 For Presocratic philosophers on religion, see Jaeger 1947 and Gregory 2013. On Socrates and Plato, see Smith and Woodruff 2000; Herrmann 2010; Lännström 2010; McPherran 2013; Benitez 2016. On popular religion, see Mikalson 2010. For philosophers' views more generally on animals, see: Sorabji 1993; Gilhus 2006; Newmyer 2017.

4 We might add those who redraw aetiological animals at the heart of religious conventions while seeking to innovate and astound, such as fabulists like Protagoras (cf. Kurke 2011: 286–288) and rationalistic interpreters like Herodorus of Heraclea (cf. Hawes 2014: 11–13). On Sophists aiming fundamentally at pleasure rather than persuasion, see Gagarin 2001.

5 Sorabji 1993: 171.

6 For full and insightful accounts of the vegetarian critique of sacrifice in antiquity, see: Dombrowski 1984a and 2014; Sorabji 1993: 170–194; Newmyer 1995 and 2014. The philosophers who promoted vegetarianism clearly had more cultural practices than religious sacrifice in their sites; see Naiden 2012: 232–275 against the sacrificial monopoly on meat.

7 Cf. Haussleiter 1935: 97–157; Sorabji 1993: 172–174; Dombrowski 2014: 537–541.

8 Diog. Laert. 8.36 (= DK 21B7 = LM Xen. D64). Cf. Diog. Laert. 8.14 on reincarnation; Diog. Laert. 8.30, which has Pythagoras grant some sort of intelligence (*noun*) and passion (*thymon*), but not mind (*phrenas*), to animals; Arist. *Protrep.* 36.7–13 (Pist.) = B29 (Dür.) on how animals possess 'some small spark of reason and intelligence but have absolutely no share of theoretical wisdom' (λόγου μὲν γὰρ καὶ φρονήσεως μικρά τινα καὶ ἐν ἐκείνοις αἰθύγματα, σοφίας δὲ θεωρητικῆς ταῦτα μὲν παντελῶς ἄμοιρα), while 'humans possess less exactness and strength of sense-perception and instinct than many animals' (ὡς αἰσθήσεσί γε καὶ ὁρμαῖς πολλῶν ἤδη ζῴων τῆς ἀκριβείας καὶ τῆς ἰσχύος λείπεται ἄνθρωπος). The gap between human and animal narrows on both sides; this fragment is included by Hutchinson and Johnson 2017: 85 as 'peripheral evidence, not in sequence' (i.e., without a speaker in the dialogue).

9 Diog. Laert. 8.22 on blood sacrifice. Diog. Laert. 8.13. (cf. 8.23) on the animal soul, though Diogenes here calls this a 'screen' (*proschēma*) for simply promoting contentedness with a simple diet (cf. 8.19).

10 Iambl. *VP* 24. His Pythagoras adds (at 30) that fellowship with animals establishes greater fellowship with humans.

11 Cf. Sorabji 1993: 174–175; Newmyer 2014: 511–513. On a Golden Age of vegetarianism, see Dombrowski 2014.

12 DK 31B21, 23 (= LM Emp. D77a, D60). On the continuous exchange of elements, see 31B26.10–12 (= LM D77b).

13 DK 31B128 (= LM D25) and B130 (= LM D26) (here and below trans. Laks and Most with modifications). On pollution, cf. *miēnē*, DK B115.3 (= LM D10). And what need is there of a sacrificial intermediary if gods, humans, and animals share the same elements and breath? Cf. Sext. Emp. *Math.* 9.126–129.

14 DK 31B136 (= LM D28).

15 DK 31B115.5–14 (= LM D10).

16 Cf. DK 31B139 (= LM D34).

17 DK 31B137 (= LM D29); cf. Heraclitus DK 22B5 (= LM Her. D15). Is there something clever in Empedocles' use of *homokleōn* – 'joint cries' (*homou-kaleō*) of human soul and animal tongue? (On the difficulties of *homoklē*, see Chantraine 1968: 799 and Beekes 2010: 1078–1079.) Here, the 'harmonising' (cf. Pind. *Isthm.* 5.27) of these appears to be a curse. But even Iphigenia's cries (λιτὰς δὲ καὶ κλη-δόνας πατρῴους, Aesch. *Ag.* 228) amount to nothing, and Lucretius' Agamemnon hears nothing out of her, *muta metu* (Lucr. 1.92).

18 Cf. Sorabji 1993: 175–178; Clark 2000; Newmyer 2014: 519–520.

19 Porph. *Abst.* 2.5–32, 3.25.

20 Porph. *Abst.* 2.5–7.

21 Porph. *Abst.* 2.7–8, 27.

22 Porph. *Abst.* 2.9–10, 27. Cf. 2.25: 'from the sacrificial animals we sacrifice not those that gratify the gods, but much more those that gratify the desires of human beings'.

23 Porph. *Abst.* 2.12. Cf. 2.24.3: how can giving thanks require treating someone else badly?

24 Porph. *Abst.* 3.25 (trans. Clark modified), *contra* Arist. *De an.* 3.20. Clark notes that one critic ends the citation from Theophrastus before *phronousi*; but even Aristotle grants intelligence (sc. *phronimos*) and other portions of judgement and knowledge to many animals (Arist. *Metaph.* 1.1), on which see Cole 1992: 49.

25 Porph. *Abst.* 2.22. Clark 2000: 149 argues for the passage's Theophrastan origin.

26 This radical turn in Theophrastus anticipates the arguments of 'equality of interest' (Singer 1975) and 'harm as deprivation' (Regan 1983) squarely in the classical context, a full four centuries before Plutarch. Cf. Newmyer 1995; Dombrowski 2014a: 548; Cole 1992: 55.

27 See Dombrowski 1984b.

28 Pl. *Plt.* 271d–e.

29 Pl. *Plt.* 272a.

30 Pl. *Plt.* 272c.

31 Pl. *Plt.* 272e, 274b–d.

32 Pl. *Resp.* 372b–d, *Leg.* 782b–d; Dombrowski 1984b: 5, which also provides evidence of Plato's ambivalence about the consumption of animals. For a list of primitive and rustic foods in Theophrastus related to the passage in *Resp.* 2, see Porph. 2.5–7 and Clark 2000: 146, n. 223.

33 Benitez 2016: 311, 315.

34 Pl. *Phd.* 114d; cf. Simmias at 85cd. That an *epōdē* can be an appeasing (cf. *synepaei-dete*, Eur. *IA* 1493) or apotropaic song 'sung over' sacrifice to influence *daimones*, see Hdt. 1.132.3 and P. Derv. Col. VI.2–3, 8–9; thus, a new myth becomes a new philosophical–religious ritual song. Elsewhere, such songs also become pleasurable stimuli for virtuous behaviour. See, e.g., Pl. *Leg.* 2.659d–e.

35 Pl. *Resp.* 382d.

36 *Ap.* 20e–21a, 28d, 30e–31c.

37 McPherran 2002: 100. For prayers, see Pl. *Phd.* 118a; *Phdr.* 237a, 257ab; *Ti.* 27b. For his 'sacrifice', see Pl. *Ap.* 23b, 31bc.

38 Pl. *Ap.* 31b.

39 Pl. *Leg.* 4.716d–e (here and below trans. Saunders with modifications).

40 Pl. *Leg.* 4.717a–b.

41 Pl. *Leg.* 4.718c–d.

42 Cf. n. 9, above. Plato suggests that such speeches arouse even those who make them as well as readers who understand priority; cf. Folch 2015: 305–309.

43 McPherran 2002: 102.

44 Lännström 2010: 271–272.

45 Lännström 2010: 273.

46 See Bell and Naas 2015.

47 Pl. *Leg.* 6.766a.

48 Pl. *Leg.* 7.808d–e.

49 Pl. *Leg.* 7.809a.

50 Pl. *Phdr.* 229c, 230b.

51 Hom. *Il.* 20.224. Though likely a late Attic interpolation (cf. Griffin 1977: 41, n. 22), a classical sign of Boreas' horsiness. Cf. Verg. *G.* 3.266–279.

52 See the merman on a stamnos (British Museum 1839.0214.70) and bull-centaur on a hydria (British Museum 1837.0609.49), both dating from the late sixth century BCE.

53 Pl. *Phdr.* 230a (trans. Nehamas and Woodruff). Upon completing the thought, Socrates immediately draws Phaedrus' attention back to their surroundings.

54 Hes. *Theog.* 830–835 (trans. Most with modifications).

55 Nightingale 1995: 134.

56 Pl. *Phdr.* 229e, 230c, 251d.

57 Pl. *Phdr.* 230d, 246a, 247c. Socrates immediately likens himself to hungry animals (*ta peinōnta thremmata*), following the earlier pattern (at 230a): how can I think about x (i.e., monsters) when I need to figure out how x-like (i.e., typhonic) I am.

58 Pl. *Phdr.* 230c, 247b.

59 Pl. *Phdr.* 248b–c.

60 See the stelae on the banks of the Cephisus: *IG* I³ 986 and 987 and nearby II² 4547–4548, which gives Hestia precedence; these lists represent gods 'prescribed by the oracle of Apollo' (Purvis 2003: 19–21).

61 Pl. *Phdr.* 247a, 230c.

62 Pl. *Phdr.* 247b–e. Alternatively, the *theōria* up the sloped ascent reverses the spectating of theatre: the charioteers and their horses leave the orchestra to stand at the top of the theatre and 'gaze upon what is outside' (*theōrousi ta exō*, 247c). For other Platonic transformations of the cultural practice of *theōria*, see Nightingale 2004.

63 Perhaps another clue that Socrates and Phaedrus occupy the orchestra of a natural theatre. Cf. Ar. *Av.* 326–327, where, from the stage, Strepsiades and Socrates look down on (*kathorō*), and draw the audience's attention to, the Clouds gathering from the wings.

64 See Ap. Rhod. 4.893 and Paus. 9.34.3 on the altar of the Winds in Boeotian Coroneia.

65 See Eur. *Hel.* 168.

66 Pl. *Phdr.* 259b, 259d.

67 Pl. *Phdr.* 259c.

68 Hes. *Op.* 115–116.

69 Pl. *Phdr.* 259b.

70 Pl. *Phdr.* 234d. When a charioteer and his horses retain memories of the Forms, and see images of them on earth, that soul, too, is 'overwhelmed' (*ekplēttontai*, Pl. *Phdr.* 250a). So the soul turns from speeches to musical dialogue and to the Forms themselves.

71 Pl. *Phdr.* 254c, 254e, 255e.

72 Pl. *Plt.* 272c.

73 Pl. *Plt.* 274b.

74 Porph. *Abst.* 3.25. Cf. Darwin 1871: 105: '[T]he difference in mind between man and the higher animals, great as it is, certainly is one of degree and not of kind. We have seen that the senses and intuitions, the various emotions and faculties, such as

love, memory, attention, curiosity, imitation, reason, etc., of which man boasts, may be found in an incipient, or even sometimes in a well-developed condition, in the lower animals.'

75 The word 'recognise' here could then have a special sense: we must re-cognise animals, not as objects of cognition, but as subjects of cognition. We must restore to them their cognition.

76 Cf. above on DK 31B137 (= LM D29).

77 Cf. DK 31B136 (= LM D28), where humans do not merely eat but 'devour' (*daptontes*) each other like animals.

78 DK 31B57 (= LM D154).

79 DK 31A72 (= LM D151).

80 DK 31B61 (= LM D156). On the role of chance in these amalgamations, see Arist. *Ph.* 2.8 198b27–32 and Sedley 2016: 116–117.

81 DK 31B117 (= LM D13).

82 DK 31B127 (= LM D36).

83 DK 31B146 (= LM D39). Cf. DK 31B129 (= LM D38) on the wisdom of Pythagoras, according to Porphyry.

84 See Woodruff 2014: 1–7.

85 DK 31B147 (= LM D40).

86 Sedley 2016: 124.

87 DK 31B135 (= LM D27a).

Bibliography

Beekes, R. (2010) *Etymological Dictionary of Greek.* Leiden.

Bell, J. and M. Naas (eds.) (2015) *Plato's Animals. Gadflies, Horses, Swans, and Other Philosophical Beasts.* Bloomington, Ind.

Benitez, R. (2016) 'Plato and the secularisation of Greek theology', in E. Eidinow, J. Kindt, and R. Osborne (eds.) *Theologies of Ancient Greek Religion.* Cambridge, 301–316.

Boedecker, D. (2008) 'Family matters: domestic religion in classical Greece', in J. Bodel and S. M. Olyan (eds.) *Household and Family Religion in Antiquity.* Oxford, 229–247.

Boyarin, D. and V. Burrus (2005) 'Hybridity as subversion of Orthodoxy? Jews and Christians in late antiquity', *Social Compass* 54, 431–441.

Chantraine, P. (1968) *Dictionnaire étymologique de la langue grecque.* Paris.

Clark, G. (2000) *Porphyry. On Abstinence from Killing Animals.* Ithaca, N.Y.

Cole, E. (1992) 'Theophrastus and Aristotle on animal intelligence', in W. Fortenbaugh and D. Gutas (eds.) *Theophrastus. His Psychological, Doxographical and Scientific Writings.* New Brunswick, 44–62.

Collins, D. (2008) 'Mapping the entrails: the practice of Greek hepatoscopy', *American Journal of Philology* 129, 319–345.

Darwin, C. (1871) *The Descent of Man, and Selection in Relation to Sex.* London.

Dombrowski, D. (1984a) *The Philosophy of Vegetarianism.* Amherst, Mass.

Dombrowski, D. (1984b) 'Was Plato a vegetarian?', *Apeiron* 18, 1–9.

Dombrowski, D. (2014) 'Philosophical vegetarianism and animal entitlements', in G. L. Campbell (ed.) *The Oxford Handbook of Animals in Classical Thought and Life.* Oxford, 535–555.

Elsner, J. and I. Rutherford (eds.) (2005) *Pilgrimage in Graeco-Roman and Early Christian Antiquity. Seeing the Gods.* Oxford.

Faraone, C. (2008) 'Household religion in ancient Greece', in J. Bodel and S. M. Olan (eds.) *Household and Family Religion in Antiquity.* Oxford, 210–228.

Faraone, C. and D. Obbink (eds.) (1991) *Magika Hiera. Ancient Greek Magic and Religion.* Oxford.

Folch, M. (2015) *The City and the Stage. Performance, Genre, and Gender in Plato's Laws.* Oxford.

Gagarin, M. (2001) 'Did the Sophists aim to persuade?', *Rhetorica* 19, 275–291.

Gilhus, I. S. (2006) *Animals, Gods and Humans. Changing Attitudes to Animals in Greek, Roman and Early Christian Ideas.* London.

Gregory, A. (2013) *The Presocratics and the Supernatural.* London.

Griffin, J. (1977) 'The epic cycle and the uniqueness of Homer', *Journal of Hellenic Studies* 97, 39–53.

Haussleiter, J. (1935) *Der Vegetarismus in der Antike.* Berlin.

Hawes, G. (2014) *Rationalizing Myth in Antiquity.* Oxford.

Herrmann, F.-G. (2010) 'Greek religion and philosophy: the god of the philosopher', in D. Ogden (ed.) *A Companion to Greek Religion.* Oxford, 385–397.

Hutchinson, D. S. and M. R. Johnson (eds.) (2017) *Aristotle. Protrepticus or Exhortation to Philosophy.* URL: www.protrepticus.info/protr2017x20.pdf (retrieved 26 April 2020).

Jaeger, W. (1947) *The Theology of the Early Greek Philosophers.* Oxford.

Kindt, J. (2009) 'Polis religion: a critical appreciation', *Kernos* 22, 9–34.

Kindt, J. (2015) 'Personal religion: a productive category for the study of ancient Greek religion?', *Journal of Hellenic Studies* 135, 35–50.

Kurke, L. (2011) *Aesopic Conversations. Popular Tradition, Cultural Dialogue, and the Invention of Greek Prose.* Princeton, N.J.

Lännström, A. (2010) 'A religious revolution? How Socrates' theology undermined the practice of sacrifice', *Ancient Philosophy* 31, 261–274.

McGuire, M. (2008) *Lived Religion. Faith and Practice in Everyday Life.* Oxford.

McPherran, M. (1996) *The Religion of Socrates.* University Park, Pa.

McPherran, M. (2002) 'Does piety pay? Socrates and Plato on prayer and sacrifice', in N. D. Smith and P. Woodruff (eds.) *Reason and Religion in Socratic Philosophy.* Oxford, 89–114.

McPherran, M. (2013) 'Socratic theology and piety', in J. Bussanich and N. Smith (eds.) *The Bloomsbury Companion to Socrates.* New York, N.Y. 257–275.

Mikalson, J. (2010) *Greek Popular Religion in Greek Philosophy.* Oxford.

Most, G. (2006) *Hesiod. Theogony, Works and Days, Testimonia.* Cambridge, Mass.

Naiden, F. (2013) *Smoke Signals for the Gods. Ancient Greek Sacrifice from the Archaic through Roman Periods.* Oxford.

Newmyer, S. (1995) 'Plutarch on the moral grounds for vegetarianism', *Classical Outlook* 72, 41–43.

Newmyer, S. (2014) 'Being the one and becoming the other: animals in ancient philosophical schools', in G. L. Campbell (ed.) *The Oxford Handbook of Animals in Classical Thought and Life.* Oxford, 507–534.

Newmyer, S. (2017) *The Animal and the Human in Ancient and Modern Thought. The 'Man Alone of Animals' Concept.* London.

Nightingale, A. (1995) *Genres in Dialogue. Plato and the Construct of Philosophy.* Cambridge.

Nightingale, A. (2004) *Spectacles of Truth in Classical Greek Philosophy. Theoria in its Cultural Context.* Cambridge.

Parker, R. (2011) *On Greek Religion.* Ithaca, N.Y.

Purvis, A. (2003) *Singular Dedications. Founders and Innovators of Private Cults in Classical Greece.* London.

Regan, T. (1983) *The Case for Animal Rights.* Berkeley, Calif.

Sedley, D. (2016) 'Empedoclean superorganisms', *Rhizomata* 4, 111–125.

Singer, P. (1975) *Animal Liberation. A New Ethic for Our Treatment of Animals.* New York, N.Y.

Smith, N. and P. Woodruff (eds.) (2000) *Reason and Religion in Socratic Philosophy.* Oxford.

Sorabji, R. (1993) *Animal Minds and Human Morals. The Origins of the Western Debate.* Ithaca, N.Y.

Sourvinou-Inwood, C. (2000a) 'Further aspects of polis religion', in R. Buxton (ed.) *Oxford Readings in Greek Religion.* Oxford, 38–55.

Sourvinou-Inwood, C. (2000b) 'What is polis religion?', in R. Buxton (ed.) *Oxford Readings in Greek Religion.* Oxford, 13–37.

Woodruff, P. (2014) *Reverence. Renewing a Forgotten Virtue.* Oxford.

Part 3
Beliefs and practices

8 Caloric codes

Ancient Greek animal sacrifice

F. Graf

In addition to the almost ubiquitous Athenian pottery, most collections of Greek antiquities contain marble votive reliefs from sanctuaries that record the felicitous interaction between worshippers and their gods (on votives, see also this volume, Chapter 11). In a variable iconographic formula, the rectangular relief depicts the meeting of gods and humans. On one side, one or several divine recipients of a sacrifice stand or sit, while, on the other, turned towards their gods, are several humans of smaller size often greeting the gods with right hands raised. Sometimes the divine and the human world come together without any marker of difference between the actors aside from size; at least as often, however, an altar separates the two worlds, functioning as the human-built interface between the spheres and the indicator of the ritual action. When there is an altar, the humans are usually accompanied by an animal, most often an ox, sometimes a pig, sheep, or goat, and in very rare cases even a deer. An inscription may name the human agents and divine recipients of the animal, with the reason for sacrifice expressed in the formulaic *kat'euchēn* ('according to my/our prayer'). It is obvious that an animal being led to the altar is a short formula for an animal sacrifice. Aside from prayer, then, animal sacrifice appears in these artefacts as a key act of Greek interaction with the gods.[1] And not just in ancient Greece: animal sacrifice – the ritual slaughter of live animals before the eyes of humans and gods – was a major ritual act in all religions of the ancient Mediterranean and far beyond before the rise of Christianity put an end to the practice.

A history of research

Before the late 19th century, antiquarians and other scholars of antiquity did not give much thought to animal sacrifice. It was a familiar ritual from both biblical Judaism and ancient authors, the double frame of reference for non-Christian religions; later Christian tradition rejected it, although Paul could accept a compromise.[2] In the ancient world, sacrifice was usually understood as a gift to the gods, following a definition in Plato's *Euthyphro* that must reflect a general opinion, although Socrates himself did not agree.[3] The modern discussion sets in with the beginning of the academic study of religion in the later

19th century, and it generally rejected the gift interpretation.[4] Animal sacrifice, after all, is a paradoxical gift in the sense that the giver receives all the material benefits and the recipient nothing but smoke. This called for more complex explanations and, in step with the dominant paradigm of the period, they had to be evolutionary.

The foundational theory goes back to the Semitist William Robertson Smith (1846–1894) and his discussion of sacrifice in pre-Islamic Arabia and early Judaism. Paramount was his claim that 'all slaughter of domestic animals for food was originally sacrificial among the Arabs as well as among the Hebrews', a view that has remained sufficiently alive that Fred Naiden in his 2013 book on Greek sacrifice feels the need to rail against it.[5] Animal sacrifice also played a role in Émile Durkheim's foundational *Elementary Forms* (1912), presumably again influenced by Smith and his colleague and friend James G. Frazer (1854– 1941).[6] Durkheim (1858–1917) understood sacrifice as the killing and eating of a totem animal, a reading that was present in his teaching well before *Elementary Forms* was published. After her absorption of Durkheimian thought, Jane Ellen Harrison imported the totemist explanation into the study of the Greek world.[7] The longer-lasting impact of Durkheim's interpretation, however, is the insight that sacrifice, like all communal rites, creates and reinforces the feeling of social bonds and community. In their study on the 'nature and function of sacrifice', Durkheim's students Marcel Mauss and Henri Hubert both rejected Smith (as well as Edward Burnett Tylor and, implicitly, Durkheim himself); their main contribution is an acute sense for the formalisation of the sacrificial act and the many variations and aims it could have in a given religious culture.[8]

Against the backdrop of these earlier discussions, in the 1960s Jean-Pierre Vernant (1914–2007) and his student Marcel Detienne (1935–2019), on the one hand, and Walter Burkert (1931–2015), on the other, developed their different interpretations of Greek sacrifice.[9] Originally independent of each other, the two paradigms coalesced into the accepted reading of the ritual for three subsequent generations of classicists, despite some fundamental differences. In both paradigms, animal sacrifice is understood as the way early Greeks turned the meat of domesticated animals into food. This makes the sacrificial feast and banquet the very centre of Greek communal religion. Both paradigms also ascribe to the ritual a communicative function that works on two levels. On the vertical level, following early Greek understanding, it was seen as connecting humans with their gods; on the horizontal level, following Durkheim, it was understood as binding together and structuring the celebrating community. The two theories differ principally on their respective attitudes towards prehistory. Unlike Vernant and Detienne, who refused to think in terms of evolution and focused entirely on Greece in the classical period, the Burkert of *Homo Necans* derived the basics of Greek animal sacrifice from a hypothetical early human hunting society. As a corollary, Burkert strongly emphasises violence and its sacralisation in sacrifice. He did so by combining the recent and at the time very influential ethological theories of the Austrian biologist Konrad Lorenz with the insights of an interesting but heretofore obscure paper by the classicist and folklorist Karl Meuli (1891–1968).[10] He also demonstrated growing opposition to the psychoanalysing evolutionary theories of the Stanford historian René Girard (1913–2015) that began to have a lasting impact around the same time.[11] During the decades following the 1960s, these converging theories stimulated intensive research into the history, phenomenology, and iconography of animal sacrifice in the Greek and, more recently, Roman worlds.[12] Less than a decade ago, however, Naiden analysed and rejected the basic tenets of the prevailing model: sacrifice was mainly about the gods, not about turning animals into food.[13] Although this coincides with a more general scholarly reappraisal of the gods in religion, we still lack a thorough appreciation of Naiden's position.[14]

All modern theories on Greek sacrifice have relied on basically the same set of almost exclusively literary texts that were collected by Paul Stengel in his authoritative *Opferbräuche der Griechen* (1910). Since then, our knowledge has been enhanced mainly by a growing corpus of inscriptions that detail local prescriptions on sacrifices, the so-called 'Sacred Laws'.[15] More recently, new insights have been gained, on the one hand, through analysis of the iconography of sacrifice and, on the other, through the rapid growth of zooarchaeology and its analysis of bone material from Greek sanctuaries.[16]

Sacrificial animals

The dominant form of animal sacrifice in Greece, as in most ancient and modern cultures, was the slaughter of domesticated animals.[17] In all animal sacrifices, all ancient sources concur that the main sacrificial animals were oxen (bovines), sheep or goats (ovicaprids), and pigs. Although it is often impossible to differentiate between bone remnants of sheep and goats, images and inscriptions demonstrate clearly that sheep, rather than goats, were the main sacrificial animals in the Greek world as early as the Bronze Age. This confirms what analysis of Greek animal husbandry has shown. The rugged and hilly landscape of mainland Greece lent itself to the systematic herding of sheep, whose products (wool, milk, meat) were central to Greek life from the Bronze Age, while goats, though equally at home on the Greek hills, were less useful because they did not produce the wool that was often a mainstay of ancient city economies.[18] Hence, goats were confined to special contexts. They were common in the cults of Dionysus and Apollo (the famous Delian altar was built from the horns of sacrificed goats), but, in marked contrast, cult laws for Apollo's son Asclepius could prohibit goat sacrifice (on Asclepius, see also this volume, Chapter 11).[19]

Unlike sheep and goats, cattle need large and preferably flat grazing areas with abundant grass. These grasslands compete with vital agricultural space and can be set aside for cattle only when enough agrarian land is available, as happened especially in Thessaly, Boeotia (etymologically: 'cow country'), and adjacent Euboea ('good-for-cows country'). This implies that in most Greek cities cattle had to be imported from other places, at least for the more lavish sacrifices that needed large numbers of animals. So, the 100 cows sacrificed to Athena at the Panathenaea might not all come from Attica, not to mention the additional cows that each of the allied cities had to send. On a more extravagant level, we hear that the tyrant Jason of Pherae in 390 BCE commanded the cities of Thessaly to send 1000 cows and bulls (ten hecatombs) and over 10,000 sheep, goats, and pigs to Delphi for the Pythia festival. The historian who records this in order to demonstrate Jason's power adds that this levy was regarded as 'moderate'. The market and herdsmen seemed to have little trouble meeting his order, and Thessaly, with its broad, open plains, was cow-country anyway.[20]

The role of pigs as sacrificial animals is less well defined. They were often kept inside settlements rather than in groups in open country; but Eumaeus talked of Odysseus' large groups of pigs, some of which were kept on the mainland opposite Ithaca.[21] Pigs were often confined to special contexts, such as the worship of Demeter, where the preparation for the mysteries was marked by the cleansing, sacrifice, and eating of a piglet, or for all sorts of purification rituals, where the piglets were slaughtered.[22] Unlike pigs and goats, cattle and sheep seem to have been almost interchangeable. Sheep were selected only because they were more economical than cattle, with the latter sacrificed on more formal occasions, such as state festivals. A private individual who sacrificed a large number of cattle to Asclepius could be censured as pretentious – or worse.[23]

A common combination of all three types of domesticated animals – what the Greeks called *trittys boarchos* and the Romans *suovetaurilia* – brought together an ox, a sheep, and a pig. Greek lexicons also attest other, rarer animal combinations. Besides the *trittys boarchos*, there were two other standard forms of animal groups. The oldest, not uncommon and certainly very impressive form of multiple sacrifice was the hecatomb: 'sacrifice of a hundred (*hekaton*)' animals. The word and the custom date back to the Indo-European past because etymologically the term means 'a hundred bovids'.[24] Earlier scholars were often incredulous at the thought of slaughtering 100 large animals in one spot and read the word simply as 'very large sacrifice'. Indeed, Homeric use seemed to confirm this interpretation: in the *Iliad*, a hecatomb sometimes consists of significantly fewer animals.[25] But archaeology has confirmed the literal understanding of the term in actual cult: large monumental altars, such as the one in the oracular shrine of Apollo at Clarus, showed an array of fifty iron rings on each side of the altar to secure the animals; and a hecatomb is probably already attested in a Linear B tablet from Cnossus.[26] The second standard group, which is almost invisible in our sources, was the *dōdekaïs* – a group of 12 animals, presumably mostly sheep. When defined as *dōdekaïs bouprōros*, 'twelve with a cattle prow', as some ancient lexicons have it, a cow or a bull led the sacrificial procession. This grouping is attested in a few local inscriptions and, with more details, explained by Greek lexicographers, and it also appears in a Linear B tablet.[27]

Ordinarily, the sacrifice proper was followed by the consumption of the meat either at a common meal in the sanctuary or in individual households outside the shrine, with meat markets as possible interfaces between sanctuary and household. The feeding of humans explains the prevalence of domesticated animals. Greek sacrificial laws sometimes forbade carrying meat outside the shrine with a standardised formula (*ou fora*, 'no carrying'), suggesting that it was normal to distribute meat from the shrine to households or markets, whereas communal consumption in the precinct was exceptional. This is confirmed by Pliny's observation that the suppression of Christians in his home province of Bithynia meant that 'sacrificial meat, which previously was almost bought no more, is again sold everywhere'.[28] In other words, meat in ancient Greek communities came from sacrifices, even in places where the meat market also relied on commercial slaughter. Paul the Apostle makes it clear that the market in Corinth sells both types of meat, and he advises Jewish or Christian guests in pagan households against asking which sort of meat they are consuming.[29]

There is much less evidence of the sacrifice of other animals, domesticated or wild, in ancient Greece. We hear of horse sacrifices to Helius in Rhodes; and bones with traces of cutting seem to confirm that the flesh was then consumed. There are also rare literary testimonies of dog sacrifices, for example to birth goddesses; it is less clear whether the meat was then eaten.[30] (Cats, however, were never sacrificed or eaten, as far as we can determine.) There are a few images of sacrifices of deer to Artemis, and bones found in sanctuary contexts suggest that the venison was then consumed. In general, though, we lack information about the status of deer in the Greek world. To judge from Xenophon's hunting park, they could be kept for hunting, which would explain their occasional appearance among sacrificial animals, because they would have been considered as somewhere between domesticated and non-domesticated animals.[31] Overall, the sacrificial role of non-domesticated animals in Greece is neither clear nor uniform. The *Odyssey* makes a distinction between the wild goats that Odysseus and his men hunt and eat without any sort of sacrificial ceremony, and the domesticated sheep of Polyphemus that they slaughter, sacrifice, then eat.[32] This leads to the conclusion that undomesticated animals – regardless of species – were generally not sacrificed.[33] Moreover, Pausanias' account of the sacrifice of wild animals, including bears, to Artemis Laphria in second-century Patrae suggests that their meat was not eaten after such rituals. At least in the Patrae ritual, these animals were driven into a corral with a huge pyre at the centre on which they were incinerated.[34] Small animals, domesticated or wild, such as fowl, small birds, and fish, are sometimes attested as well. It seems that these creatures may have been entirely burnt. Others, such as roosters, were both sacrificed and eaten by (small?) households.[35] The fact that certain fish were prohibited in some cults – such as red mullet in the cult of Eleusinian Demeter – suggests that any fish would do under normal circumstances, as long as it was sufficiently edible and substantial.[36]

In addition to species, gender and colour were important considerations when selecting sacrificial animals. As a general rule, male gods received male animals, goddesses female creatures, but as a strict rule this equation is the product of learned circles of late antiquity. It appears that the Greeks were even less rigorous in this respect than the Romans: Persephone, for example, regularly received a black ram in sacrifice.[37] Similarly, white cattle or sheep were connected with gods of the upper world, black animals with those of the underworld and the dead. To call up the soul of Tiresias, Odysseus slaughters a black ram and a black ewe.[38] The Greek Sibylline oracle that imparted the rules for Augustus' Secular Games systematically set in opposition black animals (sacrificed at night to the underworld gods into a subterranean space outside the city) and white animals (sacrificed during the day on the Capitol to the gods of the sky).[39] The oracle seems to follow Greek tradition, but, again, it might have formalised beyond the reality of earlier ritual practice.

As with everything that entailed contact with the gods, the animals had to be unblemished, pure, and beautiful; inscriptions stipulate such perfection.[40] In several places, we find sacred herds that were reserved exclusively for sacrifice, or we hear that polis officials carefully selected (*dokimazein*) the most perfect animal (usually a bull or a cow). In some cases, inscriptions describe this as a lengthy and competitive process.[41] It almost goes without saying that this stipulation also excludes the sacrifice of castrated animals, such as working oxen. Accordingly, the few exceptions to this rule, such as the sacrifice of an ox at the Athenian Buphonia, receive special ritual treatment and are remarked upon in aetiological mythology: for instance, in the oft-discussed Buphonia, the sacrificial axe is accused of murder and thrown into the sea.[42] The animal was usually fully grown (*teleios* in inscriptions), but younger animals were sacrificed in specific contexts, especially the piglets that were regularly slaughtered in purification rites. In only a few cases do we learn of the sacrifice of a pregnant animal.[43] This suggests that, ordinarily, female sacrificial animals were not supposed to be pregnant, and that pregnancy had a specific semantic function.

The performance of ordinary animal sacrifices

As far as we can tell, the basic form of ordinary animal sacrifice remained stable from the Homeric descriptions to those in late literature. The following account is based on Homer's description of Nestor's sacrifice to Athena in the *Odyssey*, with later variations and changes added.[44]

Once Nestor made the decision to offer a sacrifice to Athena, who had manifested in his palace the night before, he has a young cow brought from the meadow and the smith gild her horns 'so the goddess would delight in the offering'.[45] The implements for the rite – a bowl with water, a basket with barley, a vessel for the blood, the axe held by the sacrificer – were brought to the place of the sacrifice – the altar with its burning fire on top. Ordinarily, this was done in a sacrificial procession; the Greek term *pompē* ('procession') derives from *pempō* ('to accompany someone or something'), here the sacrificial animal. Votive reliefs and vases may show the procession of a family and sometimes other participants as well, such as a girl carrying a basket (*kanēforos*) and a slave leading the animal. Polis festivals, such as the Athenian Panathenaia, developed this into impressive demonstrations of civic power and wealth. As the images show, the animals usually walked near the head of the procession, and bovids especially were decorated not just by gilding their horns but by decking them with ribbons and wreaths.[46]

Nestor opened the rite by washing his hands and scattering the barley. In other descriptions, we see the barley thrown or water sprinkled over the animal to make it shake its head in a gesture that was construed as acquiescence to be sacrificed. Some descriptions even relate that the barley basket contained the sacrificial knife hidden under the grain: when the animal was offered the basket, it bent its head to eat, thus offering its neck to the lethal knife.[47] The importance of this initial ritual is underscored by the fact that Odysseus' companions, who had no grain on the island of Helius, sprinkled oak leaves instead of barley grains on the cattle of Helius before slaughtering them.[48] Ritual fiction constructed the animal's voluntary agreement to its sacrifice, as Meuli points out.[49] It is rather irrelevant for this fiction that in reality the animal had to be held tight, sometimes bound with ropes on its legs, or tied in front of the altar. This was necessary because it was a bad sign if the animal was not killed cleanly, as this could be read as resistance in the victim or the gods' rejection of the sacrifice. In some rare cases, a group of youths would lift the bull and carry it to the altar, where its throat was slit. In Athenian mythology, the young Theseus demonstrates his masculinity in this way.[50]

After these initial steps, Nestor prayed to the goddess (whose presence at the ritual Homer notes), cut hair from the animal's head, and threw it into the flames. The animal was now dedicated to the goddess. The sacrificer struck its neck with the axe and 'crippled its strength'.[51] As the animal sank to its knees, the women uttered the ritual shout – the *ololygē*, a semantically open vocal rite that could express either joy or fright – while the men lifted its head and the sacrificer cut its neck from below, allowing blood to flow into the bowl.[52] When the blood stopped flowing, life had left the animal; some of its blood was splashed onto the altar, and the carcass was dismembered. Flaying must have preceded dismemberment, but the sources are silent on this. We know from inscriptions that the skin was either set aside as a gift to the priest or retained by the owner. The hides from the Athenian state sacrificial were carefully registered, and their sale was part of the city's revenue.[53] After Homer, once the carcass was opened before flaying or dismemberment, the seer inspected the entrails to ascertain that the gods were accepting of the sacrifice; otherwise, it had to be repeated. However, for reasons that remain unclear, Homer does not record this divinatory act. Perhaps this is a Homeric stylisation, or it may be that the inspection was introduced later, together with reading the liver (hepatoscopy), which was a common feature of ancient Near East and later Etrurian and Roman sacrificial ceremonies. Hence, we may assume that hepatoscopy was practised in Greece as well, even though it is attested on only a few Athenian vases of the late sixth century.[54]

The meat was prepared in several steps, with several discrepancies between Homer's account and later practice. In Homer's description, first the thighs are cut out, wrapped in fat, covered with pieces of meat and burnt on the altar, while Nestor pours wine over them – presumably unmixed wine, which would have stimulated the fire due to its relatively high alcohol content. This must have been common Homeric practice, since it accounts for the formulaic praise of piety shown by burning thighs to the gods. Then the innards were dissected, put on spits, roasted, and immediately eaten before the rest of the meat was cut, prepared, again roasted on spits, and eaten in the sort of common banquet that Nestor and his sons celebrate with Telemachus and his companions. All of this took a considerable amount of time – long enough for Nestor's youngest daughter to bathe Telemachus in Homer's account. After Homer, the thigh bones (or the entire thighs) were burnt for the gods together with fat and small pieces of meat, and the innards dissected, roasted, and eaten by the sacrificial personnel. The tail was also placed on the fire; if it curled upwards, that was taken as a good omen.[55] The rest of the flesh, including the meat-rich thighs, was sometimes cut from the bones for cooking or for distribution at home. (As previously noted, the distribution of sacrificial meat to families or the market was the rule, not the exception.) There is no clear indication when the stripped thigh bones and the meat of the thighs were burnt, except where the sacrificial laws specify that the thighs are a perquisite for the priest. Osteology has provided evidence of both procedures, and, in a private sacrifice, the decision might have been left to the sacrificer.[56] At any rate, the meat that was eaten on the spot was first roasted, then boiled often with one or both thighs set aside as remuneration for the priest. Only in the Orphic inversion of the anthropophagy of young Dionysus did the boiling precede the roasting, against all reasonable ways of preparing meat for consumption.[57] Once the cooking was done, the assembled group consumed the meat, and sometimes the head of a bovid was displayed in the shrine, making the later-stylised bucranium into a symbol of piety.[58]

In other ritual forms, small pieces of meat are not burnt with the bones and the tail before general cooking; instead, they are set aside for the gods either on sacrificial tables as *trapezōmata* or, as in Athens or Chios, placed in the hands or at the knees of the divine images.[59] We must assume that priests or other shrine personnel subsequently collected this meat for themselves. This variation clarifies in an unequivocal image that these pieces of meat were thought to feed the gods (tables laden with food are very common in Egyptian sacrificial iconography); this has to be extended to the burnt pieces as well.

Sacrifices without common consumption

Greeks performed a much small number of sacrifices in which the animal was killed but not eaten. There is no common ancient term for these ceremonies. The word *sphagia*, coined by Paul Stengel as a complementary term to *thysia*, does not work because it does not cover all usages, and because *thysia* is the unmarked general term for all animal sacrifices.[60]

If we disregard isolated rituals (such as the massacre in Hermione during which women with sickles randomly killed young cows in the temple of Demeter, and where we lack information on the fate of the meat), there are a few areas where animal sacrifice did not lead to consumption.[61] One of these is purification; and if purification serves to heal mishap or illness, this shades into apotropaic rituals. In these rites, animals were killed but usually not eaten. Mostly, the slaughtered animal was a relatively inexpensive piglet, as many inscriptions show. Its blood was used to purify murderers: two Apulian vases show Apollo cutting a piglet's throat over Orestes, and Heraclitus of Ephesus objected to what he saw as the paradox of cleansing blood with blood.[62] But we should not generalise on the basis of these rites. For instance, the piglets that the Eleusinian initiates slaughtered after their preparatory bath in the sea were eaten before the initiates began their fast. In Aristophanes' *Frogs*, the slave Xanthias is thrilled when the appearance of the initiates is accompanied by the smell of 'piglet meat'.[63] And when the initiates in Andania sacrifice a white ram and later three piglets for their purification, it is unclear whether the animals were subsequently destroyed or eaten.[64] And other animals were used for purification elsewhere, too: Epimenides purified Athens with grown sheep, and some plague oracles from second-century CE Clarus prescribe different animals according to local custom that could include either a banquet or the destruction of the animals – as with a cow in a deep fire-pit (*megaron*).[65]

Another area where sacrifice did not lead to consumption was the oath. Detailed descriptions of oath rituals begin with the one that seals the abortive armistice between Greeks and Trojans in the *Iliad*. In keeping with the ominous character of the oath as a self-curse, animals were slaughtered and bled to death but never eaten: commensality would have sent the wrong message.[66]

The same holds true for the third major area where consumption did not follow slaughter: the pre-battle sacrifice, for which *sphagia* is the proper term. The most common animal in these rituals seems to have been a ewe, although there is the occasional image of a ram; and when Xenophon's mercenary army was running out of sheep because their seer could not obtain a favourable sign, they slaughtered an ox.[67] Xenophon also gives a detailed description of the complex sequence of Spartan pre-battle sacrifice that secured the help of the gods in which the divinatory character of the ceremonies was prominent.[68] First, still in Sparta, the king offered a sacrifice to Zeus Hegetor. When this was favourable, the 'fire-carrier' (*pyrforos*) led the army to the border, carrying fire from Zeus' altar. On arrival, the king used the fire to sacrifice to Zeus and Athena. If the sacrifices were favourable, the fire and animals called *sphagia* were carried at the head of the army into enemy territory, where the animals were offered (*thysia*) in the presence of dignitaries and officers. Afterwards, the king issued his orders. Xenophon is not clear on the conclusion of the ceremony, but it is likely that the rites ended with the destruction of the animals rather than a banquet; as other texts show, they served again to obtain favourable signs.

An intriguing issue is the treatment of the hides in such sacrifices. It can be assumed that piglets were completely destroyed, rather than skinned, and there is evidence that pigs were singed (*heuston*), not flayed for sacrifice.[69] On the other hand, a sacred law from the Attic deme Aixone suggests that sheep were flayed, with the skin going to the priest even when the meat was not consumed but destroyed in fire.[70] It is tempting to extrapolate this treatment to all larger animals (with the exception of pigs) whose meat was burnt (*holokautein*). Plutarch mentions a sacrifice in Smyrna to Boubrostis, 'Epidemic Hunger', where the victim was destroyed 'skin and all' (*adaptos*, lit. 'unflayed'), suggesting that, in other contexts, where hunger was not ritually displayed, a more careful treatment of the skin was the rule.[71]

Sacrificing to the heroes

Then there are the subterranean powers: the deceased and their divinities. Homer has Odysseus slaughter a black ram and ewe to attract the souls of the dead; the animals' blood flows into a *bothros*. [72] In a later interpretation, this turned into the model for necromantic rites and, more importantly, for the apotropaic rites against an epidemic that Apollo of Clarus prescribed for the town of Callipolis in a second-century CE oracle. The god advised libations to the underworldly (*hypoudaioi*) gods (whoever they may be), and a black ram and ewe, bled into a *bothros* along with libations, to Hades and Persephone. Thereafter, the animals should be completely burnt.[73]

This shades into the problem of heroic cult. In a well-known passage, Herodotus applauds the Greeks for worshipping Heracles in two ways: sacrificing (*thyousi*), as to an immortal; and making offerings (*enagizousi*), as to a hero.[74] Superficially, this passage seems straightforward: gods receive animal sacrifices with an ensuing banquet; heroes get offerings like deceased mortals – libations or animals that are fully destroyed.[75] In the past, scholars aligned this with the dichotomy between Olympian and chthonian divinities. However, even before this dichotomy was questioned (and often rejected) as an early 19th-century construct, it was clear that heroes could receive sacrifices with a banquet. After all, on votive reliefs to many heroes – not just Heracles – the worshippers bring an animal, and the dominant type of heroic relief shows the hero at a banquet (albeit with cakes rather than choice cuts of meat on the table).[76]

Inscriptions complicate the issue. A fifth-century BCE *lex sacra* from Selinous prescribes offerings to the polluted Tritopatores 'as to heroes' with libations but also an animal sacrifice, and with the sacrifice of a grown animal to the pure Tritopatores.[77] Another second-century CE plague oracle from Clarus (this time for Pergamon) prescribes: 'as it is your custom' to offer Demeter and the underworld gods (*enerterioi theoi*) fumigations, the same should be done for Aither and the gods in the sky (*epouranioi theoi*), whereas the underworld heroes (*hērōes chthonioi*) should receive libations, and Gaea a cow burnt in a holocaust.[78]

The upshot of the discussion was that, in a thorough study, Gunnel Ekroth refused to acknowledge any difference between sacrifices to gods and heroes, except in the manner in which the animal's neck and head were held.[79] But this very technical distinction might not have been all. As Robert Parker points out, even if there is no other clear and uniform dichotomy between heroic and divine sacrifices, other details might be added on a case-by-case basis.[80] The most intriguing of these might be the prohibition against eating the meat outside the sanctuary – almost common for heroes in the sacrificial calendar of Erchia. Given the role of the hero as a deceased ancestor, enforcing a common meal on the site of worship (often his grave) would make sense: the goods are much more spread out than in conventional sacrifice and might not involve a common meal for all worshippers.

Mycenaean animal sacrifice

The sacrificial practice of Mycenaean society has been the subject of intense recent research, stimulated in part by the publication of the Linear B tablets from Thebes, and in part by a much wider archaeological interest in the analysis of animal bones unearthed at ancient sites. In 2004, these studies resulted in a volume on the *Mycenaean Feast* that draws on all of the various approaches. Osteology and the study of the Linear B texts seem to be particularly informative, yielding results that often converge.[81]

The overall result is that our picture of Greek sacrifice from Homer and post-Homeric sources seems to be equally valid for the Mycenaean Bronze Age, notwithstanding its different political and economic structures.[82] The often large-scale sacrifice of domesticated animals – cattle, sheep, goats, pigs – is well attested in banquets connected with the Mycenaean palaces. The Pylus texts are crucial in this respect. One tablet attests to banquets attended by up to 1000 people, judging from the number of animals and other associated foodstuffs, although it is impossible to exclude the possibility that meat and other food were not only consumed in the palace but also distributed to individual households. Nevertheless, banquets of a large number of seated members of the elite are at least well attested by the furniture inventories.[83] In Cnossus, both a hecatomb and the *dōdekaïs* seem to be well attested, with the former comprising a state sacrifice that was held far from the find-spot of the tablets.[84] The detailed analysis of tablets that contain inventories of ritual implements points to a sacrificial technique that we find in Homer and later sources. Bridles suggest that large animals were led in a procession or tied in place; axes suggest that sacrifical victims were stunned and knives that they were bled.[85] Bone analysis suggests that red deer were sacrificed together with domesticated animals, and three Pylus texts have been interpreted as possible evidence for the keeping of deer.[86] Osteology also points to the special treatment of cattle heads and thighs. The rare presence of other large cattle bones might suggest that such bones were either burnt entirely or distributed with the meat still attached.[87] Finally, as in the Iron Age, the Bronze Age palace of Thebes imported sacrificial animals from some distance away, such as cattle from Euboea.[88]

Minoan sacrifice, on the other hand, is mainly accessible through iconography, as analysed by Nano Marinatos.[89] Despite the cultural differences between Minoans and Mycenaeans, this analysis did not identify significant differences, except that deer sacrifice seemed to be more prevalent in the Minoan civilisation than it was among either the Mycenaeans or later Greeks.

Sacrifice as a gift and meal for the gods

Several aetiological myths shed light on how the Greeks understood animal sacrifices. The best-known story is told by Hesiod in the *Theogony*, where he discusses the offspring of the Titan Iapetus and Zeus' resultant anger (*cholos*).[90] The deity's anger dates to the time when gods and humans 'separated' in Mecone (wherever that was) and Prometheus sent a large bull to deceive Zeus by making him choose between a heap of bones covered with appetising fat and a heap of entrails, and meat covered with the beast's skin and stomach. Against his better judgement, Hesiod tells us, Zeus selected the bones, which is why, ever since, 'humans burn for the immortals the white bones on their smoking altars'.[91] Enraged by the deception, Zeus took fire from humans, but Prometheus stole it back from Olympus. As punishment, Zeus had Hephaestus and Athena create Pandora – 'a beautiful evil' and the ancestor of all women, who deceive and exploit the men who marry them. Since then, all men have been caught in a trap: those who marry bring trouble into their lives, and those who reject marriage have no offspring to help and protect them in old age.

This story is not just about the paradoxical aspect of sacrifice, which causes the gods to receive the inedible parts of the animal, neatly disguised, as gifts from humans. It also concerns the use of fire, sexuality, marriage and procreation, and humans' relations with the gods. Sacrifice is the means through which humans and gods have remained in contact since their separation. To understand Zeus' anger, however, sacrifice must have been seen as a way to honour the gods with the gift of a choice piece of meat – and thus to feed them. The burning of fat thighs (*piona mēria*) in Homer's account creates an obligation between human and god. The Greek term, however, is somewhat ambiguous. It means thighs with fat, meat, and bone all intact, one of which, according to the sacrificial laws, often goes to the priest. However, the echoes of Prometheus' deception of Zeus are obvious in the *Odyssey* when Eumaeus describes Odysseus 'covering them [thighbones] under fat' before offering them to the Nymphs.[92] As osteology suggests (see above), both procedures were practised. At any rate, when sacrifices cease, as in the *Homeric Hymn to Demeter*, when the goddess halts the growth of the earth, or in Aristophanes' *Birds*, when the birds block the passage of smoke from the earth to Olympus, the threat of hunger forces the gods into negotiation. In a parodic anti-sacrifice text that was once wrongly ascribed to Lucian, the treatise *On Sacrifice*, the gods assemble like flies above the altars.[93] This same conception of the sacrifice as a meal offered to the gods was more explicit when the gods' portion was set on an offering table or, unequivocally but less frequently, when the gods' images were placed on couches as visible guests of what the Romans called *lectisternia*. There was no technical term for this ritual in Greece, but it is attested in the festival names Theoxenia and Theodaisia and in its Linear B form – *lekhestroteria*.[94] Conversely, to eat from the sacrificial animal before the meat was presented to the gods constituted a refusal of honour and was severely punished.[95]

In Hesiod's myth, the sacrificial animal is only a means to an end. Later stories provide more information about the victim, and all describe its death as a punishment. The foundational story of the Athenian bouphonia – an unusual sacrifice of a working animal – has the ox killed in an act of anger because it ate the sacred cakes which, in that still-vegetarian age, humans offered to the gods. Although the story mitigates the animal's guilt by seeing the murderous axe punished, the human slaughterer suffers no consequences, and, at the same time, his act legitimises sacrificial killing through the order of an oracle.[96]

There is much less hedging of guilt in the long list of sacrificial animals and the reasons for their slaughter in Ovid's *Fasti* (although it is not always clear what the author adopted from tradition and what he added):

- Demeter kills a pig for destroying her fields.
- Dionysus receives the death of a goat that damaged his vines.
- Cows are killed to restore the bees of Aristaeus and thus cancel his guilt for their annihilation.
- Sheep are killed for eating sacred herbs.
- The death of a deer in Iphigenia's stead started its sacrificial role in the cult of Artemis.
- And the ill-timed braying of a donkey provoked its death at the hands of frustrated Priapus.[97]

These stories contradict the willing submission that Meuli found in hunting practices and later formalised as '*Unschuldskomödie*' ('comedy of innocence').[98] On the other hand, the head-shaking prompted by the ritual sprinkling of water or barley was read as acquiescence as far back as antiquity. We are thus confronted with two different readings of the sacrificial act that must reflect a development that also led to criticism of animal sacrifice.[99]

The critics of sacrifice: philosophers

Ovid's list, in which animals are held responsible for their own sacrificial deaths, reflects an age when people started to consider the ethics of killing animals to please the gods as well as the anthropocentrism this implied. Like Porphyry, he embeds his history of sacrifice in a cultural history that begins when humans did not kill animals in order to please the gods but were content with burning herbs and flowers on altars. Both presumably derive from the now-lost treatise *On the Right Worship* (*Peri eusebeias*) by Aristotle's student Theophrastus.[100] And it should be remembered that Hesiod places his narration in a history of human development: there was a time when gods and humans had not yet fallen out. The preserved Hesiod is reticent about this era, but the late archaic continuation of the *Theogony* that was called *Catalogue of Women* described this period. It opens with the description of a time 'when immortals and mortal humans shared common meals and common seats'.[101] From the very beginning of preserved Greek reflection on the history of sacrifice, animal sacrifice belongs to a time after Paradise; the humans in the *Catalogue* did not need sacrifice because they communicated with the gods face to face.

Theophrastus and his followers had humanity living in a vegetarian age, at least with respect to communication with the gods.

Ethical discourses about the best form of sacrifice – which invariably reject animal sacrifice in favour of something much simpler – pre-date the fourth century BCE. Porphyry cites two anecdotes that have been traced back to late archaic Greek thought. In both, Apollo, through the voice of the Pythia, prefers the pious sacrifice of a small amount of ground barley prepared with a pure and pious mind to an impressive hecatomb organised by a rich but far from innocent man.[102] Importantly, neither of the anecdotes rejects hecatombs on the grounds that the gods disapprove of the killing of animals. Rather, they oppose ostentatious, expensive animal sacrifice, whose memory, as we have seen, could be kept alive by displaying the cows' heads. In any case, who could afford a hecatomb of cattle, which would have cost early fourth-century Athenians about 6000 drachmae – roughly equivalent to the daily income of 2000 unskilled laborers?[103] A similar anecdote features in the story of the Neopythagorean holy man Apollonius of Tyana's visit to the shrine of Asclepius at Aegae in Cilicia. Apollonius takes offence at the hecatombs of a rich landowner and reveals the man's immoral past. It is not the killing of animals but the landowner's use of an opulent ceremony to try to buy his way out of trouble that Apollonius finds objectionable.[104]

Late archaic Greek thought had already gone well beyond this. Towards the end of the sixth century BCE, Pythagoras of Samos developed his unique branch of Presocratic thought, first on his native island and later in southern Italy after he and his followers relocated there to escape Samian political turmoil.[105] Pythagoras coined the notions of the immortality of the soul and the migration of souls from body to body. His contemporaries, when ridiculing these concepts, tended to focus on the weird idea that a human soul could migrate into an animal body and back again.[106] This, taken to its logical extreme, forbids the killing of any animal and makes eating meat and animal sacrifice impossible. It would also prohibit Pythagoreans from participating in regular civic life, which was held together by the common sacrifice and meal.[107] The ancient tradition about Pythagorean vegetarianism is, however, less straightforward, and contradictory stories date back to the classical centuries (see also this volume, Chapter 7).[108] Whatever the historical truth, from very early on, it seems that Pythagoreans attempted to avoid a number of Greek customs. For instance, they advocated abstention from eating certain parts of the animal (especially the heart); abstention from consuming the meat of certain species, such as the ox that pulls the plough, and, in a later text, animals that had not been sacrificed; and, perhaps most ingeniously, sacrificing cakes in the shape of a bull.[109] All of these proposals indicate that animal sacrifice was a powerful and constant part of Greek religious tradition that everyone – including Pythagoreans – somehow had to accommodate.

The gradual rejection of sacrifice in later antiquity

Things started to change during the Imperial Age.[110] To judge from the few extant fragments from *On Sacrifices*, the historical Apollonius of Tyana rejected any material sacrifice: 'It is best to make no sacrifice to the divine at all, no lighting of fire.'[111] The Middle Platonists' rejection of the material world trumped Neopythagorean vegetarianism in both sacrificial ritual and diet fully two centuries before Porphyry strenuously advocated it in his treatise *On Abstinence*. Unlike modern vegetarianism, the rejection of meat was based on metaphysics rather than health considerations or empathy with animals.[112]

The quiet rejection of animal sacrifice became a possibility in ordinary cult in the second century CE, and not just in rituals performed by marginal philosophers or poor peasants who could not afford to buy a sheep, let alone a bull, but among wealthy citizens. This stands in marked contrast to the expansion of city festivals into lavish sacrificial events and international contests lasting many days.[113] Several inscriptions, two of them oracles, insist that proper worship should consist not of sacrificing animals but of singing hymns, burning incense, or pouring libations, all of which are less harmful than the blood and meat of animals. Christians, as Pliny's famous letter from Bithynia shows, had already adopted this approach, but it is difficult to gauge whether they set an example for non-Christians. It is more likely that the latter embraced a mild and popular form of Middle Platonism that did not necessarily entail a vegetarian diet.[114] The Christian resistance to animal sacrifice became visible and grew rapidly only after Constantine, when emperor worship through sacrifices quickly disappeared. In the course of the fourth century, several imperial letters preceded Theodosius' multiple, full-scale prohibitions of animal sacrifice, but even thereafter some parts of the empire were slow to abandon the practice, as the repeated imperial orders and complaints of impatient bishops testify.[115]

Conclusion: humans, animals, and sacrifice

With Vernant, scholars of Greek religion read the role of animal sacrifice as constructing a tripartite world of gods, humans, and animals. Humans are at the centre, and they use animals as tools to communicate with the gods. Human sacrifices, a ritual that would contradict this world order, belong either to the remote past or to non-Greek barbarians.[116]

Like all general abstractions, this is a bird's-eye view from high above. Closer to the ground, other structures become visible. Among the superhuman recipients of sacrifices, the main indigenous division was that between gods and heroes. We saw how this division could be expressed by ritual differences, but these were far from uniform; and, more importantly in our context, the same animals were sacrificed to the heroes and the gods.

The divisions in the world of animals were more complex. The most obvious of these was between animals that were sacrificed and those that were not. We saw that this roughly corresponded to the division between domesticated and wild animals, with deer on the borderline between these two realms and fish the exception (Greeks, after all, did not domesticate fish).[117] We also saw that the gender division of the superhuman recipients was not forcibly reproduced in the sacrificial animals. Nor did the opposition between animals that could be sacrificed and those that never were correspond to the opposition between edible and inedible meat, although we think of sacrifice as *feeding* the gods. Hunted animals, from hares to bears to lions, were not sacrificed (again with the exception of certain fish), but their meat was thought to be edible and as such could (and often did) supplement the sacrificial meal. Nor did these divisions neatly intersect with the spatial system. In the ancient Greek world, there was a conception of three types of space: settlement space (*astu*), fields (*agroi* or *chōra*), and the untamed land of forest and underbrush outside the fields (*eschatiē*). Domesticated animals that were very close to humans – so close that early Iron Age burials sometimes included them – such as dogs and horses, might belong to the *astu* or the *chōra*: horses were not stabled in settlements, but dogs could be kept inside the house.[118] The most common domesticated animals – cattle, sheep, goat, and pigs – were housed on the farms that dotted the *chōra*, but sheep and goats at least were pastured year in, year out through transhumance in the *eschatiē*.[119] Wild animals resided in all three spaces: there were mice and rats in the *astu*, and alongside deer, rabbits, and foxes in the *chōra*; and all of these, together with larger animals, also lived in the *eschatiē*. Fish and birds were at home in another type of *eschatiē*, one that was alien to human experience.

Animal sacrifice followed its own system of categorisation, overlapping only partially with others. This allowed the intricate play to generate meaning inside the world of sacrificial animals that intrigued ancient commentators, who duly noted specific cults' abstention from specific animals – no goats for Asclepius, say, and no poultry for Demeter.[120] I also suspect that this explains why the gods were usually thought to consume the *knisē*, rather than physical meat (with the rare exception of the meat that was placed on the hands and knees of statues). The uniform smoke of the burnt meat retained no trace of the visible physical animal. Visual evidence was important only for humans who wanted to be seen as sacrificers – hence the bucrania.

More complex and even less well researched is the way single animal species were used across various semantic (symbolic) systems. To give just one example: in a sacrificial context, the rooster was thought to be a small, inexpensive, and sometimes cheap sacrifice, in contrast to the large, expensive, and generous sacrifices of cows and bulls. Roosters were sacrificed to different gods, most prominently Asclepius (thanks to Socrates), to thank him for granting his petition for healing.[121] Meanwhile, they were prohibited in the cult of Eleusinian Demeter, to whom roosters were sacred, as they were to Leto.[122] The vegetarian Pythagoras allowed his less strict adherents to sacrifice a rooster or a young lamb, but not an ox; and Plutarch tells us that before the late fifth century Spartan generals routinely offered a rooster following a victorious battle but were permitted to offer an ox when victory was secured through a clever stratagem.[123] White roosters were also employed in a strange apotropaic ritual in Methane to keep a destructive wind from crops and vineyards. Similarly, King Pyrrhus was said to offer a white rooster to heal people with malfunctioning spleens; and roosters were generally thought to help ease childbirth.[124] Outside this sacrificial context, in archaic and classical Greece an adult lover would present a rooster to his *eromenos*; Ganymede holds one in the famous terracotta statue that shows his abduction by Zeus, as do young symposiasts on Attic vases; similarly, on the Locrian pinakes, Persephone holds a rooster while sitting next to Hades, and we are encouraged to think that this might be a present from her abductor, too.[125]

There have been several attempts to explain these different uses from one core of symbolic meaning, but none of these is entirely satisfactory. Indeed, such a methodology appears too rigid.[126] A hermeneutic tool from the psychology of perception that Maurizio Bettini and Sarah Iles Johnston recently applied to animal symbolism is more flexible and thus more promising. It entails the identification and analysis of the 'affordances' that Greeks connected with a specific animal.[127] The term was coined by James J. Gibson, the founder of ecological psychology, to describe the trait of an object in an environment that affords the opportunity for action to a subject in the same environment.[128] Affordances are thus determined by the characteristics of an object independent of the needs of the perceiving subject, but their perception is caused by those needs: a meadow is green and lush, but this affordance is relevant for cows and horses, not for fish or philosophers. Gibson emphasises that affordances are 'real, objective, physical properties': his is not a subjectivist theory.[129] However, they do answer the needs of the subject. In any case, they have to be consistent or form a system that gives them more flexibility than traditional or structuralist symbolism.[130] The fact that the observer does not construct affordances but perceives them when needed determines their variety inside a given historical culture: affordances might be constant, but their observation and selection are culture-specific and determined by the needs of a group or society.

What were the possible affordances of the rooster as we find them in Greek texts? Greeks perceived and described the rooster as a small animal that was edible and usually kept inside the settlement, where it crowed in the middle of the night, waking people up.[131] It was perceived as a very sexually active creature that mated with close relatives.[132] It was thought to form close bonds with its owner or with companion animals; a new owner had to perform special rituals to bind it to its new home.[133] It frightened lions and could fight with other roosters; and at least fifth-century Greeks still knew that it had links to Persia.[134] Most of these affordances were irrelevant to the bird's social roles. Its sexually active character, however, made it appropriate as a love-gift, as did its habit of forming close personal ties. Under the assumption that disease was a demonic power, as in some Clarian oracles, the rooster's role in healing and the concomitant association with Asclepius might be seen as consequences of its paradoxical power over the (much stronger) lion. This might also be the root of its power to help with childbirth. Alternatively, this might derive from its nocturnal wakefulness, which also might account for the connection with the divine (and exhausted) mothers Demeter and Leto. The rooster's role as a sacrificial animal is, thus, just one aspect of a much wider role in Greek thinking.

This is only a selective and temporary answer. The problem remains: how do we analyse the role of animals in cultural constructions? Even now no hard-

and-fast explanation is convincing. We are learning that these roles are complex and even contradictory, much like the rooster itself – that small yet fearsome creature. No simple answer will suffice.

Notes

1 For an overview, see *ThesCRA* I, 59–134.
2 See I Corinthians: 8–10.
3 Pl. *Euthphr.* 14d (τὸ θύειν δωρεῖσθαί ἐστι τοῖς θεοῖς).
4 Overviews in Lincoln 2012 and Graf 2012.
5 Smith 1894: 234; Naiden 2013.
6 Durkheim 1912.
7 Harrison 1927: 118–157, rejecting her earlier reading of sacrifice as a gift (134, n. 1).
8 Durkheim 1912; Hubert and Mauss 1964.
9 The main monographs are Burkert 1983b and Detienne and Vernant 1979; but see also, among others, the contributions of Vernant and Burkert in Reverdin and Grange 1981: 1–21 and 91–125; Vernant 1977; Burkert 1983a; Burkert 1987; and a reassessment in Georgoudi and Polignac 2018.
10 Meuli 1946 (published in the *Festschrift* for P. von der Mühll, a colleague at the University of Basel, by the Basel-based publisher Schwabe). On Meuli (who was never Burkert's teacher, contrary to popular belief), see Jung 1975.
11 See Hamerton-Kelly 1987 with essays by Burkert, Girard, and Jonathan E. Smith on sacrifice; Palaver 2010.
12 Fundamental for Rome is Scheid 2005.
13 Naiden 2013.
14 On the return of interest in the gods, see, e.g., Parker 2005a; Bremmer and Erskine 2010; Versnel 2011.
15 Collected by Prott and Ziehen 1896; Sokolowski 1955, 1962, 1969; Lupu 2004.
16 Iconography: Straten 1995; Gebauer 2002. For a recent overview of zooarchaeology, see, esp., Ekroth and Wallensten 2013; Ekroth 2017.
17 Overview: Jameson 1988.
18 Jameson 1988. On the key role of sheep in Mycenaean economy, see Killen 1964.
19 Goat sacrifice: Viscardi 2016. No goats to Asclepius: Graf 1984: 256.
20 Xen. *Hell.* 6.4.29.
21 Hom. *Od.* 14.100–118.
22 For specific cases, see, e.g., Sguaitamatti 1984; Hinz 1998; Ruscillo 2013.
23 Philostr. *VA* 1.10.
24 Linear B hecatombs: Killen 1994: 79.
25 A hecatomb consists of 50 rams in Hom. *Il.* 23.146 and just 12 oxen in Hom. *Il.* 6.115.
26 Genière and Jolivet 2003.
27 See Graf 2019.
28 Plin. *Ep.* 10.96.10. On the question, see Ekroth 2007 and Parker 2010.
29 I Corinthians:10.25–26: 'Eat anything that is sold in the meat market without asking questions for conscience's sake, for the earth is the Lord's, and all it contains.'
30 Greenewalt 1978; Lacam 2008; Sassù 2016; on eating dogs, see also Wilkens 2003.
31 Xenophon's *paradeisos*: Xen. *An.* 5.3.10. Deer sacrifice: Larson 2017. On the Mycenaean precedent, see Palaima 2004.
32 Hom. *Od.* 9.155–231.
33 Bakker 2013.
34 Pausanias 7.18; see Pirenne-Delforge 2006 (with previous literature).

35 Roosters sacrificed to Asclepius: key passage Pl. *Phd.* 118a, often repeated later; see also Artem. *Onirocritica* 5.9. To Heracles: Plut. *Quaest. conv.* 696e. Eaten after sacrifice: Ael. *NA* 5.28; Luc. *Iupp. trag.* 15 (characterised as cheap).

36 Fish sacrifice: Carboni 2016. On prohibitions against fish, see Arbesmann 1929: 50–51 (general), 76 (Eleusis).

37 Graf 1984: 282.

38 Hom. *Od.* 10.527, 11.35.

39 For the inscription: Schnegg-Köhler 2002. For the Sibylline oracle: Zos. *Historia Nova* 2.1.

40 E.g. in Athens of the cows for Athene: *IG* I^3 447 bii 26. In Delphi of a goat: *Corpus des Inscriptions de Delphes* 13.19.

41 Feyel 2006; see, esp., Sokolowski 1969: 151A (Cos) and Blümel 1995, 1997, 2000 (= *SEG* 45. 1507AB, 50.1001).

42 Porph. *Abst.* 2.29.

43 Bremmer 2005.

44 Hom. *Od.* 3.404–463.

45 Hom. *Od.* 3.438.

46 Gebauer 2002.

47 On the contents of the sacrificial basket ('barley, wreath, knife'), see Ar. *Pax* 948, with schol. Variations: Eur. *El.* 810 (Orestes' killing of Aegisthus during a sacrifice); Plato Com. F 91.

48 Hom. *Od.* 12.357–358.

49 E.g. Meuli 1975: 952–954, 1005.

50 Straten 1995: 109–113. Attic red-figured vase: Gebauer 2002: 257, no. S1. Cult of Heracles: Theophr. *Char.* 27.5.

51 Hom. *Od.* 3.450.

52 On the *ololygē*, see Deubner 1941.

53 *IG* II^2 1496, from the years 334/333 BCE (fragmentary). See Rosivach 1994.

54 Gebauer 2002: 341–351 (22 images from between ca. 525 and 500 BCE).

55 Taught by Prometheus: Aesch. *PV* 496. See Straten 1995: 118–130; Gebauer 2002: 355 and 437–441.

56 Thus Berthiaume 2004: 246.

57 Detienne 1977: 163–217.

58 Theoph. *Char.* 21.7: 'Having sacrificed a bull, he hangs its head opposite the temple gate and decks it with garlands so that everybody who comes in knows that he sacrificed a bull.'

59 Graf 1984; Straten 1995.

60 Stengel 1910: 92–101. See, on the other hand, *ThesCRA* I: 78, no. 104, following Rudhardt 1992: 272–276, 282–283.

61 Paus. 2.35.4–8; see Johnston 2012.

62 Orestes: *ThesCRA* II: 16, no. 69; Heraclitus, DK 22 B 5.

63 Ar. *Ran.* 338.

64 Sokolowski 1969: 65, 67–68; see Deshours 2006: 129–130; Gawlinski 2011: 165–166.

65 Merkelbach and Stauber 1996: banquet Pergamon, no. 2 (several bovids) and unknown city, no. 11 (no details); holocaust Hierapolis, no. 4 (cow), Kallipolis, no. 9 (male and female black goat).

66 *ThesCRA* III: 237–246. Main texts: Hom. *Il.* 3.58–120, 245–312.

67 Xen, *Hell.* 3.1.17–19. Images: *ThesCRA* I: 105, nos. 359–361.

68 Xen. *Lac.* 13.2–5; see Lonis 1979.

69 Pigs: Ackermann 2007: 124 (*Aixone lex*). The settlement among the Salaminioi decrees that the priest of Heracles will receive 'the skin and a thigh from the flayed, a thigh from the singed animals': *Agora* 19: Leases L 4a (= RO 2003, no. 37), l. 32.

70   Ackermann 2007: 122.
71   Plut. *Quaest. conv.* 6.8.1 (694ab), after Metrodoros, *FGrHist* 43 F 3; see Scullion 2000: 59, who adduces Hebrew and Punic parallels. A fragmentary *lex sacra* from Phangoria mentions 'a thigh for *holokautesis*', and thus has the animal dismembered before burning: *CIRB* 1005 = *IOSPE* II 342 (second century CE).
72   Hom. *Od.* 11.29–37.
73   Merkelbach and Stauber 1996, no. 9. For an overview of the rituals for the dead, see Johnston 1999: 36–81.
74   Hdt. 2.44; see Parker 2005b.
75   This was the perception of later commentators. See *Suda* E 1092 ('either to pour libations, or to sacrifice as to the deceased, or to destroy in fire') and E 194 (where *enagismoi* are paraphrased as *holokautōmata*).
76   Dentzer 1982.
77   Jameson *et al.* 1993, col. A 10, 13. A revised text with English translation (by R. Kotansky), detailed photos, and a series of studies on the epigraphy and religion function of the inscription is in Iannucci *et al.* 2015.
78   Merkelbach and Stauber 1996, no. 2.
79   Ekroth 2002, but see Parker 2005b (ultimately inconclusive).
80   See above, n. 77.
81   Wright 2004. See also Godart 1999 and, on Mycenaean animal husbandry, Halstead 1998–1999.
82   Cattle sacrifice in the Bronze Age: McInerney 2010: 48–73.
83   Palaima 2004: 109, based on tablet PY Un 138.
84   Hecatomb KN C 914, see Killen 1994: 77–78; *dodekais* KN C 902, see Chadwick and Ventris 1973, no. 78.
85   Palaima 2004: 112–114.
86   Deer bones: Wilkens 2003: 86 (hunt); Stocker and Davies 2004: 62–63. Deer keeping (at remote sites): Palaima 1992: 72–73.
87   Stocker and Davies 2004: 70–71.
88   Killen 1994.
89   Marinatos 1986.
90   Hes. *Theog.* 507–617; anger (*cholos*) at 533.
91   Hes. *Theog.* 356–357.
92   Hom. *Od.* 17.241.
93   Belayche 2011; Graf 2011.
94   Overall, see Jameson 1994; the Lin. B term in Pylos, PY fr. 343.
95   Petzl 1994: 1, no. 1 and 141, no. 123.
96   Porph. *Abst.* 2.29; Lebreton 2015.
97   Ov. *Fast.* 1.349–456; see Lefèvre 1976.
98   Meuli 1975: 1005. '*Unschuldskünstler*' ('artist of innocence'): Meuli 1975: 996.
99   See Dierauer 1977: 253–293.
100 For a reconstruction of Theophrastus' treatise, see Pötscher 1964.
101 Hes. fr. 1.4–5 (trans. Merkelbach and West).
102 Porph. *Abst.* 2.15–17; on the late archaic background, see Wehrli 1964: 56–57.
103 On animal prices, see Jameson 1988.
104 Philostr. *VA* 1.10; it might be a local tradition.
105 Riedweg 2005.
106 Xenoph. fr. 21 B 7 (DK).
107 For the consequence of *metempsychōsis* for animal sacrifice, see the often overlooked passage Pl. *Leg.* 781e–783b and Dombrowski 1984: 9.
108 Burkert 1972: 180–181.
109 Not eating the heart or the meat of not sacrificed animals: Sokolowski 1955: 84 (Smyrna, second century CE). Cakes: reported about Pythagoras in Porph. *VP* 36, and about Empedocles in Philostr. *VA* 11.1.

110 For an overview, see Petropoulou 2009.
111 In Euseb. *Praep. evang.* 4.12–13.
112 But Porph. *Abst.* 3.25; see Dierauer 1977: 170.
113 See Chaniotis 2003 and 2004; and, as an instructive example, Wörrle 1988.
114 Plin. *Ep.* 10.95.
115 Graf 2016: 318–322.
116 Examples and bibliography in Bonnechere and Gagné 2013; Nagy and Prescendi 2013.
117 This led Smith 1987 to the problematic thesis that sacrifice was a discourse about domestication.
118 On early Iron Age graveyards with burials of horses and dogs as proof of horseback hunting, see Wilkens 2003.
119 See, for Delos, Leguilloux 2003.
120 Goats and Asclepius: Graf 1984: 256. Domestic birds and Demeter: Porph. *Abst.* 4.16. On these taboos, see Arbesmann 1929, albeit with constant reference to 'orenda'.
121 Asclepius: key passage Pl. *Phd.* 118a, often repeated; see also Artem. *Onirocritica* 5.9. Heracles: Plut. *Quaest. conv.* 696e. Twelve gods (in a household cult): Luc. *Iupp. trag.* 15.
122 Demeter: Porph. *Abst.* 4.16. Leto: Ael. *NA* 4.29.
123 Pythagoras: Iamb. *VP* 150 and *Protr.* 116. Spartans: Plut. *Ages* 33.4 (the historicity is doubtful).
124 Methane: Paus. 2.34. Pyrrhus: Plut. *Pyrrh.* 3.7–8 (384d). Birth: Ael. *NA* 4.29.
125 Eromenos: Plut. *Quaest. conv.* 622f. For the images, see Cosentino 2016.
126 Recently Cruccas 2016 and Cosentino 2016: 190–195 (a collection of earlier views).
127 Bettini 2003: 202–209; Johnston 2018: 195–201.
128 Gibson 1979. See also Scarandino 2003. In Gibson's theory, an affordance is something an animal sees in its environment that enables it to do something; see Natsoulas 2004. In the application to culture that Bettini and Johnston pioneered, the members of a given culture perceive certain characteristics of an animal that allow them to insert it into a traditional story or ritual.
129 Gibson 1979: 129: 'an affordance is neither an objective property nor a subjective property; or it is both if you like'. See Fox *et al.* 2015: 65.
130 Gibson 1979: 139 insists that 'an affordance is not bestowed upon an object by a need of the observer'. See also Scarandino 2003: 952.
131 Crowing: Aesop. *Fab.* 16.55.124; Plut. *De Pyth. or.* 400c; Athen. *Deipn.* 12.15.
132 Sexual activity: Arist. *Hist. an.* 544a 29, 558b11, 770a7. Extreme promiscuity: Aesop. *Fab.* 16.
133 Ael. *NA* 2.30; see also 5.28.
134 Lions fear roosters: Plut. *Mor.* 537c and 981e; Ael. *NA* 8.27 and 14.9. Otherwise fearless and strong men fear them: frr. 215k, 217g. Cock-fighting: e.g. Ar. *Av.* 759; see Arnott 2007: 10. Persia: e.g. Ar. *Av.* 483–484. Roosters are attested in a Minoan seal; see Arnott 2007: 10.

Bibliography

Ackermann, D. (2007) 'Rémunération des prêtres et déroulement des cultes dans un dème de l'Attique. Le règlement religieux d'Aixônè', *Études Classiques* 75, 111–136.
Arbesmann, R. P. (1929) *Das Fasten bei den Griechen und Römern*. Giessen.
Arnott, W. G. (2007) *Birds in the Ancient World. From A to Z*. London.
Bakker, E. J. (2013) *The Meaning of Meat and the Structure of the Odyssey*. Cambridge.

Belayche, N. (2011) 'Entre deux éclats de rire: sacrifice et représentation du divin dans le traité sur les sacrifices de Lucien', in V. Pirenne-Delforge and F. Prescendi (eds.) *Nourrir les dieux? Sacrifice et représentation du divin*. Liège, 321–334.

Berthiaume, G. (2004) 'L'Aile ou les mêria: sur la nourriture carnée des dieux grecs', in S. Georgoudi, R. Koch Piettre, and F. Schmidt (eds.) *La Cuisine et l'autel. Les Sacrifices en questions dans les sociétés de la Méditerranée ancienne*. Turnhout, 241–251.

Bettini, M. (2003) *Women and Weasels. Mythologies of Birth in Ancient Greece and Rome*. Chicago (Italian orig. 1998).

Blümel, W. (1995) 'Inschriften aus Karien I', *Epigraphica Anatolica* 26, 35–64.

Blümel, W. (1997) 'Ein weiteres Fragment des Kultgsetzes aus Bargylia', *Epigraphica Anatolica* 28, 153–156.

Blümel, W. (2000) 'Ein dritter Teil des Kultgesetzes aus Bargylia', *Epigraphica Anatolica* 32, 89–93.

Bonnechere, P. and R. Gagné (eds.) (2013) *Sacrifices humains. Perspectives croisées et représentations*. Liège.

Bremmer, J. N. (2005) 'The sacrifice of pregnant animals', in R. Hägg and B. Alroth (eds.) *Greek Sacrificial Ritual. Olympian and Chthonian*. Stockholm, 155–165.

Bremmer, J. N. and A. Erskine (eds.) (2010) *The Gods in Ancient Greece. Identities and Transformations*. Edinburgh.

Burkert, W. (1972) *Lore and Science in Ancient Pythagoreanism*. Cambridge, Mass. (German orig. 1962).

Burkert, W. (1981) 'Glaube und Verhalten: Zeichengehalt und Wirkungsmacht von Opferritualen', in J. Rudhardt and O. Reverdin (eds.) *Le Sacrifice dans l'Antiquité*. Geneva, 91–125.

Burkert, W. (1983a) *Anthropologie des religiösen Opfers. Die Sakralisierung der Gewalt*. München (repr. in Graf, F. (ed.) (2011) *Kleine Schriften*. Vol. 5. Göttingen, 3–22).

Burkert, W. (1983b) *Homo Necans. The Anthropology of Ancient Greek Sacrificial Ritual and Myth*, trans. P. Bing. Berkeley, Calif. (German orig. 1972).

Burkert, W. (1987) 'The problem of ritual killing', in R. G. Hamerton-Kelly (ed.) *Violent Origins. Walter Burkert, René Girard and Jonathan Z. Smith on Ritual Killing and Cultural Formation*. Stanford, Calif., 149–176 (repr. in Graf, F. (ed.) (2011) *Kleine Schriften*. Vol. 5. Göttingen, 23–49).

Carboni, R. (2016) 'Unusual sacrificial victims: fish and their value in the context of sacrifices', in P. A. Johnston, A. Mastrocinque, and S. Papaioannou (eds.) *Animals in Greek and Roman Religion and Myth*. Newcastle, 255–279.

Chadwick, J. and M. Ventris (1973) *Documents in Mycenaean Greek*. 2nd edn. Cambridge (orig. published in 1953).

Chaniotis, A. (2003) 'Negotiating religion in the cities of the Eastern Roman Empire', *Kernos* 16, 177–190.

Chaniotis, A. (2004) 'Das Bankett des Damas und der Hymnos des Sosandros. Öffentlicher Diskurs über Rituale in den griechischen Städten der Kaiserzeit', in D. Harth and G. J. Schenk (eds.) *Ritualdynamik. Kulturübergreifende Studien zur Theorie und Geschichte rituellen Handelns*. Heidelberg, 291–304.

Cosentino, A. (2016) 'Persephone's cockerell,' in P. A. Johnston, A. Mastrocinque, and S. Papaioannou (eds.) *Animals in Greek and Roman Religion and Myth*. Newcastle, 189–212.

Cruccas, E. (2016) 'Ho Persikos Ornis: the symbology of the rooster in the cult of the Kabeiroi', in P. A. Johnston, A. Mastrocinque, and S. Papaioannou (eds.) *Animals in Greek and Roman Religion and Myth*. Newcastle, 171–187.

Dentzer, J.-M. (1982) *Le motif du banquet couché dans le Proche-Orient et le monde grec du VIIe au IVe siècle avant J.-C.* Paris.

Deshours, N. (2006) *Les Mystères d'Andania. Étude d'épigraphie et d'histoire religieuse.* Pessac.

Detienne, M. (1977) *Dionysus mis à mort.* Paris.

Detienne, M. and J.-P. Vernant (1979) *La Cuisine du sacrifice en pays grec.* Paris.

Deubner, L. (1941) *Ololyge und Verwandtes.* Berlin (repr. in Deubner, O. (ed.) (1982) *Kleine Schriften zur klassischen Altertumskunde.* Königstein, 607–634).

Dierauer, U. (1977) *Tier und Mensch im Denken der Antike.* Amsterdam.

Dombrowski, D. A. (1984). *The Philosophy of Vegetarianism.* Amherst, Mass.

Durkheim, É. (1912) *Les Formes élémentaires de la vie religieuse. Le système totèmique en Australie.* Paris.

Ekroth, G. (2002) *The Sacrificial Rituals of Greek Hero-Cults in the Archaic to the Early Hellenistic Periods.* Liège.

Ekroth, G. (2007) 'Meat in ancient Greece: sacrificial, sacred or secular?', *Food and History* 5, 249–272.

Ekroth, G. (2017) 'Bare bones: zooarchaeology and Greek sacrifice', in S. Hitch and I. Rutherford (eds.) *Animal Sacrifice in the Ancient Greek World.* Cambridge, 15–47.

Ekroth, G. and J. Wallensten (eds.) (2013) *Bones, Behaviour and Belief. The Zooarchaeological Evidence as a Source for Ritual Practice in Ancient Greece and Beyond.* Stockholm.

Feyel, C. (2006) 'La *Dokimasia* des animaux sacrifiés', *Revue de Philologie* 80, 33–55.

Fox, R., D. Panagiotopoulos, and C. Tsouparopoulou (2015) 'Affordanz', in T. Meier, M. R. Ott, and R. Sauer (eds.) *Materiale Textkulturen: Konzepte – Materialien – Praktiken.* Berlin, 63–70.

Gawlinski, L. (2011) *The Sacred Law of Andania. A New Text with Commentary.* Berlin.

Gebauer J. (2002) *Pompe und Thysia. Attische Tieropferdarstellungen auf schwarz- und rotfigurigen Vasen.* Münster.

Genière, J. de la and V. Jolivet (2003) *Cahiers de Claros II. Les sanctuaires D'Apollon à Claros: l'aire des sacrifices.* Paris.

Georgoudi, S. and F. de Polignac (eds.) (2018) *Relire Vernant.* Paris.

Gibson, J. J. (1979) *An Ecological Approach to Visual Perception.* Boston, Mass.

Godart, L. (1999) 'Les Sacrifices d'animaux dans les textes mycéniens', in S. Deger-Jalkotzy, S. Hiller, and O. Panagl (eds.) *Floreant Studia Mycenaea. Akten des X. Mykenologischen Colloquims, Salzburg.* Vienna, 249–256.

Graf, F. (1984) *Nordionische Kulte. Religionsgeschichtliche und epigraphische Untersuchungen zu den Kulten von Chios, Erythrai, Klazomenai und Phokaia.* Rome.

Graf, F. (2011) 'A satirist's sacrifices: Lucian's On Sacrifices and the contestation of religious traditions', in J. W. Knust and Z. Várhelyi (eds.) *Ancient Mediterranean Sacrifice.* New York, N.Y., 203–213.

Graf, F. (2012) 'One generation after Burkert and Girard: where are the great theories?', in C. A. Faraone and F. Naiden (eds.) *Greek and Roman Sacrifice. Ancient Victims, Modern Observers.* Cambridge, 32–51.

Graf, F. (2016) *Roman Festivals in the Greek East.* Cambridge.

Graf, F. (2019) 'Δωδεκαῖς', *Zeitschrift für Papyrologie und Epigraphik* 211, 95–96.

Greenewalt, C. H.Jr. (1978) *Ritual Dinners in Early Historic Sardis.* Berkeley, Calif.

Halstead, P. (1998–1999) 'Texts, bones, and herders; approaches to animal husbandry in late Bronze Age Greece', *Minos* 33/34, 149–189.

Hamerton-Kelly, R. G. (ed.) (1987) *Violent Origins. Walter Burkert, René Girard and Jonathan Z. Smith on Ritual Killing and Cultural Formation.* Stanford, Calif.

Harrison, J. E. (1927) *Themis. A Study of the Social Origins of Greek Religion*. Cambridge. (orig. published in 1911).

Hinz, V. (1998) *Der Kult von Demeter und Kore auf Sizilien und in der Magna Graecia*. Wiesbaden.

Hubert, H. and M. Mauss (1964) *Sacrifice. Its Nature and Function*, trans. W. D. Halls. Chicago (French orig. 1899).

Iannucci, A., F. Muccioli, and M. Zaccarini (eds.) (2015) *La città inquieta. Selinunte tra lex sacra e defixiones*. Milan.

Jameson, M., D. Jordan, and R. Kotansky (1993) *A Lex Sacra from Selinous*. Durham, N.C.

Jameson, M. H. (1988) 'Sacrifice and animal husbandry in classical Greece', in C. R. Whittaker (ed.) *Pastoral Economies in Classical Antiquity*. Cambridge, 87–119 (repr. in Jameson, M. H. (2014) *Cults and Rites in Ancient Greece. Essays on Religion and Society*. Cambridge, 198–231).

Jameson, M. H. (1994) 'Theoxenia', in R. Hägg (ed.) *Ancient Greek Cult Practice from the Epigraphical Evidence*. Stockholm, 35–57 (repr. in Jameson, M. H. (2014) *Cults and Rites in Ancient Greece. Essays on Religion and Society*. Cambridge, 145–176).

Jameson, M. H. (2014) *Cults and Rites in Ancient Greece. Essays on Religion and Society*. Cambridge.

Johnston, P. A., Mastrocinque, A., and S. Papaioannou (eds.) (2016) *Animals in Greek and Roman Religion and Myth*. Newcastle.

Johnston, S. I. (1999) *Restless Dead. Encounters between the Living and the Dead in Ancient Greece*. Princeton, N.J.

Johnston, S. I. (2012) 'Demeter in Hermione: sacrifice and ritual polyvalence', *Arethusa* 45, 211–241.

Johnston, S. I. (2018) *The Story of Myth*. Cambridge, Mass.

Jung, F. (1975) 'Biographisches Nachwort', in K. Meuli, *Gesammelte Schriften II*. Basel, 1153–1209.

Killen, T. J. (1964) 'The wool industry of Crete in the late Bronze Age', *Annual of the British School in Athens* 59, 1–15.

Killen, T. J. (1994) 'Thebes sealings, Knossos tablets and Mycenaean state banquets', *Bulletin of the Institute of Classical Studies* 39, 67–84.

Lacam, J.-C. (2008) 'Le Sacrifice du chien dans les communeautés grecques, étrusques et romaines. Approche comparatiste', *Mélanges de l'École Française de Rome. Antiquités* 120, 29–80.

Larson, J. (2017) 'Venison for Artemis? The problem of deer sacrifice', S. Hitch and I. Rutherford (eds.) *Animal Sacrifice in the Ancient Greek World*. Cambridge, 48–62.

Lebreton, S. (2015) 'Zeus Polieus à Athènes: les Bouphonies et au-delà', *Kernos* 28, 85–110.

Lefèvre, E. (1976) 'Die Lehre von der Entstehung der Tieropfer in Ovids "Fasten" 1.335–456', *Rheinisches Museum* 119, 39–64.

Leguilloux, M. (2003) 'The Delian chora in classical and Hellenistic times: an island landscape planned for pastoralism', in E. Kotjabopoulou *et al.* (eds.) *Zooarchaeology in Greece. Recent Advances*. London, 251–256.

Lincoln, B. (2012) 'From Bergaigne to Meuli: how animal sacrifice became a hot topic', in C. A. Faraone, and F. Naiden (eds.) *Greek and Roman Sacrifice. Ancient Victims, Modern Observers*. Cambridge, 13–31.

Lonis, R. (1979) *Guerre et religion en Grèce à l'époque classique*. Paris.

Lupu, E. (2004) *Greek Sacred Law. A Collection of New Documents*. Leiden.

Marinatos, N. (1986) *Minoan Sacrificial Ritual. Cult Practice and Symbolism*. Göteborg.

McInerney, J. (2010) *The Cattle of the Sun. Cows and Culture in the World of the Ancient Greeks.* Princeton, N.J.

Merkelbach, R. and J. Stauber (1996) 'Die Orakel des Apollon von Klaros', *Epigraphica Anatolica* 27, 1–54 (repr. in Merkelbach, R. (1997) *Philologica. Ausgewählte Kleine Schriften.* Leipzig, 155–218).

Meuli, K. (1946) 'Griechische Opferbräuche', *Phyllobolia für Peter von der Mühll zum 60. Geburtstag am 1. August 1945.* Basel, 185–288.

Meuli, K. (1975) *Gesammelte Schriften*, ed. T. Gelzer. Basel.

Nagy, A. A. and F. Prescendi (eds.) (2013) *Sacrifices humains. Dossiers, discours, comparaisons. Actes du colloque de Genève, 19–20 Mai 2011.* Louvain.

Naiden, F. S. (2013) *Smoke Signals for the Gods. Ancient Greek Sacrifice from the Archaic through Roman Periods.* Oxford.

Natsoulas, T. (2004) '"To see things is to perceive what they afford": James J. Gibson's concept of affordance', *Journal of Mind and Behavior* 25, 323–347.

Palaima, T. (1992) 'Mycenaean scribal aesthetics', in R. L. Crowley and J. L. Crowley (eds.) *Eikon. Aegean Bronze Age Iconography Shaping a Methodology.* Liège, 63–74.

Palaima, T. (2004) 'Sacrificial feasting in the Linear B documents', in J. C. Wright (ed.) *The Mycenaean Feast.* Princeton, N.J., 97–126.

Palaver, W. (2010) 'Religion und Gewalt. Walter Burkert und René Girard im Vergleich', in A. Bierl and W. Braunert (eds.) *Gewalt und Opfer. Dialog mit Walter Burkert.* Berlin, 247–266.

Parker, R. T. (2005a) *Polytheism and Society at Athens.* Oxford.

Parker, R. T. (2005b) 'Ὡς ἥρωι ἐναγίζειν', in R. Hägg and B. Alroth (eds.) *Greek Sacrificial Ritual. Olympian and Chthonian.* Stockholm, 37–45.

Parker, R. T. (2010) 'Eating unsacrificed meat', in P. Carlier and C. Lerouge-Cohen (eds.) *Paysage et religion en Grèce antique. Mélanges offerts à Madeleine Jost.* Paris, 137–145.

Petropoulou, M.-Z. (2009) *Animal Sacrifice in Ancient Greek Religion, Judaism and Christianity, 100 BC–AD 200.* Oxford.

Petzl, G. (1994) 'Die Beichtinschriften Westkleinasiens', *Epigraphica Anatolica* 22, 1–143.

Pirenne-Delforge, V. (2006) 'Ritual dynamics in Pausanias: the Laphria', in E. Stavrianopoulou (ed.) *Ritual and Communication in the Graeco-Roman World.* Liège, 111–129.

Pötscher, W. (ed.) (1964) *Theophrastos. Περ Εὐσεβείας. Griechischer Text herausgegeben, übersetzt und eingeleitet von Walter Pötscher.* Leiden.

Prott, J. von and L. Ziehen (1896) *Leges Graecorum Sacrae e Titulis Collectae. I. Fasti Sacri.* Leipzig.

Reverdin, O. and B. Grange (eds.) (1981) *Le Sacrifice dans l'antiquité.* Genève.

Riedweg, C. (2005) *Pythagoras. His Life, Teaching, and Influence.* Ithaca, N.Y. (German orig. 2002).

Rosivach, V. J. (1994) *The System of Public Sacrifice in Fourth-Century Athens.* Atlanta, Ga.

Rudhardt, J. (1992) *Notions fondamentales de la pensée religieuse et actes constitutifs du culte dans la Grèce classique.* Paris. (orig. published in 1958).

Ruscillo, D. (2013) 'Thesmophoriazousai. Mytilenaean women and their secret rites', in G. Ekroth and J. Wallensten (eds.) *Bones, Behaviour and Belief. The Zooarchaeological Evidence as a Source for Ritual Practice in Ancient Greece and Beyond.* Stockholm, 181–196.

Sassù, A. (2016) 'Through impurity: a few remarks on the role of the dog in purification rituals of the Greek world', in P. A. Johnston, A. Mastrocinque, and S. Papaioannou (eds.) *Animals in Greek and Roman Religion and Myth.* Newcastle, 393–418.

Scarandino, A. (2003) 'Affordances, explained', *Philosophy of Science* 70, 949–961.

Scheid, J. (2005) *Quand faire, c'est croire. Les Rites sacrificiels des Romains.* Paris.

Schnegg-Köhler, B. (2002) 'Die augusteischen Saekularspiele', *Archiv für Religionsgeschichte* 4, 201–205.

Scullion, S. (2000) 'Heroic and chthonian sacrifice: new evidence from Selinous', *Zeitschrift für Papyrologie und Epigraphik* 132, 163–171.

Sguaitamatti, M. (1984) *L'Offrante de porcelet dans la coroplathie géléenne. Étude typologique.* Mainz.

Smith, J. Z. (1987) 'The domestication of sacrifice', in R. G. Hamerton-Kelly (ed.) *Violent Origins. Walter Burkert, René Girard and Jonathan Z. Smith on Ritual Killing and Cultural Formation.* Stanford, Calif., 191–205.

Smith, W. R. (1894) *Lectures on the Religion of the Semites*, ed. J. S. Black. 2nd edn. London.

Sokolowski, F. (1955) *Lois sacrées de l'Asie mineure.* Paris.

Sokolowski, F. (1962) *Lois sacrées des cités grecques. Supplément.* Paris.

Sokolowski, F. (1969) *Lois sacrées des cités grecques.* Paris.

Stengel, P. (1910) *Opferbräuche der Griechen.* Leipzig.

Stocker, S. R. and J. L. Davies (2004) 'Animal sacrifice, archives, and feasting at the palace of Nestor', in J. C. Wright (ed.) *The Mycenaean Feast.* Princeton, N.J., 59–75.

Straten, F. T. van (1995) *Hierà Kalá. Images of Animal Sacrifice in Archaic and Classical Greece.* Leiden.

Vernant, J.-P. (1977) 'Sacrifice et alimentation humaine: à propos du Prométhée d'Hésiode', *Annali della Scuola Nazionale Superiore di Pisa* 7, 905–940.

Vernant, J.-P. (1981) 'Théorie générale du sacrifice et mise à mort dans la θυσία grecque', in O. Reverdin and B. Grange (eds.) *Le Sacrifice dans l'antiquité.* Vandoeuvres-Genève, 1–21 (Eng. trans. in Vernant, J.-P. (1991) *Mortals and Immortals. Collected Essays*, ed. F. I. Zeitlin. Princeton, N.J., 290–302).

Versnel, H. S. (2011) *Coping with the Gods. Wayward Readings in Greek Theology.* Leiden.

Viscardi, G. P. (2016) 'Constructing humans, symbolising the gods: the cultural value of the goat in Greek religion', in P. A. Johnston, A. Mastrocinque, and S. Papaioannou (eds.) *Animals in Greek and Roman Religion and Myth.* Newcastle, 115–139.

Wehrli, F. (1964) *Hauptrichtungen des griechischen Denkens.* Zurich.

Wilkens, B. (2003) 'Hunting and breeding in ancient Crete', in E. Kotjabopoulou *et al.* (eds.) *Zooarchaeology in Greece. Recent Advances.* London, 85–90.

Wörrle, M. (1988) *Stadt und Fest im kaiserzeitlichen Kleinasien: Studien zu einer agonistischen Stiftung aus Oinoando.* Munich.

Wright, J. C. (2004) 'A survey of evidence for feasting in Mycenaean society', in J. C. Wright (ed.) *The Mycenaean Feast.* Princeton, N.J., 13–58.

9 Animals in ancient Greek divination

Oracles, predictions, and omens

J. Kindt

Introduction

Animals feature prominently in the varied ways the ancient Greeks sought to participate in the knowledge of the divine.[1] In particular, various forms of what Cicero in *De divinatione* (*On Divination*) has termed 'artificial divination' – prophetic insights gained through the obtaining and interpretation of signs – draw on the movement and behaviour of animals as meaningful articulations of the supernatural.[2] Yet, animals figure in the other ways in which the ancient Greeks obtained knowledge from the gods, too. They offered themselves as chance omens that could emerge anywhere and at any time without being solicited for a particular purpose. Furthermore, in dreams and oracular utterances, they served as complex symbols requiring careful consideration to be decoded. Animals, then, are variously present in Greco-Roman oracles, predictions, and omens of all kinds, whether from Delphi or one of the other centres of oracular divination, in the utterances of an inspired prophet or a seer with special skills, or as natural signs believed to convey supernatural knowledge.

This chapter explores the role of animals within and across different forms of oracles, predictions, and omens. Parallels emerge not only in which animals are chosen as divinatory signs, but also in how animals and animal behaviour are deemed meaningful to humans wishing to gain a better understanding of past, present, or future events. Differences emerge in how this symbolic system infuses the individual strategies by which the supernatural was thought to reveal itself in ancient Greece.

I will show that there is a common symbolic system that informs the different ways in which the ancient Greeks sought out and interpreted divine signs. This system casts gods and the supernatural more generally as providers of superior knowledge, humans as those who seek this knowledge, and animals as a medium facilitating the obtaining of this knowledge in various ways. The way this tripartite symbolic division informs various means of divination suggests that, in ancient Greece, the different modes of gaining knowledge with the help of the supernatural may have more in common than we have previously acknowledged. Overall, this chapter illustrates that the practice of divination supports the larger picture of ancient Greek religion as a symbolic language based on the tripartite division of gods, humans, and animals that is also at play in other areas of the ancient Greek religious experience.

Why animals? The natural and the supernatural

As in ancient Greek religion more generally, the practice of divination is deeply grounded in the natural world.[3] Outstanding aspects of the physical environment – springs, caves, mountain groves – feature prominently in numerous oracular sanctuaries and divinatory centres in the ancient world. Their ubiquitous presence suggests that such noticeable locations in the physical landscape were considered privileged sites for human communication with the supernatural and the divine.[4] Other aspects of the natural world – the oak tree at Dodona, the vapours at Delphi – were thought to facilitate the transmission of divine knowledge from gods to humans. Moreover, certain natural phenomena, such as a flash of lightning, an earthquake, or an eclipse of the sun or moon, served directly as divine signs.[5] All these links between divination and the natural world illustrate that in ancient Greece there was a close connection between the natural and the supernatural, with the latter thought to manifest itself in the former.

Animals, then, come into the picture as part of the physical environment and the idea of nature as potentially enchanted, and as a medium for the divine to reveal itself. As such, they have an important capacity that is significant to their role as preferred divine signs: they are able to act independently – that is, without human intervention. This capacity matters because many divinatory practices are based on the reading of animal movements and behaviours that are not instigated by humans and so can be interpreted as reflecting supernatural involvement.

The scanning of nature for meaningful signs, which is at the core of many ancient Greek divinatory practices, plays into a basic human need that dates back to primordial time: to identify agents in our surroundings that (potentially) matter to us. The human brain is physically hardwired to detect agency and gauge the many ways in which something may relate to us.[6] The practice of divination draws on this propensity, redirecting and institutionalising it practically by taking animal agency to stand for a parallel situation in the human realm (see below). In their likeness to humans both physically and in terms of behaviour, animals lend themselves to the drawing of such parallels and analogies.

At the same time, there is another way in which the observation of animals in nature may have informed the idea that they can reveal the future. As Fritz Graf and others have pointed out, ancient Greek observation of animals in nature morphs at times seamlessly into religious considerations.[7] Aelian's eclectic anthology of naturalistic observations, for example, includes plenty of animals with an uncanny capacity to anticipate future events: bees are endowed with 'the faculty of divination' (*mantikos*) because they seem able to predict rain or frost.[8] The Egyptian antelope is believed to mark the rising of the dog star with a sneeze.[9] Finally, Aelian states that chaffinches 'are cleverer than man in predicting the future' (σοφώτεροι καὶ ἀνθρώπων τὸ μέλλον προεγνωκέναι) because they know when winter is coming and prepare themselves accordingly.[10] In these and similar examples, the idea of supernatural intervention is abandoned in favour of natural explanations for animals' capacity to anticipate the future.[11] Did such examples of animal predictions contribute to their role as divinatory signs? We cannot know for sure, but the way an animal's capacity to forecast is linked here to divination suggests as much.

Regardless, the way in which nature and religion intersect in the practice of divination suggests that the natural world provides a key to our understanding of how animals feature in ancient Greek divination. As I will show throughout this chapter, the different divinatory practices draw on the order of nature by either following or openly deviating from it. The reason for this is that the natural world is an ordered system with certain features, processes, and patterns: day and night, birth and death, summer and winter. As such, it can provide a structure for the articulation of supernatural knowledge, thus enabling it to present itself as an ordered system of signs.

Before we delve into the principles and practices of the way in which animals feature in ancient Greek oracles, predictions, and omens, it should be said that ancient Greek divination is by no means unique in assigning animals such an important role. Other religious traditions also treat the animal kingdom as a preferred aspect of the natural environment for the purpose of obtaining knowledge from the supernatural. We know of several divinatory systems that draw on animals as divine signs, including the poison oracle of the Azande, which revolves around the behaviour of poisoned chicken.[12] Differences emerge mainly in how these and other religious traditions have framed the scope and meaning of animal signs as well as the methods by which they are derived. It is at this point that cultural and historical analyses come into the picture. And it is to this kind of information that we now proceed.

Animals as divine signs in 'artificial' divination

The most prominent use of the animal in ancient Greek divination was as a medium in various methods of obtaining supernatural knowledge. Indeed, two of the most common forms of 'artificial' divination relied on animals: the observation of birds (ornithomancy) and the reading of the entrails of sacrificial victims, most notably the livers of various domestic animals (hepatomancy). Each of these forms of divination, in effect, singled out a small segment of nature − a bird (or birds) or the liver (or other body part) of a slaughtered animal − as particularly meaningful for the purpose of gaining access to the superior knowledge of the supernatural. In both, an animal (or animal part) drew the attention of the onlooker (in what one may call 'the divinatory gaze') to certain features that were then interpreted by aligning them with a set of predetermined meanings.[13]

Ornithomancy

Ornithomancy involved the observation of the behaviour of birds, mostly birds of prey, such as eagles, hawks, herons, and vultures.[14] The practice was probably Anatolian in origin (as was hepatoscopy).[15] Because they were much rarer than songbirds, raptors' appearance seemed particularly meaningful; and they were easier to observe from a distance on account of their size. As meat-eaters they may also have evoked associations with the reading of entrails (see below).[16] When circling the skies to look for prey, these birds were clearly visible and showed complex behaviours that lent themselves to the attribution of further symbolic meanings. It therefore comes as no surprise that in Greek thought and literature, birds of prey are widely associated with the gods even beyond their use in ornithomancy.[17]

This form of divination was practised either in semi-institutionalised form at certain specially designated observatories, such as the *oiōnoskopeion* at the Tiresias oracle at Thebes or the *skiron* close to Eleusis in Attica.[18] More frequently, however, it was carried out whenever and wherever a divine sign was warranted. It was in this context that the Trojan king Priam, when setting out to meet Achilles, prayed to receive a positive bird sign:

> Ζεῦ πάτερ Ἴδηθεν μεδέων κύδιστε μέγιστε
> δός μ' ἐς Ἀχιλλῆος φίλον ἐλθεῖν ἠδ' ἐλεεινόν,
> πέμψον δ' οἰωνὸν ταχὺν ἄγγελον, ὅς τε σοὶ αὐτῷ
> φίλτατος οἰωνῶν, καί εὖ κράτος ἐστὶ μέγιστον,
> δεξιόν, ὄφρά μιν αὐτὸς ἐν ὀφθαλμοῖσι νοήσας
> τῷ πίσυνος ἐπὶ νῆας ἴω Δαναῶν ταχυπώλων.

> Father Zeus, who rules from Ida, most glorious, most great, and grant that I may come to Achilles' hut as one to be welcomed and pitied; and send a bird of omen, the swift messenger that to yourself is dearest of birds and is mightiest in strength; let him appear on my right hand, so that noting the sign with my own eyes, I may have trust in it, and go to the ships of the Danaans of swift steeds.[19]

These evocative words, addressed to Zeus as the most powerful of the Greek gods, did not go unanswered: soon after Priam's prayer, a large black eagle appeared to the king's right, much to the delight of those witnessing this 'surest of omens among winged birds' (τελειότατος πετεηνῶν).[20] The omen not only endorsed Priam's plan but also illustrated his close alliance with Zeus, who responded swiftly to his request for a divine sign.

As is clear in this example, what mattered most was the movement of the bird or birds in question, and whether this was to the right or left of the observer.[21] The former was considered to be a positive sign, the latter negative. Here as elsewhere, this form of divination lent itself in particular as an aid to decision-making in situations calling for a simple yes/no response.[22]

We know that in the ancient world there was a specific literature featuring instructions on how to read birds, including an *Ornithomanteia* attributed to the poet Hesiod.[23] Unfortunately, this and similar works have been lost; yet, we are probably not far off the mark if we assume that their instructions were similar to those included in the first part of an inscription we have from Ephesus. Dating from the sixth or fifth century BCE, the inscription illustrates how in the ancient Greek practice of ornithomancy the behaviour of birds was ascribed certain meanings:

[. . . ἐκ μὲν τῆς δεξιῆ]-
[ς εἰς τὴν ἀριστερὴν πετ]-
[όμεν]ος: ἦμ μὲν: ἀποκρύψε-
[ι δε]ξιός: ἢν δὲ: ἐπάρει: τὴ-
[ν ε]ὐώνυμον: πτέρυγα: κἂν
[ἐπά]ρει: κἂν ἀποκρύψει: ε-
[ὐώ]νυμος: ἐγ δὲ: τῆς ἀριστ-
[ερ]ῆς: ἐς τὴν δεξιὴν: πετό-
[μ]ενος: ἦμ μὲν: ἰθὺς: ἀποκρ-
[ύ]ψει: εὐώνυμος: ἢν δὲ: τὴν
[δεξ]ιὴν: πτέρυγα: ἐπάρας
[δεξιός —]
ρ[—]
ε: υ[—]
ἐγ δ[ὲ —]
ιαν[—]
ι̣: μ[—]
ι̣: μη[—]
οντ[—]
ο: ἂν [—]
ναι: [—]

[I]f (the bird) [fly]ing [from the right to left] disappear(s) (from view) (the omen is) [fav]ourable; if it raises it[s left] wing, [flies a]way and disappears (the omen is) unfavourable; if fl[y]ing from l[ef]t to right it disap[p]ears on a straight course (the omen is) unfavourable; but if after raising its [rig]ht wing, [it flies away and disappears the omen is favourable].[24]

Even though, as Matthew Dillon has rightly pointed out, this inscription is the only extant ancient Greek source in which the raising of wings is considered meaningful, it is nonetheless typical in the way it links a bird's particular gesture to a particular meaning. It also neatly illustrates the simple answers that could be generated by this form of divination.

Due to the straightforward way the divinatory system is set out here, it becomes clear why reading birds was a skill that could (at least in principle) be learnt by anybody. In practice, however, it seems that those with a special expertise in this area had a competitive advantage and were specifically enlisted to deploy their skills. Seers, therefore, feature with some regularity in the ancient sources whenever the supernatural reveals itself through the behaviour of birds.[25]

In the ancient Greek world, ornithomancy was one of the most widely practised forms of divination – sufficiently widespread for the ancient Greek word for 'bird of prey' (*oiōnos*) to double as the word for 'divine sign'.[26] Ornithomancy seems to have been especially popular during the archaic period; later, it was partially supplanted by other forms of divination, most notably the reading of entrails, which was altogether unknown to Homer. However, throughout antiquity, it remained a powerful decision-making tool that variously informed other forms of divination (see below).[27]

Extispicy and hepatomancy

The reading of entrails (extispicy) was a very popular form of divination that required little more than the availability of a sacrificial victim (to provide the entrails) and some expertise in what to look for.[28] It was the preferred method of divination especially in situations when much was at stake. Due to the straightforward answers it generated, the reading of entrails was a particularly useful tool in processes of decision-making.

Different kinds of *splanchna* (entrails) were considered to be of significance for the purpose of divination. In addition to thighbones, the gods received some other animal parts, such as the gall bladder and the tail, both of which featured in divinatory practices. The way in which an animal's gall bladder burst on the sacrificial fire, for example, could serve as a meaningful divine sign, as could the way in which the tail of a sacrificial victim kinked or twisted when roasting on the flames.[29]

Yet, by far the most popular divinatory organ, especially on the battlefield, was the liver. Hepatomancy routinely involved reading the livers of sheep, goats, and cattle, but there are also accounts of the use of pigs' livers and dogs' livers for the same purpose.[30] The colour, size, and form of the organ were all important, as were the presence or absence of a lobe (*lobos*), 'gates' (*pylai*), and a 'head' (*kephalē*).[31]

As in the case of ornithomancy, this kind of divination usually generated straightforward, yes/no answers to questions.[32] The absence of the lobe, for example, was invariably considered to be a negative sign. When the Spartan king Agesilaus, in 388 BCE, hoped to fortify a garrison post at the entrance to Argive territory, he first sacrificed to obtain divine endorsement of his plan. Unfortunately, the livers of the sacrificial victims were *aloba* ('lacking a lobe'), so he promptly demobilised his troops.[33]

Hepatomancy, again like ornithomancy, was frequently practised by a seer (*mantis*) with special expertise in how to read the signs. However, this was a technical skill (*technē*) that could, at least in principle, be acquired by anyone. For instance, the Greek philosopher, historian, and military commander Xenophon claimed to know how to read a liver, due to the fact that he had observed many rituals.[34]

An advantage of this particular form of divination over ornithomancy was that it could be repeated as often as necessary until a positive sign that reflected the aims and objectives of those seeking the assistance of the gods was achieved. The ancient sources report several instances in which more than one liver was studied until the desired outcome was reached, whereupon those in charge promptly ceased looking for confirmation so as not to jeopardise their plans. The aforementioned Agesilaus, for example, at one point went through several readings of entrails, all of which produced negative signs. He then sacrificed to the deities in charge of averting evil and granting safety. Once a favourable omen was finally obtained, no further samples were assessed.[35]

In addition to the reading of birds and the interpretation of the entrails of a sacrificial victim, the ancient Greeks practised a number of less significant forms of artificial divination that relied on animals as signs. Yet, practices such as the reading of fish (ichthyomancy) always remained local curiosities, tied to a particular place and time.[36] They never reached the level of interest and popularity enjoyed by the two principal forms of divination.

Animal omens

In parallel with the major, institutionalised forms of artificial divination, animals offered themselves as impromptu signs (omens) that were not part of specifically orchestrated mantic procedures. Such omens did not emerge in response to a specific question or situation. Their reading was also not restricted to a number of preordained characteristics (the flight of birds, the features of the liver). Rather, a much wider array of circumstances could be considered in their interpretation, with regard to both an animal's behaviour and the broader context in which it occurred.

Such impromptu signs offered themselves above all in moments of heightened importance when the mind was particularly attuned to possible signs of supernatural intervention. If a seer was present in such a situation, he might suggest an explanation.[37] In other instances, however, it was incumbent upon those perceiving the sign to formulate a plausible interpretation. At first, one needed to establish the existence of such a supernatural sign against the background of mere natural occurrences. In forms of artificial divination, the institutional set-up and the ritual context answered the question of what should count as a divine sign from the outset. But the situation was not as clear cut in the case of animal omens, which could offer themselves practically anywhere and at any time. So, how should one determine what was merely a natural occurrence and what pointed to the realm of the symbolic and the divine?

Again, the naturalistic observation of typical animal behaviour and the knowledge it generated enter the picture here. For what passed as a divine sign in ancient Greece was frequently established with reference to the order of nature: in particular, that which is outside of – or a deviation from – the natural and expected offered itself as a meaningful divine sign. Take, for example, the strange incident that Herodotus included in a story at the very end of his

Histories. Apparently, the Greek guard of some Persian prisoners of war experienced the following peculiar incident while preparing a meal: '[H]e was frying dried fishes, and these, as they lay over the fire, began to leap and writhe as though they were fishes newly caught.'[38] The point is that dried fish leaping away from a flame as if still alive is extraordinary and thus draws the onlooker's attention. It ties in with other strange occurrences recounted earlier in the *Histories* – a mare giving birth to a hare, a hermaphroditic mule – unnatural or rare incidents that turn out to be divinely inspired.[39] In these examples, the order of nature (that is, the patterns and processes in which nature typically presents itself) provides the norm against which the supernatural stands out and thus identifies itself as meaningful.

Once the existence of a divine sign was firmly established, the focus quickly shifted to the question of reference. Unlike artificial divination, in which particular signs were sought and interpreted as answers to specific questions or problems, impromptu signs raised questions of reference. There was a pressing need to establish to whom or what the animal sign referred, as well as its meaning. That this was not always an uncontested process is evident in the response that the jumping fish elicit in Herodotus' account. The Persian general immediately informs the Athenian guard: 'This prodigy ... has no reference to you, my Athenian friend. It applies to me.'[40] By addressing head-on the question of the intended recipient, the general was able to steer the sign's interpretation in a particular direction. At the same time, his status helped him to monopolise the interpretation: divination is never without power.

Finally, attention turned to the all-important question of the sign's interpretation. On this point, too, the reading of omens drew on the order of nature. Referring to Protesilaus, a famous Homeric hero who was the first Greek to die at Troy, the Persian general suggests:

ἐμοὶ σημαίνει ὁ ἐν Ἐλαιοῦντι Πρωτεσίλεως ὅτι καὶ τεθνεὼς καὶ τάριχος ἐὼν δύναμιν πρὸς θεῶν ἔχει τὸν ἀδικέοντα τίνεσθαι. νῦν ὦν ἄποινά μοι τάδε ἐθέλω ἐπιταχθῆναι, ἀντὶ μὲν χρημάτων τῶν ἔλαβον ἐκ τοῦ ἱροῦ ἑκατὸν τάλαντα καταθεῖναι τῷ θεῷ, ἀντὶ δ᾽ ἐμεωυτοῦ καὶ τοῦ παιδὸς ἀποδώσω τάλαντα διηκόσια Ἀθηναίοισι περιγενόμενος.

Protesilaus of Elaeus is telling me that though he is as dead as dried fish, he yet has power from the gods to punish the man who wrongs him. Look now; I am willing to pay him a hundred talents in compensation for the treasure I took from the shrine, and I will pay the Athenians two hundred, on condition that they spare my life and the life of my son.[41]

This interpretation starts from the fact that dried fish cannot move of their own accord, just as dead people usually do not have the capacity to act and harm others. It is the power of the supernatural that is at play here, and the Persian general enlists its help to strike a deal in his favour. What makes this interpretation compelling is that it does not proceed randomly. Rather, the general aligns it with statements about plausibility that refer in turn to conceptions of nature and the natural.

There is a similar example of the interpreter of an animal sign aligning it with naturalistic observations in Xenophon's *Anabasis*. When the opportunity to become the sole commander of the Greek contingents presents itself to Xenophon, he recalls that an eagle had screamed to his right when he was about to leave Ephesus to meet Cyrus.[42] The fact that the bird appeared on his right-hand side recalls the principles and practices of ornithomancy as a form of artificial divination (see above). Yet, there is nothing to indicate that the reading of this sign was in any way limited by certain preconceived meanings. Indeed, a seer's subsequent interpretation ventured far from any established schema. First, he confirmed that the eagle was indeed related to Xenophon and that it denoted glory – probably because of the bird's association with power in ancient Greek thought and literature. His interpretation of the animal omen then drew on knowledge of the typical ways in which eagles usually behave. For example, he took the fact that the eagle was sitting rather than flying as a sign of suffering, because eagles are usually attacked by other birds when they are sedentary, not in the air.[43] Similarly, the omen did not indicate future gains, because eagles hunt in the air, not when sitting still. It was this alignment of the sign with eagles' typical behaviour that convinced Xenophon to accept the seer's interpretation.[44]

Here and elsewhere, drawing analogies between the human and animal realms is at the core of making sense of divine signs. The behaviour of certain animals is interpreted in a way that stands directly for a parallel situation in the human realm. In the process, animal omens invite those wishing to make sense of them to think about the manifold ways in which the human and animal planes align. The result is a cosmos in which the animal realm can seamlessly point to the human realm – and vice versa.

Indeed, different omens and divinatory practices variously explore the continuum, parallels, and analogies between the human and animal realms. In Book 15 of the *Odyssey*, for example, Helen interprets the meaning of an eagle flying by on her right-hand side, carrying a tame white goose, followed by a group of shouting people:

ὡς ὅδε χῆν' ἥρπαξ' ἀτιταλλομένην ἐνὶ οἴκῳ / ἐλθὼν ἐξ ὄρεος, ὅθι οἱ γενεή τε τόκος τε, / ὡς Ὀδυσεὺς κακὰ πολλὰ παθὼν καὶ πόλλ' ἐπαληθεὶς / οἴκαδε νοστήσει καὶ τείσεται· ἠὲ καὶ ἤδη / οἴκοι, ἀτὰρ μνηστῆρσι κακὸν πάντεσσι φυτεύει.

Even as the eagle came from the mountain, where are his kin, and where he was born, and snatched up the goose to his home after many toils and many wanderings, even so shall Odysseus return to his home after many toils and many wanderings and shall take vengeance; or even now he is at home, and is sowing the seeds of evil for all the suitors.[45]

This interpretation of the divine sign, in effect, unpacks the image by relating it to the parallel situation of Odysseus taking revenge on the suitors back home. All the myriad differences that distinguish Odysseus from an eagle are brushed aside to move the spotlight squarely on to the structural similarities between the two: Odysseus and the eagle are both heading home after a lengthy and fraught absence. In addition, both demonstrate their strength and dominance through their handling of physically weaker creatures (suitors and goose, respectively).

Animals in oracles and dreams (inspired divination)

We have seen that animals did not merely provide simple signs in omens; rather, they provided complex symbols, the interpretation of which required the establishment of parallels between the order of nature and the human cosmos. The same holds true for non-human creatures' appearances in oracles and prophetic dreams as forms of inspired divination.[46] Here, too, animal images prevailed in some of the most famous prophecies of the ancient world, again aligning the human and animal realms in complex ways and encouraging the establishment of parallels between them.

In the body of dreams and inspired prophecies that have come down to us from the ancient Greek world, animal imagery figures in oracles and dreams that form part of fantastic tales of prediction and fulfilment.[47] In Joseph Fontenrose's classification of oracles from Delphi, for example, animals feature exclusively in responses that were written down long after their alleged delivery; therefore, as Fontenrose notes, these responses were probably products of storytelling and the later historiographic tradition.[48] The same holds true for animal imagery in extraordinary tales of prophetic dreams, prediction, and fulfilment that are important elements within timeless legends and other forms of fiction-making. Animal images are thus part of the oracular tradition and lie right at the intersection of oral tradition, historical imagination, and storytelling (see also this volume, Chapter 4).

In these tales, animals serve as complex signs with the capacity to point to the human world through analogy and parallelism. On one occasion, according to Diodorus Siculus, a group of Spartans who had recently suffered a defeat and were keen to leave Sparta enquired at Delphi whether they would seize Sicyon. They received the following response:

καλόν τοι τὸ μεταξὺ Κορίνθου καὶ Σικυῶνος·
ἀλλ' οὐκ οἰκήσεις οὐδ' εἰ παγχάλκεος εἴης.
Σατύριον φράζου σὺ Τάραντός τ' ἀγλαὸν ὕδωρ
καὶ λιμένα σκαιὸν καὶ ὅπου τράγος ἁλμυρὸν οἶδμα
ἀμφαγαπᾷ τέγγων ἄκρον πολιοῖο γενείου·
ἔνθα Τάραντα ποιοῦ ἐπὶ Σατυρίου βεβαῶτα.

Fair is the plain 'twixt Corinth and Sicyon;
But not a home for thee, though thou wert clad

Throughout in bronze. Mark thou Satyrion
And Taras' gleaming flood, the harbour on
The left, and where the goat (*tragos*) catches with joy
The salt smell of the sea, wetting the tip
Of his gray beard. There build thou Taras firm
Within Satyrion's land.[49]

The *tragos* (goat) here denotes a specific place where a new city should be built. Yet, in order to build it, those receiving the prophecy first have to deduce what kind of goat wets its beard in water and where it might do this. The homonymy between the ancient Greek words for 'goat' and 'fig tree' provides the key that links the animal sign to its referent in the real world. The goat (*tragos*) turns out to be a wild fig tree (also *tragos*, at least among Messenian Greeks), which has a habit of trailing its branches in water.

Here – and in several other responses – the animal image serves as an 'animal guide'.[50] Yet, as far as the goat is concerned, the oracle seems to describe something impossible: it is not very likely that a goat would dip its beard in seawater. Both here and elsewhere, animal images allude to the unlikely or even the impossible in order to stand out. Frequently, they constitute so-called *adynata* ('impossibilities') because they contain inherent contradictions, such as a dog with a human voice, or fish and deer residing on the same pasture.[51] In these examples, the animals are metaphors, metonyms, or other tropes that carry a surplus of meaning. As with the reading of animal omens, the task is to find an interpretation that successfully and plausibly links the animal sign to a parallel situation in the human world.

Again, in many instances, this involves juxtaposing the human and animal realms. The dream that the Persian queen Atossa recounts in Aeschylus' *Persians*, for example, includes an encounter between hunter and hunted:

ὁρῶ δὲ φεύγοντ' αἰετὸν πρὸς ἐσχάραν
Φοίβου, φόβωι δ' ἄφθογγος ἐστάθην, φίλοι·
μεθύστερον δὲ κίρκον εἰσορῶ δρόμωι
πτεροῖν ἐφορμαίνοντα καὶ χηλαῖς κάρα
τίλλονθ'· ὁ δ' οὐδὲν ἄλλο γ' ἢ πτήξας δέμας
παρεῖχε·.

Then I saw an eagle fleeing for refuge to the altar of Phoebus – and I was rooted speechless to the spot with terror, my friends. Next I saw a hawk swooping on him at full speed with beating wings, and tearing at his head with its talons – and he simply cowered and submitted.[52]

For Atossa, there is no doubt that this dream is bad news. In her own words:

ταῦτ' ἔμοιγε δείματ' εἰσιδεῖν,
ὑμῖν δ' ἀκούειν. εὖ γὰρ ἴστε, παῖς ἐμὸς
πράξας μὲν εὖ θαυμαστὸς ἂν γένοιτ' ἀνήρ,

κακῶς δὲ πράξας, οὐχ ὑπεύθυνος πόλει,
σωθεὶς δ᾽ ὁμοίως τῆσδε κοιρανεῖ χθονός.

This was terrifying for me to behold, and must be terrifying for you to hear; for you know well that if my son were successful he would be a very much admired man, but were he to fail – well, he is not accountable to the community, and if he comes home safe he remains ruler of this land.[53]

Here, although Atossa falls short of interpreting the dream (this is left to the audience), she feels inclined to defend her son and emphasise his position as the head of the Persian state, irrespective of the outcome of the war with the Greeks. The eagle in this dream surely refers to Xerxes. The fact that the king of the birds flees from a mere hawk and ultimately submits to it is a sign of the impending defeat of the mighty Persian army by the much smaller Greek forces. On this point (and this point alone), the animal points to the human realm.

Thanks to their presence in some of the most famous prophetic dreams and oracular utterances in Greek thought and literature, animal images seem to represent the typical oracular voice itself. This is why, in *Knights*, Aristophanes has the first slave circulate a comic prophecy that features a 'crook-taloned rawhide eagle' (βυρσαίετος ἀγκυλοχήλης) and a 'dim-witted blood-guzzling serpent' (δράκων κοάλεμος αἱματοπώτης).[54] It is also why Lucian centres his oracle parody in *Zeus Rants* on a response that features four different animals: a 'hook-taloned vulture' (αἰγυπιὸς γαμψώνυχος), crows, a mule and, intriguingly, a grasshopper.[55] With the exception of the grasshopper, all of these animals are well known from other famous oracles (the mule), prophetic dreams, or omens (eagles and vultures). In oracle parodies, then, animal signs serve as shorthand for the ways in which prophecies *mean* – in particular, their propensity to use enigmatic images that have the capacity to mislead.[56]

Therefore, throughout the various forms of divination practised in the ancient Greek world, it may be said that animals served as complex intermediaries between the superior knowledge of the gods and the much more limited understanding of humans. Both as artificial signs and as complex symbols, they provided prompts for human interpretation. More often than not, this involved the drawing of parallels between the natural world of which the animals were part and the human realm. In mediating between gods and humans, nature and culture, and the visible and the invisible, animals were at the core of a tripartite symbolic system that allowed those versed in it to make complex statements about the world.

Before we cast a final glance at this symbolic language in action, it should be said that there are various crossovers and intermediate forms between the different ways in which animals were used for divination. Indeed, many examples defy the rigid categories into which classical scholarship – this chapter included – divide the material. For example, animal signs were also used to enhance the authority of oracular sites. A Delphic origin myth relates that Zeus dispatched two eagles from opposite poles of the earth with the intention of finding the planet's centre.[57] As it happened, the two birds met above Delphi and thus provided a pseudo-geographical marker for the religious centrality of the oracle in the ancient Greek world.[58] Moving beyond the realm of mythology, in historical times the priests at Delphi used another animal to reassure themselves of the continued presence of Apollo at the sanctuary. On mornings when the oracle was open for business, they would pour water over a goat. If the goat shuddered, this was taken as a sign that the god was present and ready for consultation.[59] Meanwhile, at the oracle of Zeus at Dodona, doves were said to speak in human voices.[60] A later tradition took them to be female priests, who were compared to birds because they spoke in an unintelligible tongue that reminded the locals of birdsong.[61] Be that as it may, given their prominent role across different forms of divination, it is no coincidence that birds represented female priests. Such examples illustrate some of the manifold ways in which animals in general, and birds in particular, were interpreted as divine signs.

Symbolic language in practice: animals and divination in Herodotus' *Histories*

This chapter's brief survey of animals' functions in the various forms of ancient Greek divination has shown that they invariably acted as intermediaries between the omniscient gods and humans who wished to access the superior knowledge of the divine. They were thus at the core of a tripartite symbolic system – with gods and humans as the other components – that informed the ways in which the ancient Greeks sought to gain a better understanding of past, present, and future events.

In this section, we will consider the centrality of this system in the work of one author – Herodotus – and the world he describes. Oracles, predictions, and omens, including several that feature animals, play major roles in Herodotus' account of the Greco-Persian Wars and their extensive prehistory.[62] Yet, the aim of this section is not to present numerous examples of these forms of divination in Herodotus' *Histories*, nor to explore his historiographic strategies when recounting these and other omens (a matter on which I have commented elsewhere).[63] Rather, I wish to use this brief case study to illustrate the myriad ways in which an individual author can draw on the tripartite symbolic language in contexts that fall outside of the cultural practices described so far.

In Book 1 of the *Histories*, Herodotus reports the visit of a certain Aristodicus from the Greek city of Cyme to the oracle of Apollo near Miletus (better known as the oracle of Apollo at Didyma).[64] The purpose of his consultation is to check the accuracy of a response that the same oracle issued to an earlier delegation. This was called into question because it suggested that the Cymaeans should hand over a suppliant who had sought refuge with them.[65] Contrary to Aristodicus' expectation, the oracle reiterates its previous answer.[66] Yet, Aristodicus still hesitates to comply and resorts to walking around the temple and scattering some sparrows and other birds that are nesting on the other side of the shrine. The oracle's response is as instant as it is defamatory. A voice from the shrine proclaims: 'Impious wretch, how dare you do this wicked thing? Would you destroy those who have come to my temple for protection?' (Ἀνοσιώτατε ἀνθρώπων, τί τάδε τολμᾷς ποιέειν; τοὺς ἱκέτας μου ἐκ τοῦ νηοῦ κεραΐζεις).[67] Aristodicus is quick to respond: 'Lord Apollo, do you protect your suppliants yet tell the men of Cyme to abandon theirs?' (Ὦναξ, αὐτὸς μὲν οὕτω τοῖσι ἱκέτῃσι βοηθέεις, Κυμαίους δὲ κελεύεις τὸν ἱκέτην ἐκδιδόναι).[68] The final response from the shrine, however, leaves no room for doubt as to the god's intentions: 'Yes, answered the god; I do indeed, that you may suffer the sooner for the sacrilege and never come here again to consult my oracle about handing over suppliants' (Ναὶ κελεύω, ἵνα γε ἀσεβήσαντες θᾶσσον ἀπόλησθε, ὡς μὴ τὸ λοιπὸν περὶ ἱκετέων ἐκδόσιος ἔλθητε ἐπὶ τὸ χρηστήριον).[69] Apollo, it seems, really meant what he said – and he was not best pleased about being challenged.

What is most interesting about this exchange is that Aristodicus addresses Apollo with the kind of language that the gods usually use to convey their knowledge to humans. In addition to utilising the enigmatic mode that is typically associated with the oracular voice itself, he refers to animals (the sparrows and other birds) as images in order to convey to Apollo his concern about handing over the suppliant. For, just as the birds are suppliants at Apollo's temple, so is the human who sought refuge at Cyme. Again, it is through a very specific parallelism that the human and animal realms speak to each other. This example reveals an astonishing versatility in the use of animals as symbols in human attempts to converse with the supernatural.[70]

Herodotus here makes a strong point about the presence of the supernatural. At the moment when the god's authority is challenged by a human enquirer, Apollo quite literally speaks with a human voice to reassert his authority. The presence of the divine is not always quite so clear elsewhere in the *Histories*. Animals (or animal parts) sometimes feature in situations where the presence of the supernatural is merely suggested. Is it mere coincidence that a fish snaps up Polycrates' infamous ring and returns it to its owner, or is this incident a key to the meaning of the story?[71] Alternatively, is the fish (also) a sign that hints at the possibility of divine agency and thus represents the view in Greek thought and literature that the gods stand for a world order in which one cannot escape one's fate?[72] And what should we make of Herodotus' account of the Spartan general Leotychides, who hands his mother the entrails of a recently sacrificed oxen and asks her to speak the truth in the hope of discovering the name of his father?[73] As Lionel Scott has pointed out, touching fresh entrails was one way in which those swearing an oath gained additional credibility.[74] It seems certain that this symbolic gesture had its origins in entrails' central role in divination.

Of course, these are not situations in which divination is practised. Yet, the associations that spring from their role in divine revelations of all kinds surely make animals (or their parts) potent symbols in these and other contexts where divine agency is not a given but a mere possibility. Such examples reveal considerable flexibility in the use of animals as part of the symbolic language of ancient Greek religion. This is important because it shows the versatility of the symbolic language that informed the ancient Greek practice of divination. In particular, it illustrates that humans were not always merely passive recipients and interpreters of divine images. Rather, they sometimes used such images themselves in their interactions with the supernatural.

Conclusion

This chapter has explored the roles that animals played in ancient Greek attempts to access the superior knowledge of the supernatural through the interpretation of divine signs. I have shown that they featured in all the major ways in which information was obtained from the gods: divination (including artificial divination), chance omens, oracles, and prophetic dreams. In artificial divination, animals (or their parts) served as signs that were interpreted according to certain predetermined meanings. In omens, animals and their actions were complex symbols, the interpretation of which frequently aligned itself with the typical behaviour of these animals in (or deviations from) nature. Finally, in forms of inspired divination, animals served as complex images that pointed to parallel situations in the human realm.

Revealing parallels among the ways in which oracles, predictions, and omens used animal signs are evident in the symbolic values of particular species. Even though, at least in principle, a wide variety of animals could be seen as delivering divine signs, in practice only a handful of privileged species served this purpose. Lions and eagles feature particularly prominently, due to their association with royalty, as do other birds, due to their ubiquity and their role in ornithomancy.

In all the examples discussed in this chapter, animals (or their parts) serve as intermediaries that mediate symbolically between the omniscient gods and the humans who need information from the divine realm. This tripartite symbolic structure – gods as providers of supernatural knowledge, animals as carriers or mediators of that knowledge, and humans as both recipients and interpreters of the divine signs – was one way, among several, in which ancient Greek religion conceived of the triangular symbolic relationship between gods, humans, and animals.

Notes

1 Even though the main focus of this chapter is on the role of animals in different kinds of divination, I also include other, non-ritualised human attempts to participate in the superior knowledge of the gods, as well as those not embedded in some sort of institutional structure, such as chance omens and certain dreams.

2 See Cic. *Div.* 2.11. In Greek myth, Prometheus is said to have taught humans these divinatory techniques (see Aesch. *PV* 476–506). On the distinction between artificial and natural divination, see Johnston 2008: 8–9; Johnston 2015.

3 On the link between ancient Greek religion and the natural world, see the essays collected in Scheer 2019.

4 Such physical features of oracular sites are discussed in detail in Friese 2010, esp. 241–266, 331–344. On springs, see also Johnston 2008: 65–68.

5 Lightning and thunder as a divine signs: e.g. Hdt. 3.86. Earthquake: Hdt. 6.98, 8.64; Thuc. 1.128; Xen. *Hell* 4.7.4–5. Eclipse of the sun: Hdt. 7.37, 9.10. Eclipse of the moon: Thuc. 1.128.

6 On cognitive approaches to (ancient Greek) religion, see Larson 2016: 73–80; Driediger-Murphy and Eidinow 2019

7 Graf 2005: 2 observes that the 'Grenzen zwischen "rationalem" Beobachtungswissen und Zeichen-Glauben sind fliessend.' On this point, see also Johnston 2008: 5–6; Struck 2014: 314. On ancient zoological knowledge, see Bodson 2014.

8 Ael. *NA* 1.11.

9 Ael. *NA* 7.8.

10 Ael. *NA* 4.61 (trans. A. F. Schofield, with changes).

11 For further prophetic animals in Aelian, see, e.g., *NA* 1.48, 2.46, 2.51, 8.4., 11.6.

12 On which, see the seminal study of Evans-Pritchard 1937. On animals in divination, see also Meyer 1991; Hammond-Tooke 1999.

13 Michel Foucault 1963 first made the point that gazing (in contrast to merely 'looking on') entails a particularly focused and conditioned way of observation in *Naissance de la clinique* (*The Birth of the Clinic*). I use the term 'divinatory gaze' here because this particularly focused form of observation is analogous to other forms of gazing in the ancient world, such as the ekphratic gaze (on which, see, e.g., Elsner 2007: 67–109).

14 Hom. *Od.* 2.182 mentions eagles, falcons, and hawks.

15 See, e.g., Mouton and Rutherford 2013. On the origins of hepatoscopy, see Bachvarova 2012; Rollinger 2017.

16 As first suggested by Bouché-Leclerq 1879–1882: Vol. 1: 129–130; see also Struck 2014: 312.

17 The eagle, for example, carried divinatory significance due to its close association with Zeus. On the eagle, see, in detail, Keller 1909–1912: Vol. 2: 1–6; Arnott 2007: 2–4 on the *aetos*, with cross-references to other kinds of eagles. Other famous associations of birds with deities include Apollo's association with the falcon and Athena's link to the owl.

18 Ornithomancy at the Tiresias oracle at Thebes: Soph. *Ant.* 999–1005; Paus. 9.16.1. On this and the other Theban oracles, see Symeonoglou 1985; Bonnechere 1990; Friese 2010: 98, 385. The *skiron* near Eleusis in Attica: Hesych. s.v. *Skeiromantis*. On the Athenian festival of the Skira and the *skiron*, see Deubner 1932: 40–50; Burkert 1972: 161–168; Parker 2005: 173–177, 480. On ornithomancy, see also Collins 2002.

19 Hom. *Il.* 24.308–313 (here and below trans. Murray, with changes).

20 See Hom. *Il.* 24.314–321.

21 See Arist. *Cael.* 285a3.

22 See, in more detail, Johnston 2008: 128–132; Friese 2010: 98.

23 Graf 2005: 5; Johnston 2008: 7.

24 Syll.[3] 1167/*IEph* V. 1678 (trans. Dillon 1996).

25 See, e.g., Hom. *Il.* 1.69–99 and Aesch. *Ag* 122–137 (both Calchas); Eur. *Phoen.* 834–844 (Tiresias); Apollod. 1.9.11 (Melampus' inability to understand the voices of birds).

26 See, e.g., Thuc. 6.27; Ar. *Av.* 716–22.

27 Starting with Homer, the reading of birds features throughout Greek thought and literature, including in the historiographic tradition, in comedy and tragedy, right through to the literature of Roman Greece (Plutarch and Pausanias). A few examples: Hom. *Il.* 10.274–276; Hom. *Od.* 2.177–186, 15.171–178; Hes. *Op.* 825–828; Aesch. *PV* 488–493, 826–828; Paus. 9.16.1.

28 On the reading of entrails, see also Collins 2008.

29 Graf 2005: 7; Johnston 2008: 128. On the body parts offered to the gods in Greek blood sacrifice, see also Straten 1988; Ekroth 2009.
30 Routinely used animals: Johnston 2008: 126. Dogs: Paus. 6.2.4. In Plutarch's treatise *On Isis and Osiris* (380b), the sacrifice of a dog is presented as a local curiosity practised by some Egyptians.
31 See, in detail, Johnston 2008: 125–128; Struck 2014: 315–318. The meaningful parts of the liver are named repeatedly in the ancient sources. See, e.g., Eur. *El.* 825, 828; Pl. *Ti.* 71C; Xen. *Hell.* 4.7.7.
32 See, e.g., Hdt. 6.76, 9.45 (unfavourable omens are eventually ignored); Xen. *An.* 1.8.15–16 (favourable omens).
33 Xen. *Hell.* 4.7.7.
34 Xen. *An.* 5.6.29.
35 Xen. *Hell.* 3.3.4.
36 E.g. ichthyomancy: Ath. 8.333d–f; see also Friese 2010: 99–100.
37 On the figure of the seer, see Bremmer 1996; Flower 2008.
38 Hdt. 9.120.
39 Both examples are mentioned in Hdt. 7.57. The latter omen apparently appeared earlier but was recalled at the moment when Xerxes crossed into Europe.
40 Hdt. 9.120.
41 Hdt. 9.120. On Protesilaus, see also Hom. *Il.* 2.705.
42 Xen. *An.* 6.1.23.
43 Xen. *An.* 6.1.23.
44 Xen. *An.* 6.1.24.
45 Hom. *Od.* 15. 174–178 (trans. Murray, with changes).
46 A few examples of animals in ancient Greek dreams: Hdt. 5.56, 6.131; Aesch. *PV* 651–654, *Cho.* 526–539; Plut. *Alex.* 2.2–6, *Phyrrh.* 11.2; Ap. Rhod. *Argon.* 3.616–617; Callim. *Aet*, fr. 2; Ael. *VH* 12.1; Nonnus *Dion.* 44.46–79.
47 On divinatory dreams in ancient Greece, see, e.g., Corno 1982; Bonnechere 2003.
48 That is, in 'quasi-historical' and 'legendary' responses, rather than 'historical' ones (in Fontenrose's terms). See, e.g., Q6, 23, 34, 43, 44, 60, 81, 99, 101, 119, 134, 138, 152, 161, 172, 180, 190, 199, 213, 217, 233, 360, L27, 33, 50, 54, 82, 83, 86, 99, 127, 133, 136, 147, 155, 163 (Fontenrose's numbering in his catalogue of responses from Delphi in Fontenrose 1978: 244–416).
49 Diod. Sic. 8.21.3 (trans. Oldfather).
50 On the animal guide, see Fontenrose 1978: 73–74.
51 On *adynata*, see also Fontenrose 1978: 64. The dog with a human voice features in a Delphic oracle reported by Livy in 1.50.4–10. The fish and deer in the same pasture figure in Steph. Byz. 190 (Billerbeck/Zubler).
52 Aesch. *Pers.* 205–210.
53 Aesch. *Pers.* 210–214 (trans. Sommerstein).
54 Ar. *Eq.* 195–201 (trans. J. Henderson). The 'leather-eagle' is of course a reference to Cleon, the tanner.
55 Lucian. *Iupp. trag.* 31 (trans. A. M. Harmon). This oracle is discussed in more detail in Kindt 2017.
56 This is also why Croesus, in his famous oracle test, literally cooks up a complex animal image by dissecting a tortoise and a lamb and boiling them together in a bronze pot (see Hdt. 1.47–48). By putting a test question to the gods that itself contains an animal image, he both imitates and reverses the way in which oracles typically 'mean' (see, in detail, Kindt 2006). On enigmatic oracles from Delphi, see also Kindt 2016: esp. 159–164.
57 Str. 9.3.6.
58 See Kindt 2016: 1–2.
59 Plut. *De def. or.* 438b.

60 See, e.g., Hdt. 2.55. On doves and divination at Dodona, see Franke 1956; Dakaris 1963; Parke 1967: 34–45; Johnston 2008: 63–65.
61 Hdt. 2.57.
62 A few examples: Hdt. 1.55–56 (the Delphic oracle likening Cyrus to a mule); 1.78 (snake omen); 3.153–154 (a mule bearing offspring read as an omen); 5.56 and 6.131 (two dreams featuring lions); 7.57–58 (a mare giving birth to a hare as an omen); 7.220 (an oracle featuring bulls and lions); 8.20 (an oracle of Bacis featuring goats).
63 See Kindt 2006; Kindt 2016: 16–54.
64 Hdt. 1.157–160. On Didyma and the responses attributed to it, see Fontenrose 1988.
65 In ancient Greek religion, supplication was an obligation that was usually protected by the gods. On supplication in ancient Greek thought and culture, see Naiden 2006.
66 On the political and historiographic context of this consultation, see Asheri et al. 2007: 181–183 (with further literature).
67 Hdt. 1.159.
68 Hdt. 1.159.
69 Hdt. 1.159.
70 At the same time, the example also recalls the other recorded attempt of a human using an animal symbolically in the context of divination: Croesus' oracle test (see Hdt. 1.47–48).
71 As told in Hdt. 3.40–43. For other interpretations of this passage, see Versnel 1977 and Asheri et al. 2007: 441–442 (with further literature).
72 Incidentally, the same question could be asked about the famous passage in which a dolphin rescues the Greek singer Arion after he jumps into the sea in full attire to escape from pirates. See Hdt. 1. 23–24; Asheri et al. 2007: 91–92 (with further literature).
73 See Hdt. 6.68.
74 Scott 2005: 272 (with further examples).

Bibliography

Arnott, W. G. (2007) *Birds in the Ancient World from A to Z*. London.
Asheri, D., A. Lloyd, and A. Corcella (2007) *A Commentary on Herodotus Books I–IV*. Oxford.
Bachvarova, M. (2012) 'The transmission of liver divination from East to West', *Studi Micenei ed Egeo-Anatolici* 54, 1–22.
Bodson, L. (2014) 'Zoological knowledge in ancient Greece and Rome', in G. L. Campbell (ed.) *Animals in Classical Thought and Life*. Oxford, 556–579.
Bonnechere, P. (1990) 'Les Oracles de Béotie', *Kernos* 3, 53–65.
Bonnechere, P. (2003) *Trophonios de Lébadée. Cultes et mythes d'une cité béotienne au miroir de la mentlité antique*. Leiden.
Bouché-Leclerq, A. (1879–1882) *Histoire de la divination dans l'antiquité*. 4 vols. Paris.
Bremmer, J. (1996) 'The status and symbolic capital of the seer', in R. Hägg (ed.) *The Role of Religion in the Early Greek Polis*. Stockholm, 97–109.
Burkert, W. (1972) *Homo Necans. Interpretationen altgriechischer Opferriten und Mythen*. Berlin.
Collins, D. (2002) 'Reading the birds: oionomanteia in early epic', *Colby Quarterly* 38, 17–41.
Collins, D. (2008) 'Mapping the entrails: the practice of Greek hepatoscopy', *American Journal of Philology* 129, 319–345.

Corno, D. del (1982) 'Dreams and their interpretation in ancient Greece', *Bulletin of the Institute of Classical Studies* 29, 55–62.

Dakaris, S. (1963) 'Das Taubenorakel von Dodona und das Totenorakel bei Ephyra', *Antike Kunst*, Beiheft 1, 35–55.

Deubner, L. (1932) *Attische Feste*. Berlin.

Dillon, M. (1996) 'The importance of ornithomanteia in Greek divination', in M. Dillon (ed.) *Religion in the Ancient World. New Themes and Approaches*. Amsterdam, 99–121.

Driediger-Murphy, L. G. and E. Eidinow (eds.) (2019) *Ancient Greek Divination and Experience*. Oxford.

Ekroth, G. (2009) 'Thighs or tails? The osteological evidence as a source for Greek ritual norms', in P. Brulé (ed.) *La Norme en matiere religieuse en Grece ancienne*. Liege, 125–151.

Elsner, J. (2007) *Roman Eyes. Visuality and Subjectivity in Art and Text*. Princeton, N.J.

Evans-Pritchard, E. E. (1937) *Witchcraft, Oracles, and Magic among the Azande*. Oxford.

Flower, M. A. (2008) *The Seer in Ancient Greece*. Berkeley, Calif.

Fontenrose, J. (1978) *The Delphic Oracle. Its Responses and Operations with a Catalogue of Responses*. Berkeley, Calif.

Fontenrose, J. (1988) *Didyma. Apollo's Oracle, Cult and Companions*. Berkeley, Calif.

Foucault, M. (1963) *Naissance de la clinique. Une archéologie du regard médical*. Paris.

Franke, P. R. (1956) 'Das Taubenorakel zu Dodona und die Eiche als der heilige Baum des Zeus Naios', *Athener Mitteilungen* 71, 60–65.

Friese, W. (2010) *Den Göttern so nah. Architektur und Topographie griechischer Orakelheiligtümer*. Stuttgart.

García Valdés, M., L. A. Llera Fueyo, and L. Rodríguez-Noriega Guillén (2009) *Claudius Aelianus. De natura animalium*. Berlin.

Graf, F. (2005) 'Divination: Greek', in *ThesCRA*. III, 1–48.

Hammond-Tooke, W. D. (1999) 'Divinatory animals: further evidence of San/Ngui borrowing?', *South African Archaeological Bulletin* 54, 128–132.

Johnston, S. I. (2008) *Ancient Greek Divination*. Oxford.

Johnston, S. I. (2015) 'Oracles and divination', in E. Eidinow and J. Kindt (eds.) *The Oxford Handbook of Ancient Greek Religion*. Oxford, 477–489.

Keller, O. (1909–1912) *Die antike Tierwelt*. 2 vols. Leipzig.

Kindt, J. (2006) 'Delphic Oracle stories and the beginning of historiography: Herodotus' Croesus Logos', *Classical Philology* 101, 34–51.

Kindt, J. (2016) *Revisiting Delphi: Religion and Storytelling in Ancient Greece*. Cambridge.

Kindt, J. (2017) 'The inspired voice: enigmatic oracular communication', in F. S. Naiden and R. J. A. Talbert (eds.) *Mercury's Wings. Exploring Modes of Communication in the Ancient World*. Oxford, 211–228.

Larson, J. (2016) *Understanding Greek Religion. A Cognitive Approach*. London.

Meyer, P. (1991) 'Divination among the Lobi of Burkina Faso', in P. M. Peek (ed.) *African Divination Systems. Ways of Knowing*. Bloomington, Ind., 91–100.

Mouton, A. and I. Rutherford (2013) 'Luwian religion – a research project: the case of "Hittite" augury', in A. Mouton *et al*. (eds.) *Luwian Identities. Culture, Language and Religion between Anatolia and the Aegean*. Leiden, 329–343.

Naiden, F. S. (2006) *Ancient Supplication*. Oxford.

Parke, H. W. (1967) *The Oracles of Zeus. Dodona, Olympia, Ammon*. Cambridge, Mass.

Parke, H. W. and D. E. W. Wormell (1956) *The Delphic Oracle*. 2 vols. Oxford.

Parker, R. (2005) *Polytheism and Society at Athens*. Oxford.

Rollinger, R. (2017) 'Hauspici from the ancient Near East to Etruria', in A. Naso (ed.) *Etruscology*. Berlin, 341–356.

Scheer, T. S. (ed.) (2019) *Natur – Mythos – Religion im antiken Griechenland.* Stuttgart.

Scott, L. (2005) *Historical Commentary on Herodotus, Book 6.* Leiden.

Straten, F. T. van (1988) 'The god's portion in Greek sacrificial representations: is the tail doing nicely?', in R. Hägg, N. Marinatos, and G. C. Nordquist (eds.) *Early Greek Cult Practice. Proceedings of the Fifth International Symposium at the Swedish Insitute at Athens, 26–29 June 1986.* Stockholm, 51–67.

Struck, P. (2014) 'Animals and divination', in G. L. Campbell (ed.) *The Oxford Handbook of Animals in Classical Thought and Life.* Oxford, 310–323.

Symeonoglou, S. (1985) *The Topography of Thebes from the Bronze Age to Modern Times.* Princeton, N.J.

Versnel, H. S. (1977) 'Polycrates and his ring: two neglected aspects', *Studi Storico-Religiosi* 1, 17–46.

10 Animals in ancient Greek dedications[1]

M. Gaifman

Introduction

Dedications to the gods lie at the heart of ancient Greek religious practice. From the rise of the polis ca. 750 BCE to late antiquity, objects of varying sizes and forms – from hairpins to grand monuments – were placed in sacred spaces by worshippers.[2] These offerings were made in thanks for – or in the hope of – divine grace (*charis*), or both, possibly with the intention of exchange with the gods, as often described in the Latin phrase *do ut des* ('I give so that you give').[3] Among these, representations of real-life animals are common, including a wide range of species: insects, birds, reptiles, fish and marine animals, amphibians, and wild and domesticated mammals. These depictions vary vastly in size, form, material, facture, and technique. They can be miniature or life-size, three- or two-dimensional. They can be made of clay, marble, wood, metal, or other materials. They can be carved, moulded, hand-shaped, painted, or produced some other way. Together, this broad array of zoological imagery in sacred spaces throughout Greek antiquity speaks to the importance of animals in human interactions with the divine. It is a material manifestation of the conceptual triangular relationships in ancient Greek religion between gods, humans, and animals that are explored throughout this book.

The immense range of dedications portraying animals cannot be accounted for in a single volume, let alone a single chapter.[4] In what follows, I take the rich evidence of the central sanctuary of Olympia in the eighth century BCE as the basis for a general discussion of the religious meanings of votive offerings portraying various species. I begin by examining the interpretative framework by assessing a horse statuette before considering other types of animal votives that were uncovered in this major Panhellenic shrine. In the final part of the chapter I turn to a group of dedications from a sixth-century BCE sanctuary in the Peloponnese that provides a helpful starting point for contemplating human and divine interactions with animals. I focus primarily on bronze figurines. Although, as seen in Olympia, simpler clay figurines were very popular, bronze statuettes tend to be better preserved and are therefore more amenable for analysis.[5] The examples discussed here are from mainland Greece from the eighth to the fourth century BCE. This chronological and geographical spread hardly accounts for the full range of representations of animals in dedications, which were ubiquitous for many centuries throughout the entire ancient Greek world. Rather than attempting to provide a comprehensive account, the cases I discuss demonstrate how particular meanings of dedications representing animals are historically contingent and demand contextual examination.

As we shall see, dedications representing animals provide a physical testimony of what we may conceive of as the symbolic triangles in Greek religious practice comprising gods, men, and animals. Such dedications may be linked to the animals' place in the world of the worshippers, whether as pets, expensive possessions, agricultural aids, or any other identities they held in the lives of individuals or larger groups, which could indicate the social statuses of their owners. The dedications may speak to ties between a certain species and a divinity or a cult, whether in belonging to a divine sphere of influence or in manifesting the deity itself. In addition, dedications depicting animals may reference the roles of those creatures in rituals, specifically as sacrificial offerings (on sacrifice, see also this volume, Chapter 8). Meanings, however, are not mutually exclusive, and I will suggest a range of possibly concurrent associations linked to representations of animals in dedications.

A bronze horse from Olympia

In 1880, the German archaeological expedition to Olympia uncovered a bronze statuette of a horse south of the temple of Hera (Figure 10.1).[6] This stylised animal, which is little more than 12 centimetres in height, was made with care and great attention to detail; it has a smooth surface and delicate lines engraved along its body. The flat base attached to the legs and tail indicates that it was intended for display. Produced of bronze, a metal prized in antiquity, it was likely of some value originally.[7] It may be described as an *agalma* – an object made with the intention of delighting the gods.[8] And as it was found in one of the ancient world's most sacred sites, from its discovery in 1880 it was recognised as a votive offering – a dedication to the gods.

Let us consider first what we may learn from one miniature horse from Olympia. The discussion of this example – and all other representations of Greek animals in dedications – lies at the intersection of several scholarly fields: archaeology, art history, ancient history, anthropology, and the history of ancient Greek religion.[9] For the archaeologist, the statuette is one of thousands of artefacts deposited at the site in the eighth century BCE – an indication of a dramatic rise in activities at the sanctuary.[10] The art historian would assert that the same object is in the geometric style, likely the product of Argive workmanship, and that, while its equine features are recognisable, its representation indicates choices that deviate from normal horse anatomy: its abdomen is abnormally thin, and it has no eyes.[11] The historian is likely to note the value of real-life horses in ancient society and their relatively high maintenance costs, suggesting that the animal connotes the Greek upper class of the eighth century BCE.[12] This observation corresponds with this particular statuette's probable

Figure 10.1 Horse statuette from Olympia, ca. 775–750 BCE
Image: German Archaeological Institute D-DAI-ATH 1971/39 (public domain)
Courtesy of the German Archaeological Institute at Athens

higher value when compared with terracotta figurines and other less carefully wrought bronzes from Olympia.[13] The social anthropologist may also note the phenomenon of human behaviour whereby the deposition of one offering elicits comparable offerings, a tendency that led our bronze horse to be clustered with thousands of similar objects. Such an amalgamation of votives is not unique to ancient Greek society; indeed, it is evident across broad geographical and chronological expanses – from prehistoric times to the present.[14]

For the historian of ancient Greek religion, the statuette may be taken as one among numerous pieces of evidence for the rise of Olympia as a central Panhellenic sanctuary in the eighth century BCE. Our miniature horse, along with thousands of other bronze and clay figurines of equines, bovines, birds, deer, and other animals deposited at Olympia in this period, bears witness to the immense growth in the Greek practice of making dedications to the gods.[15] What should we make of this development in religious practice? First, the choice to deposit an equine representation indicates at the very least that some importance was ascribed to horses in Olympia at the time. Second, when trying to reach a more nuanced understanding of this and many similar representations of animals in holy sites, we must acknowledge a number of interpretative challenges. Generally, we approach offerings in relation to one or a combination of the following aspects: the worshipper(s), the divine power(s) involved, and the cult(s) engaged, together with any ritual actions, such as incense burning, libations, or animal sacrifice. So, for instance, depictions of mortals are usually taken as references to the dedicators, and images of deities as portrayals of the venerated gods. In contrast, ritual implements that were deposited as dedications are assumed to connote particular actions performed at a holy site. Yet, as neat as this interpretative frame may appear, it is often impossible to pin down specific meanings for votives. In certain cases, we cannot even be sure whether a figure represents a deity or a mortal.[16] The realities of ancient religions are often far more surprising than we may have assumed; we may be confronted with cases that do not fall within any of the categories I have just outlined.

With these preliminaries in mind, let us first consider what this bronze horse can tell us about its dedicator. Since real-life horses in the eighth century BCE constituted valuable possessions of an elite class, the deposition of an image of this particular species could have been made either in thanks for its dedicator's current good fortune, in the hope of future wealth, or both.[17] It may reflect its patron's current standing, aspirations, or both.

Could the statuette also be connected to the gods that were worshipped at Olympia? Given its findspot near the Heraion, it is logical to consider Hera first. She is associated with horses in the *Iliad*, and Pausanias describes the altar of Hera Hippia at Olympia in his second-century CE text.[18] We are, however, uncertain whether the goddess was worshipped at Olympia in the eighth century BCE.[19] Perhaps the statuette should be linked instead with Zeus, the primary deity worshipped at the sanctuary from its early phases and the patron of Olympia's chariot races.[20] However, this idea is problematic because scholars are in general agreement that the races started after the eighth century BCE, and the Father of the Gods otherwise lacks any particular hippic affinities.[21] We may also consider Pelops, reputed to have been worshipped at Olympia from deep antiquity onwards. This mythological hero won both a chariot race and the hand of a local princess, Hippodameia (lit. 'tamer of the horse'), and thus became king of Elis. Yet, it seems that the cult of Pelops was established no earlier than the sixth century BCE.[22] We may also hypothesise, with Elinor Bevan, that some other horse-related deity was worshipped at Olympia at this time.[23]

Ultimately, then, any attempt to establish connections between our horse and a particular divine sphere is likely to yield only speculative conclusions. It is significant to note, however, that the horse's association with a particular Greek social class need not undermine its force as a religious artefact that is designed to delight the gods. And we cannot completely rule out the possibility that the decision to dedicate an image of a horse was somehow connected to a specific cult or deity, even if we cannot determine which one.[24] One layer of meaning does not preclude another.[25]

Finally, we may turn to the question of the horse's possible role in the activities that took place at Olympia. As noted above, it seems that chariot races were introduced to the Olympic Games after the eighth century BCE, so it is difficult to link the statuette to any races. But could it be associated with the blood rituals that took place at Olympia around the time of its deposition? All of the evidence suggests that equines were rarely sacrificial victims at the burning altar, either at Olympia or elsewhere. Although some ancient authors describe the sacrifice of horses, and some osteological analyses of bones from Greek sanctuaries suggest that their meat was occasionally consumed at certain holy sites, there is no reason to link our bronze horse, nor any of the other representations of equines found at Olympia, to sacrifice.[26]

So far, I have traced the various hypotheses and conclusions that may be drawn from a dedication representing a particular animal. This discussion demonstrates the need to consider each example in context and in relation to similar cases. This is particularly true with respect to the analysis of objects that were deposited as part of Greek dedicatory practice, which was, by its nature, repeated and emulated. There remain, of course, questions that cannot be answered with complete certainty. In the case of our bronze statuette, we will never know precisely why an image of a horse was dedicated, by whom, and on what occasion. Was it deposited at Olympia by a visitor from Argos, or perhaps by someone from Laconia who happened upon it at the Argive workshop in Olympia?[27] Nevertheless, certain observations may be made through contextual analyses and comparisons with other evidentiary material that will help us gain a better understanding of the pertinence of animals in Greek religious experience.

The zoological array in dedications

Bronze horses from Olympia often feature at the beginnings of surveys of Greek religion and art.[28] Yet, finds at the sanctuary from this period present a range of species and provide a fruitful ground for broad, not comprehensive, discussion. Consider the bronze representations of cattle from Olympia (see the three examples in Figure 10.2).[29]

Bovines constitute the largest cohort of all of the animal representations found at the site, numbering in more than 1800 statuettes, including both cows and bulls.[30] This group must be examined in relation to sacrifice, especially given the emphasis on hecatombs in Homeric literature and all the textual, archaeological, and osteological evidence confirming that cattle were among the chief victims in Greek blood rituals, along with other primarily domesticated mammals, such as sheep, goats, and pigs.[31] Additionally, cattle had particular associations with Zeus. In myth, the god transformed himself into a bull when he fell in love with Europa and carried off the maiden. Zeus is shown as a bull in imagery of this mythological episode dating from the seventh century BCE, suggesting that in context an image of the animal may be understood as the god himself.[32] The other major divinity with a bovine connection that may have been worshipped in Olympia in the eighth century BCE is Hera. She is named in the Homeric poems as *boōpis* (lit., 'cow-eyed' or 'cow-faced').[33]

Such strong affinities between cattle and the gods worshipped at Olympia do not preclude the possibility that the figurines also evoke sacrifice. An animal closely affiliated with a deity can equally be offered in rituals to that deity.[34] Deer, for instance, are the principal companions of Artemis, yet archaeological

Figure 10.2 Bull figurines from Olympia, early eighth century BCE
Image: Gösta Hellner, D-DAI-ATH-1969/407
Courtesy of the German Archaeological Institute at Athens

excavations have unearthed the remains of deer that were sacrificed to the goddess.[35] Similarly, fish depicted in votive imagery uncovered in sanctuaries of Poseidon could have been consumed during holy meals along with other marine fauna. Archaeological and textual evidence also suggests that tuna were sacrificed to the god of the sea.[36]

Let us scrutinise further the possible significance of dedications in relation to sacrifice. In antiquity, images of animals could have been conceived of as valid alternatives to living victims, as seen, for instance, in an episode reported by Pausanias. The travel writer of the second century CE reports that the people of Orneae in the Argolis were at war with the Sicyonians and vowed to Apollo that, should they defeat their enemy, they would make a daily procession and sacrifice in his honour at Delphi. They won the war but could not afford to fulfil their vow, so, instead, they dedicated a group of bronzes depicting a sacrifice (*thysia*) and a procession.[37] These artefacts substituted for the promised ceremonial animal sacrifice.[38] Notably, in his account of the vow, Pausanias mentions the procession first and the sacrifice second; yet, in his description of the fulfilment of the promise after the war, he reverses the order, recording the sacrifice first and the procession second. He thereby calls attention to the bronzes, for in real life obviously the procession always precedes the rites at the altar. When his description is compared to Greek sacrificial imagery, Pausanias' nuanced rhetoric becomes evident. Greek visual culture, especially of a dedicatory nature, features plenty of sacrificial scenes, yet portrayals of the actual slaughter of victims are relatively rare.[39] Most often, living animals are shown in scenes of worship at a sacrificial altar, such as in a fourth-century BCE votive relief to Demeter and Kore from Eleusis, in which a family brings a large pig to the altar (Figure 10.3).[40]

The people of Orneae's ingenious solution was to portray *both* the procession *and* the sacrifice in lieu of the real thing. Indeed, the image of a *thysia* is a remarkable solution to the difficulty of performing the task every day.

The archaeological record provides another instance of a representation used in place of a real act of sacrifice. Ronald Stroud and the archaeological team working at the sanctuary of Demeter and Kore in Corinth uncovered a sacrificial pit that was constructed at the site in the sixth century BCE.[41] It measured 1.00 × 0.95 metres, had a depth of 1.00 metre, and was without any stratification all the way to the bedrock. It was full of ash containing animal bones identified in osteological analysis as primarily the remains of piglets. Moreover, its stone walls were heavily calcined, confirming without doubt that it was a site of pig sacrifices. In the same location there were cooking pots and broken pottery dating to the late fourth and early third centuries BCE – around the time when the pit fell into disuse. In addition, the site yielded some 26 figurines, mostly of women and children, as well as a comic mask. Among these finds

Figure 10.3 Votive relief to Demeter and Kore from Eleusis, ca. 340–320 BCE. Musée du Louvre, Dist. RMN-Grand Palais/ Daniel Lebée/ Carine Déambrosis/ Art Resource, N.Y.

was a small clay pig with traces of burning. Apparently, it was the only find with such traces, as Stroud does not mention any other figurines with burn marks. It seems likely that the burning of this figurine was intentional. According to Stroud's report, a worshipper who was unable to afford a live animal probably used the terracotta model instead.[42] Whatever the dedicator's economic circumstances, the archaeological record indicates that the represented creature was treated similarly to the living animals whose remains were found with it.[43] This discovery ought not to be too surprising given the long tradition of treating images as though they are the actual subjects they represent, as evidenced by both their worship and their purposeful destruction throughout history.[44] When looking at the vast numbers of representations of animals, we should always consider the possibility that, within ritual contexts, these representations may have been conceived of and treated as substitutes for living animals.

Let us return to Olympia to consider representations of birds, the third-largest group of animals in dedications after bovines (numbering around 1800) and equines (around 1600). This cohort is much smaller, consisting of barely 20 examples.[45] Elsewhere in the Greek world, representations of birds are common among votive offerings, whether they depict identifiable species, such as peacocks and doves, or generic winged and beaked creatures.[46] This prevalence correlates with the strong general association of birds with the realm of the divine and the supranatural, presumably because of their capacity for flight. In antiquity, birds are seen as divine messengers, as omens (see this volume, Chapter 11),[47] or indeed as the gods themselves (see this volume, Chapter 5),[48] and numerous deities had specific ornithological associations,[49] such as Zeus and his eagle or Athena and her owl.[50] The archaeological record of eighth-century BCE Olympia does not include an eagle, yet we might assume that, in general, a dedication portraying this bird of prey is likely to reference the Father of the Gods. Historic context, however, can alter meanings dramatically. Take, for instance, the marble eagle found in the Athenian Agora.[51] Superficially, we may assume that the artefact is related to the worship of Zeus. Yet, its second–century CE inscription indicates that it was dedicated to the two goddesses of the Athenian Eleusinion. When Athens was under Roman rule, the marble eagle likely connoted Roman power, for which the bird became a symbol. Yet, simultaneously, it may have evoked Zeus, Jupiter, or both in the minds of Athenian worshippers.[52] This case, an outlier in the present survey, exemplifies how the specific significance of dedications representing animals must be assessed contextually, and that a particular species may accrue or change meanings over time.

It goes without saying that birds were also integral to daily human life, whether partridges killed through hunting or trapping, or domestic fowl kept in the household. They also served as sacrificial victims.[53] So, when examining Olympia's figurines, all the various roles of birds – whether in the sphere of the gods or in the realm of mortals – ought to be kept in mind. We must also acknowledge the limits of our interpretation of this group of figurines as we

Figure 10.4 Figurine of a bronze bird (possibly a goose) from Olympia, ca. 775–750 BCE
Image: Hermann Wagner, DAI, ATH-Olympia-1242
Courtesy of the German Archaeological Institute at Athens

cannot be completely sure about the particular species represented. For instance, a miniature bronze dating from the eighth century BCE is said to be a goose – a viable identification – yet its legs are quite elongated for this type of fowl (see Figure10.4).[54] So, perhaps the statuette was not intended to depict a single species. Nevertheless, since other examples from Olympia resemble chickens, it seems that the avian group represents domesticated fowl and hence pertains to the sphere of the *oikos*.[55] This interpretation can be developed further if we note the long association of birds, and particularly geese, with the female sphere and the fertility of the household.[56] Thus, the bird figurines of Olympia may be related to one of the sanctuary's eighth-century BCE cults of female goddesses, to the domestic sphere, or to both.[57]

Far fewer bronzes of other animals have been found at Olympia: eight deer, three beetles, and two hares.[58] Since both deer and hares are prey animals, they may be interpreted as references to the hunt.[59] At the same time, both may be associated with Artemis, who was worshipped at nearby Kombothreka.[60] The three beetles remind us of two classes of animals that we have not considered thus far: insects and reptiles.[61] For example, a silver serpent is listed in the treasurers' accounts of the Athenian Acropolis from the fourth century BCE.[62] While snakes have broad cultic and religious meanings, in fourth-century Athens this valuable snake dedication was likely connected with Athena's earthborn child, Erichthonios, who was known for his reptilian associations.[63] Olympia's three beetles raise an additional question since there is scarcely any evidence that these insects were of religious significance in the eighth century BCE.[64] They may bring to mind the dung beetle in Aristophanes' *Peace* (421 BCE), yet it seems that, in general, such insects were of little importance in Greek culture.[65] Of course, they are primarily known for their significance in ancient Egypt.[66] Olympia's beetles are also a reminder that some species are not easily linked with a deity, a particular type of devotee, or any sacrificial or ritual activities. Instead, the beetles may be interpreted as products of Phoenician or Egyptian influence. As such, their value may be in evoking connections and familiarity beyond mainland Greece.[67]

Carriers, caretakers, and hunters

So far, I have analysed representations of certain species in isolation, yet a broad class of votives presents anthropomorphic figures carrying animals. Consider, for instance, a small bronze figurine of a man with a calf that was uncovered in a votive deposit at a sanctuary of Pan on the slopes of Mount Lykaion at the heart of Arcadia in the Peloponnese (Figure 10.5).[68]

Figure 10.5 Figurine of a man carrying a calf from the sanctuary of Pan, Mount
Lykaion, ca. 540–520 BCE
Image: Carl Blümel, D-DAI-ATH-2129-30, 2132
Courtesy of the German Archaeological Institute at Athens

The bearded man, wearing a broad hat and a short tunic, has a young bovine slung over his shoulders as he strides forward. Therefore, he may be labelled a *moschophoros* ('calf-bearer'). Since, as we have seen, cattle were among the most common sacrificial victims, the figurine may easily be interpreted as a worshipper carrying an offering to the altar. This example, like numerous other depictions of men and women bearing various species – whether birds, hares, or larger mammals – are often viewed as referencing animal sacrifice.[69] Perhaps the best case in point is the renowned calf-bearer from the Athenian Acropolis (Figure 10.6).[70] This large marble statue, which was found in 1864 at the site of the Old Acropolis Museum on the Athenian Acropolis, is usually dated to ca. 570–560 BCE. The inscription on its base asserts that Rhonbos dedicated the life-size sculpture, and it may be seen as self-referential – a gift portraying the

Figure 10.6 Calf-bearer from the Athenian Acropolis, ca. 560 BCE
Image: Nimatallah/ Art Resource, N.Y.
Courtesy of the Acropolis Museum, Athens

delivery of a gift to the goddess, presumably by Rhonbos himself.[71] Due to its location on the Acropolis, the statue must be considered in relation to sacrificial ritual at the nearby altar. Richard Neer interprets the accentuated haunches that the bearer clasps across his chest as proleptic references to the victim's impending death and dismemberment.[72]

At the same time, the dedication presents a calm occasion marked by harmony and intimacy. The calf hugs the man's neck; its body fits perfectly across his shoulders, neither too large nor too small. Their heads are at precisely the same level. The man steps forward with ease, with no indication of struggle or strain in his upper body. His eyes, which were originally inlaid with reflective stone, are directed at the viewer; his mouth is set in the familiar so-called 'archaic smile'. While we can imagine the calf resisting its bearer both before and after the moment portrayed by the statue – which will likely be followed by the creature's slaughter – at this instant it is calm and quiet. The artwork celebrates the connection between the devotee and the young bovine.

We may also recognise a harmonious composition in the small Peloponnesian calf-bearer (Figure 10.5). Here, the carrier's bent left arm effortlessly supports the animal's front legs, while his extended right arm echoes the hoof that rests on his chest. As with the Athenian calf-bearer, there is no sense of struggle between the two. A similar sense of peace pervades another figurine unearthed in the region of Mount Lykaion, likely from the same sanctuary of Pan, of a bearded nude (he wears only boots and a pointed hat) who carries a ram tucked under his left arm.[73] As the animal's head and forelegs project forward, the two bodies seem to blend into each other. There is a comparable connection between man and animal in a third miniature bronze ram-bearer from the same region. Dating to ca. 525–500 BCE, its dedicatory inscription asserts that Ainneas offered it to Pan (see Figure 10.7).[74] The man, who wears a heavy cloak and a pointed shepherd's hat, carries what is presumably one of his own flock in the crook of his left arm, and a cup in his right hand. The relationship between man and beast again seems congenial.

A similarly harmonious relationship between carrier and animal is evident in yet another statuette from Mount Lykaion. Once again, a bearded figure in a short tunic has a ram under his left arm (Figure 10.8).[75] However, unlike the other examples from Mount Lykaion, the man's boots are winged, and his headgear terminates in what appears to be elaborate feathers, indicating that he is the god Hermes *kriophoros*, the 'ram-bearer'.[76] This deity is well known in the literature and evident across the Greek and Greco-Roman world, with a long afterlife into the Christian era in the iconography of Christ as the Good Shepherd.[77] Hermes, in his ram-bearer guise, is the patron of shepherds – the deity who cares for the flock. His representation in this role fits the statuette's provenance in the rural Arcadian sanctuary of Pan, as he has strong rustic affinities and was commonly worshipped by shepherds. The statuette of this divinity with a ram cradled in his arm casts new light on the figurines of anonymous men carrying equally peaceful rams. It is possible that, rather than references to the sacrificial act, the whole group of bearers of living animals

Figure 10.7 Statuette of a shepherd carrying a ram, ca. 525–500 BCE
New York Metropolitan Museum of Art, 43.11.3 (public domain)
Courtesy of the New York Metropolitan Museum of Art

Figure 10.8 Hermes carrying a ram, ca. 540–525 BCE
National Archaeological Museum, Athens, 12347 (public domain)
Courtesy of the National Archaeological Museum, Athens

may be interpreted as caretakers of their herds. Hermes and his worshippers share the stewardship of their animals.[78] Indeed, looking again at the large Athenian calf-bearer, we may wonder whether it too had connotations beyond sacrifice. Could Rhonbos have made his dedication in thanks for his ownership of a calf, in the hope of future good fortune, or both?

Against this group of bronzes, another sixth-century BCE figurine from the area of Mount Lykaion, possibly from the same sanctuary of Pan, presents a rather different relationship between a human and an animal.[79] It features the familiar man with a pointed hat and a heavy cloak, but on this occasion he is carrying a fox by its thick tail. This contrasts sharply with the representations of men bearing calves and rams with the tenderness of parents carrying young children over their shoulders or cradling them by their side. In this case, the fox is gripped by its tail so its entire body falls unsupported. Most scholars describe

Figure 10.9 Figurine of a dead fox tied to a pole from Mount Lykaion, ca. 550–500 BCE
National Archaeological Museum Athens, 13054
Image: Courtesy of the German Archaeological Museum at Athens, D-DAI-ATH-4129

the dangling animal as dead.[80] It resembles a figurine of a dead fox hanging by its paws that was found in the sanctuary of Pan in Mount Lykaion (Figure 10.9).[81] The animal's head sags downwards, and its front paws are tied together. These two dedications serve to present the god with miniaturised portrayals of booty from the hunt. They may be interpreted as thanks-offerings to Pan, a deity who is sometimes shown in Greek art carrying a dead animal.[82] Unlike the herdsmen who nurture their flocks, hunters kill their prey, yet both groups express their gratitude to the gods for their animals via dedicatory images.

Conclusion

The final example of a statuette portraying a dead fox is striking among the vast corpus of ancient Greek dedications. In the archaeological record, animals represented in dedications are usually shown as whole.[83] In general, allusions to dismemberment, killing, violence, or any form of aggression are rare in the visual record of Greek art.[84] While we may take this portrayal of animals for granted, the dead fox provides us with a powerful warning against making assumptions. Representations of death were part of the Greek visual vocabulary even prior to the rise of naturalism. The choice to portray a dedicatory animal as dead or alive carries meaning. In the case of our final example, the lifeless victim may be seen as a celebration of a successful hunt. Similarly, the norm of portraying animals as alive may be read as extolling the existence of the various species. Some of the dedications that portray animals may refer to past or future sacrifices, or may even serve as substitutes for real animal sacrifices. Above all else, however, the vast array of offerings with zoological subjects speaks to the fact that animals were valued as living beings. Even when portrayed by an altar, they are still alive. These dedications acknowledge animals' centrality across various spheres in Greek antiquity – in real life and in the imagination, in daily experience, and in myth. Simultaneously, they may have concurrent meanings referring to the dedicator, the deity, and/or the ritual. As most of the species represented were pertinent to both mortals and immortals, their images were most suitable *agalmata* to delight the gods.

Notes

1 My thanks to Julia Kindt for inviting me to contribute to this volume and sharing her valuable notes. I am also grateful to Jaś Elsner, Pauline LeVen, and the anonymous readers for their helpful comments on an earlier draft.

2 The bibliography on dedications in Greek religion is vast and keeps growing. See, e. g., Linders and Nordquist 1987; Straten 1992; Parker 2005; Salapata 2002; Gaifman 2008; Patera 2012; Hughes 2017; Platt 2018. For the phenomenon of votives from a global perspective, see the essays in Weinryb 2016.

3 On dedications in the context of exchange and *charis*, see Parker 2011: x. For a critique of the notion of religious exchange, see Veyne 2000: 18. For more on reciprocity in Greek religion, see Parker 1998. On dedications in ancient religions in

the context of exchange with the gods, see Polignac 1995: 29–30; Linders and Nordquist 1987.

4 For a very helpful overview of representations of animals in dedications, see Bevan 1986.

5 For Olympia's terracotta animal figurines that generally resemble bronze figurines, see Heilmeyer 1972: 87–88.

6 Athens, National Archaeological Museum 6224. See Heilmeyer 1979: 210, no. 153, pl. 22; Furtwängler 1880: 35, no. 197, pl. 14.

7 On perceptions of bronze and its value, see Neer 2010: 76; Stewart 2015.

8 For the primary meaning of *agalma*, see ἄγλμα in the *LSJ*. For further discussion of the term specifically in relation to dedicatory practice, see Scheer 2000: 8–18; Bettinetti 2001: 27–37; Jim 2012; Patera 2012: 27–28, 156–158.

9 See the recent discussion in Elsner 2018.

10 Snodgrass 1980: 52–55; Whitley 2001: 144–145.

11 Markman 1943: 23; Heilmeyer 1979: 67.

12 See, e.g., Osborne 1998: 24–27; Lewis and Llewellyn-Jones 2017: 135–136. For an overview of horses in ancient societies, see Gardeisen 2005. For more on the social status of visitors to Olympia in the eighth century BCE, see Morgan 1990: 30–47.

13 See discussion in Heilmeyer 1979: 196.

14 Elsner 2018: 17–22.

15 For the primary publications, see Heilmeyer 1979 and 1972. For an overview of changes in the course of the eighth century BCE, see Morgan 2009.

16 A classic example is the statuette dedicated by Mantiklos to Apollo in the seventh century BCE, whose identity as a man or the god Apollo is unclear. See, e.g., Mitten 1967: 16; True 1988; Depew 1997: 238–239.

17 Herrmann 1972: 72.

18 For Homeric associations between Hera and horses, see O'Brien 1993: 200. See Pausanias' account of the altar of Hera Hippia at 5.15.5–6.

19 On a fifth-century BCE date for the cult of Hera at Olympia, see Moustaka 2002; Sinn 2004: 83. For the argument in favour of an eighth-century BCE date, see Fuchs 2006: 627.

20 On the earliest history of the cult of Zeus at Olympia, which can be traced back to the late eleventh century BCE, see Kyrieleis 2006: 61–79.

21 Heilmeyer 1972: 38–40. The introduction of four-horse chariot racing is dated to ca. 680 BCE, while two-horse racing can be dated precisely to 408 BCE. See further discussion in Morgan 1990: 90–92; Kindt 2012: 127–128.

22 Kyrieleis 2006: 79–83.

23 Bevan 1986: 205–206.

24 Notably, Jean-Louis Zimmermann emphasises the social aspect and excludes any discussion of possible cultic associations (Zimmermann 1989: 323–324).

25 For more on how objects may accrue meanings, see Gosden and Marshall 1999.

26 Georgoudi 2005; Ekroth 2014; Ekroth 2007: 265.

27 On the production of dedications in Olympia, see Morgan 1990: 35–43.

28 See, e.g., Pollitt 1972; Osborne 1998.

29 Rome, Deutsches archäologisches Institut, DAI Neg. 69/407; Heilmeyer 1979: 206, nos. 106, 103, 104, pl. 18.

30 Heilmeyer 1979: 185, 275; Heilmeyer does not provide a comprehensive count by gender.

31 Ekroth 2014: 330–331.

32 On the myth of Zeus and Europa, see Marconi 2007: 93–96. For more on the associations between Zeus and the bull, see McInerney 2010: 115–116.

33 On this epithet, see McCartney 1951.

34 This point is made repeatedly throughout Elinor Bevan's work (e.g. Bevan 1986: 18, 100). See, more recently, Larson 2017; Villing 2017: esp. 75 on the complexity of the sacrifice of victims that are also sacred to a divinity.

35 Bevan 1986: 100–114. On deer sacrifice, see Larson 2017. On the remains of sacrificed deer found in the sanctuary of Artemis at Ephesos, see Bammer 1998: 38. See further examples in Ekroth 2007.

36 For dedications representing fish, see Bevan 1986: 133–135. For fish sacrifice, see Theodoropoulou 2013: 204; Ekroth 2017: 18–19; Mylona 2015, esp. 406–410 (with further bibliography).

37 Paus. 10.18.5. For discussion, see Elsner 2007: 42–45; Platt 2018: 141–142.

38 For more on votives as substitutes, see Platt 2018. For a cautionary approach to this idea, see Patera 2015.

39 Straten 1995: 103 notes only one relief that may be a votive depicting killing and relatively few scenes on Greek vases portraying slaughter.

40 Paris, Louvre, Ma 752.

41 See Stroud 1965. For a more extensive overview of the site, see Bookidis *et al.* 1999.

42 Stroud 1965: 10.

43 For a discussion of the notion of the 'cheap substitute', see Salapata 2018.

44 In the context of worship, see, more recently, Hölscher 2017: 84–174 (with earlier bibliography). For a negative treatment of images, see Kousser 2017, esp. 37–42 for a discussion of voodoo dolls and votives.

45 I follow here Wolf-Dieter Heilmeyer, who does not provide an exact number of bird votives, presumably because of the difficulty in drawing distinctions between various species, including geese and cocks (Heilmeyer 1979: 185).

46 Bevan counted over 1000 representations of birds in dedications across various sanctuaries (Bevan 1986: 42). She and others have noted a recurring association between birds and female deities. On Aphrodite and doves, see Rosenzweig 2004: 14, 41, 43; Villing 2008; Villing 2017: 73 (with further references).

47 On birds and omens, see Zografou 2011; Dillon 2017.

48 On the appearance of gods in the form of birds generally, see Pollard 1977: 155–161.

49 See, e.g., Bevan 1986: 39, 57; Villing 2008 and 2017; Vidal-Naquet 1993; Beaulieu 2016: 46.

50 On Zeus and the eagle, see Hemingway 2015. On Athena's owl, see Shapiro 1993.

51 Miles 1998: 193, no. 24; Geagan 2011: 308.

52 Miles 1998: 88. For Roman associations of the eagle, see Hawtree 2014: 73–74.

53 Stafford 2008; MacKinnon 2014; and Villing 2017 (with further bibliography).

54 Heilmeyer 1979: 270, no. 933.

55 Heilmeyer 1979: 196.

56 Villing 2008.

57 On the cults of Themis and Gaia in this period, see Morgan 1990: 42–43.

58 Heilmeyer 1979: 185.

59 Heilmeyer 1979: 196.

60 Sinn 1981: 41–43 argues for the presence of Artemis at Olympia at the time, given her cult at Kombothreka. For counter-arguments, see Morgan 1990: 271, n. 67; Bevan 1986: 191–192; Larson 2017: 52, for a discussion of Artemis as a protector of hunted animals.

61 Heilmeyer 1979: 272, no. 948, pl. 121.

62 *IG* II^2, 1414, l. 21 (385/4 BCE). Harris 1995: 153, V 108.

63 For a general discussion of snakes in Greek religion, see Küster 1913. For snakes in sanctuaries and their various cultic associations, see Bevan 1986: 260–277; Salapata (2006), particularly in religious art of Lakonia. For snakes and Erichthonios, see Sourvinou-Inwood 2011: 37–38.

64 Here I follow Bevan 1986: 224.

65 Dung beetle in Aristophanes: Bowie 1993: 134–139.

66 Lewis and Llewellyn-Jones 2017: 621–624.

67 Heilmeyer 1979: 191.

68 Athens, National Archaeological Museum, 13053; Lamb 1925: 138, no. 8; Hübinger 1992: no. A 1, fig. 9; Stibbe 2007: 22, no. 35, fig. 14.
69 On figurines holding birds as evidence for bird sacrifice, see, e.g., Bevan 1986: 42.
70 Athens, Acropolis Museum, Akr 624; Brouskari 1974: 40–41; Payne and Young 1950: 2–3; Stewart 1990: 120.
71 See Neer 2012.
72 Neer 2012: 106.
73 Berlin, Antikensammlung, 10782; Lamb 1925: 137, no. 6; Hübinger 1992: Appendix 2.6. The figurine was uncovered in the area of Pan's sanctuary in Mount Lykaion prior to the Greek excavations at the site in 1902. Ulrich Hübinger considers the figure as likely connected to the worship of Pan in Mount Lykaion.
74 New York, Metropolitan Museum of Art, 43.11.3; Richter 1944: 5–6; Straten 1995: 55–56; Hübinger 1992: Appendix 3.11.
75 Athens, National Archaeological Museum, 12347; Hübinger 1992: Appendix 2.1, figs. 4–6; Stibbe 2007: no. 34, fig. 13.
76 For the *kriophoros* type in Greek and Greco-Roman art, see Bevan 1986: 247; Perdrizet 1903; Himmelmann 1980; Fullerton 1990: 165–167; Siebert 1990: 311, nos. 260–266.
77 On the motif of the ram-bearer and the Good Shepherd, see Gomola 2018: 24, 49–50 (with further bibliography). On the theological consequences of labelling images of ram-bearers as either *kriophoros* or the Good Shepherd, see also Taylor 2002.
78 See, similarly, Straten 1995: 55–56.
79 Berlin, Antikensammlung, Ident. Nr. Misc. 10784; Hübinger 1992: Appendix 2.7.
80 Hübinger 1992: Appendix 2.7; Straten 1995: 56.
81 Hübinger 1992: Appendix 1 A.2.
82 For more on Pan and hunting, see Hübinger 1992. On the cult of Pan, see Borgeaud 1988. For an image of Pan carrying his prey, see, e.g., the fourth-century BCE votive relief from Mount Penteli in Athens (National Archaeological Museum, Athens, NM 4465). For a discussion, see Gaifman 2008: 94–95.
83 A terracotta leg of a goat found at the sanctuary of Asclepius in Corinth may seem a likely candidate for an exception to this observation. However, Roebuck 1951, no. 38 notes the peg at its top suggests that it was intended to be inserted into the animal's shoulder.
84 See discussion in Straten 1995: 103–114; and more recently Gaifman 2018: 28–31 (with further bibliography).

Bibliography

Bammer, A. (1998) 'Sanctuaries in the Artemision of Ephesos', in R. Hägg (ed.) *Ancient Greek Cult Practice from the Archaeological Evidence. Proceedings of the Fourth International Seminar on Ancient Greek Cult, Organized by the Swedish Institute at Athens, 22–24 October 1993*. Stockholm, 27–47.
Beaulieu, M.-C. (2016) *The Sea in the Greek Imagination*. Philadelphia, Pa.
Bettinetti, S. (2001) *La statua di culto nella pratica rituale greca*. Bari.
Bevan, E. (1986) *Representations of Animals in Sanctuaries of Artemis and Other Olympian Deities*. Oxford.
Bookidis, N. *et al.* (1999) 'Dining in the sanctuary of Demeter and Kore at Corinth', *Hesperia* 68, 1–54.
Borgeaud, P. (1988) *The Cult of Pan in Ancient Greece*. Chicago, Ill.
Bowie, A. M. (1993) *Aristophanes. Myth, Ritual, and Comedy*. Cambridge.
Brouskari, M. S. (1974) *The Acropolis Museum. A Descriptive Catalog*, trans. J. Binder. Athens.

Depew, M. (1997) 'Reading Greek prayers', *Classical Antiquity* 16, 229–258.

Dillon, M. (2017) *Omens and Oracles. Divination in Ancient Greece.* Abingdon.

Ekroth, G. (2007) 'Meat in ancient Greece: sacrificial, sacred or secular?', *Food and History* 5, 249–272.

Ekroth, G. (2014) 'Animal sacrifice in antiquity', in G. L. Campbell (ed.) *The Oxford Handbook of Animals in Classical Thought and Life.* Oxford, 324–354.

Ekroth, G. (2017) 'Bare Bones: Zooarchaeology and Greek Sacrifice', in S. Hitch and I. Rutherford (eds.) *Animal Sacrifice in the Ancient Greek World.* Cambridge, 15–47.

Elsner, J. (2007) *Roman Eyes. Visuality & Subjectivity in Art and Text.* Princeton, N.J.

Elsner, J. (2018) 'Place, shrine, miracle', in I. Weinryb (ed.) *Agents of Faith. Votive Objects in Time and Place.* New Haven, Conn., 3–25.

Fuchs, W. (2006) 'Review of "*Das antike Olympia. Götter, Spiel und Kunst* by Ulrich Sinn"', *Gnomon* 78(7), 624–630.

Fullerton, M. D. (1990) *The Archaistic Style in Roman Statuary.* Leiden.

Furtwängler, A. (1880) *Die Bronzefunde aus Olympia und deren kunstgeschichtliche Bedeutung. Aus den Abhandlungen der Königl. Akademie der Wissenschaften zu Berlin 1879.* Berlin.

Gaifman, M. (2008) 'Visualized rituals and dedicatory inscriptions on votive offerings to the nymphs', *Opuscula* 1, 85–103.

Gaifman, M. (2018) *The Art of Libation in Classical Athens.* New Haven, Conn.

Gardeisen, A. (ed.) (2005) *Les Équidés dans le monde méditerranéen antique. Actes du colloque organisé par l'Ecole rançaise d'Athènes, le Centre Camille Jullian et l'UMR 5140 du CNRS, Athènes, 26–28 novembre 2003.* Lattes.

Geagan, D. J. (2011) *Inscriptions. The Dedicatory Monuments: The Athenian Agora.* Princeton, N.J.

Georgoudi, S. (2005) 'Sacrifice et mise à mort: aperçus sur le statut du cheval dans les pratique rituelles grecques', in A. Gardeisen (ed.) *Les Équidés dans le monde méditerranéen antique.* Lattes, 137–142.

Gomola, A. (2018) *Conceptual Blending in Early Christian Discourse. A Cognitive Linguistic Analysis of Pastoral Metaphors in Patristic Literature.* Boston, Mass.

Gosden, C. and Y. Marshall (1999) 'The cultural biography of objects', *World Archaeology* 31, 169–178.

Harris, D. (1995) *The Treasures of the Parthenon and Erechtheion.* Oxford.

Hawtree, L. (2014) 'Animals in epic', in G. L. Campbell (ed.) *The Oxford Handbook of Animals in Classical Thought and Life.* Oxford, 73–83.

Heilmeyer, W. (1972) *Frühe olympische Tonfiguren.* Berlin.

Heilmeyer, W. (1979) *Frühe olympische Bronzefiguren. Die Tiervotive.* Berlin.

Hemingway, S. (2015) 'The eagle of Zeus in Greek art and literature', in K. F. Daly and L. A. Riccardi (eds.) *Cities Called Athens. Studies Honoring John McK. Camp II.* Lewisburg, Va., 89–114.

Herrmann, H. (1972) *Olympia. Heiligtum und Wettampfstätte.* Munich.

Himmelmann, N. (1980) *Über Hirten-Genre in der antiken Kunst.* Opladen.

Hölscher, F. (2017) *Die Macht der Gottheit im Bild. Archäologische Studien zur griechischen Götterstatue.* Heidelberg.

Hübinger, U. (1992) 'On Pan's iconography and the cult in the sanctuary of Pan on the slopes of Mount Lykaion', in R. Hägg (ed.) *The Iconography of Greek Cult in the Archaic and Classical Periods. Proceedings of the First International Seminar on Ancient Greek Cult, Organised by the Swedish Institute at Athens and the European Cultural Centre of Delphi (Delphi, 16–18 Novembre 1990).* Liége, 189–207.

Hughes, J. (2017) *Votive Body Parts in Greek and Roman Religion*. New York, N.Y.

Jim, T. S. (2012) 'Naming a gift: the vocabulary and purposes of Greek religious offerings', *Greek, Roman and Byzantine Studies* 52, 310–337.

Kindt, J. (2012) *Rethinking Greek Religion*. Cambridge.

Kousser, R. M. (2017) *The Afterlives of Greek Sculpture. Interaction, Transformation, and Destruction*. New York, N.Y.

Küster, E. (1913) *Die Schlange in der griechischen Kunst und Religion*. Giessen.

Kyrieleis, H. (2006) *Anfänge und Frühzeit des Heiligtums von Olympia. Die Ausgrabungen am Pelopion, 1987–1996*. Berlin.

Lamb, W. (1925) 'Arcadian bronze statuettes', *Annual of the British School at Athens* 27, 133–148.

Larson, J. (2017) 'Venison for Artemis? The problem of deer sacrifice', in S. Hitch and I. Rutherford (eds.) *Animal Sacrifice in the Ancient Greek World*. Cambridge, 48–62.

Lewis, S. and L. Llewellyn-Jones (2017) *The Culture of Animals in Antiquity. A Sourcebook with Commentaries*. London.

Linders, T. and G. Nordquist (1987) *Gifts to the Gods. Proceedings of the Uppsala Symposium 1985*. Uppsala.

MacKinnon, M. (2014) 'Animals in epic', in G. L. Campbell (ed.) *The Oxford Handbook of Animals in Classical Thought and Life*. Oxford, 269–281.

Marconi, C. (2007) *Temple Decoration and Cultural Identity in the Archaic Greek World. The Metopes of Selinus*. Cambridge.

Markman, S. D. (1943) *The Horse in Greek Art*. Baltimore, Md.

McCartney, E. S. (1951) 'The epithet "Boopis"', *Classical Journal* 46, 348–350.

McInerney, J. (2010) *The Cattle of the Sun. Cows and Culture in the World of the Ancient Greeks*. Princeton, N.J.

Miles, M. M. (1998) *The City Eleusinion*. Princeton, N.J.

Mitten, D. G. (1967) 'The earliest Greek sculptures in the museum', *Boston Museum Bulletin* 65, 4–18.

Morgan, C. (1990) *Athletes and Oracles. The Transformation of Olympia and Delphi in the Eighth Century BC*. Cambridge.

Morgan, C. (2009) 'The early Iron Age', in K. A. Raaflaub and H. van Wees (eds.) *A Companion to Archaic Greece*. Chichester, 43–63.

Moustaka, A. (2002) 'On the cult of Hera at Olympia', in R. Hägg (ed.) *Peloponnesian Sanctuaries and Cults. Proceedings of the Ninth International Symposium at the Swedish Institute at Athens, 11–13 June 1994*. Stockholm, 199–205.

Mylona, D. (2015) 'From fish bones to fishermen: view from the sanctuary of Poseidon at Kalaureia', in D. C. Haggis and C. M. Antonaccio (eds.) *Classical Archaeology in Context. Theory and Practice in Excavation in the Greek World*. Boston, Mass., 385–417.

Neer, R. T. (2010) *The Emergence of the Classical Style in Greek Sculpture*. Chicago, Ill.

Neer, R. T. (2012) 'Sacrificing stones: on some sculpture, mostly Athenian', in C. A. Faraone and F. S. Naiden (eds.) *Greek and Roman Animal Sacrifice. Ancient Victims, Modern Observers*. Cambridge, 99–150.

O'Brien, J. V. (1993) *The Transformation of Hera. A Study of Ritual, Hero, and the Goddess in the Iliad*. Lanham, Md.

Osborne, R. (1998) *Archaic and Classical Greek Art*. Oxford.

Parker, R. (1998) 'Pleasing thighs: reciprocity in Greek religion', in C. Gill, N. Postlethwaite, and R. Seaford (eds.) *Reciprocity in Ancient Greece*. Oxford, 105–127.

Parker, R. (2005) 'Dedications', in *ThesCRA*. IV, 269–281.

Parker, R. (2011) *On Greek Religion*. Ithaca, N.Y.

Patera, I. (2012) *Offrir en Grèce ancienne. Gestes et contextes.* Stuttgart.

Patera, I. (2015) 'Objects as substitutes in ancient Greek ritual', *Religion in the Roman Empire* 1, 181–200.

Payne, H. and G. M. Young (1950) *Archaic Marble Sculpture from the Acropolis. A Photographic Catalogue.* 2nd edn. London.

Perdrizet, P. (1903) 'Hermès Criophore', *Bulletin de Correspondance Hellénique* 27, 300–313.

Platt, V. (2018) 'Clever devices and cognitive artifacts: votive giving in the ancient world', in I. Weinryb (ed.) *Agents of Faith. Votive Objects in Time and Place.* New Haven, Conn., 141–157.

Polignac, F. de (1995) *Cults, Territory, and the Origins of the Greek City-State*, trans. J. Lloyd. Chicago, Ill.

Pollard, J. (1977) *Birds in Greek Life and Myth.* London.

Pollitt, J. J. (1972) *Art and Experience in Classical Greece.* Cambridge.

Richter, G. (1944) 'Five bronzes recently acquired by the Metropolitan Museum', *American Journal of Archaeology* 48, 1–9.

Roebuck, C. (1951) *The Asklepieion and Lerna.* Princeton, N.J.

Rosenzweig, R. (2004) *Worshipping Aphrodite. Art and Cult in Classical Athens.* Ann Arbor, Mich.

Salapata, G. (2002) 'Greek votive plaques: manufacture, display, displosal', *Bulletin antieke Beschavung* 77, 19–42.

Salapata, G. (2006) 'The tippling serpent in the art of Lakonia and beyond', *Hesperia* 75, 541–560.

Salapata, G. (2018) 'Tokens of piety: inexpensive dedications as functional and symbolic objects', *Opuscula* 11, 97–109.

Scheer, T. S. (2000) *Die Gottheit und ihr Bild. Untersuchungen zur Funktion griechischer Kultbilder in Religion und Politik.* Munich.

Shapiro, H. A. (1993) 'From Athena's owl to the owl of Athens', in R. M. Rosen and J. Farrell (eds.) *Nomodeiktes. Greek Studies in Honor of Martin Ostwald.* Ann Arbor, Mich., 213–224.

Siebert, G. (1990) 'Hermès', in *LIMC.* Vol. 5.1, 285–387.

Sinn, U. (1981) 'Das Heiligtum der Artemis Limnatis bei Kombothekra', *Mitteilungen des Deutschen Archäologischen Instituts, Athenische Abteilung* 96, 25–71.

Sinn, U. (2004) *Das antike Olympia. Götter, Spiel und Kunst.* Munich.

Snodgrass, A. M. (1980) *Archaic Greece. The Age of Experiment.* London.

Sourvinou-Inwood, C. (2011) *Athenian Myths and Festivals. Aglauros, Erechtheus, Plynteria, Panathenaia, Dionysia*, ed. R. Parker. Oxford.

Stafford, E. (2008) 'Cocks to Asklepios: sacrificial practice and healing cult', in V. Mehl and P. Brulé (eds.) *Le Sacrifice antique. Vestiges, procédures et stratégies.* Rennes, 205–221.

Stewart, A. (2015) 'Why bronze?', in J. Daehner and K. D. S. Lapatin (eds.) *Power and Pathos. Bronze Sculpture of the Hellenistic World.* Los Angeles, Calif., 35–47.

Stewart, A. F. (1990) *Greek Sculpture. An Exploration.* New Haven, Conn.

Stibbe, C. M. (2007) 'Three silens from Olympia and "the international style" in late archaic Greek bronze statuettes', *Bulletin Antieke Beschaving* 82, 1–28.

Straten, F. T. van (1992) 'Votives and votaries in Greek sanctuaries', in J. Bingen and A. Schachter (eds.) *Le Sanctuaire grec. Huit exposés suivis de discussions par A. Schachter et al.* Genève, 247–284.

Straten, F. T. van (1995) *Hiera Kala. Images of Animal Sacrifice in Archaic and Classical Greece.* Leiden.

Stroud, R. S. (1965) 'The sanctuary of Demeter and Kore on Acrocorinth. Preliminary Report I: 1961–1962', *Hesperia* 34, 1–24.

Taylor, A. (2002) 'The problem of labels: three marble shepherds in nineteenth-century Rome', *Memoirs of the American Academy in Rome* S1, 47–59.

Theodoropoulou, T. (2013) 'The sea in the temple? Shells, fish and corals from the sanctuary of the ancient town of Kythnos and other marine stories of cult', in J. Wallensten and G. Ekroth (eds.) *Bones, Behaviour and Belief. The Zooarchaeological Evidence as a Source for Ritual Practice in Ancient Greece and Beyond.* Stockholm, 197–222.

True, M. (1988) 'Mantiklos Apollo', in A. P. Kozloff, D. G. Mitten, and S. Fabing (eds.) *The Gods Delight. The Human Figure in Classical Bronze.* Cleveland, Oh., 52–57.

Veyne, P. (2000) 'Inviter les dieux, sacrifier, banqueter: Quelques nuances de la religiosité gréco-romaine', *Annales* 55, 3–42.

Vidal-Naquet, P. (1993) 'Le Chant du cygne d'Antigone: À propos des vers 883–884 de la tragédie de Sophocle', in A. Machin and L. Pernée (eds.) *Sophocle. Le Texte, les personnages, Actes du colloque international d'Aix-en-Provence, 10, 11, et 12 janvier 1992.* Aix-en-Provence, 285–297.

Villing, A. (2008) 'A wild goose chase? Geese and goddesses in classical Greece', in D. C. Kurtz and H. Meyer (eds.) *Essays in Classical Archaeology for Eleni Hatzivassiliou, 1977–2007.* Oxford, 171–180.

Villing, A. (2017) 'Don't kill the goose that lays the golden egg? Some thoughts on bird sacrifices in ancient Greece', in S. Hitch and I. Rutherford (eds.) *Animal Sacrifice in the Ancient Greek World.* Cambridge, 63–102.

Weinryb, I. (2016) *Ex Voto. Votive Giving across Cultures.* New York, N.Y.

Whitley, J. (2001) *The Archaeology of Ancient Greece.* Cambridge.

Zimmermann, J. (1989) *Les Chevaux de bronze dans l'art géométrique grec.* Mainz.

Zografou, A. (2011) 'Des Sacrifices qui donnent des ailes: PGM XII, 15–95', in V. Pirenne-Delforge and F. Prescendi (eds.) *Nourrir les dieux?Sacrifice et représentation du divin. Actes de la VIe rencontre du groupe de recherche européen "Figura, représentation du divin dans les sociétés grecque et romaine" (Université de Liège, 23–24 octobre 2009).* Liège, 149–163.

11 Animals in Asclepian medicine

Myth, cult, and miracle healings

F. Steger and F. Ursin (trans. D. Hanigan)

Introduction

In Greco-Roman medicine, animals had a distinct significance in the curing of illness. Asclepian medicine is a famous example of this.[1] There are 28 different animals affiliated with Asclepius.[2] The principal animal is the snake, which is symbolic of Asclepius and points to the fact that human and animal were closely related in ancient Greek religion.[3] This is because they were attributed with the capacity to cure diseases, as is, for example, evident in the accounts of miracle healings in inscriptions at Epidaurus. In this chapter, the snake and some lesser-known animals will be studied in relation to Asclepian medicine.

We shall consider three areas in which animals relate to medicine: first, the central cultural–historical tradition of animals as it traces its origin to the myth of Asclepius; second, the fact that the cult of Asclepius features the same animals as we find in myth; and, third, the role that these animals play in temple healing.[4] The objective of the chapter is to show the triangular relations among the divine, animal, and human spheres as they are rendered symbolically in Asclepian medicine.

This chapter constitutes a systematic presentation and analysis of the sources attesting to the importance of animals in the myth, cult, and healing associated with Asclepius. Because the source material for Asclepius and medicine is rich and complex, inscriptions, coins, and archaeological evidence are analysed alongside literary texts. The period considered spans from classical Greece to the Roman Empire.

Animals in the myth of Asclepius

The myth of Asclepius features snakes, dogs, a centaur, and a raven. In the Augustan period, Hyginus relates a short fable about the role of the raven:

> Apollo cum Coronida Phleg<y>ae filiam grauidam fecisset, coruum custodem ei dedit, ne quis eam uiolaret. cum ea <Ischys> Elati filius concubuit; ob id ab Ioue fulmine est interfectus. Apollo Coronidem grauidam percussit et interfecit; cuius ex utero exsectum Asclepium educauit, at coruum qui custodiam praebuerat ex albo in nigrum commutauit.[5]

When Apollo had made Coronis, daughter of Phlegyas, pregnant, he put a raven in guard, so that no one should violate her. But Ischys, son of Elatus, lay with her, and because of this he was killed by the thunderbolt of Zeus. Apollo struck the pregnant Coronis and killed her. He took Asclepius from her womb and reared him, but the raven who had guarded her he turned from white to black.[6]

Apollo turned the originally white raven black because the bird was not only the bearer of bad news but had neglected its duties. The raven is a relatively recent addition to the myth of Asclepius, appearing for the first time in the first or second century CE.[7]

In the ancient core myth, which features in Pindar's *Third Pythian Ode* (474 BCE), the centaur Chiron appears as Asclepius' foster-father, having taken over his guardianship after the death of Koronis.[8] Chiron is half-human, half-horse, and thought to be the child of Zeus and Philyra.[9] Asclepius learns about medicine from him. In the *Iliad*, one of Asclepius' sons, Machaon, heals an arrow wound using the herbs that Chiron had shown his father.[10] In Homer, Chiron is well known for his *pharmaka* and is called the 'justest of the centaurs'.[11] The cultural and medico-historical importance of the centaur endures until late antiquity, as evidenced in Apuleius' book of herbal medicine, which the author claims to have received from Chiron himself.[12] Even as late as Isidore of Seville (560–636 CE), Chiron is described as the inventor of beneficial medicine.[13]

In addition to playing a central role in the Greek myth of Asclepius, the dog indicates a cultural encounter between the Greeks and ancient Babylon. As a motif, it provides a unifying theme between the two civilisations.[14] For the Greeks, Pausanias provides an account of the myth of the exposure and subsequent rediscovery of the infant Asclepius:

> ἐκκειμένῳ δὲ ἐδίδου μέν οἱ γάλα μία τῶν περὶ τὸ ὄρος ποιμαινομένων αἰγῶν, ἐφύλασσε δὲ ὁ κύων ὁ τοῦ αἰπολίου φρουρός. Ἀρεσθάνας δὲ – ὄνομα γὰρ τῷ ποιμένι τοῦτο ἦν – ὡς τὸν ἀριθμὸν οὐχ εὕρισκεν ὁμολογοῦντα τῶν αἰγῶν καὶ ὁ κύων ἅμα ἀπεστάτει τῆς ποίμνης, οὕτω τὸν Ἀρεσθάναν ἐς πᾶν φασιν ἀφικνεῖσθαι ζητήσεως, εὑρόντα δὲ ἐπιθυμῆσαι τὸν παῖδα ἀνελέσθαι·[15]

> As the child lay exposed he was given milk by one of the goats that pastured about the mountain and was guarded by the watch-dog of the herd. And when Aresthanas (for this was the herdsman's name) discovered that the tale of the goats was not full, and that the watch-dog also was absent from the herd, he left, they say, no stone unturned, and on finding the child desired to take him up.[16]

The motif of a goat suckling a child was already familiar from the myth of Zeus.[17] In the myth of Asclepius, a watchdog is added. In yet another version, Asclepius is suckled by a female dog after being exposed on Mount Kynortion.[18]

The name Kynortion, from the Greek *kyōn* ('dog'), is itself a reference to dogs.[19] The dog was also represented iconographically in the cult image of the temple of Asclepius at Epidaurus, as we know from the city's coins and Pausanias' account.[20] In an *ekphrasis*, the latter describes the opulent cult image that was on display in the temple:

τοῦ δὲ Ἀσκληπιοῦ τὸ ἄγαλμα μεγέθει μὲν τοῦ Ἀθήνησιν Ὀλυμπίου Διὸς ἥμισυ ἀποδεῖ, πεποίηται δὲ ἐλέφαντος καὶ χρυσοῦ· [...] κάθηται δὲ ἐπὶ θρόνου βακτηρίαν κρατῶν, τὴν δὲ ἑτέραν τῶν χειρῶν ὑπὲρ κεφαλῆς ἔχει τοῦ δράκοντος, καί οἱ καὶ κύων παρακατακείμενος πεποίηται.

The image of Asclepius is, in size, half as big as the Olympian Zeus at Athens, and is made of ivory and gold. The god is sitting on a seat grasping a staff; the other hand he is holding above the head of the serpent; there is also a figure of a dog lying by his side.

Another connection to dogs comes in the from of an inscribed *lex sacra* from the Piraeus. It mentions sacrifices for Maleatas, Apollo, Hermes, Jason, Akeso, Panakeia, and, finally, for dogs and their handlers.[21] The connection between Asclepius and dogs cannot be mere coincidence and may well have originated in older sources than his Greek myth. Dogs in the context of healing are likewise known from ancient Babylon.[22] For instance, three small bronzes depicting a praying man were unearthed in the sanctuary of Hera in Samos. They were all dedicated to the Babylonian goddess of healing, Gula of Isin, also called Azugallatu ('great healer').[23] Gula could both inflict and heal illnesses, so she was a typical example of an ambivalent healing deity.[24]

It is clear that the strikingly frequent motif of Asclepius with a dog was imported to Greece from ancient Babylon.[25] The dog refers to the canine victims for Gula of Isin, who was always depicted with dogs, and several dog burials have been found in her temple precinct.[26] Further evidence of a Near Eastern connection comes in form of the sacrificial remains of dogs and puppies that were found in the temple of Astarte and Mukol in Kition on Cyprus. A further connection may be made by equating Rešep-Mukol and Apollo at Idalion on Cyprus, where Apollo is given the epithet *Amuklos*.[27] Among all inedible animal sacrifices, the dog is widespread in Greek temples outside of the Asclepeia.[28] No dogs were sacrificed in the Asclepeia. This is probably due to the fact that 'sacred dogs' were kept there.[29] These temple dogs helped to maintain order in a place where large numbers of people congregated, and they guarded expensive votive offerings.

By gathering the evidence of animals in the myth of Asclepius in conjunction with the evidence of Near Eastern healing cults, it may be suggested that the Greek myth was influenced by the animals that featured in the Near Eastern healing cult of Gula of Isin. In the Greek myth of Asclepius, animals have several functions: the raven is a messenger, the dog is a protector, the goat is a nurturer, and the centaur is a teacher. The features that are ascribed to

Asclepius himself are reflected in the features of the animals that are attributed to him. With respect to incubation rites and dreams, Asclepius appears to the adorant and transmits the healing procedure.[30] He protects the healthy against illness and nurtures the sick to recover their health. Finally, he is the teacher of physicians.

The iconography of the serpent

The snake of Asclepius has considerable cultural and historical value. Just as Asclepius is a symbol of medicine, so, too, is his snake.[31] In antiquity, the snake was connected not only to Asclepius personally but to all physicians. Here, healing cults and the origins of naturalistic medicine did not come together without tensions.[32] For example, the so-called 'Berliner Arztrelief' (ca. 100 BCE–100 CE) depicts a throned doctor with three attributes: a book-roll in his hand as a symbol of erudition; a case of surgical implements, including forceps and scalpels; and, in the background, a snake coiled around a tree.[33] The fact that the iconography of a throned Asclepius is reflected in the representation of the throned doctor is striking.[34] Today the snake of Asclepius is the paradigmatic symbol of medicine.[35] However, in antiquity the snake was also the symbol of heroes, particularly the physical incarnation of the *hērōs* who lives under the earth.[36] It has been suggested that the snake of the 'Berliner Arztrelief' should not be identified as the symbol of medicine, but as an attribute of the heroised physician who is depicted in the relief.[37]

The snake is also a symbol of the transfer of Greek medicine to Rome, since the history of Roman medicine starts with the cult transfer of Asclepius' snake from Epidaurus to Rome. A temple was erected to Asclepius on the island in the Tiber in the city where the snake supposedly settled. In Ovid's *Metamorphoses*, Asclepius transforms into the serpent and indicates where the temple should be built.[38] The incentive to build the temple was a plague that the Romans were unable to cure with their own medications.[39]

The plague was thought to be a divine punishment for a human crime. Envoys were sent to oracles and miracle-workers in a bid to learn how the angry deity might be assuaged.[40] The ambassadors returned with the snake from Epidaurus, which designated the site in 293 BCE; the temple was completed four years later. The snake thus symbolises the transfer of Asclepius and his healing cult from Epidaurus to Rome. This cult transfer is similar to those to Athens, Sicyon, and Pergamum.[41] A Roman bronze medallion from the mid-second century CE commemorates the event (Figure 11.1).[42] It shows, with a bridge and a boat, the reception of Asclepius' snake on the island in the Tiber. The figure who receives the snake is either Asclepius himself or the personified deity of the Tiber – more likely the latter, since, according to the literary sources, Asclepius is introduced to Rome in the form of the snake, so he could hardly have welcomed himself.[43]

To commemorate the snake's voyage, the island was given the architectural form of a stone hull.[44] At its downstream tip, the remains of an ancient ship are

Figure 11.1 Medallion, Antoninus Pius: the serpent arrives at the island in the Tiber, ca. 138–161 CE
Medaillon: British Museum, London, 1853,0512.238
Image: Florian Steger (2018, fig. 2).

modelled in stone.[45] On the left side of the bow is a relief depicting the bust of Asclepius accompanied by the snake coiled around a staff.[46] The snake's arrival marked the beginning of a long medical tradition on the island: in 1582, the Order of the Brothers of Charity established a hospital there that still exists today.

Other iconographic depictions of the snake decorate numerous votive reliefs for Asclepius that have been found in various parts of the ancient world.[47] In total, 159 reliefs for Asclepius have been identified, many of which include snakes.[48] When these are added to votive reliefs for other healing deities who are depicted with snakes, such as Amphiaraus, the grand total exceeds 200 – more than for any other deity.[49] However, the snake is not exclusive to the iconography of Asclepius. It is also often associated with Demeter, Kore, Helius, Hecate, and Zeus.[50] Indeed, the latter is regularly depicted on a throne with a serpent at his feet.[51] The seated Asclepius, with a snake winding under his throne, was modelled on this image. It can be traced back to the cult image in the temple of Asclepius at Epidaurus, created by Thrasymedes in 370 BCE.[52]

A second important variation, known as the 'Giustini type', dates from roughly 380 BCE (see Figure 11.2).[53] A bearded, aged, yet still muscular Asclepius leans on his walking staff while a snake coils around it.[54] In other depictions, Asclepius is often accompanied by his mythical daughter, Hygieia. There are six different iconographic types of Hygieia, all of which feature her with a snake.[55]

As we have seen, Pausanias provides a detailed description of the gilded ivory cult statue in the temple at Epidaurus.[56] The god is seated on a throne, holding his staff in one hand while guarding the head of a snake that is coiling freely with the other. A dog is on the ground.[57] This type of image is also found on coins.[58] Again, the snake and the staff are associated with the healing cult of Asclepius. The snake coiling around the staff was readopted in the Renaissance as a symbol of the healing

Figure 11.2 'Giustini type' depiction of Asclepius, Epidaurus
Epidaurus Museum, 813. Image: Florian Steger.

god Asclepius.[59] However, this close association with the deity eventually faded
and the reptile became a general symbol of medicine and pharmacy.[60]

A noticeable feature of the iconographic association between Asclepius and
the snake is the frequent presence of an egg.[61] Reliefs from Thrace, Cyprus,
Pergamum, Kos, and Epidaurus all show the deity feeding a snake.[62] A total of
18 sculptures have been attested, forming the Nea–Paphos–Alexandria–Trier
type.[63] Eggs are indeed a favourite food of tree snakes – and especially of
Asclepius colubrids – a fact that is reflected in the ancient iconography. The
exact species of the Asclepius colubrids is subject to scholarly debate.[64]

As we have seen, then, the snake was first a symbol for Asclepius himself, but later
it came to symbolise medicine more generally. At the same time, it also remained
associated with other hero cults and the gods in general. Given this symbolic function, the snake was perceived as introducing a divine medicine that helps the local
population, as in the case of Rome in the early third century BCE. In this way, it also
symbolised the transfer of healing cults.

The cock as a sacrificial animal for Asclepius

Gula of Isin, the goddess who is affiliated with Asclepius, received dog sacrifices in her role as Azugallatu ('great healer'). There are no traces of dog victims for Asclepius, but there is evidence that cattle, sheep, pigs, goats, birds, and chickens all served as sacrificial animals.[65] As attested in three distinct source traditions, the rooster is particularly important as a sacrificial animal for Asclepius. A first strand of evidence can be found in Plato's *Phaedrus*, in which Socrates insists on the sacrifice a rooster to Asclepius:

Ἤδη οὖν σχεδόν τι αὐτοῦ ἦν τὰ περὶ τὸ ἦτρον ψυχόμενα, καὶ ἐκκα-
λυψάμενος – ἐνεκεκάλυπτο γάρ – εἶπεν – ὃ δὴ τελευταῖον ἐφθέγξατο –
Ὦ Κρίτων, ἔφη, τῷ Ἀσκληπιῷ ὀφείλομεν ἀλεκτρυόνα· ἀλλὰ ἀπόδοτε καὶ
μὴ ἀμελήσητε. Ἀλλὰ ταῦτα, ἔφη, ἔσται, ὁ Κρίτων· ἀλλ' ὅρα εἴ τι ἄλλο
λέγεις. Ταῦτα ἐρομένου αὐτοῦ οὐδὲν ἔτι ἀπεκρίνατο.[66]

By now he was growing cold somewhere around his abdomen and uncovering himself – he had wrapped himself up – he said – and these were the last words he uttered – 'Crito,' he said, 'we owe Asclepius a cock. See that you all buy one, and don't forget.' 'So it shall be,' said Crito. 'But see if you have anything else to say.' There was no further answer to his question.[67]

Socrates' dying words, in which he requests the sacrifice of a rooster to Asclepius, are variously cited in the ancient literature.[68] However, their interpretation is controversial.[69] Most scholars assume that Socrates considered death to be a cure for life.[70] Then again, it may have been a simple domestic matter that motivated his request for the sacrifice.[71]

The second tradition that attests to the fact that the rooster was a preferred sacrificial animal for Asclepius can be found in the fourth *Mimiambus* of Herodas (ca. 250 BCE). Here, the value of a rooster sacrifice is compared with those of other animals:

ὅντιν' οἰκίης †τοίχων†
κήρυκα θύω, τἀπίδορπα δέξαισθε.
οὐ γάρ τι πολλὴν οὐδ' ἕτοιμον ἀντλεῦμεν,
ἐπεὶ τάχ' ἂν βοῦν ἢ νενημένην χοῖρον
πολλῆς φορίνης, κοὐκ ἀλέκτορ', ἴητρα
νούσων ἐποιεύμεσθα τὰς ἀπέψησας
ἐπ' ἠπίας σὺ χεῖρας, ὦ ἄναξ, τείνας.
ἐκ δεξιῆς τὸν πίνακα, Κοκκάλη, στῆσον
τῆς Ὑγιείης.[72]

May ye graciously come hither and receive this cock which I am sacrificing, herald of the walls of the house, as your dessert. For our well is far from abundant or ready-flowing, else we should have made an ox or a

sow heaped with much crackling, and not a cock, our thank-offering for
the diseases which thou hast wiped away, Lord, stretching out thy gentle
hands. Coccale, set the tablet on the right of Hygieia.[73]

Kynno, one of the two female characters, wants to sacrifice a rooster to
Asclepius in gratitude for a successful cure. Her reason for not sacrificing an ox
or a pig is poverty. Although the sacrifice of cattle and pigs was more common,
a rooster could be chosen as an economical alternative.[74] While the accounts of
miracle healings at Epidaurus never include the sacrifice of roosters, and the
votive reliefs never show a rooster as a sacrificial animal, it is nonetheless
probable that their sacrifice was quite common in the cult of Asclepius.[75] After
all, the sick from a wide variety of socioeconomic backgrounds would have
wished to consult him and, given that the overwhelming majority of the
population was poor, we may assume that roosters were routinely sacrificed in
place of cow and pigs. At the end of Herodas' *Mimiambus*, a rooster is sacrificed
and a portion is offered to the temple servant (*neōkoros*):

> Κοκκάλη, καλῶς
> τεμεῦσα μέμνεο τὸ σκελύδριον δοῦναι
> τῶι νεωκόρωι τοὔρνιθος· ἔς τε τὴν τρώγλην
> τὸν πελανὸν ἔνθες τοῦ δράκοντος εὐφήμως,
> καὶ ψαιστὰ δεῦσον·[76]

Coccale, remember to cut carefully the bird's little leg and give it to the
temple-warden, and place the batter reverently in the snake's hole and dip
the cakes.

As it happens, terracotta replicas of roosters have been found in the Asclepeia
of Athens and Corinth.[77] These have been interpreted as replicas of real sacrificial animals.[78]

The third and final tradition – which scholars have barely recognised as evidence for rooster sacrifice to Asclepius – can be found in Artemidorus' *Oneirocritica* ('dream key'). Here, a dream is related during which Asclepius himself
comments on the practice of rooster sacrifice in his honour:

> Ηὔξατό τις τῷ Ἀσκληπιῷ, εἰ διὰ τοῦ ἔτους ἄνοσος ἔλθοι, θύσειν αὐτῷ
> ἀλεκτρυόνα· ἔπειτα διαλιπὼν ἡμέραν ηὔξατο πάλιν τῷ Ἀσκληπιῷ, εἰ μὴ
> ὀφθαλμιάσειεν, ἕτερον ἀλεκτρυόνα θύσειν. καὶ δὴ εἰς νύκτα ἔδοξε λέγειν
> αὐτῷ τὸν Ἀσκληπιὸν 'εἷς μοι ἀλεκτρυὼν ἀρκεῖ'. ἄνοσος μὲν οὖν ἔμεινεν,
> ὠφθαλμίασε δὲ ἰσχυρῶς· καὶ γὰρ μιᾷ εὐχῇ ὁ θεὸς ἀρκούμενος τὸ ἕτερον
> ἠρνεῖτο.[79]

A certain man prayed to Asclepius that, if he should make it through the
year without illness, he would sacrifice a cock to him. Then, after waiting
a day, he prayed again to Asclepius that, if he should not contract ophthalmia, he would sacrifice another cock. And indeed, that night, he

imagined that Asclepius said to him: 'One cock is enough for me.' And so he remained without illness but was afflicted terribly with ophthalmia. For in fact the god, satisfied with one prayer, rejected the other.[80]

According to the literary sources, Asclepius thus accepted a rooster as a sacrificial victim; yet, the rooster is not attested in the iconographical record. Presumably, this is because the rooster was a modest sacrificial animal and, therefore, not depicted in prestigious votive reliefs, which tend to feature expensive animals, such as cattle and pigs.

As has been shown, beside the common sacrificial animals, another is closely associated with Asclepius. The rooster was a cheap sacrificial animal and, therefore, more people could afford one. Given that everyone can suffer from diseases, the poor were also able to connect themselves to Asclepius via the rooster and thereby gain access to Asclepeia. In this respect, the rooster became an inclusive symbol, because it did not exclude the poor. There is even some evidence that Asclepius actually favoured the rooster. The work of Aelian includes a reference to the healing power of a rooster, most likely a one-legged fighting cock, which praises Asclepius with his morning crow and is healed by sundown.[81] While this is a bilateral connection between an animal and Asclepius, the triangle is completed by the sacrificial practice when it is performed by his human worshippers.

Miracle healing in Asclepeia: the animal as healer

Since Asclepius was able to appear in both anthropomorphic and zoomorphic epiphanies, here we focus on his zoomorphic appearance.[82] Healings by animals have scarcely featured in the scholarship to date. Indeed, there is only a single paragraph on the subject in the relevant commentary on Asclepius testimonials.[83] There are some incomplete lists of incidents in which animals are related to healings in Asclepeia.[84] However, neither the extent nor the symbolic meaning of animal healings in Asclepeia is known. Several reports from Epidaurus of miracle cures involving animals have survived as inscriptions.[85] Snakes are identifiable in six instances, dogs in two, a goose in one, and a horse in another (see Table 11.1).[86] The reports indicate that the sacred animals healed those seeking a cure either during the day or at night. When the patient awoke in the morning and left the *Abaton*, he or she had been healed.

In one of the inscriptions from Epidaurus, a snake emerges from the healing room, cures the malignant ulcer on a man's toe with its tongue, then retreats back to whence it came.[87] Another sick man is disappointed that he has not been cured at the Asclepeion and returns home. However, one of the sacred snakes makes the journey with him and eventually heals him in his sleep. The man, unsure what to do with the holy serpent, consults the oracle at Delphi, which recommends that his home town should build a temple to Asclepius and house the serpent there.[88] Snakes cure female patients, too. One barren woman is asleep in the healing room and dreams that a snake is lying on her stomach.

Thereafter, she bears five children.[89] Another patient is cured of her childlessness after dreaming that she slept with a snake.[90] When a mute girl spots a snake slithering down from a tree in the sanctuary, she screams in fear and is thus healed.[91] Another patient has an ulcer on her hand, but she is restored to full health after a viper (*echis*) bites it.[92] A snake (*drakōn*) also features in a seventh inscription, but the text is so badly damaged that it is unclear whether the reptile is part of the healing procedure.[93]

In other inscriptions, a goose cures a man's podagra by nipping his feet, making them bleed and then heal; a dog cures a blind boy; and a sacred dog licks another boy's neck and thereby heals an ulcer.[94] Finally, a man, paralysed at the knees, dreams of being trampled by the horses that are pulling Asclepius' cart.[95] His knees immediately return to full strength.

In reverse analogy, perhaps, to the hellhound Cerberus, which was thought to use his saliva to bring death, the sacred temple dogs at Asclepeia were able to heal the sick by licking them.[96] This healing lick – or licking cure – was also performed by other animals.[97] In Aristophanes, snakes lick the eyelids of the blind Plutus, and the following morning he can see.[98] Finally, there are pictorial representations of the way in which the 'kiss' of a snake can cure a sick person.[99] However, precisely why the ancient Greeks credited serpents with healing power remains subject to debate.[100] Since snakes shed their skin, they were thought to rejuvenate, so perhaps the belief was that this rejuvenation could be passed on to humans.[101] Similarly, snake venom might have been considered beneficial in some circumstances. That said, it could be inferred that Asclepian snakes are non-venomous.

Figure 11.3 Dedication from Archinus at the shrine of Amphiaraus, Oropos, featuring a healing scene with a sacred snake, ca. 500 BCE
National Museum of Athens, 3369. Image: Wellcome Collection.
Courtesy of the Wellcome Collection.

It should also be noted that the snake plays no part in the myth of Asclepius; it first appears during the transfer of the cult from Epidaurus to Athens in 420 BCE.[102] It is, therefore, impossible to derive the snake's healing function from the myth, and it remains unclear why snakes appear more often in miracle cures than all other animals combined. Gil H. Renberg's theory is that the hero Asclepius himself appears as the healing snake, whereas other animals, such as dogs, are mere agents of the deity.[103] This suggestion is based on Renberg's assumption that snakes only ever treat sleeping patients, whereas dogs treat people when they are awake. However, this assumption is incorrect, as two of the inscriptions from Epidaurus show serpents healing fully conscious patients (see Table 11.1). We cannot know for sure whether the Epidaurian snake was a symbol of the god's presence (epiphany), a fragment of Asclepius' divine essence, or a zoomorphic manifestation of the deity.[104] However, there is strong evidence that the first two options are simply opposite sides of the same coin. Furthermore, the notion that the sacred snakes were conceived as zoomorphic manifestations of the god is a modern one that would not have occurred to ancient worshippers and pilgrims.

Sacred serpents in Asclepeia feature not only in the Epidaurian *iamata* ('healing stories') but also in Aristophanes' *Plutus* (388 BCE).[105] In addition, Pausanias informs us that non-venomous Asclepian snakes occur naturally in

Table 11.1 Healing miracles at Epidaurus involving animals

No.	Healing animal	Condition	Healed person	Patient's state of consciousness	Evidence
1	Serpent	Ulcer	Man	Asleep	Wunder 17 (Herzog 1931)
2	Serpent	Disease	Man	Asleep	Wunder 33 (Herzog 1931)
3	Serpent	Child-lessness	Woman	Asleep	Wunder 39 (Herzog 1931)
4	Serpent	Child-lessness	Woman	Asleep	Wunder 42 (Herzog 1931)
5	Serpent	Muteness	Girl	Awake	Wunder 44 (Herzog 1931)
6	Serpent	Ulcer	Woman	Awake	Wunder 45 (Herzog 1931)
7	Goose	Podagra	Man	Awake	Wunder 43 (Herzog 1931)
8	Dog	Blindness	Boy	Awake	Wunder 20 (Herzog 1931)
9	Dog	Ulcer	Boy	Awake	Wunder 26 (Herzog 1931)
10	Horse	Paralysed knees	Man	Asleep	Wunder 38 (Herzog 1931)

Based on data from Herzog, R. (1931) Die *Wunderheilungen von Epidauros. Ein Beitrag zur Geschichte der Medizin und der Religion*. Leipzig.

the area around Epidaurus.[106] This evidence, and records of relocation rituals in which snakes were transported from Epidaurus to other sanctuaries, leads to the conclusion that the majority of Asclepeia probably kept snakes.[107] For instance, Aelian tells us that five large snakes were transported from Ethiopia to the Asclepeion at Alexandria during the reigns of Ptolemy Philadelphos and Ptolemy Euergetes III.[108] Moreover, in Herodas' *Mimiambus*, there is mention of a 'snake-hole' (*trōglē tou drakontos*).[109] According to Festus, snakes were kept on Rome's island in the Tiber.[110] And, finally, researchers have hypothesised that the labyrinth beneath the tholos at Epidaurus might have served as a snake-holding facility.[111] However, it should be pointed out that none of this has been confirmed by archaeological evidence, and it has been noted that snakes prefer sun and warmth to the dark, cold conditions of a cellar.[112]

Healing animals, especially snakes, emerge as symbols of the healing hero Asclepius himself. They play active roles in the healing process at the Asclepeia because they connect human patients with the divine Asclepius. On a symbolic level, the triangular divine/human/animal relationship is constituted by the healing procedures of the Asclepeia. As we have seen from the miraculous cures effected at Epidaurus, either the god himself is the healing animal or he sends such an animal as his agent to the human patient, whereupon it performs the healing procedure.

Miracle healing in the cult of Asclepius Glycon

As in Asclepian medicine, the serpent was at the heart of the healing cult at Asclepius Glycon in Abonuteichus. There are, however, noticeable differences between these two healing cults as they belong to two distinct medicinal traditions. There is ample evidence of a wide and eclectic range of medical options in the Roman Empire, including physicians from a number of discrete traditions, midwives, nurses, pharmacists, the priests of countless gods and goddesses, heroes and their cults, and finally magicians and miracle healers.[113] One such miracle healer was a certain Alexander of Abonuteichus, who represented himself as 'Neos Asclepius Glycon'.[114] The founding of a cult for Neos Asclepius Glycon is attested in several literary sources, coins, and sculptures.[115] In 'Alexander the False Prophet', Lucian portrays Alexander as a charlatan. This assessment was based on the author's visit to Abonuteichus (on the Paphlagonian coast of the Black Sea) around 162 CE, roughly 20 years after the cult was founded, although he did not write his scathing report until 180 CE.[116] He describes the establishment of the cult in some detail. Reportedly, Alexander deposited a drained goose egg into which he had placed a newborn snake in the building pit of the temple when it was first built.[117] In contrast to the healing cults that were transferred to Athens and Rome in 420 and 293 BCE, respectively, in this instance it seems the snake was born in Abonuteichus itself. As we have seen, both egg and snake are easily identifiable attributes of Asclepius.[118]

Asclepius Glycon himself is represented in the form of a snake.[119] Thus, the founder of the cult, Alexander, directly emulates the iconography of the Asclepian snake. Yet, there are also some significant iconographical differences. The snake of Asclepius Glycon does not coil around a staff; rather, it twines around itself with a raised head. Moreover, it has a lion's tail, human ears, long hair, and a sheep-like muzzle. A complete, three-dimensional sculptural representation was discovered in ancient Tomi (modern-day Constanta in Romania) during excavations of a fourth-century CE treasure hoard (see Figure 11.4). The same iconographic type was also represented on coins mentioned by Lucian and confirmed by the numismatic record.[120] The cult of Asclepius Glycon seemed to persist in the eastern Mediterranean until the fourth century CE. So, what type of medicine was practised at Abonuteichus? And did animals have a role to play in the healing?

Although Lucian's text tells us a great deal about the relationship between the healing cult and Asclepius worship at Abonuteichus, the precise form of medicine that was practised there remains unclear.[121] In part, this may be attributed to the author's evident lack of familiarity with contemporaneous medical textbooks.[122] Moreover, his main goal was to expose Alexander's fraudulent oracular activity, to record his medical methods. Nevertheless, one or two details of the treatment that was dispensed at Abonuteichus do emerge:[123]

Figure 11.4 Statue of Neos Asclepius Glycon, late second century CE
    Image: C. Chirita; National Museum Constantia, Romania
    Courtesy of the National Museum Constantia

Τοὺς δὲ ἀπέτρεπεν ἢ προῦτρεπεν, ὡς ἂν ἄμεινον ἔδοξεν αὐτῷ εἰκάζοντι·
τοῖς δὲ θεραπείας προῦλεγεν καὶ διαίτας, εἰδώς, ὅπερ ἐν ἀρχῇ ἔφην, πολλὰ
καὶ χρήσιμα φάρμακα. μάλιστα δὲ εἰδοκίμουν παρ' αὐτῷ αἱ κυτμίδες,
ἀκόπου τι ὄνομα πεπλασμένον, ἐκ λίπους ἀρκείου συντεθειμένου.[124]

Some people he dissuaded or encouraged as seemed best to him at a guess.
To others he prescribed medical treatments and diets, knowing, as I said in
the beginning, many useful remedies. His 'cytmides' were in highest favour
with him – a name which he had coined for a restorative ointment com-
pounded of bear's grease.[125]

In addition to such general comments about the remedies that were offered at
Abonuteichus, Lucian notes that Alexander provided medical advice as a part of
his oracular activity.[126] The cost of an oracle was one drachma and two obols –
a great deal of money at the time, particularly when compared with the tariffs
for other oracular institutions and a worker's average daily earnings, which
might be in the region of four obols.[127] Alexander might have justified his high
fee by emphasising his expert medical training, as he was supposedly a second-
generation pupil of Apollonius of Tyana. Indeed, it seems that his magical and
healing knowledge followed the Apollonian tradition.[128]

In addition, in the so-called Antonine Plague of 165 CE, Alexander sold
protective oracles and told his clients to inscribe them above their front doors.
Lucian sardonically notes that the epidemic inflicted more damage on these
homes than anywhere else.[129] That said, earlier in the text, he acknowledges
that Alexander did sometimes dispense useful drugs.[130] The oracles were
delivered not only by Alexander himself but also by the big snake that he
always carried as his companion. The physician allegedly made full use of his
talent for ventriloquism to bolster the illusion.[131] His snake did not participate
directly in the healing process, in contrast to those that resided in the Asclepeia.
In addition, Lucian does not record any incubation rites at Abonuteichus,
which may explain why there is no mention of snake healings during patients'
dreams in his account.

As we have seen throughout this chapter, the serpent does not only symbolise
Asclepius' healing powers but has itself curative capacities. Alexander's serpent, by
contrast, merely dispenses healing oracles and represents the deity. It was the
creature's lack of independent healing power that differentiated Alexander's cult
from the common Asclepius cult, as practised in the Asclepeia, regardless of
Alexander's attempts to connect the two. Nevertheless, both cults epitomised the
triangular god/animal/human relationship.

Conclusion

This chapter has explored the role of animals at the intersection of myth,
healing cults, and miracle healings in Asclepeia. The myth features several animals and human/animal hybrids. First, the foster-father of Asclepius, the

centaur Chiron, introduces him to medicine.[132] Thereafter, a raven, dog, and goat all appear in the story. Apollo changes the raven's plumage from white to black after the bird delivers the unwelcome news of Coronis' adultery. Later, the dog and goat both protect the young Asclepius. The dog's appearance in the myth attests to close connections between Greece and ancient Babylon. However, while the goddess Gula of Isin, as Azugallutu ('great healer'), received dog sacrifices, the Greeks did not use them in their blood rituals; indeed, they were regarded as sacred in the Asclepeia.[133] The animals that appear in the myth all have symbolic meaning in that they help to explain the characteristics that are ascribed to Asclepius.

Although Asclepius' snake is absent from the myth, it, too, was heavily laden with symbolic meaning. It made its first appearance in the cult during the transfer from Epidaurus to Athens in 420 BCE.[134] Thereafter, although the snake's healing power is not extolled in the myth, it was credited with as many miracle healings as all other animals put together. This is attributable to the Greek notion that the snake is the physical incarnation of the *hērōs*. By its presence, the triangular divine/animal/human relationship is completed: the healing animal (snake, dog, etc.) bridges the gap between gods and humans.

At the iconographic level, Asclepius is closely affiliated with a snake coiling around his staff.[135] This image eventually gained immense historico–cultural significance as it transmuted into a symbol of both Asclepius himself and the field of medicine. A further meaning of the snake derives from its role in the transfer of cult. Roman medical history begins with the transportation of an Asclepian snake from Epidaurus to Rome. A temple of Asclepius was built on the island in the Tiber where the snake supposedly settled; in this way, Greek medicine was symbolically transferred to Rome. While this is a symbolic rendering of the triangular relationship on a meta level, it is rooted in the individual level – that is, the specific cult transfer. Although just one cult was transferred to Rome, this act inaugurated a completely new form of medicine.

The rooster held special sacrificial significance in the cult of Asclepius, as both literary and archaeological sources attest. Three discrete traditions are identifiable. The first originates in Plato's *Phaedrus*, where the dying Socrates asks for the sacrifice of a rooster to Asclepius, the second in Herodas' *Mimiambus*, and the third in Artemidorus' *Oneirocritica*. Social historians tentatively explain the sacrifice of this relatively cheap animal with reference to the socioeconomic circumstances of those who sought cures at the Asclepeia. In this respect, the rooster is an inclusive symbol because it does not exclude those who cannot afford a more expensive sacrificial offering.

According to the sources, animals were frequently involved in the healing that occurred in the Asclepeia. For instance, the literary evidence includes the case of a blind man who dreamt that his eyes were touched by a snake and awoke to find that he could see. There are also visual depictions of the 'kiss' of a snake healing a sick person. Moreover, the keeping of snakes within Asclepeia is attested in the Greek literature. The triangular relationship of Asclepius, his sacred animals, and the patients who seek cures has at its core the symbolic connection between humans and the divine.

The snake also played a central role in the healing cult of Asclepius Glycon, even though Alexander of Abonuteichus' serpent was not directly associated with his cures. The type of medicine that was practised at Abonuteichus was distinct from the standard Asclepian tradition in other ways, too. For instance, there is no evidence of incubation rites or animal healings at Abonuteichus, and the temple's main source of revenue was oracular pronouncements that offered medical advice. That said, the symbolic rendering of the triangular divine/animal/human relationship was fundamental to the cult of Glycon, just as it was to every other branch of Greek religion.

Notes

1 Steger 2018, 2016, 2004.
2 Riethmüller 2005: Vol. 2: 493–494.
3 On animals in the thinking of Greeks and Romans, see Newmyer 2018.
4 Gröpl 2003.
5 Hygin. *Fab.* 202 (ed. Rose).
6 Trans. Grant.
7 Stafford 2008: 206.
8 Pind. *Pyth.* 3.1, 38–46, 54–60.
9 Apollod. *Bibl.* 1.2.4.
10 Hom. *Il.* 4. 190–219.
11 Hom. *Il.* 11.828–832.
12 Brodersen 2015.
13 Isid. *Orig.* 4.9.12.
14 Steger 2018: 18–20; Lorenz 2016 and 2000; Burkert 1984: 75–77.
15 Paus. 2.26.4–5.
16 Here and below, trans. Jones.
17 Callim. *Hymn.* 1; Ov. *Fast.* 5.111–128; Pherec. *FGrH* 3 F 42.
18 Apollod. *FGrH* 244 F 138.
19 Lorenz 2000: 211–212.
20 Franke 1969: 62–63, fig. 2; *BMC Peloponnesus*, pl. 29, no. 14.
21 *IG* II/III² 4962.
22 Lorenz 2000: 260–266.
23 Lorenz 1988: 5–6; Kyrieleis 1979.
24 Maul 2001: 20; Avalos 1995: 99–232.
25 Steger 2018: 18–20.
26 British Museum no. 130814; Ornan 2004; Wapnish and Hesse 1993; Livingstone 1988; Shaffer 1974.
27 Lorenz 2000: 266.
28 Orth 1913b: 2575; Orth 1910.
29 Ael. *NA* 7.13; National Museum of Athens no. 1426; Renberg 2017: Vol. 1: 185, n. 165; Orth 1913b: 2576.
30 Renberg 2017: Vol. 1: 215, n. 239.
31 Edelstein and Edelstein 1998: T467–481; Petridou 2015: 184.
32 Edelstein 1937.
33 Pergamonmuseum no. 152; for the date, see Krug 2008: 48.
34 *ThesCRA* 1.2a gr. Taf. 16, figs. 85–86; Straten 1995, figs. R6, 8, 10, 23, 35, 97–98, 113, 126, 137, 149–150.

35 Cavanaugh 2017; Steger 2000; Schouten 1967.
36 Farnell 1921: 240.
37 Krug 2008: 22.
38 Ov. *Met.* 15.622–744.
39 Liv. 10.47.7.
40 Horstmanshoff 1992.
41 Schnalke 2005; Clinton 1994.
42 Penso 1984: 12; British Museum no. 1853.0512.238.
43 See Ov. *Met.* 15.622–744.
44 Pfeffer-Küppers 1969: 22–27 and 98–102.
45 Krauss 1944.
46 Steger 2018: 72, figs. 9a, 9b.
47 See Stafford 2008: 205, n. 1.
48 Hausmann 1948.
49 Straten 1995: 63.
50 Błaśkiewicz 2014: 58.
51 Hausmann 2019: 94, fig. 57.
52 *IG* IV^2 1,102; Meyer 1994; National Archaeological Museum Athens, nos. 173, 1330, 1338, 1339.
53 *LIMC* II,1 s.v. 'Asclepius', nos. 154–233.
54 Steger 2018: 41, fig. 3; Meyer 1988.
55 Ogden 2013: 318.
56 Paus. 2.27.2.
57 Lorenz 2000: 211–214.
58 Franke 1969: 62–63, fig. 2; *BMC Peloponnesus*, pl. 29, no. 14.
59 Schouten 1967.
60 Steger 2018: 7, fig. 1; Steger 2000: 21–25, figs. 1–10.
61 Strohmaier 1970.
62 Riethmüller 2005: Vol. 1: 323.
63 Mazzuca 2014: 292–293.
64 Ogden 2013: 373–375.
65 Riethmüller 2005: Vol. 1: 134; Vol 2: 236.
66 Plat. *Phaedr.* 118a.
67 Trans. Jones and Preddy.
68 Luc. *Bis accusatus* 5; Olymp. *In Phlb.* 205.24, 244.17; Tert. *Apol.* 46.5; Lactant. *Div. inst.* 3.20.16–17; Lact. *Inst. epit.* 32.4–5; Prudent. *Apoth.* 203–206.
69 See, e.g., Kloss 2001; Leimbach 2008; Stafford 2008; Renberg 2017: Vol. 1: 263.
70 Orth 1913a: 2533.
71 Stafford 2008: 211.
72 Herod. 4.13–20: T482 (Edelstein).
73 Here and below, trans. Rusten and Cunningham.
74 Straten 1995: 181.
75 Błaśkiewicz 2014: 64; Dillon 1994: 255.
76 Herod. 4.87–92.
77 Stafford 2008: 211, fig. 2.
78 Straten 1995: 54.
79 Artem. 5.9.
80 Trans. Harris-McCoy.
81 Ael. fr. 98 (T466 Edelstein).
82 Petridou 2015: 171–194.
83 Edelstein and Edelstein 1998: 167.
84 Renberg 2017: Vol. 1: 215, n. 239; Petridou 2015: 93, n. 357; Solin 2013: 26, 185.
85 *IG* IV^2, 1, 121–124; Schäfer 2000; LiDonnici 1995; Herzog 1931.

86   Snakes: Herzog 1931: Wunder ('miracle') 17, 33, 39, 42, 44, 45. Dogs: Herzog
      1931: Wunder 20, 26 . Goose: Herzog 1931: Wunder 43. Horse: Herzog 1931:
      Wunder 38.
87   Herzog 1931: Wunder 17.
88   Herzog 1931: Wunder 33.
89   Herzog 1931: Wunder 39
90   Herzog 1931: Wunder 42.
91   Herzog 1931: Wunder 44.
92   Herzog 1931: Wunder 45.
93   Herzog 1931: Wunder 58.
94   Goose restores health: Herzog 1931: Wunder 43. Dog cures a blind boy: Herzog
      1931: Wunder 20. Sacred dog cures an ulcer: Herzog 1931: Wunder 26.
95   Herzog 1931: Wunder 38.
96   Orth 1913b: 2576.
97   Scholz 1937: 12–13 and 23.
98   Ar. *Plut.* 730–734; Weinreich 2015: 96–97.
99   National Museum of Athens no. 3369.
100 Mähly 1867: 9–10; Ogden 2013: 347–382.
101 Giebel 2003: 166–167.
102 Ogden 2013: 310, n. 1.
103 Renberg 2017: Vol.1: 216, n. 239.
104 Petridou 2015: 93.
105 Ar. *Plut.* 653–725; Renberg 2017: Vol.1: 135–136, 215; Petridou 2015: 186, 191.
106 Paus. 2.28.1; Ael. *NA* 8.12; Keller 2013: Vol. 2: 299.
107 Krug 1993: 127; Ogden 2013: 347.
108 Ael. *NA* 16.39.
109 Herod. 4.89–90.
110 Fest. P. 110 M.
111 Riethmüller 2005: Vol.1: 318–319.
112 Krug 1993: 132.
113 Steger 2002.
114 Steger 2005; Victor 1997.
115 *LIMC* IV.1 s.v. 'Glykon'; Petsalis-Diomidis 2010: 14–41.
116 Flinterman 1997.
117 Luc. *Alex.* 13; Aston 2011: 125.
118 Schnalke 2005; Strohmaier 1970.
119 Victor 1997: figs. 1–3.
120 Luc. *Alex.* 58; Robert 1980: 396, figs. 2–5.
121 Steger 2005.
122 Langholf 1996.
123 Victor 1997: 3, 15.
124 Luc. *Alex.* 22.
125 Trans. Harmon.
126 Luc. *Alex.* 25.
127 Luc. *Alex.* 23, *Tim.* 6, *Ep. Sat.* 21.
128 Luc. *Alex.* 5; Frede 1996; Bowie 1987.
129 Luc. *Alex.* 36.
130 Luc. *Alex.* 22; Renberg 2017: Vol 1: 228, n. 280.
131 Luc. *Alex.* 26.
132 Aston 2011: 91–109 and 271–272.
133 Lorenz 2016.
134 Ogden 2013: 310, n. 1.
135 Schouten 1967.

Bibliography

Aston, E. (2011) *Mixanthrôpoi. Animal–Human Hybrid Deities in Greek religion.* Liège.

Avalos, H. (1995) *Illness and Health Care in the Ancient Near East. The Role of the Temple in Greece, Mesopotamia, and Israel.* Atlanta, Ga.

Błaśkiewicz, M. (2014) 'Healing dreams at Epidaurus: analysis and interpretation of the Epidaurian iamata', *Miscellanea Anthropologica et Sociologica* 15, 54–69.

Bowie, E. (1987) 'Apollonius of Tyana: tradition and reality', in *ANRW.* Vol. 2, 16.2, 1652–1699.

Brodersen, K. (ed.) (2015) *Apuleius Heilkräuterbuch. Herbarius.* Wiesbaden.

Burkert, W. (1984) *Die orientalisierende Epoche in der griechischen Religion und Literatur.* Heidelberg.

Cavanaugh, T. A. (2017) *Hippocrates' Oath and Asclepius' Snake. The Birth of the Medical Profession.* New York, N.Y.

Clinton, K. (1994) 'The Epidauria and the arrival of Asclepius in Athens', in R. Hägg (ed.) *Ancient Greek Cult Practice from the Epigraphical Evidence. Proceedings of the Second International Seminar on Ancient Greek Cult, Organized by the Swedish Institute at Athens, 22–24 November 1991.* Jonsered, 17–34.

Dillon, M. P. J. (1994) 'The didactic nature of the Epidaurian iamata', *Zeitschrift für Papyrologie und Epigraphik* 105, 239–260.

Edelstein, E. J. L. and L. Edelstein (1998) *Asclepius. Collection and Interpretation of the Testimonies.* Baltimore, Md.

Edelstein, L. (1937) 'Greek medicine in its relation to religion and magic', *Bulletin of the Institute of the History of Medicine* 5, 201–246.

Farnell, L. R. (1921) *Greek Hero Cults and Ideas of Immortality.* Oxford.

Flinterman, J.-J. (1997) 'The date of Lucian's visit to Abonuteichos', *Zeitschrift für Papyrologie und Epigraphik* 119, 282.

Franke, P. R. (1969) 'Asklepios: Aesculapius auf antiken Münzen', *Medizinischer Monatsspiegel* 3, 60–67.

Frede, M. (1996) 'Apollonios von Tyana', in *DNP.* Vol. 1, 887.

Giebel, M. (2003) *Tiere in der Antike. Von Fabelwesen, Opfertieren und treuen Begleitern.* Stuttgart.

Gröpl, T. J. M. (2003) 'Das Tier in der Medizin. Eine ideengeschichtliche Abhandlung der Beziehung des Menschen zum Tier unter besonderer Berücksichtigung der Antike anhand Galens anatomischer Schrift Anatomikai encheireseis ("Anatomische Handgriffe")'. Ph.D. diss., Technische Universität München.

Hausmann, U. (1948) *Kunst und Heiltum. Untersuchungen zu den griechischen Asklepiosreliefs.* Potsdam.

Hausmann, U. (2019) *Griechische Weihreliefs.* Berlin.

Herzog, R. (1931) *Die Wunderheilungen von Epidauros. Ein Beitrag zur Geschichte der Medizin und der Religion; mit einer Tafel.* Leipzig.

Horstmanshoff, H. F. J. (1992) 'Epidemie und Anomie: Epidemien in der griechischen Welt (800–400 v. Chr.)', *Medizinhistorisches Journal* 27, 43–65.

Keller, O. (2013) *Die antike Tierwelt*, Vol. 2: *Vögel, Reptilien, Fische, Insekten. Mit Gesamtregister von Emil Staiger (Leipzig 1920).* Hildesheim.

Kloss, G. (2001) 'Sokrates, ein Hahn für Asklepios und die Pflege der Seelen: ein neuer Blick auf den Schluss von Platons "Phaidon"', *Gymnasium* 108, 223–239.

Krauss, F. (1944) 'Die Prora an der Tiberinsel in Rom', *Mitteilungen des Kaiserlich Deutschen Archäologischen Instituts, Römische Abteilung* 59, 159–172.

Krug, A. (1993) *Heilkunst und Heilkult. Medizin in der Antike*. Munich.

Krug, A. (2008) *Das Berliner Arztrelief*. Berlin.

Kyrieleis, H. (1979) 'Babylonische Bronzen im Heraion von Samos', *Jahrbuch des Deutschen Archäologischen Instituts* 94: 32–48.

Langholf, V. (1996) 'Lukian und die Medizin: Zu einer tragischen Katharsis bei den Abderiten (De historia conscribenda §1)', in *ANRW*. Vol. 2, 37.3, 2793–2841.

Leimbach, R. (2008) 'Was hat Asklepios für Sokrates getan?' *Hermes* 136, 275–292.

LiDonnici, L. R. (1995) *The Epidaurian Miracle Inscriptions: Text, Translation, and Commentary*. Atlanta, Ga.

Livingstone, A. (1988) 'The Isin "dog-house" revisited', *Journal of Cuneiform Studies* 40, 54–60.

Lorenz, G. (1988) 'Apollon, Asklepios und Hygieia: Drei Typen von Heilgöttern aus der Sicht der vergleichenden Religionsgeschichte', *Saeculum* 39, 1–11.

Lorenz, G. (2000) *Tiere im Leben der alten Kulturen. Schriftlose Kulturen, Alter Orient, Ägypten, Griechenland und Rom*. Wien.

Lorenz, G. (2016) *Asklepios, der Heiler mit dem Hund, und der Orient. Religion und Medizin in alten Kulturen in universalhistorischer Sicht: gesammelte Schriften*. Innsbruck.

Mähly, J. (1867) *Die Schlange im Mythus und Cultus der classischen Völker*. Basel.

Maul, S. M. (2001) 'Die Heilkunde im Alten Orient', *Medizinhistorisches Journal* 36, 3–22.

Mazzuca, V. (2014) 'Asclepius with egg: type Nea Paphos–Alexandira–Trier: new data and some new reflections', *Arheologia Moldovei* 37, 291–298.

Meyer, M. (1988) 'Erfindung und Wirkung: Zum Asklepios Giustini', *Mitteilungen des Deutschen Archäologischen Instituts Abteilung Athen* 103, 119–159.

Meyer, M. (1994) 'Zwei Asklepiostypen des 4. Jahrhunderts v. Chr. Asklepios Giustini und Asklepios Athen-Macerata', *Antike Plastik* 23, 7–55.

Newmyer, S. T. (2018) 'Tiere im Denken der Griechen und Römer: eine schwierige Sache', in T. Pommerening and J. Althoff (eds.) *Kult, Kunst, Konsum: Tiere in alten Kulturen*. Darmstadt, 33–47.

Ogden, D. (2013) *Drakōn. Dragon Myth and Serpent Cult in the Greek and Roman Worlds*. Oxford.

Ornan, T. (2004) 'The goddess Gula and her dog', *Israel Museum Studies in Archaeology* 3, 13–30.

Orth, F. (1910) *Der Hund im Altertum*. Schleusingen.

Orth, F. (1913a) 'Huhn', in *RE*. Vol. 8. 2, 2519–2536.

Orth, F. (1913b) 'Hund', in *RE*. Vol. 8. 2, 2540–2582.

Pabst, A. (2008) 'Hasen und Löwen: Tiere im politischen Diskurs des klassischen Griechenland', in A. Alexandridis, M. Wild, and L. Winkler-Horacek (eds.) *Mensch und Tier in der Antike. Grenzziehung und Grenzüberschreitung*. Wiesbaden, 83–97.

Penso, G. (1984) *La Médecine romaine. L'Art d'Esculape dans la Rome antique*. Paris.

Petridou, G. (2015) *Divine Epiphany in Greek Literature & Culture*. Oxford.

Petsalis-Diomidis, A. (2010) *Truly beyond Wonders. Aelius Aristides and the Cult of Asklepios*. Oxford.

Pfeffer-Küppers, M. E. (1969) *Einrichtungen der sozialen Sicherung in der griechischen und römischen Antike, unter besonderer Berücksichtigung der Sicherung bei Krankheit*. Berlin.

Pommerening, T. and J. Althoff (eds.) (2018) *Kult, Kunst, Konsum. Tiere in alten Kulturen*. Darmstadt.

Renberg, G. H. (2017) *Where Dreams May Come. Incubation Sanctuaries in the Greco-Roman World*. 2 vols. Leiden.

Riethmüller, J. W. (2005) *Asklepios. Heiligtümer und Kulte*. 2 vols. Heidelberg.

Robert, L. (1980) *A Travers l'Asie mineure. Poètes et prosateurs, monnaies grecques, voyageurs et géographie*. Athens.

Schäfer, D. (2000) 'Traum und Wunderheilung im Asklepios-Kult und in der griechisch-römischen Medizin', in A. Karenberg and C. Leitz (eds.) *Heilkunde und Hochkultur*. Vol. 1. Berlin, 259–274.

Shaffer, A. (1974) 'Enlilbani and the "dog house" in Isin', *Journal of Cuneiform Studies 2*, 251–255.

Schnalke, T. (2005) 'Asklepios-Schlange', in K. H. Leven (ed.) *Antike Medizin. Ein Lexikon*. Munich, 112–113.

Scholz, H. (1937) 'Der Hund in der griechisch-römischen Magie und Religion'. Ph.D. diss., Friedrich-Wilhelms-Universität.

Schouten, J. (1967) *The Rod and Serpent of Asklepios. Symbol of Medicine*. Amsterdam.

Solin, H. (2013) 'Inschriftliche Wunderheilungsberichte aus Epidauros', *Zeitschrift für Antike und Christentum* 17, 7–50.

Stafford, E. J. (2008) 'Cocks to Asklepios: sacrificial practice and healing cult', in V. Mehl and P. Brulé (eds.) *Le Sacrifice antique. Vestiges, procédures et stratégies*. Rennes, 205–221.

Steger, F. (2000) 'Erinnern an Asklepios: Lektüre eines gegenwärtigen Mythos aus der antiken Medizin', in B. von Jagow (ed.) *Topographie der Erinnerung: Mythos im strukturellen Wandel*. Würzburg, 19–39.

Steger, F. (2002) 'Der kulturelle Ort des Heilens: die Koexistenz medizinischer Kulturen im Imperium Romanum', in F. Steger (ed.) *Kultur: ein Netz von Bedeutungen: Analysen zur symbolischen Kulturanthropologie*. Würzburg, 137–158.

Steger, F. (2004) *Asklepiosmedizin: Medizinischer Alltag in der römischen Kaiserzeit*. Stuttgart.

Steger, F. (2005) 'Der neue Asklepios Glykon', *Medizinhistorisches Journal* 40, 3–18.

Steger, F. (2016) *Asclepios. Medizin und Kult*. Stuttgart.

Steger, F. (2018) *Asclepius. Medicine and Cult*, trans. M. M. Saar. Stuttgart (German orig. 2016).

Straten, F. T. van (1995) *Hiera Kala. Images of Animal Sacrifice in Archaic and Classical Greece*. Leiden.

Strohmaier, G. (1970) 'Asklepios und das Ei: Zur Ikonographie in einem arabisch erhaltenen Kommentar zum hippokratischen Eid', in R. Stiehl and H. E. Stier (eds.) *Beiträge zur alten Geschichte und deren Nachleben. Festschrift für Franz Altheim zum 6.10.1968*. Vol. 2. Berlin, 143–153.

Victor, U. (1997) *Lukian von Samosata. Alexandros oder der Lügenprophet*. Leiden.

Wapnish, P. and B. Hesse (1993) 'Pampered pooches or plain pariahs? The Ashkelon dog burials', *Biblical Archaeologist* 56, 55–80.

Weinreich, O. (2015) *Antike Heilungswunder. Untersuchungen zum Wunderglauben der Griechen und Römer*. Berlin.

12 Circe's Ram[1]

Animals in Ancient Greek Magic

K. Dosoo

Introduction

Both human/animal studies and the field of ancient magic have seen considerable growth in recent decades, and their intersections, though few, have produced some significant works.[2] These demonstrate two overlapping foci. The first of these is the rich corpus of Greco-Egyptian magical papyri, dating largely to the third and fourth centuries CE. In these texts, animals are found as both 'ingredients' in ritual prescriptions and as beings closely linked to the invoked gods, following Egyptian concepts of the potential divinity of the animal form (on which, see also this volume, Chapter 6).[3] The second focus is on earlier Greek and Latin zoological material, such as Pliny's *Natural History*, within which animal parts play an important role in the construction of amuletic and ritual power.[4] Both bodies of material can be supplemented by the sparser information from other textual and artefactual evidence, as has often been done to write discussions of particular animals or practices, such as the famous *echenēis* fish, capable of rooting ships in place and binding rivals and lovers, or the *iynx*, a 'magical' wheel that took its name from the wryneck and might once have had living birds bound to it.[5]

This discussion does not aim to provide an exhaustive survey or comprehensive theory of animals in Greek magic. Instead, it investigates three motifs – human/animal metamorphoses, curses, and magical sacrifice (on the latter, see also this volume, Chapter 8). These represent only a few of many possible examples, but they are recurrent themes within the discursive field of magic, and, more importantly, they constitute cases in which more general principles are made explicit. These 'magical' practices, and their literary reflexes, both delineate and interrogate the boundary between humans and non-human animals within the symbolic system of Greek religion. I argue that the tracing and retracing of this boundary serves to reveal the ways in which human and non-human animals, and superhuman beings, were conceived of as simultaneously alike and unlike.

Talking about Greek magic

It is not easy to write a history of Greek magic. We are confronted first with the question of the viability of 'magic' as a concept, which was cast into doubt by developments in anthropology over the course of the 20th century that favoured contextual studies over essentialising categories.[6] While several authors have suggested either jettisoning or replacing the term, these moves have not, generally speaking, changed the range of sources used in discussions of 'magic', although they have led to new approaches and analyses.[7] Taking inspiration from these, I understand 'magic' not as a property inherent in the sources being studied, but as a category that allows us to bring different materials into contact with one another. That is, describing a practice as 'magical' does not tell us that it is subversive, marginal, mistaken, dishonest, or fraudulent (although it may be), but rather that we can observe in it features it shares with other 'magical' practices that make it useful to study within this frame. Most obviously, these practices involve the performance by humans (and, more rarely, other animals) of marvellous feats through ritual, knowledge of the natural properties of plants, minerals, and animals, and special relationships with superhuman powers. It is important to note that this working definition does not distinguish 'magic' from either 'science' or 'religion'. While these categories may be at least notionally distinct in particular cultural settings, 'magical' practices in the ancient Greek-speaking world generally drew upon similar logics to those we might call 'technical' or 'religious'.

The second major problem relates to sources: those typically captured by the category 'magic' are very diverse. They include references to and discussions of magical practices in literary sources from the archaic to the Roman period; curse tablets, primarily on lead, found throughout the Greek world from the sixth century BCE onwards; and the richest ritual material, the Roman-era 'Greek magical papyri', which are part of a larger corpus of Greco-Egyptian magical artefacts.[8] How can these sources – diverse in terms of form, nature, date, and geographical origin – be integrated? Despite the undeniable relationships scholars have observed across these types of evidence, there are equally undeniable methodological problems. Do the richer discussions of magic found in Roman-era sources represent fuller expressions of earlier concerns, or rather new anxieties, informed by changed social and political circumstances? Should the Greco-Egyptian magical texts be understood as preserving much older culturally Greek material? Or do they translate Egyptian ritual practices into the Greek language? Or, perhaps most likely, some combination of the two?[9] (On sources, see also this volume, Chapter 2).

These problems arise from the way in which our surviving sources are haunted by the much larger body of material that has been lost: the writings attributed to Orpheus, which were in circulation by at least the fifth century BCE, for example, or the Hellenistic works of the *magos* Ostanes and other authors to whom Pliny alludes, as well as the innumerable conversations, speeches, and rituals that were never transcribed or described.[10] It is for this reason that it is tempting to use the richer material from the Common Era, often from Egypt, the Latin West, or the Near East, to reconstruct the more allusive mentions to practices in Homer or Plato, and to assume that literary texts refer more or less directly to the same kinds of rituals attested by surviving artefacts.

Some of these issues can be resolved if we give up the attempt to discuss 'Greek magic' in a hypothetical 'pure' or 'classical' form. While the Persian, Macedonian, and Roman conquests increased the degree of cultural inter-penetration, Greek-speaking cultures were in dialogue with other traditions long before these events. Greek borrowing from – and influence on – surrounding peoples must be taken as the norm, rather than as a confounding factor. We must also acknowledge that literary texts and ritual artefacts do not comprise a single kind of evidence; rather, they draw upon and feed into the same symbolic and proto-scientific systems and therefore exist in a complex relationship of mutual influence. Understanding the history of magic as an unfolding of texts and practices in discourse with one another allows us to acknowledge both temporal discontinuities and persistent themes, as the overlapping discourses develop magic as a 'discursive field'. This discursive field, which offered the possibility of talking about and attempting to enact marvellous deeds, does not need to be understood as culturally homogeneous. Speakers of Latin, Egyptian, Aramaic, and other languages could participate in the construction of Greek magic, parti-cularly as Hellenism became the dominant cultural model of the Mediterranean. Speakers of these languages would bring with them new material from their own cultural backgrounds while interacting with and building upon existing ideas from the Greek tradition. Using this model, the following discussion will sketch out the position of animals within this discursive field, focusing primarily on Greek material from the end of the eighth century BCE to the fourth century CE. That said, sources from other places and eras will be utilised if they have the potential to enrich the discussion.

Animalising the human: transformation

We begin, as Daniel Ogden does in his recent survey, with Circe, the first 'magician' of Greek literature.[11] Odysseus encounters her in Book 10 of Homer's *Odyssey*, arriving at her island having lost 11 of his 12 ships to Laes-trygonian cannibals. For two days and nights, he is afraid to venture ashore, but on the third day he scouts the island, spying the smoke from Circe's home before returning to report his findings. He encounters a huge stag en route and kills it to feed his crew. The size of the stag is stressed repeatedly – it is 'great and high-horned' (ὑψίκερων ἔλαφον μέγαν), an 'exceedingly great beast' (μάλα γὰρ μέγα θηρίον ἦεν), and a 'terrible monster' (δεινοῖο πελώρου).[12] From the beginning, then, Circe is defined as simultaneously divine and human – a 'ter-rible goddess of human speech' (δεινὴ θεὸς αὐδήεσσα) – as well as surrounded by uncanny animals.[13]

After a night of feasting, half of the men are chosen by lot to explore Circe's dwelling. They are greeted by her human voice, singing as she weaves, sur-rounded by wolves and lions that fawn on the humans like tame dogs. She offers the men a meal but laces it with *pharmaka* – which, translated into Eng-lish, can mean either magic potion or drug – before turning them into pigs with her wand and leading them to a sty. Only one, Eurylochus, is left human, having been too suspicious to accept Circe's invitation into her home. He flees back to Odysseus, who eventually overcomes the goddess with the help of Hermes.

This scene has inspired many retellings and artistic depictions, both ancient and modern (see, e.g., Figure 12.1). As Ogden observes, the images of Circe and her victims on Greek pottery focus on the transitional moment when they are in mid-transformation, neither human nor animal: they crawl on all fours, with pigs', lions', or sheep's heads and tails sprouting from human bodies.[14] The *Argonautica* of Apollonius Rhodius (ca. 250 BCE) stretches this moment into a tableau, replacing the men's final pig-shape with that of hybrids resembling the primeval creatures of Empedocles who had not yet evolved into their fixed forms: οὐ θήρεσσιν ἐοικότες ὠμηστῇσιν, οὐδὲ μὲν οὐδ᾽ ἄνδρεσσιν ὁμὸν δέμας, ἄλλο δ᾽ ἀπ᾽ ἄλλων συμμιγέες μελέων ('neither flesh-eating animals nor yet humans in any consistent form, but having a mixture of limbs from each').[15] The scene's fascination lies in its transgression of the boundary between human and animal, mediated by the goddess/witch Circe. But why did she do it, and what does it signify?

Odgen suggests that the reason for the transformation, 'inexplicit but inevitable', is that Circe intends to eat the men, like the Cyclops whom Odysseus encountered earlier, and the Laestrygonians who speared his men 'like fish' (ἰχθῦς δ᾽ ὣς).[16] However, this explanation is not fully convincing in light of

Figure 12.1 Bronze figurine of one of Odysseus' crew transforming from a human into a pig, Peloponnesus, fifth century BCE
The Walters Art Museum, 54.1483 (public domain)
Courtesy of the Walters Art Museum, Baltimore

other ancient authors' inference that the lions and wolves that surround Circe are also transformed humans. Dio Chrysostom, for example, suggests that the lions' tameness is due to their essentially human nature, which means they lack the leonine ferocity that would have made them effective guards.[17] If Circe's main goal in transfiguring humans was to eat them, we might expect sheep and cattle alongside pigs, not the lions, wolves, and donkeys that are mentioned in the *Odyssey* and elsewhere.[18] When we look for possible instances of cannibalism on the island, the clearest (though still uncertain) instances are committed not by Circe herself, but by Odysseus and his men, who eat the uncanny stag and other meats (*krea*) during their year-long stay. As Ogden points out, it would be easy to read this monstrous stag as one of Circe's transfigured humans.[19]

The only stories in which Circe's motivations are clear are those in which her transformations are directly instrumental, as is particularly common in Roman-era retellings. For example, she transforms Scylla into a monstrous hybrid out of spite, and Picus into woodpecker after he spurns her advances.[20] Such stories imply that transformation is simply what Circe does, just as the Laestrygonians eat humans, or the Sirens entice sailors to their doom. Transformation, and the humiliation of being forced to live like an animal, are the particular threats that she represents.

The horror of this transformation arises from the idea, explicitly mentioned by Dio Chrysostom but present in Homer, too, that the pig-men retained their human minds (*nous*) while trapped in their alien, animal bodies.[21] However, a rather different perspective eventually emerged to rival this original understanding. This is often evident in examples where the transformation is understood as metaphorical. For example, Xenophon records Socrates telling his friends that it was through overindulgence that Circe turned her guests into pigs.[22] A fragment of Porphyry preserved by Stobaeus similarly understands the story as an allegory for the Platonic myth of transmigration, according to which those souls who have lived lives unworthy of their human form will be drawn to those of 'lower' animals in their next incarnation.[23] Here the negatively charged human drives of greed and gluttony are identified with an animal, and while the minds of the pig-men are understood to remain unchanged, their altered form reflects an exteriorisation of their previously hidden bestial nature.

This theme of transformation, and the tension between animal and human – and body and mind – is one that recurs in later stories of magic. The most developed example is in the story of Lucius' transformation into a donkey, best known in its Latin telling, Apuleius' *Metamorphoses*, which drew upon an older Greek version that is represented by a surviving epitome, the *Onos*, attributed to Lucian of Samosata.[24] The rationales behind the transformations are clearer in these accounts, and the witches transform not only their victims but also themselves. Yet, the stories contain numerous different types of transformation: the witches turn into birds, dogs, mice, flies, weasels, and, above all, owls – creatures whose small size and/or ability to fly give them access to otherwise barred places and enable them to pass by unnoticed.[25] These transformations might be understood as similar to those of the gluttonous sailors: the habitual form of the witch Pamphile is that of an owl (*korax nykterinos, bubo*), a bird of ill-omen that Aelian suggests already resembles a witch (*pharmakis*) as it is a wily, nocturnal creature that binds both humans and other birds with its incantation-like call.[26] Once again, then, the transition from human to animal reveals an inner, inhuman truth.

By contrast, the incongruity of the transformations that the witches inflict upon their (usually) male victims marks them as horrific, and at times ironic, punishments. Apuleius describes an innkeeper-turned-frog who is forced to swim, trapped, in a jar of his own wine. Elsewhere in the story, a lawyer-turned-ram still vainly tries to plead cases. Even more brutal is the example of a witch's former lover who is turned into a beaver, and doomed by his new animal nature to chew off his own genitals when pursued by hunters.[27] The story's central transformation, though, is that of the protagonist, Lucius, who is turned into a donkey after his own curiosity and the incompetence of a witch's slave leads to him being slathered with the wrong transforming salve.[28] Both versions of his story tell of his subsequent misadventures, as he is passed from owner to owner, constantly beaten, mistreated, and threatened with death, castration, and even sexual abuse. This abject picture of the life of a domestic animal is made all the more horrific – and indeed, in both versions, perversely funny – by the fact that Lucius, like Odysseus' men, retains his human mind but loses the ability to express it through either speech or gestures.[29]

Keith Bradley has argued that this transformation may be understood as a metaphor for slavery. Lucius' sudden fall from free human to chattel, the way he is passed from one owner to the next, and the regular threats of physical and sexual violence all parallel the experiences of human slaves in the Greek and Roman worlds.[30] Indeed, Lucius himself makes this connection by explicitly referring to his condition as 'slavery' (*seruitium*), and to other owned humans and animals as his 'fellow-slaves' (*homodouloi, conserui*).[31] Bradley explains that the process of 'animalisation', to which slaves were subject, 'offered the prospect of converting human beings to a state of mute and unquestioning docility and obedience in which there were virtually no limits to the demands of work, punishment, and disposal that might be made of them, and in which the slaves' ability to exercise their will and make independent decisions might be completely destroyed.'[32]

The degradation of humans through animalisation was facilitated by both the material realities of animal domestication in the ancient world and the supporting ideology that developed around these realities. Ingvild Sælid Gilhus has traced the persistent idea in Greek and Latin literature that animals existed for human benefit, and so could be used instrumentally without qualms.[33] In one of his lowest moments – when he is engaged in the Sisyphean and body-destroying work of turning a millstone – Lucius describes the baker who owns him as a generally good man, and even helps him by uncovering his wife's adultery.[34] His degradation is not a moral failing of his master, but rather a consequence of his own animal nature. Through animalisation, certain

categories of humans – here the enslaved – could be assimilated to this discourse: the slaves who work alongside the donkey Lucius in the mill are
equally stunted and deformed by their labours.[35] Bradley notes many instances
of the animalisation of slaves in both the literature and the law. Most striking is
the designation of slaves as 'human-footed animals' (*andrapoda*), analogous to
the 'four-footed animals' (*tetrapoda*) that comprised the bulk of domestic
creatures.[36]

   While Lucius' transformation reveals the reality of animalisation through an
accident of curiosity, there are suggestions that this notion formed a larger part
of the discourse of magical transformation. In a story that is reminiscent of the
Metamorphoses, Augustine of Hippo relates stories of Italian landladies who fed
their guests enchanted cheese, transforming them into beasts of burden
(*iumenta*) that they then forced to work for them.[37] Here, again, turning
humans into animals, like enslaving them, transforms them into malleable
instruments.

   In an interesting passage of his *Advice to a Bride and Groom*, Plutarch suggests
that magic (*pharmaka, philtra, goēteia*) allows fish to be caught easily, and wives
to gain power over their husbands, but renders the fish inedible and the men
'stupid and broken' (ἀνοήτοις καὶ διεφθαρμένοις), just like the useless animals
that surrounded Circe.[38] However, the transformation he describes – mental
rather than physical – is an inversion of that in the *Odyssey*. Is he implying that
love spells effect a kind of mental transformation, analogous to the physical
transformation into an animal? David Frankfurter has discussed this theme in
later Christian Egypt. Two fifth-century CE versions of the story of Saint
Macarius tell of a magician who seemingly turns a woman into a horse through
a love spell.[39] If the purpose of turning a human into a horse for erotic purposes is unclear, the implications are elucidated in a still later variation on the
same theme in the Arabic-language *History of the Patriarchs*. Here, a magician
turns a woman into a donkey, rides her when he is in the city, then transforms
her back into a woman so that he can sexually abuse her when they are alone
in the desert.[40] Once again, animal transformation seems to function as a
metaphor for slavery. No surviving ritual texts present the physical transformation of human bodies into those of animals as a serious goal, but Frankfurter
points out that several do aim to effect a mental transformation.[41] They follow
Plutarch in inverting the body/mind distinction that we find in Homer: the
body remains human, but the mind becomes animalistic. Most of these texts
were written in Coptic Egyptian and appeared later than the material under
consideration here. A typical eleventh-century example calls upon a woman to
lust for a man 'like a female donkey under her male … as she whinnies like a
mare, bellows like a camel, as she is crazed like a bear and a crocodile'.[42] The
persuasive similes in such texts envision a complete mental transformation:
unavailable human women becoming animals in heat.

   Clear examples of such animalisations are absent in surviving Greek magical
papyri, though not in the accompanying Demotic texts, and I would argue that
we can trace the spectral outlines of the lost Greek spells in literary texts.[43] For

instance, in Vergil's *Eclogue 8*, a fictionalised love spell calls for a man to be seized by 'such a love … as when a heifer, tired out by searching for a bullock through the groves and the deep woods, collapses in despair on the green sedge beside a stream of water'.[44] A more material practice involved a substance known as *hippomanes* ('horse-madness'), which was used as an ingredient in love potions from at least the time of Aristotle. Its reputation as a powerful aphrodisiac was based on the widely held belief that female horses were the most sexually eager of all animals.[45] While its source – a discharge from a mare's vagina, a substance found on the heads of newborn foals, or a plant – was disputed, its function was clear: to animalise its victim, leaving them unrestrained by human culture and reason, unprotected by human custom, and a slave to whoever used the love spell.[46]

From Aristotle onwards, Greek philosophical discourse often conceived of an abyssal rupture between humans and other animals that was supposedly created by the human faculties of speech and reason – faculties that Circe, but not her beasts, also possessed.[47] Yet, the persistent mythological theme of metamorphosis reveals a fascination with the possibility of leaping across this abyss. The examples we have examined here suggest that such a leap can both undermine and reinforce the human/animal distinction. If the incongruous horror of a human mind in an animal body highlights the unbridgeable divide, the idea that some humans might already have porcine or owl-like minds just waiting to be revealed by magic suggests that the chasm might actually cut through the human species itself. In material terms, this idea is manifest in slavery, a system in which animalised humans are brutalised alongside domestic beasts of burden, and a state to which those who cast love spells hoped to reduce their victims.

Objectifying the human, humanising the animal: binding curses

If Circe is the first magician of Greek literature, the curse tablets are the earliest physical evidence of rituals that we call 'magical' – objects intended to bind sexual partners, romantic rivals, and opponents in the spheres of law, business, and competitive sports. First appearing in sixth-century BCE Sicily, they are found soon after in other Greek-speaking areas, and ultimately throughout the entire Roman Empire from Britain to Palestine. The earliest examples often consist of simple lists of names written on lead tablets; later varieties also use other material, such as selenite (in Cyprus) or papyrus (in Egypt). By at least the fifth century BCE, the writers of these texts were frequently using more elaborate formulaic phrases, often built on the verb 'I bind [the victim] down' (*katadeō*), which is the origin of the common Greek term for curse tablets, *katadesmoi*.[48] The basic ritual process involved the deposition of these objects in significant places – bodies of water, temples, or burial sites – often accompanied by folding, piercing with nails, or burying with small 'voodoo dolls', which could themselves be bound and/or pierced, representing the victims of the curse. Instructions for such practices survive from third- and fourth-century CE Greco-Egyptian handbooks.[49] These suggest that the writing of the texts might be accompanied by the recitation of verbal formulae and the burning of incense. Again, though, we must acknowledge that our evidence is haunted by what is lost: the verbal component suggests that the earliest curse spells may have been purely oral. Moreover, as Christopher Faraone has pointed out, any *katadesmoi* written on wood and wax will have been lost, as will any papyrus examples from beyond Egypt with its dry climate.[50]

The simple texts of the early examples, even those consisting of binding or dedication formulae, lack references to animals, and we have no evidence that animal sacrifice played a regular role in the rituals that accompanied them. Instead, the texts often focus on describing their human victims as a catalogue of fragmented body parts and actions that may be enumerated in order to be controlled:

> καταδῶ δὲ [καὶ Σ]εύθου γλῶτταγ καὶ ψυχὴν καὶ λόγον ὃμ με[λ]εται καὶ πόδας καὶ χεῖρας ὀφ[θ]αλμοὺς [καὶ στόμ]α
>
> I also bind Seuthēs' tongue and soul and speech that he is practising and his feet and hands and eyes and mouth.[51]

Examples from the Roman period are often illustrated with depictions of the bodies of the victims, either bound or as skeletal or mummified figures, mimicking the textual content of the curses. These texts regularly project a state of death-like passivity onto victims, creating a persuasive analogy with the cold, dead lead on which they are written and the cold, dead bodies of the corpses with which they are deposited.[52] Animals occasionally appear in the illustrations on the texts as threatening figures in animal or hybrid form, divine or demonic (the distinction is not necessarily salient here): serpents that bite the victims (see, e.g., Figure 12.2), or the threatening, equine-headed figure that is usually identified as Seth-Typhon – visual signifiers of the supernatural threat.[53]

But the relationship between binding and animals can also be examined from a different perspective. If we look at the earliest literary attestations in Homer, we see that the verb *katadeō* ('I bind down'), so common in curse tablets, is most often used to describe the binding of animals. Of the fourteen occurrences of the verb in the *Odyssey* and the *Iliad*, eight refer to the binding of animals – horses, mules, sheep, and goats tethered so that they cannot move. Only twice is it used to refer to the binding of humans: once to describe an enslaved man bound in a ship, and once to describe a slave's fear of being caught and bound by her master.[54] Given the animalisation of slaves, in both cases the underlying conceptual metaphor seems to be the binding of domestic animals. This early use of *katadeō* recurs in later texts, although by then it is no longer primary.

The 'binding song' (*hymnos ... desmios*) of the Erinyes in Aeschylus' *Eumenides* suggests yet another relationship between animals and those who are cursed.[55] Faraone has argued that this is a literary representation of a verbal *katadesmos* that might be used to bind a litigant in court.[56] Preparing for the

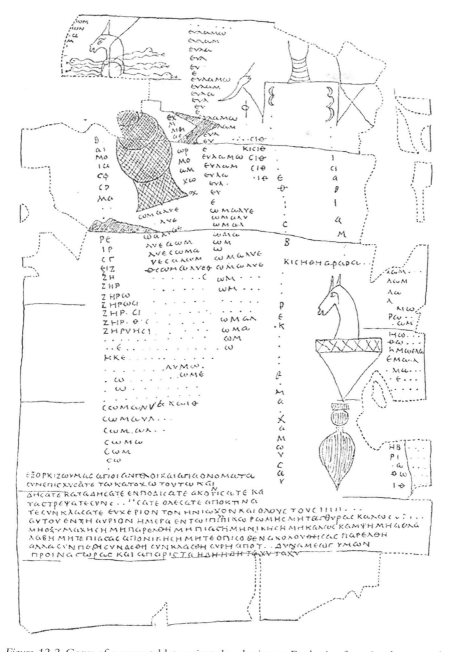

Figure 12.2 Copy of a curse tablet against the charioteer Eucherios featuring horses and snakes, Rome, ca. 300 CE

Image: R. Wünsch (1898) *Sethianische Verfluchungstafeln aus Rom*. Leipzig, p. 51, no. 49 (public domain)

murder trial in which they will face Orestes, the Erinyes sing the song over their enemy, describing him as a 'sacrificial victim' (*tethymenos*).[57] As with the cases of transformation, the alignment of curse victims with bound or sacrificial animals serves to render them powerless.

This verbal animalisation, though, seems to have had a corresponding ritual component. The manipulation of lead, clay, and wax tablets and figures was intended to have a parallel effect upon the victims – as the objects were bound and pierced, so, too, were the victims to be bound and pierced. Faraone has recently written about several instances in which man-made 'voodoo dolls' are replaced by animal bodies.[58] The earliest of these is a young chicken from the third-century BCE Athenian Agora, whose head and feet were removed and placed in a buried jar inscribed with more than 20 names, through which a nail was driven.[59] This example demonstrates many of the features we have already discussed: the inscribing of names, the piercing with nails, and the fragmentation of bodies. Faraone lists nearly a dozen examples of similar rituals. An excavation at a second-century BCE site on the Rhône unearthed an infant red fox, its body pierced with three bronze needles. This find evokes a well-known Latin curse from first-century CE Aquitania that describes the piercing of a puppy, as an analogy to the curse's victim:[60]

> Quomodo hic catellus nemin[i] nocuit, sic … nec illi hanc litem uincere possint; quomodo nec mater huius catelli defendere potuit, sic nec aduo‐cati eorem e[os d]efendere ‹non› possint … quomodo hic catellus auersus est nec surgere potesti, sic nec illi; sic traspecti sin[t] quomodo ille.
>
> Just as this puppy harmed no one, so, too, may [the victims harm no one] and may they be unable to win this lawsuit. Just as the mother of this puppy is unable to protect it, so, too, may their lawyers be unable to protect them … Just as this puppy is on its back and unable to rise up, so too [may] they be. (May) they be pierced, just as this (puppy) is pierced.[61]

The helplessness of the young animals (and the puppy's mother) is of most relevance here, rather than the passivity of domesticity. Much later, the orator Libanius (ca. 314–393 CE) described a dream in which he witnessed the sacrifice of two children in the temple of Zeus, one of whom was to be buried at night, which he understood as presaging a ritual by sorcerers (*goētes*) against him.[62] Afterwards, he was unable to read, write, or speak, and suffered a life-threatening attack of gout. He finally identified the cause as a chameleon, deposited in his classroom, which had been mutilated by having its head placed between its feet, one foreleg removed, and the other placed at its mouth in a gesture of silence. The ritual described – or imagined – by Libanius creates a dual symmetry between human and animal: the sacrifice of human children in the dream is instantiated in the real killing of a chameleon, and the mutilated body of the animal corresponds in a one-to-one fashion to the human body of Libanius – his mouth silenced and one arm (which Faraone tentatively identifies as the gesturing right arm of an orator) removed to hinder his performance further.[63] As Faraone observes, the use of animal 'voodoo dolls' was based on a simple yet profound principle: the anatomical similarity between humans and animals, in which each human member had a parallel in the animal body.[64]

A still deeper instance of human/animal symmetry is evident in another example, from second-century CE Carthage, in which a rooster, bound by its limbs and head, is assimilated to a charioteer.[65] Faraone observes that this goes beyond a simple part-for-part equivalence: a rooster, like a charioteer, was a male animal that might be highly trained and take part in competitive sport – cockfighting.[66] This curse is unlike the others, however, in that it has more than one victim: not only the human charioteer but also his horses. Indeed, each horse is named in the curse and their fragmented selves are enumerated and bound, just as would be done for a human:

κατάδησον αὐτῶν τὰ σκέλη καὶ τὴν ὁρμὴν καὶ τὸ πήδημα καὶ τὸν δρόμον, ἀμαύρωσον αὐτῶν τὰ ὄμματα ἵνα μὴ βλέπωσιν, στρέβλωσον αὐτῶν τὴν ψυχὴν καὶ τὴν καρδίαν ἵνα μὴ [π]νέωσιν

Bind their legs, their dash, their bounding, and their course, blind their eyes so that they cannot see and twist their spirit and heart so that they cannot breathe.[67]

Such racing curses are the only examples that target animal bodies directly, rather than using them as the means to harm human victims. They are, therefore, worth considering in more detail.[68]

Richard Gordon identifies 79 known binding curses against charioteers – a significant portion of the tablets with explicit purposes. He points out that the majority of them come from only eight sites, with the earliest from Africa Proconsularis, and specifically the cities of Carthage and Hadrumetum in modern Tunisia.[69] The oldest of these have been dated palaeographically to the second and third centuries CE; the latest, from Roman Syria, to the sixth. The oldest possible reference to a charioteer curse, however, is in Pindar, whose first *Olympian Ode* (476 BCE) describes Pelops calling upon Poseidon to bind (*pedason*) the spear of his rival Oenomaus and thereby give him victory.[70] A connection between this story and curse rituals is suggested by Pausanias' discussion of the racecourse at Olympia, where the race took place. He reports that the altar known as the *taraxippos* ('horse-troubler') terrified horses because the magician Amphion had given Pelops 'something' (*ti*) to bury at the spot where it stood; this object is probably best understood as some type of curse.[71] We should not presume that curse tablets against charioteers like those of the Roman period were fashioned centuries earlier, however. If earlier charioteer curses did exist, they may have taken different forms. As ever, we should be wary of assuming that our surviving evidence represents a complete picture.[72]

Gordon suggests that the charioteer curses were commissioned by three groups.[73] The first of these were the charioteers themselves, who wanted to secure victory by causing competitors to become distracted or crash; the second were punters, who wanted to safeguard their bets; and the third, whom Gordon suggests were the most numerous group, were rival factions and stable-owners. The latter group bore the massive costs and risks of racing, and they could use their insider knowledge to provide the names of charioteers and horses that were necessary for successful cursing.

What do the appearances of horses in curses tell us about the relationship between human and non-human animals? Horses normally appear alongside the human charioteers who guide them, forming, in the words of Florent Heintz, a 'unified target'.[74] This is analogous to the lists of presumably human victims found from the earliest tablets, which bundle groups of individuals into composite targets. Yet we also find instances where individuals of only one species – human or horse – are named. In these cases, the horses – apparently the more vital part of the composite target – feature alone most often.[75]

The treatment of horses in curse tablets is very similar to that of humans. Their names are given, sometimes without any indication that they belong to a different species than the charioteers; their images are sometimes drawn on the tablets; and they are described synecdochically through lists of their parts.[76] Gordon suggests that the 'parts' listed on the curses from Carthage – 'course' (dromos), 'power' (dynamis), 'spirit' (psychē), 'dash' (hormē), 'speed' (tachytēs), for example – represent 'specialized circus jargon'.[77] We might think, then, that the different natures of human and horse victims were expressed by their different constituent parts, drawn from different domains of vocabulary. It is true, of course, that humans are not usually bound by their 'course' or 'dash', but, as Faraone has pointed out, curses do not always use generic lists of human body parts. Rather, they adapt themselves to their targets, focusing on salient features according to the situation – binding the 'tongues' of legal opponents, for example.[78] Similarly, curses against wrestlers attack their 'wrestling' (palē), while those against human runners do mention their 'course' (dromē) and 'dash' (hormē) – two of the properties that are bound in racing horses.[79] More profoundly, though, we may note that the listing of 'power' (dynamis) and 'spirit' (psychē) aligns horses exactly with humans. As John Gager has observed, this pairing is found regularly in curse texts, representing, he suggests, 'the inner and outer aspect of human life in its totality'.[80] This focus on inner life is even more striking in curses against horses which contain phrases such as 'may they not eat, may they not drink, may they not sleep'.[81] This formula finds a close parallel in binding love spells, in which a state of infatuated longing is described as sleepless restlessness: μὴ ἐάσῃς αὐτὴν φαγῖν μήτε πῖν μήτε ὕπνου τυχῖν ἕως δὰν ἔλθῃ πρὸς ἐμέ ('do not allow her to eat or drink or sleep until she comes to me').[82]

While the practices of transformation discussed earlier animalise humans in order to enslave them, katadesmoi humanise horses, recognising them as possessing physical and mental characteristics that are analogous, if not identical, to those of humans. These similarities allow both horses and humans to be subjected to the same techniques of binding. In curses, humans and animals alike are hindering objects, reduced to bodies whose parts may be enumerated so that they may be bound or destroyed.

Transgressing the boundary: life, death, and undeath in magical sacrifice

As Odysseus leaves Circe's island for the first time, the goddess slips unseen past the weeping sailors and binds (*katedēsen*) two sheep – a ram and a ewe – by the ship, to have their blood offered to the human dead on the borders of the underworld in the first, and most influential, scene of Greek consultation of the dead (*nekyomanteia*; 'necromancy').[83]

As many scholars have recognised, sacrifice served as a nexus in Greek culture, linking human and divinity, individual and community, and community and super-community through the medium of animal bodies.[84] This tight knot of meaning rendered it highly charged, allowing for multiple interpretations, involving numerous rules and taboos, and taking on many forms. As Ogden has observed, the type of animal sacrifice that features in the necromantic procedure in the *Odyssey* seems to be based on the normal offerings to the dead and to heroes within Greek cults: the jugulation (throat-slitting) of a black animal, usually a sheep, whose blood is drained into a pit before the carcass is burnt whole, accompanied by offerings of mixed honey, water, olive oil, and sprinkled barley.[85] In his consultation, Odysseus stands by the pit with his sword drawn, selectively allowing the spectral ghosts (*eidōla*) to come forward and drink the blood, restoring their faculties so that they may talk to him. Actual consultations of the dead, in the sparse attestations identified by Ogden from the fifth century BCE onwards, often took place at hero shrines or underground sanctuaries near bodies of water. The ghosts seem to have appeared in dreams, while the questioner slept on the skin of the sacrificed animal.[86]

Following Ogden, we may note that the *Odyssey* points us again to the idea of an equivalence between human and animal substance.[87] The dead lack bodies, but they can take on a temporary materiality as they drink the blood of sheep. Similar ideas can be found in later, more graphic accounts of magical procedures in which human bodies are brought back to life: an unfortunate dead soldier is pumped full of new blood by the witch Erichtho in Lucan's *Pharsalia*; an Egyptian woman uses her own blood in place of that of a sacrificial animal in Heliodorus' *Aethiopica*.[88] The possibility of the substitution of human for animal blood, and vice versa, implies an equivalence between the dead human and the dying animal, and thus the spectre of human sacrifice. Indeed, we can catch a glimpse of this in the *Odyssey* itself: was Circe's ram, like her pigs, her lions, and perhaps the stag, a transfigured human?

Human sacrifice is associated with the *magoi* as early as the writings of Herodotus, but the commonplace that it was a regular feature of magical rituals is best attested in Roman literature from the first century BCE onwards.[89] Cicero accuses his enemy, the Pythagorean Vatinius, of sacrificing human beings to the ghosts of the dead; Pliny describes Nero as delighting in human sacrifice under the influence of the *magi*; and Cassius Dio claims that Didius Julianus (one of the five emperors of 193 CE) sacrificed several boys in some kind of divinatory or apotropaic ritual.[90] We have already mentioned that a dream of child

Figure 12.3 Odysseus and two of his companions have just sacrificed two sheep to the
dead; the head of one of the animals lies between Odysseus' feet, facing the
head of the seer Tiresias, who is summoned by this ritual; Lucanian calyx
crater, Pisticci, Italy, ca. 400–375 BCE

Image: A Furtwängler and K. Reinhold (1904) *Griechische Vasenmalerei*. Vol.
1, pl. 60. Munich (public domain)

sacrifice warned Libanius of a curse, foretelling or standing in for the ritual
mutilation of a chameleon, and the rhetorician reports that he himself was fal-
sely accused of beheading two girls to use in malign magic.[91] The exact purpose and nature of these sacrifices is unclear: in some cases, they seem to be
offerings to the dead, analogous to the black rams in necromancy; in others,
they are used in haruspicy, with their innards examined to foretell the future in
the same way as those of the animal victims in public sacrifices to state gods.[92]
Even if these human sacrifices constitute a literary fantasy, it seems that at least

some individuals in the Roman Mediterranean believed in them. A well-known funerary epitaph for Iucundus, slave of the sister of the Emperor Claudius, asserts that he was killed by a witch (*saga*) while still a child.[93]

These fantastical human sacrifices follow the outlines of normative offerings even as they invert them. The choice of children as victims may reflect the fact that the animals used in sacrifices were usually juveniles, and the ideal of the blackness of the victims in necromancy-inspired magical rituals finds a strange parallel in a story by Zacharias of Mytilene (ca. 460–post-536 CE) that relates the attempted sacrifice of an Ethiopian slave in a magical ritual in Antioch.[94] The close link between meat-eating and sacrifice – almost all meat in the Greek world was theoretically sacrificial, and providing meat for the masses was a major function of public sacrifices – led to a logical link between human sacrifice and cannibalism in literary texts.[95] Human sacrifice was often linked to a pre-civilisational state marked by a different relationship between humans and animals. While some visions of this primeval age posit a peaceful world in which humans, like Circe's pigs, ate nuts and roots, others describe one marked by human sacrifice and its corollary, cannibalism.[96] Both, however, point to a lack of differentiation between humans and other animals. Civilisation, then, arrives when human and animal are clearly distinguished, marked by the act of defining one category as sacrificial, and hence edible, and the other as neither sacrificial nor edible.[97]

Nonetheless, this uncivilised past could always intrude on the present. Greco-Roman writers associated human sacrifice and cannibalism with barbarian Others such as the Taurians, who sacrificed a woman to their Artemis every year, or the Judaeans, who were accused of fattening up a man in their temple to be sacrificed to their god each year.[98] Human sacrifice, as James Rives has argued, thus became a signifier of 'bad religion' and 'bad humanity' more broadly.[99] We may think here of the stories of would-be tyrants, such as Apollodorus of Cassandreia, who, according to Polyaenus, marked the oath he made with his co-conspirators with the sacrifice and tasting of a human boy in a perverse imitation of the normative oaths solemnised by the sacrifice of non-human animals.[100]

The notion of human sacrifice in necromantic rituals takes on another dimension when we consider the role and nature of the spirits invoked. The line between necromancy and other forms of magic, such as cursing, is very thin in literary depictions. Thus, the ghosts called upon in magic are most often those who died violently (*biaiothanatoi*), or whose deaths, before they had completed the transition to adulthood, left them trapped in a liminal space – the 'untimely dead' (*aōroi*).[101] Human sacrifices would often fulfil both of these criteria – killed as children and, by necessity, in pain and fear. The equivalence between the *offering* and the *being offered to* becomes identity. This idea – that humans could be killed not as offerings but to create familiar spirits – is implicit in several texts, but explicit in the *Clementine Recognitions* (ca. 301–400 CE), which describe how Simon Magus killed a boy in order to produce a helper for his magic.[102]

Here, though, the logic of human sacrifice poses a problem. It was common knowledge in the Greco-Roman world that the violently dead could and did seek vengeance on their killers. To give one example among many, Strabo reports that the people of Temesa murdered Polites, one of Odysseus' men. His spirit then tormented them until he was appeased with a hero shrine and regular tribute.[103] Following the same logic, we might expect to encounter allusions to sacrificed humans seeking revenge on the magicians and witches who killed them. Such a logic is indeed suggested by certain texts: in Horace's fifth *Epode*, for example, a boy starved by witches threatens to torment them after his death; and in the *Recognitions*, Simon Magus' companions ask why the spirit of the boy he killed does not seek revenge against him.[104] Simon's response is theological: he claims that the dead are capable of enacting justice, but refrain from doing so because they know that those who kill them will receive an even greater punishment after death. This response, however, is contradicted by the more common stories of ghostly revenge. The idea of human sacrifice, then, generated a contradiction: if magicians killed humans to use in magic, how did they escape the vengeance of the restless spirits they created?

One possible way to resolve this conflict would be to make the sacrifice consensual. When telling the story of the death of Antinous, the lover of Hadrian, all ancient historians agree that the emperor killed him in a ritual that was designed to extend Hadrian's life or produce some kind of oracle, and that Antinous died willingly.[105] Similarly, Libanius describes a fictitious situation in which the son of a magician is selected by lot for sacrifice to end a plague afflicting his town. The magician wants to sacrifice a different child, but Libanius mocks him, pointing out that, through necromancy, he would still be able to see his son, who would serve him more willingly than other ghosts because of their pre-existing relationship.[106]

Again, it should be stressed that there is no reason to believe that real 'magicians' killed human beings either as offerings or to produce familiar spirits. Where human bodies are used in magic – as in the case of three fourth-century CE instructions for necromantic rituals – there is no suggestion that they have been expressly killed for this purpose.[107] It is far more likely that already deceased humans are opportunistically used, as is the case where curse tablets are deposited with corpses known to belong to the categories of the violent or untimely dead. The purpose of this extended digression has not been to reveal the truth of human sacrifice, but rather to draw attention to features of the discourse of animal sacrifice that become clearer when the animal is a human.

Greco-Roman religious discourse established the line between human and animal life, and between civilised and uncivilised humans, through the practice of rendering particular bodies available for sacrifice and consumption. This distinction had implications for the way in which animal and human deaths were also conceptually different: a human death could be violent or untimely, but every animal death was simply part of the ritual cycle. This links into a third difference: the concept of individual volition, which might be violated through an unwilling death, and result in the creation of a vengeful ghost. We see some suggestion of this in the common fiction that sacrificial victims had to give their consent, which they supposedly indicated in normative state sacrifice by tossing their heads when sprinkled with water, but the problem seems to be more acute in the case of humans than it is for other animals.[108] This is likely due to what we may call personhood – the fact that humans are understood to have distinct individual identities and to exist in meaningful relationships to other persons. The importance of these relationships is apparent in cases where the problems of using a restless spirit can be allayed by reference to the specific relationship that exists between the dead ghost and the living magician. By contrast, sacrificial animals can be seen as interchangeable parts of a larger whole, indistinct non-persons identified by species and physical features (young, black, unblemished), symbols in a system of exchange whose distinctiveness is denied. We see some acknowledgement of this in Cato's instruction that the names of animal victims should not be spoken during offerings.[109]

While the magical creation of familiar spirits through the killing of humans is a literary fantasy, there are echoes of this idea in surviving ritual instructions. Yet, these instructions reflect the normative human/animal boundary by using non-human animals as their raw material. The clearest examples of such rituals are the instructions in the Greco-Egyptian magical papyri for creating 'blessed ones' (*esiēs*) by drowning animals.[110] Though often written in Greek, these draw upon Egyptian ideas, probably dating to around the Thirtieth Dynasty (389–343 BCE), of the divinising force of death in water, mimicking the death of the god Osiris in the Nile (on Osiris, see also this volume, Chapter 6).[111] Here, I will focus on the most complex of the 20 or so spells of this type, which is preserved in the third-century Greek-language roll *PGM* III.[112] This ritual likely began as a curse against charioteers, since it involves the creation of *lamellae* inscribed with the figure of the equine-headed Seth-Typhon threatening two skeletal charioteers, and suggests that the victims might be charioteers and horses. A note at the end, however, says that it may also be used to send dreams, bind lovers, or separate couples.[113]

The killing of the animal is carried out not as a traditional Greek sacrifice, but rather as a drowning in water, as is the case with the other rituals of this type. Similarly, the choice of a cat, rather than one of the domestic birds or quadrupeds typically used in sacrifices, is explained by its relationship to the sun god in the Greco-Egyptian religious system. The cat's body is wrapped, as a mummy, in a papyrus before interment. The ritualist uses the animal's whiskers as phylacteries, and the water in which it has been drowned, which has taken on some of its sacred power, is sprinkled over the racecourse. The formula invokes Seth-Typhon in his traditional role as steersman of the sun's barque, calling upon him to strike the spell's victim. So far, each element of the ritual is clearly Egyptian: the relationship between the cat and the sun god; the death through drowning, which is described as 'making into an *esiēs*' (*ekpoiein esiēn*); and the cat's subsequent mummification.[114] But it then diverges from the other examples by drawing on elements with clearly Greek origins, implicating the ritual in the discursive field of Greek magic. The cat has inscribed *lamellae* inserted into its body before it is buried, and the names of the human and horse victims are written on its papyrus shroud. This practice might be seen to align the cat with the mutilated animals used in other curse assemblages, which represent the curses' victims. However, in this instance, it has a different function. Because of its violent death, the cat is invoked as a restless ghost, and thus corresponds to the *human* corpses with which curse tablets were typically deposited. The description of animals as violently dead is occasionally explicit in the magical papyri, and this ritual represents a rare example where the Greek idea of the *biaiothanatos* is aligned with the Egyptian idea of the drowned *esiēs*.[115] This difference is evident in the characterisation of the animals: the example of the pierced puppy cited above stresses its profound helplessness, projected on the curse's victim; by contrast, the cat's spirit, assimilated to Seth-Typhon, is seen as an angry and powerful deity, which is called upon to 'rouse [itself]' (ἔγειρόν μοι σεαυτόν), 'take on strength and power' (ἴσχυσον καὶ εὐτόνησον), and 'destroy and be lawless' (ἀπόλεσον καὶ ἀνόμησον).[116] The association of the drowned cat with the originally human conception of the *biaiothanatos* has a further consequence: killing the cat is described as a 'wrong-doing' (*adikein*), a crime, which the now-divine spirit is called upon to avenge (*antapodēs*).[117] Whereas the literary examples of human sacrifice discussed above must either deny or find solutions to the problem of the power of the unjustly killed, this ritual text draws upon its full force. Here, though, the text of its invocation plays a final sleight of hand. Following the common Egyptian pattern known in Greek as the *diabolē*, or slander, the ritualist absolves himself of the killing, blaming it instead on the spell's victim, so that the power of the invoked curse is strengthened by the wrath of a vengeful ghost. As we come full circle, from animal to human to animal death, this example illustrates the ways in which the two categories of being could be considered both alike and fundamentally different.

Conclusion

This discussion has understood magical rituals and their literary descriptions as constituting a discursive field within the larger religious symbolic system, within which particular ideas could be explored in novel ways.[118] Three case studies – focusing on metamorphosis, curses, and sacrifice – have served as points of departure from which the geography of this field could be surveyed.

In the first thematic study, we traced the line from the sorceress Circe's apparently unmotivated transformations of human bodies into those of pigs to the later ritual practices that aimed to transform human minds, drawing upon discursive techniques of animalisation to reconstruct the human being as an animal-like slave, a living tool, or an instrument. In this example, the lines between free human and enslaved animal are, at least notionally, clear, so that their deliberate transgression allows the status of humans to be radically altered.

The second case study considered the way in which binding curses construct human and animal selves as (physically and mentally) isomorphic; this parallelism allows the mutilation and binding of helpless animals to prefigure the binding of human targets, and, conversely, for horses to be targeted according to ritual patterns developed for humans. Here, a fundamental symmetry between human and non-human animals allows both to be considered as objects that hinder or threaten the ritual subject – objects that can be broken up, controlled, or destroyed.

The third case study looked at the ways in which human and animal life, death, and undeath circumscribe one another. The fundamental equivalence of human and animal life implied by necromantic sacrifice raises concerns that magicians might invert normative religion, and develop techniques of human sacrifice, merging the sacrificed animal with the (dead) human recipient of sacrifice. Yet, this apparent collapse in the distinction between human and animal life reveals the ways in which the two categories are constructed as fundamentally different: human life as individual, relational, and subject to being avenged; animal life as generic and symbolic. In actual rituals, this contradiction is resolved by the exclusive use of living animals and already-dead humans. But the curse spell using the drowned cat stands as a unique example, a text perched between Greek and Egyptian conceptions of ritual efficacy that draws its power from the tensions within the triangular human/animal/divine relationship.

All three case studies show that examining non-human animals within the frame of magic not only tells us about these animals but reveals broader societal conceptions of humans – their nature, distinctiveness, and relationship with superhuman beings. As Julia Kindt has noted, the undeniable similarities between human and non-human animals allow the latter to serve as 'complex symbols' within religious thought and action.[119] Literary representations of magic could manipulate these symbols in the fashion of thought experiments, inverting common rituals so that the tensions and contradictions within practices such as sacrifice could be explored, and animals could do the cultural work of defining relationships among humans. Yet, animals are not mere symbols: the horses listed on lead tablets were as real as the humans mentioned alongside them, as, too, were the economies of chariot racing and slavery, and the religious practices that death produced and that produced death. Simultaneously, and unavoidably, the discursive field of magic could not only reflect existing material and social realities but shape them.

Notes

1 Thanks to Christopher Faraone, Richard Gordon, Raquel Martín Hernández, and Joseph Sanzo for sharing work with me, both published and unpublished, which was of great value in preparing this discussion, and to Julia Kindt, both for inviting me to write this contribution and for her helpful work as editor.
2 For a recent overview, see Ogden 2014.
3 See, e.g., Sicherl 1937; Eitrem 1939; Galoppin 2015 and 2016; Lucarelli 2017; Salayová 2017; Dosoo and Galoppin forthcoming; Dosoo forthcoming a.
4 See, e.g., Gordon 2010; Watson 2019b; Galoppin forthcoming; see also Galoppin 2015 and 2016; Dosoo and Galoppin forthcoming.
5 For the *echenēis*, see Watson 2010 and Faraone forthcoming b. For the *iynx*, see Tavenner 1933; Faraone 1993b; Johnston 1995.

6   See, e.g., Tambiah 1990. For examples of the critical reflection provoked in the field of ancient magic studies, see, e.g., Faraone and Obbink 1991; Johnston *et al.* 1999; Smith 2001; Otto 2013.

7   Cf. the comments of Sanzo forthcoming.

8   By Greco-Egyptian magical material, I mean the texts surviving from Roman Egypt, primarily those from the first four centuries CE, written on papyrus in Greek, Demotic, and Old Coptic. The largest collections of these are *PGM* and Daniel and Maltomini 1990–1992. Cf. the translations in Betz 1986 and the review in Brashear 1995.

9   For two representative views on the cultural origin of the practices contained in the Greco-Egyptian magical material, see Ritner 1995 and Faraone 2000. Cf. Brashear 1995: 3422–3438.

10   For the books attributed to Orpheus, see, e.g., Pl. *Resp.* 364e–365a; cf. Eur. *Hipp.* 952–954, *Alc.* 966–969. Cf. Martín Hernández 2010: 44–56 *et passim*. On Ostanes, see Plin. *HN* 30.2; Bidez and Cumont 1938: Vol. 1: 167–212; Vol. 2: 267–356. Cf. Quack 2006: 267–282. On the relationship between Ostanes and Pseudo-Democritean literature, see Dickie 1999: 172–177.

11   Hom. *Od.* 10.158, 10.168, 10.171. See Ogden 2014: 295.

12   Cf. Hom. *Od.* 11.634, where the same phrase is used of the Gorgon.

13   Hom. *Od.* 10.136.

14   Ogden 2014: 295. Humans with sheep's, lions', pigs', and dogs' heads: Boston Museum of Fine Arts, no. 99.518 (sixth century BCE). Pig-men crawling on all fours: Athens, National Museum, no. 9685 (fifth century BCE).

15   Ap. Rhod. *Argon.* 4.672–674 (trans. Race). Cf. Hunter 2015: 175–178.

16   Hom. *Od.* 10.124. Ogden 2014: 294.

17   Dio Chrys. *Or.* 77/78.34–35; cf. Dio Chrys. *Or.* 8.21 and 33.58, where Dio Chrysostom mentions that some became wolves.

18   Hom. *Od.* 10.212. Although the text states that Circe had 'given them evil *pharmaka*' (κακὰ φάρμακ' ἔδωκεν; 10.213), it is unclear whether this has transformed them from humans, or whether the *pharmaka* allows the witch to control real wild animals. For clearer references to other animal transformations effected upon Odysseus' men, see Verg. *Aen.* 7.15–20 (lions, boars, bears, wolves); Plut. *Mor.* 985d (pigs, wolves, lions), 139a (pigs, donkeys); Ath. 1.18 (lions, wolves); cf. n. 17, above.

19   Hom. *Od.* 10.468, 10.477. See Ogden 2002: 98.

20   For Scylla, see Ov. *Met.* 14.40–67. On Picus, see Verg. *Aen.* 7.187–191; Ov. *Met.* 14.386–415; cf. the story of Calchus, turned into a pig by Circe, in Parth. 12.1–3.

21   Hom. *Od.* 220.

22   Xen. *Mem.* 1.3.7–8. See also Ar. *Plut.* 302–308; Ath. 1.18; Pall. *Anth.* 10.50.

23   Flor. 1.49.60.

24   On the complex and unresolved debates about the authorship of the Greek *Onos* and its precise relationship to the Latin *Metamorphoses*, see Mason 2005: 87–95.

25   Apul. *Met.* 2.22, 25; cf. Phillips, 2009: 25–27.

26   Apul. *Met.* 3.21, 3.23, *Onos* 12. On the call of the owl, see Ael. *NA* 1.29. Cf. Men. fr. 620 ll. 11–13; Ael. *NA* 10.37; Horap. 2.25.

27   Apul. *Met.* 1.9. The *Onos* goes into less detail here but still describes the witch as having transformed many of those who spurn her into animals (*zōa*, 4).

28   Cf. *Onos* 13 where Lucius' motivation is to become a bird, to fly, and to see if his soul will become avian, a concern echoed in the Latin version, where he describes the advantages of transformation as the ability to explore the whole sky (3.23). This is reminiscent of the persistent theme in Christian literature that birds, able to fly and thus closer to heaven, are in some ways superior to humans; see Gilhus 2006: 247–250.

29 *Onos* 13: φωνὴν δὲ ἀνθρώπου … οὐκέτι εἶχον ('I no longer had a human voice'; cf. 15, 38); *Met.* 3.25: *iam humano gestu simul et uoce priuatus* ('now I was deprived of both human gestures and voice'; cf. 7.26–27, etc.). The ability to speak was, of course, often considered one of the primary differences between humans and animals, along with the closely related faculty of rationality; see Gilhus 2006: 3–58.

30 Bradley 2000: 110–125.

31 *Onos* 42; *Met.* 7.3, 9.11, 32, 11.15. Cf. *Onos* 36, where the priests of Atargatis describe the donkey Lucius as their new slave (*doulos*). For a discussion, see Bradley 2000: 117–119.

32 Bradley 2000: 118.

33 Gilhus 2006: 37–44.

34 Apul. *Met.* 9.14: *bonus alioquin vir.*

35 Apul. *Met.* 9.12–13.

36 Bradley 2000: 110–112; cf. Harvey 1988: 42–52.

37 August. *De civ. D.* 18.18.

38 Plut. *Mor.* 139a.

39 Pall. *Hist. Laus.* (recensio G) 17.6–9; *Hist. Mon.* 21.93–101. See Frankfurter 2001; Dosoo forthcoming b.

40 Evetts 1910: 205–206.

41 Frankfurter 2001: 484–487; cf. Dosoo forthcoming b. There were, however, 'party tricks' (*paignia*), transmitted by the Pseudo-Democritean tradition into the Middle Ages, which aimed to make the people at a dinner party appear to have horses' or donkeys' heads (Plin. *HN* 28.49 and *PGM* XIb.). Note also the occasional mentions in the Greek magical papyri of the ability to change the ritualist's form (e.g. *PGM* XIII.275–277). As I have argued in the case of the witches in the story of Lucius, the latter should be understood as an appropriation of the powers of animals rather than animalisation of the type discussed here.

42 P.Bad. V 122, ll. 114–120.

43 The surviving Greek love spells more often seem to use the listing of body parts discussed in the following section, but cf. the third-century bilingual (Demotic and Greek) *PDM* XIV, which contains a love spell that uses the simile of 'the longing which a female cat feels for a male cat, a longing which a female wolf feels for a male wolf, a longing which a female dog feels for a male dog' (ll. 1029–1031).

44 *talis amor Daphnin, qualis cum fessa iuuencum per nemora atque altos quaerendo bucula lucos propter aquae riuum uiridi procumbit in ulua perdita.* Verg. *Ecl.* 8.85–9 (trans. Ogden). Cf. Aristotle's comments on 'bull-struck' cows in *Hist an.* 572a–b.

45 Arist. *Hist an.* 572a; cf. 575b. For uses of *hippomanes* not mentioned below (n. 46), see also Columella, *Rust.* 6.27.3–4; Prop. 4.5.17–18; Juv. 6.133–135.

46 Arist. *Hist an.* 572a, 577a, 605a; Verg. *G.* 3.280–283; Tib. 4.58; Plin. *HN* 7.66, 28.49; Ael. *NA* 3.17, 14.18; Theoc. 2.48–51.

47 Sorabji 1993: 12–16, 80–82 *et passim*; Gilhus 2006: 38–44. I borrow the term 'abyssal rupture' (*rupture abyssale*) from Derrida 2006: 52.

48 See, e.g., Pl. *Resp.* 365c, *Leg.* 933a, 933d–e.

49 E.g. *PGM* III.1–164, IV.296–466, VII.429–458.

50 Faraone 1985; Lamont 2015: 166–167; Faraone 1991: 7.

51 DT 49, ll. 12–14 (Athens, ca. 300 BCE; trans. Gager with changes). For a fuller discussion, see Versnel 1998: 217–267; cf. Gordon 2000.

52 A full study of the images in *katadesmoi* remains a vital desideratum. For some images of bound, skeletal, or mummified figures, often threatened by animal or animal-headed figures, on curse tablets, see *PGM* III.1–164; Wünsch 1898, nos. 11, 16, 17, 19, 20B, 29, 35, 43; Gager 1992: 53–56, no. 5; Sánchez Natalías 2011: 201–217. For the 'persuasive analogies' of coldness and death, see Faraone 1991: 5–10.

53 For examples, see the texts from *PGM* III and Wünsch 1898 listed in n. 52, above. For discussions of the identity of the figure, see Martín Hernández forthcoming; Love forthcoming; cf. Preisendanz 1926.

54 References to the binding of animals: Hom. *Il.* 8.434, 10.567, 23.654, 24.274; Hom. *Od.* 4.40, 10.572, 20.176, 20.189. References to the binding of slaves: Hom. *Od.* 14.345, 15.443. There are a few other uses referring to the binding of inanimate objects: Hom. *Od.* 5.383 and 10.20 (the paths of the winds); 7.272 (the path of Odysseus); 10.23 (the bag containing the winds).

55 Aesch. *Eum.* 331–332.

56 Faraone 1985: 150–154.

57 Aesch. *Eum.* 328.

58 Faraone forthcoming a.

59 Faraone forthcoming a.

60 Bouloumie 1985.

61 *DT* 111–112 (ca. 101–200 CE; trans. Gager with changes).

62 Lib. 1.245–249.

63 Faraone forthcoming a.

64 Faraone forthcoming a.

65 *DT* 241 (ca. 1–300 CE, Carthage). Since the rooster is bound by its 'hands' (χῖρας) rather than its wings, Galoppin 2015: 354 suggests that the model of the curse may have featured an anthropomorphic figurine, replaced here by a rooster.

66 Faraone forthcoming a.

67 *DT* 241, ll. 12–15.

68 While I focus on curses here, we should note that they were only one of many 'magical' practices connected with the circus and horses. Others included amulets to make run horses faster or to protect them, as well as divination and healing charms, which were whispered into the horses' ears. These charms often state explicitly that they may be used for the same maladies in humans and horses, demonstrating again the symmetries in the capacities and vulnerabilities of different animal bodies. See Heintz 1999: 2–3, 36; Gitton-Ripoll forthcoming.

69 Gordon 2012: 47–74.

70 Pind. *Ol.* 1.75–78. See Heintz 1999: 65–67.

71 Paus. 6.20. See Heintz 1999: 72–74.

72 Cf. Gordon 2012: 41, n. 71.

73 Gordon 2012: 54–59.

74 Heintz 1999: 93.

75 Rengen 1984: 220 and n. 47.

76 For the naming of horses unmarked in lists, see, e.g., Jordan 2002: 141–147 (text from Rome, ca. 300–400 CE). For drawings of horses, see, e.g., Wünsch 1898: no. 49; *DT* 285. Cf. the nine lead figurines of horses from Antioch, apparently part of some kind of magical assemblage. See Seyrig 1935: 42–50; Heintz 1999: 219–220.

77 Gordon 2012: 45.

78 Faraone 1985: 151–152.

79 For curses against wrestlers, see Jordan 1985: nos. 1, l. 6; 2, ll. 4, 7; 3, l. 6; 5, l. 5 (restored). These curses are described as 'late Roman' by their editor. For the curse against a runner, see Tomlin 2007: 161–166, ll. 2, 5, 20. The text is from Oxyrhynchus, Egypt, and dated by its editor to the fourth century CE.

80 Gager 1992: 140, n. 86.

81 Tablet A, ll. 6–7 (Apamea, ca. 501–600 CE): Μὴ φάγωσιν, μὴ πίωσιν, μὴ κοιμηθῶσιν, in Rengen 1984: 215. Cf. *DT* 289, B l.16: 'may you take sweet sleep from them' (of horses; *auferas illis dulce somnum*).

82 *SM* 43, ll. 8–10 (Egypt, ca. 300–400 CE). See Martinez 2001.

83 Hom. *Od.* 10.488–11.332.

84 Detienne 1989; Burkert 1983; Gordon 1990.

85 Ogden 2001: 7–11.
86 Ogden 2001: 17–92; cf. 163–190.
87 Ogden 2001: 173.
88 Luc. 6.667–669; Heliod. *Aeth.* 6.14.4. Cf. Ogden 2001: 206–207.
89 *Hdt.* 7.114. Cf. Watson 2019a: 203–226; Rives 1995; Ogden 2001: 197–201; Hughes 1991.
90 Cic. *Vat.* 14; Plin. *HN* 30.6; Cass. Dio 73.16.5; cf. SHA *Did. Iul.* 7.
91 Lib. *Oration* 1.98, 245–249.
92 For humans as offerings, see, e.g., Cic. *Vat.* 14; Tert. *Apol.* 23.1; Kugener 1904: 58–59. For humans used in haruspicy, see Philostr. *VA* 7.11; cf. Paulus *Sent.* 5.23.16.
93 *CIL* VI 19747; cf. Graf 2007.
94 Naiden 2012: 64; Kugener 1904: 58–59.
95 Detienne 1989: 3; but cf. McInerney 2010: 182–184. I thank Julia Kindt for pointing out the exception of hunted meat, which, though marginal, was probably not understood as sacrificial; see Detienne 1989: 8–9; MacKinnon 2014.
96 On primeval vegetarianism, see Dombrowski 1984: 19–34; Haussleiter 1935: 57–64. Cf. Dio Chrys. *Or.* 6.62, in which the philosopher says he will live on vegetable foods like those eaten by Circe's pigs, and Plut. *Mor.* 991c–d, in which a transformed pig points out to Odysseus that animals display more temperance than humans by eating only appropriate foods. On primeval cannibalism, see Ar. *Ran.* 1032; Pl. *Leg.* 782c; Sext. Emp. *Math.* 2.31–33.
97 Cf. Detienne 1979: 53–67.
98 Rives 1995: 67–72.
99 Rives 1995: 77–83.
100 Polyaenus *Strat.* 6.7.2; cf. Diod. Sic. 22.5; Plut. *Mor.* 556d. For other examples, see Rives 1995: 72–73. For animal sacrifice in normative oaths, see Faraone 1993a; Cole 1996.
101 Johnston 1999: 76–80, 127–160.
102 Ps.-Clem. *Rec.* 2.13.
103 Stra. 6.1.5; cf. Paus. 6.6.7–11.
104 Hor. *Epod.* 5.87–102; Ps.-Clem. *Rec.* 2.13 in Migne, *PG* 1 1254c–1255c.
105 Cass. Dio 69.11.2–4; Aur. Vict. *Caes.* 14.7–9; SHA *Hadr.* 14.5–7; Origen *C. Cels.* 3.36. Dio tells us that Antinous was sacrificed (*hierourgētheis*) but gives no reason for it, and the *Hist. Aug.* calls him a *devotum*. Aurelius Victor says that Hadrian killed him *fatum producere*, which is usually translated as 'to extend [his own] life' but could also mean 'to produce an oracle'. Origen implies that Egyptian priests falsified his transformation into a god by setting up a false oracular spirit of Antinous in his temple. For a more detailed discussion, see Dosoo forthcoming a.
106 Lib. *Declamation* 41.51.
107 *PGM* IV.1928–2005, 2006–2125, 2140–2144; for a discussion of these, see Faraone 2005.
108 Burkert 1983: 3–4; Detienne 1989: 9–10. Cf. Philostr. *VA* 8.7, in which the holy man argues that the traumatic deaths of humans, afraid of death, would render their entrails unusable in haruspicy, in contrast to other animals (in particular lambs and female goats), which lack understanding of their fate and are 'simple and almost senseless' (εὐήθη τὰ ζῷα καὶ οὐ πόρρω ἀναισθήτων).
109 *Agr.* 141: *nominare vetat Martem neque agnum vitulumque.* As Gilhus 2006: 277, n. 6 points out, *Martem* should probably be corrected to *porcem*.
110 The Greek *esiēs* is a borrowing from the Egyptian *ḥsy* ('blessed one'), probably specifically from a northern form (represented by the Bohairic Coptic *esie*) in which the initial aspiration had been lost. For more on this concept, see Dosoo forthcoming a; Griffith 1909; Wagner 1998.
111 For early documents attesting to this usage, see Rowe 1940; Pestman 1993: 470–473.

112   *PGM* III.1–64.
113   See ll. 162–164. For the figure, cf. the references in n. 53.
114   This is almost certainly a calque of the Demotic *r n ḥsy* (trans. 'make into a *hesy*';
       intrans. 'become a *hesy*'; e.g. *PDM* XIV.360–361); see Dosoo forthcoming a.
115   *PGM* XII.108; cf. *PGM* XIXb.
116   *PGM* III.9, 13, 121–122.
117   *PGM* III.5–6, 7, 112–113.
118   Cf. the comments of Kindt 2012: 114 on binding curses.
119   Kindt 2019: 155–156.

Bibliography

Arnott, W. G. (2007) *Birds in the Ancient World from A to Z*. London.

Audollent, A. (1904) *Defixionum Tabellae*. Paris.

Bell, S. and C. Willekes (2014) 'Horse racing and chariot racing', in G. L. Campbell
(ed.) *The Oxford Handbook of Animals in Classical Thought and Life*. Oxford, 478–490.

Betz, H. D. (ed.) (1986) *The Greek Magical Papyri in Translation including the Demotic Spells*. Chicago, Ill.

Bidez, J. and F. Cumont (1938) *Les Mages hellénisés. Zoroastre, Ostanès et Hystape d'après la tradition grecque*. 2 vols. Paris.

Bouloumie, B. (1985) 'Dépôt votif du IIe s. av. J.-C. à Sainte–Blaise (13): un rite d'envoûtement?' *Archéologie du midi méditerranéen* 11, 63–67.

Bradley, K. (2000) 'Animalizing the slave: the truth of fiction', *Journal of Roman Studies* 90, 110–125.

Brashear, W. (1995) 'The Greek magical papyri: an introduction and survey; annotated bibliography (1928–1994)', in *ANRW*. Vol. 2, 18.5, 3380–3684.

Burkert, W. (1983) *Homo Necans. The Anthropology of Ancient Greek Sacrificial Ritual and Myth*, trans. P. Bing. Berkeley, Calif.

Cameron, A. (1976) *Circus Factions. Blues and Greens at Rome and Byzantium*. Oxford.

Cole, S. G. (1996) 'Oath ritual and the male community at Athens', in J. Ober and C. Hedrick (eds.) *Dēmokratia. A Conversation on Democracies, Ancient and Modern*. Princeton, N.J., 227–248.

Daniel, R. W. and F. Maltomini (1990–1992) *Supplementum Magicum*. 2 vols. Opladen.

Derrida, J. (2006) *L'Animal que donc je suis*. Paris.

Detienne, M. (1979) *Dionysos Slain*, trans. M. Muellner and L. Muellner. Baltimore, Md.

Detienne, M. (1989) 'Culinary practices and the spirit of sacrifice', in M. Detienne and J.-P. Vernant (eds.) *The Cuisine of Sacrifice among the Greeks*. Chicago, Ill., 1–20.

Dickie, M. W. (1999) 'The learned magician and the collection and transmission of magical lore', in D. R. Jordan, H. Montgomery, and E. Thomassen (eds.) *The World of Ancient Magic. Papers from the First International Samson Eitrem Seminar at the Norwegian Institute at Athens, 4–8 May 1997*. Bergen, 163–193.

Dombrowski, D. A. (1984) *The Philosophy of Vegetarianism*. Amherst, Mass.

Dosoo, K. (forthcoming a) 'Living death and deading life: animal mummies in Graeco-Egyptian ritual', in K. Dosoo and J.-C. Coulon (eds.) *Magikon Zōon. Animal et magie*. Paris.

Dosoo, K. (forthcoming b) 'Suffering doe and sleeping serpent: animals in Christian magical texts from late Roman and early Islamic Egypt', in K. Dosoo and J.-C. Coulon (eds.) *Magikon Zōon. Animal et magie*. Paris.

Dosoo, K. and T. Galoppin (forthcoming) 'The animal in Graeco-Egyptian magical practice', in K. Dosoo and J.-C. Coulon (eds.) *Magikon Zōon. Animal et magie*. Paris.

Dufault, O. (2017) 'Who wrote Greek curse tablets?', in R. Evans (ed.) *Prophets and Profits. Ancient Divination and Its Reception*. London, 31–49.

Eitrem, S. (1939) 'Sonnenkäfer und Falke in der synkretistischen Magie', in T. Klauser and A. Rücker (eds.) *Pisciculi. Studien zur Religion und Kultur des Altertums*. Münster, 94–101.

Evetts, B. (1910) *History of the Patriarchs of the Coptic Church of Alexandria*, Vol. 3: *Agathon – Michael I*. Paris.

Faraone, C. A. (1985) 'Aeschylus' ὕμνος δέσμιος (Eum. 306) and Attic judicial curse tablets', *Journal of Hellenic Studies* 105, 150–154.

Faraone, C. A. (1991) 'The agonistic context of early Greek binding spells', in C. A. Faraone and D. Obbink (eds.) *Magika Hiera. Ancient Greek Magic and Religion*. New York, N.Y. 3–32.

Faraone, C. A. (1993a) 'Molten wax, spilt wine and mutilated animals: sympathetic magic in Near Eastern and early Greek oath ceremonies', *Journal of Hellenic Studies* 113, 60–80.

Faraone, C. A. (1993b) 'The wheel, the whip and other implements of torture: erotic magic in Pindar Pythian 4.213–19', *Classical Journal* 89, 1–19.

Faraone, C. A. (2000) 'Handbooks and anthologies: the collection of Greek and Egyptian incantations in late Hellenistic Egypt', *Archiv für Religionsgeschichte* 2, 195–213.

Faraone, C. A. (2005) 'Necromancy goes underground: the disguise of skull- and corpse-divination in the Paris magical papyri (PGM IV 1928–2144)', in S. I. Johnston and P. T. Struck (eds.) *Mantikê. Studies in Ancient Divination*. Leiden, 255–282.

Faraone, C. A. (forthcoming a) 'Animal-effigies in ancient Greek curses: the role of gender, age and natural behavior in their selection'.

Faraone, C. A. (forthcoming b) 'The Echenêis–fish and magic', in K. Dosoo and J.-C. Coulon (eds.) *Magikon Zōon. Animal et magie*.

Faraone, C. A. and D. Obbink (1991) *Magika Hiera. Ancient Greek Magic and Religion*. New York, N.Y.

Frankfurter, D. (2001) 'The perils of love: magic and countermagic in Coptic Egypt', *Journal of the History of Sexuality* 10, 480–500.

Gager, J. G. (ed.) (1992) *Curse Tablets and Binding Spells from the Ancient World*. New York, N.Y.

Galoppin, T. (2015) 'Animaux et pouvoir ritual dans les practiques 'magiques' du monde romain'. Ph.D. diss., EPHE Paris.

Galoppin, T. (2016) 'Animaux et pouvoir rituel dans les pratiques "magiques" du monde romain', *Asdiwal* 11, 187–190.

Galoppin, T. (forthcoming) 'Des Animaux merveilleux dans la fabrique gréco-romaine de la magie', in K. Dosoo and J.-C. Coulon (eds.) *Magikon Zōon. Animal et magie*. Paris.

Gilhus, I. S. (2006) *Animals, Gods and Humans. Changing Attitudes to Animals in Greek, Roman and Early Christian Ideas*. London.

Gitton-Ripoll, V. (forthcoming) 'Incantations pour les chevaux', in K. Dosoo and J.-C. Coulon (eds.), *Magikon Zōon: Animal et magie*. Paris.

Gordon, R. (1990) 'The veil of power: emperors, sacrificers and benefactors', in M. Beard and J. North (eds.) *Pagan Priests. Religion and Power in the Ancient World*. London, 199–231.

Gordon, R. (2000) '"What's in a list?" Listing in Greek and Graeco-Roman malign magical texts', in D. R. Jordan, H. Montgomery, and E. Thomasson (eds.) *The World of Ancient Magic*. Bergen, 239–277.

Gordon, R. (2010) 'Magian lessons in natural history: unique animals in Graeco-Roman natural magic,' in J. Dijkstra, J. Kroesen, and Y. Kuiper (eds.) *Myths, Martyrs and Modernity. Studies in the History of Religions in Honour of Jan N. Bremmer.* Leiden, 249–269.

Gordon, R. (2012) 'Fixing the race: managing risks in the North African circus', in M. Piranomonte and F. Marco Simón (eds.) *Contesti magici / Contextos mágicos*. Rome, 47–74.

Graf, F. (2007) 'Untimely death, witchcraft, and divine vengeance: a reasoned epigraphical catalog', *Zeitschrift für Papyrologie und Epigraphik* 162, 139–150.

Griffith, F. L. (1909) 'Herodotus II.90: apotheosis by Drowning', *Zeitschrift für Ägyptische Sprache und Altertumskunde* 46, 132–134.

Harvey, F. D. (1988) 'Herodotus and the man-footed creature', in L. Archer (ed.) *Slavery and Other Forms of Unfree Labour*. London, 42–52.

Haussleiter, J. (1935) *Der Vegetarismus in der Antike*. Berlin.

Heintz, F. G. P. (1999) 'Agonistic magic in the late antique circus'. Ph.D. diss., Harvard University.

Hughes, D. D. (1991) *Human Sacrifice in Ancient Greece*. London.

Humphrey, J. H. (1986) *Roman Circuses. Arenas for Chariot Racing*. Berkeley, Calif.

Hunter, R. (2015) *Apollonius of Rhodes. Argonautica: Book IV*. Cambridge.

Hyland, A. (1990) *Equus. The Horse in the Roman World*. New Haven, Conn.

Johnston, S. I. (1995) 'The Song of the Iynx: magic and rhetoric in Pythian 4', *Transactions of the American Philological Association* 125, 177–206.

Johnston, S. I. (1999) *Restless Dead. Encounters between the Living and the Dead in Ancient Greece*. Berkeley, Calif.

Johnston, S. I. *et al.* (1999) 'Panel discussion: *Magic in the Ancient World* by Fritz Graf', *Numen* 46, 291–325.

Jordan, D. R. (1985) 'Defixiones from a well near the southwest corner of the Athenian Agora', *Hesperia* 54, 205–255.

Jordan, D. R. (2002) 'A curse on charioteers and horses at Rome', *Zeitschrift für Papyrologie und Epigraphik* 141, 141–147.

Junkelmann, M. (2000) 'On the starting line with Ben Hur: chariot-racing in the Circus Maximus', in E. Köhne (ed.) *Gladiators and Caesars. The Power of Spectacle in Ancient Rome*. Berkeley, Calif., 86–102.

Kindt, J. (2012) *Rethinking Greek Religion*. Cambridge.

Kindt, J. (2019) 'Animals in ancient Greek Religion: divine zoomorphism and the anthropomorphic divine body', in T. S. Scheer (ed.) *Natur – Mythos – Religion im antiken Griechenland*. Stuttgart, 155–170.

Love, E. O. D. (2017) 'The *PGM* III archive: two papyri, two scripts, and two languages', *Zeitschrift für Papyrologie und Epigraphik* 202, 175–188.

Love, E. O. D. (forthcoming) '"Crum's chicken": demonised donkeys in the context of the Demotic and Greek magical papyri and the tradition of Coptic magic', in K. Dosoo and J.-C. Coulon (eds.) *Magikon Zōon: Animal et magie*. Paris.

Kugener, M.-A. (1904) *Vie de Sévère par Zacharie*. Paris.

Lamont, L. L. (2015) 'A new commercial curse tablet from classical Athens', *Zeitschrift für Papyrologie und Epigraphik* 196, 159–174.

Lucarelli, R. (2017) 'The donkey in the Graeco-Egyptian papyri', in S. Crippa and E. M. Ciampini (eds.) *Languages, Objects, and the Transmission of Rituals. An Interdisciplinary Analysis on Ritual Practices in the Graeco–Egyptian Papyri (PGM)*. Venice, 89–104.

MacKinnon, M. (2014) 'Hunting', in G. L. Campbell (ed.) *The Oxford Handbook of Animals in Classical Thought and Life*. Oxford, 203–215.

Martín Hernández, R. (2010) *Orfeo y los magos. La literatura orfica, la magia y los misterioso*. Madrid.

Martín Hernández, R. (forthcoming) 'Eulamo vs. Seth. On the equine-headed demon represented in the defixiones from Porta S. Sebastiano (Rome)', in R. Martín Hernández (ed.) *Drawing Magic. Images of Power and the Power of Images in Ancient and Late Antique Magic*. Leuven.

Martinez, D. (2001) '"May she neither eat nor drink": love magic and vows of abstinence', in M. Meyer and P. Mirecki (eds.) *Ancient Magic and Ritual Power*. Boston, Mass., 335–359.

Mason, H. J. (2005) 'The metamorphoses of Apuleius and its Greek sources', in H. Hofmann (ed.) *Latin Fiction. The Latin Novel in Context*. London, 87–95.

McInerney, J. (2010) *The Cattle of the Sun. Cows and Culture in the World of the Ancient Greeks*. Princeton, N.J.

Naiden, F. S. (2012) 'Blessed are the parasites', in C. A. Faraone and F. S. Naiden (eds.) *Greek and Roman Animal Sacrifice. Ancient Victims, Modern Observers*. Cambridge, 55–83.

Ogden, D. (2001) *Greek and Roman Necromancy*. Princeton, N.J.

Ogden, D. (2002) *Magic, Witchcraft, and Ghosts in the Greek and Roman Worlds. A Sourcebook*. Oxford.

Ogden, D. (2014) 'Animal magic', in G. L. Campbell (ed.) *The Oxford Handbook of Animals in Classical Thought and Life*. Oxford, 294–309.

Otto, B. C. (2013) 'Towards historicizing "magic" in antiquity', *Numen* 60, 308–347.

Pestman, P. W. (1993) *The Archive of the Theban Choachytes*. Leuven.

Phillips, R. L. (2009) *In Pursuit of Invisibility. Ritual Texts from Late Roman Egypt*. Durham, N.C.

Preisendanz, K. (1926) *Akephalos. Der kopflose Gott*. Leipzig.

Quack, J. F. (2006) 'Les Mages égyptianisés? Remarks on some surprising points in supposedly magusean texts', *Journal of Near Eastern Studies* 65, 267–282.

Rengen, W. van (1984) 'Deux Défixions contre les Bleus à Apamée (VIe siècle apr. J.-C.)', in J. Balty (ed.) *Apamée de Syrie. Bilan des recherches archéologiques 1973–1979. Actes du 3ᵉ Colloque tenu à Bruxelles du 29 au 30 mai 1980: aspects de l'architecture domestique d'Apamée*. Brussels, 213–238.

Ritner, R. K. (1995) 'Egyptian magical practice under the Roman Empire: the Demotic spells and their religious context', in *ANRW*. Vol. 2, 18.5, 3333–3379.

Rives, J. (1995) 'Human sacrifice among pagans and Christians', *Journal of Roman Studies* 85, 65–85.

Rowe, A. (1940) 'Newly-identified monuments in the Egyptian Museum showing the deification of the dead together with brief details of similar objects elsewhere', *Annales du service des antiquités de l'Égypte* 40, 1–50.

Salayová, A. (2017) 'Animals as magical ingredients in Greek magical papyri: preliminary statistical analysis of animal species', *Graeco-Latina Brunensia* 22, 191–206.

Sánchez Natalías, C. (2011) 'The Bologna defixio(nes) revisited', *Zeitschrift für Papyrologie und Epigraphik* 179, 201–217.

Sanzo, J. E. (forthcoming) 'Deconstructing the deconstructionists: a response to recent criticisms of the rubric "ancient magic",' in A. Mastrocinque, J. E. Sanzo, and M. Scapini (eds.) *Ancient Magic. Then and Now*. Nordhausen.

Seyrig, H. (1935) 'Notes archéologiques', *Berytus* 2, 42–50.

Sicherl, M. (1937) 'Die Tiere in der griechisch–aegyptischen Zauberei, hauptsächlich nach den griechischen Zauberpapri'. Ph.D. diss., Charles University, Prague.

Smith, J. Z. (2001) 'Trading places', in M. Meyer and P. Mirecki (eds.) *Ancient Magic and Ritual Power*. Boston, Mass., 13–27.

Sorabji, R. (1993) *Animal Minds and Human Morals. The Origins of the Western Debate*. Ithaca, N.Y.

Tambiah, S. J. (1990) *Magic, Science, Religion, and the Scope of Rationality*. Cambridge.

Tavenner, E. (1933) 'Iynx and Rhombus', *Transactions and Proceedings of the American Philological Association* 64, 109–127.

Thompson, D. W. (1895) *Glossary of Greek Birds*. London.

Tomlin, R. S. O. (2007) '"Remain like stones, unmoving, un–running": another Greek spell against competitors in a foot–race', *Zeitschrift für Papyrologie und Epigraphik* 160, 161–166.

Versnel, H. S. (1998) 'καὶ εἴ τι λ[οιπὸν] τῶν μερ[ῶ]ν [ἔσ]ται τοῦ σώματος ὅλ[ο]υ (... and any other part of the entire body there may be ...). An essay on anatomical curses', in F. Graf and W. Burkert (eds.) *Ansichten griechischer Rituale. Geburtstags-Symposium für Walter Burkert*. Stuttgart, 217–267.

Wagner, G. (1998) 'Le Concept de "Ḥsy" à la lumière des inscriptions Grecques'", in W. Clarysse, A. Schoors, and H. Willems (eds.) *Egyptian Religion. The Last Thousand Years. Studies Dedicated to the Memory of Jan Quaegebeuer*. Vol. 2. Leuven, 1074–1078.

Watson, L. C. (2010) 'The *Echeneis* and erotic magic', *Classical Quarterly* 60, 639–646.

Watson, L. C. (ed.) (2019a) *Magic in Ancient Greece and Rome*. London.

Watson, P. (2019b) 'Animals in magic', in L. C. Watson (ed.) *Magic in Ancient Greece and Rome*. London, 127–165.

Wünsch, R. (1898) *Sethianische Verfluchungstafeln aus Rom*. Leipzig.

13 Gods, humans, and animals revisited

J. Kindt

To say that ancient Greek religion brought together gods and humans in a variety of real and symbolic relationships is to state the obvious.[1] And yet this observation, commonplace and uncontroversial as it may seem, does not tell the whole story. For it leaves out the sustained presence of a third creature across the spectrum of ancient Greek religious beliefs and practices, including those commonly referred to as 'magic': the animal.

Taken together, the individual chapters of this book illustrate that ancient Greek religion frequently drew on the animal as a third player and point of reference besides gods and humans. This applies not merely to the cultural practice of blood sacrifice, in which the place of the animal has traditionally been well researched. It also pertains to a number of other religious beliefs and practices in which the presence of animals has received considerably less, if any, scholarly attention to date. Whether in divination, epiphany, healing, the setting up of dedications, the writing of a binding spell, or the instigation of other 'magical' means, the contributions in this book show exemplarily that animals feature widely in numerous areas of the ancient Greek religious experience.

As mentioned in the introductory chapter to this volume, several pioneering works have demonstrated the richness of this line of enquiry.[2] In particular Liliane Bodson's *Hiera zôia* (1975) has illustrated how productive it is to include animals firmly within the picture we sketch of ancient Greek religion by pointing to the roles and significance of individual species and classes. And yet, despite this promising start, the role of animals across different areas of the ancient Greek religious experience has, up to this point, not received the level of scholarly attention it deserves. This is due to a number of factors: some are grounded in the history of scholarship on ancient Greek religion, as detailed expertly by Emily Kearns (this volume, Chapter 3); others emerge from the way in which the category of 'the animal' has fared beyond antiquity in philosophical, ethical, and political debate, all the way to the present. In the thought and literature of what is traditionally referred to as 'the West', the animal has come to be regarded as inferior to both gods and humans.[3] This way of thinking has itself emerged out of the classical tradition. The clear symbolic relationship – gods at the top, animals at the bottom, and humans sandwiched somewhere in between – originated in classical antiquity. It was articulated forcefully and prominently in the works of certain philosophers (most notably Aristotle) who sought to establish essentialist distinguishing criteria separating man from beast. And yet, even in classical philosophy, it always remained just one position among many.[4] With the advent of Christianity, however, these views became enshrined in a value system, the normative force of which extended well beyond the sphere of the religious.[5] And once this relationship was firmly established, the path led right down the slippery slope to such thinkers as René Descartes (1596–1650), who sought to sustain the idea of the categorical inferiority of the animal by reifying it.[6]

Against this background, arguably the most significant insight emerging from this book concerns the diversity of relationships in which gods, humans, and animals come together in ancient Greek religion. As its chapters show, there was no single tripartite symbolic system underlying ancient Greek religion but several. The triad was flexible, not fixed. Moreover, in the transactions and negotiations among its individual categories, animals did not always come last. This point becomes evident if we consider, for example, the ways in which animals could stand in for both gods and humans in ancient Greek religion. Due to their real or perceived otherness, they could articulate the otherworldly nature of the divine (see, e.g., this volume, Chapter 5). In other contexts, however, it was the notion that they shared with humans a physical existence in this world that facilitated their use as substitutes for the human body (see, e.g., some of the magical rituals described in this volume, Chapter 12).

Multiplicity and 'entanglement'

The notion of 'entanglement' has been central to how various contributors to this book have conceived the tripartite relationships between gods, humans, and animals in ancient Greek religion. It is addressed in detail in Jeremy McInerney's methodological opening chapter (this volume, Chapter 1). Applied to ancient Greek religion, 'entanglement' has both a real and a symbolic dimension. It not only articulates how real human and animal lives intersected with each other in the ancient Greek religious experience, drawing on the role, value, and functions of animals in other areas of culture and society; it also points to the way in which human, divine, and animal identities reference and define one another in ancient Greek religious beliefs and practices. As McInerney points out, the notion of 'entanglement' articulates more dynamic and creative relationships than the mere notion of a tripartite hierarchy of gods, humans, and animals would suggest. It points to the fact that the human existed in negotiation with both the conception of the divine and the conception of the animal. In other words, thinking about humans, humanity, and the human place in the world frequently involves thinking about the nature of the divine *and* the nature of animals.

At the same time, the notion of 'entanglement' also means that answers to the questions 'What is a god?' and 'What is a human being?' – and, of course, by implication 'What is an animal?' – are never complete, never final. Rather, they change over time and space, depending on which human, divine, and animal natures are brought into play in a particular context. The individual chapters in this book show that ancient Greek religious beliefs and practices answered these questions in a variety of ways. Taken together, they draw an invariably rich and multifaceted picture.

This insight into the richness and plurality of human/animal/divine relationships and the value systems that inform them is significant beyond the immediate socio-religious contexts from which it derives as it affects the core of what we think ancient Greek religion might be. It has frequently been argued that ancient Greek religion is a symbolic language designed to 'make sense' of the world.[7] This symbolic language drew upon gods, humans, *and animals* as individual entities and sources of meaning and the way in which they were entangled with one another.

Overlaps and correspondences

What remains to be done now is to tie up some loose ends and consider some of the insights that emerge between the lines and from a broader, bird's-eye view of the arguments contained in the individual chapters. What kind of issues can be discerned from the contributions to this book taken together? What larger themes emerge? And in the process of considering the bigger picture, what productive avenues suggest themselves for further enquiry into the role of animals in ancient Greek religion?

First, it appears that, despite the diversity in relationships mentioned above, there are discernible overlaps, influences, and correspondences in the way animals feature in different areas of the ancient Greek religious experience. A few examples: the idea that animals can, in one way or another, facilitate human/divine communication informs various aspects of ancient Greek religion, as described in several contributions to this volume. It is present in the ancient Greek practice of divination (this volume, Chapter 9) and manifests itself in the kind of symbolic transactions central to ancient Greek blood sacrifice (this volume, Chapter 8). Likewise, the notion of the animal as invariably 'other' and a potential threat to human life and well-being informs the way in which animals feature in some forms of myth and magic, while the idea of the proximity of humans and animals is present in certain aspects of ritual healing and certain kinds of dedication (this volume, Chapters 11 and 10, respectively). Finally, the fact blood sacrifice features prominently in several other chapters (see, e.g., this volume, Chapters 9, 10, and 12) in addition to Fritz Graf's chapter on the subject confirms the centrality of this ritual to ancient Greek religion. It appears that multiple religious beliefs and practices drew on its structures, processes, and imagery for their own purposes, thus extending its meanings and functions into other areas of the ancient Greek religious experience.

We could broaden the list of examples here, but the larger point is already clear: such overlaps, influences, and correspondences are significant in their own right because they speak to the vexed question of the unity and diversity of ancient Greek religion.[8] They illustrate the existence of underlying patterns that manifest across different areas of the religious as well as the significance of the singular and parochial.

Indeed, as this volume shows, the way in which animals feature in ancient Greek religion cuts across the way classical scholars have traditionally divided up the subject. Animals are present in both the material and the literary record. They bring together belief and practice, myth and ritual, the real and the imaginary; some serve in the same role across different regions of Greece, while the roles of others are highly localised – the Brauronian 'bears' are a prominent example here (see, e.g., this volume, Chapter 3). Overall, then, this study maintains the case for both unity and diversity. It provides a powerful example of how universal and local dimensions intersect and allows us to talk of both ancient Greek religion and the *religions* of the ancient Greeks.[9]

Species matters

Several, if not all, chapters explicitly articulate the need to move away from a simple and singular conception of the role of 'the animal' in ancient Greek religion – itself a by-product of Greco-Roman philosophical efforts to differentiate the category of 'the human' from 'the non-human' – and instead investigate the role of individual species within and across different religious beliefs and practices (see, e.g., this volume, Chapters 2, 3, and 5). As Milette Gaifman shows in her contribution (this volume, Chapter 10), dedications featuring animals derive much of their symbolic dimension from specific animals. They do not make a point about the category of *the* animal *per se* but target meanings emerging from different species, sometimes even featuring in specific contexts and situations (see, e.g., in Gaifman's chapter, the bronze figurines of deer and hares from Olympia that use the hunt as a point of reference for their meaning).

Individual animal species thus differed in the value and meanings they brought to – and received from – ancient Greek religious beliefs and practices. And yet here, too, we find overlaps and correspondences. Birds, for example, feature especially prominently. They were used in divination and as images in oracles (this volume, Chapter 9); at the same time, they were one of the preferred forms in which the major ancient Greek gods chose to reveal themselves to humans (see, e.g., this volume, Chapter 5).[10] Moreover, the specific species of bird that appeared in a particular situation was crucial (this volume, Chapter 2). Different birds carried different cultural connotations, which played into how they featured in ancient Greek religion. Birds of prey, for example, carry cultural meaning as powerful agents that frequently strike and kill smaller creatures, thus illustrating the more threatening and uncanny features of the supernatural.

Similarly, several contributors represent the snake as a potent religious symbol, expanding on Liliane Bodson's work in this area.[11] For instance, it is discussed as a 'visual epithet' for some impersonations of Zeus, such as Zeus Meilichios and Zeus Ktesios (this volume, Chapters 2 and 5, with further literature). In addition, we find it on an Attic hydria depicting Odysseus' men blinding the Cyclops Polyphemus (this volume, Chapter 2); it serves as a symbol for Asclepius, the god of healing (this volume, Chapter 11); and, finally, it is an agent of supernatural intervention in one of the curse tablets discussed by Korshi Dosoo (this volume, Chapter 12). What brings these different uses and representations together is the notion of the snake as a powerful, potentially threatening, and somewhat uncanny creature.[12] Given its strong symbolic value, it should come as no surprise that it was also appropriated by Alexander of Abonuteichus, who aimed to set himself up as a quasi-oracular voice and authority on all things supernatural (this volume, Chapters 5 and 11).

The differentiated look at how individual animal species feature across the spectrum of ancient Greek religious beliefs and practices also affects ancient Greek blood sacrifice as its central ritual. Many traditional interpretations, including the influential and long-dominant positions of both Walter Burkert and the Paris School around Jean-Pierre Vernant paid little attention to the species of animals that were sacrificed in particular situations. What mattered to their social reading of this cultural practice was merely that *an animal* was sacrificed for the purpose of reinforcing group solidarity (Burkert) or to restrain violence (Vernant).[13] In his contribution (this volume, Chapter 8), Fritz Graf variously points to the fact that meanings could emerge especially from the species of animal that was chosen. Was the creature male or female? Young or mature? Expensive or cheap? Domesticated or wild? The differences in 'value' (broadly conceived) across different species enhance the picture here, giving further layers of meaning to blood sacrifice as an already overdetermined cultural practice, and help to explain the centrality of the ritual.

Overall, then, it seems that not all animals are created equal when it comes to their use in Greek religious beliefs and practices. They are not paraded according to the frequency of their occurrence in nature, but according to their significance in other aspects of Greek culture and society.[14] Hence, by far the most common animals in ancient Greek religion are mammals, and especially livestock (oxen, cows, sheep, pigs, and goats). We have already commented on the frequency of birds; and fish make occasional appearances, for example as sacrificial victims or divine signs.[15] By contrast, one or two intriguing exceptions aside, such as the religious lore surrounding the honeybee, invertebrates are rarely visible in the extant record, even though they comprise about 99 per cent of all animal life on the planet.[16]

While the domestic, accessible, and familiar usually prevail, sometimes the focus is firmly on the wild and untamed nature of a particular animal: think, for example, of the Calydonian boar; or the Nemean lion, whose principal claim to fame in Greek mythology was that he was killed by Heracles.[17] And every so often we find ourselves face-to-face with utterly bizarre creatures that defy the laws of nature, such as the Minotaur, the Chimera, or Circe's famous pig-men (see this volume, Chapters 5, 7, and 12, respectively). Some of the more exotic creatures inhabiting the marvellous world of Greek mythology shine a light on further aspects of the roles of animals in ancient Greek religion: for example, they reveal a distinct taste for hybridisation (the creation of composite figures; see this volume, Chapter 2) and metamorphosis (the transformation from one category of being to another).[18] As such, they point us away from the meaning of individual species and back to the larger categories of which they are part. Both hybridisation and metamorphosis compel us to reconsider the categories we use to 'make sense' of the world. By their mere existence, creatures such as centaurs illustrate that, at least sometimes, those categories are inadequate.

Moreover, there is something unsettling about hybridity and transformation, especially if it involves the human form. It is the predominant anthropomorphism of the ancient Greek gods that gives urgency and weight to the idea of gods transforming physically from human into animal and back again. Gods that pull off such a trick demonstrate their power to transcend; any humans who wish to emulate them must rely on magic, which always carries the whiff of transgression.

Against this background, it is especially fitting that Schrödinger's infamous cat makes an appearance early on in this book (this volume, Chapter 1). In its uncertain ontological status as both dead and alive, the cat mirrors the mode of existence of some ancient mythological creatures: it is in equal parts elusive, unsettling, and subverting of established truths, and thus, as McInerney argues, representative of the dilemmas that are central to the notion of 'entanglement' discussed above.

The cross-cultural perspective

Finally, as Emily Kearns points out (this volume, Chapter 3), 'the place of animals in Greek religion cannot be fully explored solely from within the Greek domain: a wider remit is needed'. Several other contributors confirm this view by pointing to the manifold ways in which the role of animals in ancient Greek religion either resembles or differs from those in other ancient cultures. In his chapter on divine theriomorphism (this volume, Chapter 5), for example, Jan Bremmer points to the Near East in general (and Hittite myth in particular) as a possible origin of the concept of metamorphosis into birds, and to the Indo-European origin of the Dioscuri's connection with horses. Likewise, Florian Steger and Frank Ursin trace the presence of dogs in the imagery and lore pertaining to Asclepius to ancient Babylonia (this volume, Chapter 11). Such insights are significant beyond the history of religion because they shed light on wider cultural influences and transfers of meaning.

And yet, the cross-cultural perspective does more than just speak to questions of origin: it also reveals those aspects that are uniquely Greek and those that ancient Greek religion shares with other ancient cultures. As Fritz Graf remarks, the cultural practice of blood sacrifice as 'a major ritual act' is accounted for in every religion of the ancient Mediterranean world (this volume, Chapter 8). However, as he explains, Greek religion is distinguishable from the others on account of particular values and meanings associated with individual species and the ritual practices to which they were subjected.

Finally, the cross-cultural perspective also reveals the complex way in which ancient Greek religion intersected with and integrated aspects of the religions of adjacent cultures. This was most evident during the Hellenistic and Roman periods, when there was increased cultural exchange between ancient Greek religion and those of other parts of the Mediterrenean. Some of the magical documents discussed by Korshi Dosoo combine Egyptian and Greek imagery (this volume, Chapter 12). The cross-cultural encounter also sparked a conceptual debate about the principles and practices of divine representation (this volume, Chapter 6). And the incorporation of material from Egypt and the ancient Near East can help us make sense of some of the human/animal hybrid deities of ancient Greek religion (this volume, Chapter 2, informed by the work of Emma Aston).[19] It illustrates the way in which ancient Greek culture was just one component in several much wider networks. At the same time, an understanding of how deeply ancient Greek religion is grounded in the broader Mediterranean world reminds us that cross-cultural transfer and influence is not a one-way process. Ancient Greece had a profound influence on other ancient cultures, too, especially with respect to the role of animals in religious belief and practice, as is evident, for example, in the spread of the Asclepius cult from Greece to Rome (this volume, Chapter 11).

It has sometimes been argued that the study of ancient Greek religion can be quite insular and disengaged from current debates in the interdisciplinary study of religions.[20] The understanding of ancient Greek religion as a symbolic system encompassing gods, humans, and animals sets ancient Greek religion on a par with other religious traditions, both ancient and modern, that have attributed supernatural powers to animals or otherwise used them to facilitate human/divine contact.[21] Further lines of productive enquiry will likely emerge from a deeper consideration of how Greek religion sits within this larger picture of the comparative study of religions in this respect.

Change over time

Throughout the individual chapters of this volume, the focus is strictly thematic. This structure was deemed preferable to any other for the purpose of drawing attention to the variety of ways in which animals feature across different religious beliefs and practices. It can also be justified by pointing to the sometimes astonishing continuity of ancient Greek religious beliefs and practices over time; but, of course, we should be careful not to adopt a research design that merely confirms our existing (pre-)conceptions.[22]

The temporal dimension variously enters the picture, then, in some of the individual case studies that appear in this book. It is here that continuities and changes come into play. For example, in his chapter on philosophical attitudes to animals in ancient Greek religion, James Collins shows how arguments in favour of vegetarianism evolved over the long history of the ancient world, culminating in Porphyry's position in support of it but integrating much earlier material from Theophrastus (this volume, Chapter 7). This argument finds a natural extension in Fritz Graf's subsequent chapter on sacrifice (this volume, Chapter 8). Graf sketches the emergence of the rejection of animal sacrifice in certain philosophically inclined circles during the Imperial Age against the background of a ritual practice that shows remarkable continuity from the Mycenean period onwards. Further continuities and differences will no doubt emerge as more research is done on how human and animal lives intersected in ancient Greek religion.

Outlook

A number of extra chapters could have been included in this volume to flesh out certain dimensions of the topic. For example, the roles of animals and animal parts in specific magical beliefs and practices could have been investigated in greater detail. And the same could be said of the link between animals and religion in the writings of the ancient Greek philosophers (this volume, Chapter 7), or indeed hybridity and metamorphosis with regard to gods, humans, and animals. Further contributions could have focused full attention on subjects that are touched on only in passing here, such as the roles of animals in epiphany and prayer, or the affiliation between animals and some of the minor Greek gods. (Think of the ancient Greek river god Achelous, who is sometimes represented as a human with a fish tail, or Pan, the god of shepherds and their flocks with his goat's feet and horns.[23]) A whole chapter could have been devoted to divine epithets that indicate a special connection between a deity and a particular animal, and yet another on the way in which animals featured in ancient Greek mystery cults. Finally, the place of animals in all these areas could – and should – be explored within the much larger context of ancient Greek religion's engagement with the natural world.[24]

As mentioned in the introductory chapter, this book was conceived as a succinct and exemplary study rather than a full and comprehensive account. While the potential contributions outlined above would undeniably have added extra fabric and detail, they would not have changed the overall picture. At the same time, this book offers more than mere snapshots of the roles of animals in various aspects of the ancient Greek religious experience. It also informs the reader about the sources and methodologies that are available to study these roles and functions (see, in particular, this volume, Chapters 1, 2, and 3), and it provides insights into the relevant debates both past and present. The individual chapters shed light on the history of scholarship and point to productive areas for future research in the hope that some readers will take up the thread.

Notes

1 I say 'real and symbolic relationships' because the gods were involved with humans in a variety of ways that would have felt invariably real to an ancient Greek.
2 See esp. this volume, introductory chapter, n. 14 (with further literature).

3 See, in detail, Newmyer 2017. In certain non-Western cultural traditions, animals always retained a different status without a clear subordinate role to humans (see, e. g., animals' roles in certain Australian Aboriginal myths: Reed 1978). The category of 'the West' is itself somewhat problematic, because it frequently involves a certain normative dimension that sets it against other cultural traditions, most notably 'the East'. See, e.g., Bavaj 2011; McNeil 1997; Appiah 2016. On the logocentric and anthropocentric tradition in philosophy, see Sorabji 1993. See also Calaro 2008 for some of the modern debates.

4 See, e.g., Newmyer 2005; Osborne 2007 (with evidence).

5 See, in detail, Gilhus 2006.

6 See, e.g., Descartes 1982: Vol. 1: 118 ('Discourse on Method V') with Harrison 1992. It was only with Charles Darwin's theory of evolution that the insight of the fundamental relatedness of all animals (man included) prevailed. Darwin's theory illustrated that not only biological features but also capacities and faculties of all kinds are distributed across the animal kingdom (man included). See Darwin 1859.

7 Gould 1985 with Kindt 2012: 75–80.

8 On the unity and diversity of ancient Greek religion, see, e.g., Pirenne-Delforge and Pironti 2015; Osborne 2015.

9 I am referring here to Price 1999, in which he emphasises the diversity of Greek religious beliefs and practices.

10 On individual species of birds in the cultures and societies of the ancient world, see, in detail, Keller 1909–1912: Vol. 2: 1–246, and, more recently, Arnott 2007.

11 Bodson 1975: 68–91.

12 On snakes in the cultures and societies of the ancient world, see, e.g., Keller 1909–1912: Vol. 2: 284–305.

13 Burkert 1983; Detienne and Vernant 1979. On these authors' influential positions, see, e.g., this volume, Chapters 3 and 8.

14 On which, see, e.g., the essays in Kalof and Resl 2007: Vol. 1 and Campbell 2014.

15 See this volume, Chapters 8 and 9, respectively (with further examples). On the cultural significance of fish in the ancient world, see also Keller 1909–1912: Vol. 2: 323–393. On mammals in ancient Greek religion, see also Bodson 1975: 121–158.

16 On the honeybee in ancient Greece and ancient Greek religion, see Ransome 2004: 75–82, 91–111, 119–139. On insects in the societies of the ancient world, see, in detail, Keller 1909–1912: Vol. 2: 395–460; Davies and Kathirithamby 1986; Beavis 1988; Rory 2014. On insects in ancient Greek religion, see Bodson 1975: 9–43.

17 Examples: *LIMC* II.2: 561, nos. 33b, 173, 176, 284, 1395, and this volume, Chapter 3.

18 On hybrids, see Aston 2011. On metamorphosis, see Forbes Irving 1990; Buxton 2009. On the related topic of epiphany, see Petridou 2015.

19 Aston 2011.

20 See, e.g., Roubekas 2018.

21 On animals in other religious traditions, see, e.g., Kemmerer 2012.

22 On continuity and change in ancient Greek religion, see Dietrich 1986 with Sourvinou-Inwood 1989; Mikalson 2006; Pirenne-Delforge and Pironti 2015.

23 On which, see, in detail, Aston 2011: 79–89, 287–298 (Achelous), and 196–199 (Pan).

24 On which, see, e.g., Scheer 2019.

Bibliography

Appiah, K. A. (2016) 'There is no such thing as Western civilisation', *Guardian*, 9 November. URL: www.theguardian.com/world/2016/nov/09/western-civilisation-appiah-reith-lecture (retrieved 11 April 2020).

Arnott, W. G. (2007) *Birds in the Ancient World from A to Z*. London.

Aston, E. (2011) *Mixanthrôpoi. Human–Animal Hybrid Deities in Greek Religion*. Liège.

Bavaj, R. (2011) '"The West": a conceptual exploration', *European History Online*. URL: www.ieg-ego.eu/bavajr-2011-en (retrieved 11 April 2020).

Beavis, I. C. (1988) *Insects and Other Invertebrates in the Classical World*. Exeter.

Bodson, L. (1975) *Hiera zôia. Contribution à l'étude de la place de l'animal dans la religion grecque ancienne*. Brussels.

Burkert, W. (1983) *Homo Necans. The Anthropology of Ancient Greek Sacrificial Ritual and Myth*. Berkeley, Calif. (German orig. 1972).

Buxton, R. (2009) *Forms of Astonishment. The Question of the Animal from Heidegger to Derrida*. New York, N.Y.

Calaro, M. (2008) *Zoographies. The Question of the Animal from Heidegger to Derrida*. New York, N.Y.

Campbell, G. L. (ed.) (2014) *The Oxford Handbook of Animals in Classical Thought and Life*. Oxford.

Darwin, C. (1859) *On the Origin of Species by Means of Natural Selection*. London.

Davies, M. and J. Kathirathamby (1986) *Greek Insects*. London.

Descartes, R. (1982) *The Philosophical Works of Descartes*, ed. E. Haldane and G. Ross. 2 vols. Cambridge.

Detienne, M. and J.-P. Vernant (1979) *La cuisine du sacrifice en pays grec*. Paris.

Dietrich, B. C. (1986) *Tradition in Greek Religion*. Berlin.

Forbes Irving, P. M. C. (1990) *Metamorphosis in Greek Myth*. Oxford.

Gilhus, I. S. (2006) *Animals, Gods, and Humans. Changing Attitudes to Animals in Greek, Roman and Early Christian Thought*. London.

Gould, J. (1985) 'On making sense of Greek religion', in P. Easterling and J. V. Muir (eds.) *Greek Religion and Society*. Cambridge, 1–33.

Harrison, P. (1992) 'Descartes on animals', *Philosophical Quarterly* 42(167), 219–227.

Johnston, P., A. Mastrocinque, and S. Papaionannou (eds.) *Animals in Greek and Roman Religion and Myth. Proceedings of the Symposium Grumentinum Grumento Nova (Potenza) 5–7 June 2013*. Cambridge.

Kalof, L. and B. Resl (eds.) (2007) *A Cultural History of Animals*. 6 vols. London.

Keller, O. (1909–1912) *Die antike Tierwelt*. 2 vols. Leipzig.

Kemmerer, L. (2012) *Animals and World Religions*. Oxford.

Kindt, J. (2012) *Rethinking Greek Religion*. Cambridge.

Larson, J. (2007) 'A land full of gods: nature deities in Greek religion', in D. Ogden (ed.) *A Companion to Greek Religion*. London, 56–70.

McNeil, W. H. (1997) 'What we mean by "the West"', *Orbis* 41, 513–524.

Mikalson, J. (2006) 'Greek religion: continuity and change in the Hellenistic period', in G. R. Bugh (ed.) *The Cambridge Companion to the Hellenistic World*. Cambridge, 208–222.

Newmyer, S. T. (2005) *Animals, Rights, and Reason in Plutarch and Modern Ethics*. London.

Newmyer, S. T. (2017) *The Animal and the Human in Ancient and Modern Thought. The 'Man Alone of Animals' Concept*. London.

Osborne, C. (2007) *Dumb Beasts and Dead Philosophers. Humanity and the Humane in Ancient Philosophy and Literature*. Oxford.

Osborne, R. (2015) 'Unity vs. diversity?', in E. Eidinow and J. Kindt (eds.) *The Oxford Handbook of Ancient Greek Religion*. Oxford, 11–19.

Petridou, G. (2015) *Divine Epiphany in Greek Literature and Culture*. Oxford.

Pirenne-Delforge, V. and G. Pironti (2015) 'Many vs. one?', in E. Eidinow and J. Kindt (eds.) *The Oxford Handbook of Ancient Greek Religion*. Oxford, 39–47.

Price, S. (1999) *Religions of the Ancient Greeks*. Cambridge.

Ransome, H. M. (2004) *The Sacred Bee in Ancient Times and Folklore*. New York, N.Y.

Reed, A. W. (1978) *Aboriginal Legends. Animal Tales*. Sydney.

Rory, E. (2014) 'Insects', in G. L. Campbell (ed.) *The Oxford Handbook of Animals in Classical Thought and Life*. Oxford, 180–192.

Roubekas, N. P. (2018) 'The insularity of the study of ancient religions and "religion"', *Bulletin for the Study of Religion* 47, 2–7.

Scheer, T. S. (ed.) (2019) *Natur – Mythos – Religion im antiken Griechenland*. Stuttgart.

Sorabji, R. (1993) *Animal Minds and Human Morals. The Origins of a Western Debate*. Ithaca, N.Y.

Sourvinou-Inwood, C. (1989) 'Review: continuity and change in ancient Greek religion', *Classical Review* 39, 51–58.

Index